AF689552

GLOBAL ECONOMIC STUDIES

DIRECT INVESTMENT ABROAD

GLOBAL ECONOMIC STUDIES

Additional books in this series can be found on Nova's website under the Series tab.

Additional E-books in this series can be found on Nova's website under the E-books tab.

GLOBAL ECONOMIC STUDIES

DIRECT INVESTMENT ABROAD

CALEB J. BLACKWELL
EDITOR

Nova Science Publishers, Inc.
New York

Copyright © 2010 by Nova Science Publishers, Inc.

All rights reserved. No part of this book may be reproduced, stored in a retrieval system or transmitted in any form or by any means: electronic, electrostatic, magnetic, tape, mechanical photocopying, recording or otherwise without the written permission of the Publisher.

For permission to use material from this book please contact us:
Telephone 631-231-7269; Fax 631-231-8175
Web Site: http://www.novapublishers.com

NOTICE TO THE READER

The Publisher has taken reasonable care in the preparation of this book, but makes no expressed or implied warranty of any kind and assumes no responsibility for any errors or omissions. No liability is assumed for incidental or consequential damages in connection with or arising out of information contained in this book. The Publisher shall not be liable for any special, consequential, or exemplary damages resulting, in whole or in part, from the readers' use of, or reliance upon, this material. Any parts of this book based on government reports are so indicated and copyright is claimed for those parts to the extent applicable to compilations of such works.

Independent verification should be sought for any data, advice or recommendations contained in this book. In addition, no responsibility is assumed by the publisher for any injury and/or damage to persons or property arising from any methods, products, instructions, ideas or otherwise contained in this publication.

This publication is designed to provide accurate and authoritative information with regard to the subject matter covered herein. It is sold with the clear understanding that the Publisher is not engaged in rendering legal or any other professional services. If legal or any other expert assistance is required, the services of a competent person should be sought. FROM A DECLARATION OF PARTICIPANTS JOINTLY ADOPTED BY A COMMITTEE OF THE AMERICAN BAR ASSOCIATION AND A COMMITTEE OF PUBLISHERS.

LIBRARY OF CONGRESS CATALOGING-IN-PUBLICATION DATA
Direct investment abroad / editor, Caleb J. Blackwell.
p. cm.
Includes index.
ISBN 978-1-61668-857-8 (hardcover)
1. Investments, American. 2. Corporations, American--Law and legislation--Foreign countries. 3. International business enterprises. I. Blackwell, Caleb J.
HG4538.D558 2010
332.67'373--dc22
2010012868

Published by Nova Science Publishers, Inc. ✦ New York

CONTENTS

Preface		**vii**
Chapter 1	U.S. Direct Investment Abroad: Trends and Current Issues *James K. Jackson*	**1**
Chapter 2	The Overseas Private Investment Corporation: Background and Legislative Issues *Shayerah Ilias*	**9**
Chapter 3	Foreign Investment: Laws and Policies Regulating Foreign Investment in 10 Countries *United States Government Accountability Office*	**21**
Chapter 4	The International Markets of Multinational Firms *Mihir A. Desai, C. Fritz Foley and James R. Hines, Jr.*	**101**
Chapter 5	U.S. Multinational Companies: Operations in the United States and Abroad in 2007 *Kevin B. Barefoot and Raymond J. Mataloni, Jr.*	**113**
Chapter 6	Do Intangible Assets Explain High U.S. Foreign Direct Investment Returns? *Benjamin Bridgman*	**183**
Chapter 7	Direct Investment Positions for 2008: Country and Industry Detail *Marilyn Ibarra and Jennifer Koncz*	**207**
Index		**245**

PREFACE

The United States is the largest investor abroad and the largest recipient of direct investment in the world. For some Americans, the national gains attributed to investing overseas are offset by such perceived losses as displaced U.S. workers and lower wages. Even more striking is the fact that the share of investment going to developing countries has fallen in recent years. Most economists conclude that direct investment abroad does not lead to fewer jobs or lower incomes overall for Americans and that the majority of jobs lost among U.S. manufacturing firms over the past decade reflect a broad restructuring of U.S. manufacturing industries. This book explores the trends and current issues of Direct Investment Abroad.

Chapter 1 - The United States is the largest investor abroad and the largest recipient of direct investment in the world. For some Americans, the national gains attributed to investing overseas are offset by such perceived losses as displaced U.S. workers and lower wages. Some observers believe U.S. firms invest abroad to avoid U.S. labor unions or high U.S. wages, however, 70% of U.S. foreign direct investment is concentrated in high income developed countries. Even more striking is the fact that the share of investment going to developing countries has fallen in recent years. Most economists conclude that direct investment abroad does not lead to fewer jobs or lower incomes overall for Americans and that the majority of jobs lost among U.S. manufacturing firms over the past decade reflect a broad restructuring of U.S. manufacturing industries.

Chapter 2 - The Overseas Private Investment Corporation (OPIC) was established in 1969 and began operations in 1971 as a development agency to promote and assist U.S. business investment in developing nations. Today, OPIC is a U.S. government agency that provides project financing, investment insurance, and other services for U.S. businesses in over 150 developing nations and emerging economies. To date, OPIC has funded, guaranteed, or insured over $180 billion in investments.

OPIC's activities are guided by U.S. foreign policy objectives. Geographical priority areas for OPIC-supported activities are sub-Saharan Africa, the Broader Middle East and North Africa, and Asia. Sectoral priorities for the agency are renewable energy and access to credit for micro-, small-, and medium-sized enterprises. OPIC-supported projects must not have negative economic effects on U.S. employment and industry and must fulfill other statutory requirements.

OPIC's budget is fully self-sustaining from its own revenues. Congress, as part of its oversight activities, annually provides OPIC with the authority to cover its administrative expenses and credit subsidy funding from user fees and its own income. The Omnibus Appropriations Act of 2009 (P.L. 111-8) extended OPIC's authority through September 30, 2009. The Act provided $50.6 million for OPIC's administrative expenses and authorized a transfer of $29 million from OPIC's noncredit account to conduct its credit and insurance programs. Legislation to extend OPIC reauthorization until September 30, 2013 (S. 705) has been introduced in the 111th Congress.

Chapter 3 - Foreign acquisitions of U.S. companies can pose a significant challenge for the U.S. government because of the need to balance the benefits of foreign investment with national security concerns. The Exon-Florio amendment to the Defense Production Act authorizes the President to suspend or prohibit foreign acquisitions of U.S. companies that may harm national security.

To better understand how other countries deal with similar challenges, GAO was asked to identify how other countries address the issues that Exon-Florio is intended to address. Specifically, this chapter describes selected countries' (1) laws and policies enacted to regulate foreign investment to protect their national security interests and (2) implementation of those laws and policies.

This chapter updates a 1996 GAO report that describes how four major foreign investors in the United States—France, Germany, Japan, and the United Kingdom— monitored foreign investment in their own countries to protect national security interests. It also examines foreign investment in six additional countries: Canada, China, India, the Netherlands, Russia, and the United Arab Emirates (UAE). GAO reviewed selected laws and regulations and interviewed foreign government officials and others concerning their implementation and any planned changes to their foreign investment laws, regulations, and policies.

Chapter 4 - The rising economic importance of multinational firms has been accompanied by significant changes in their structure and functioning. Multinational firms, historically characterized as webs of autonomous subsidiaries spread across countries, now represent globally integrated production systems serving worldwide customers. These changes are manifest in the rising significance of intrafirm trade and financial flows for these firms. While there is extensive analysis of aggregate patterns in intrafirm flows of goods and capital, few firm-based studies examine the workings of the internal markets of multinational firms, largely because of the difficulty in accessing the necessary data.

A number of our recent projects investigated the internal markets of U.S. multinational firms. Our research demonstrates that internal market operations represent a critical aspect of firm responses to costly external finance, capital controls, and currency fluctuations. Our research also shows that the changing nature of internal markets has influenced how firms operate and finance themselves around the world. An important insight emerging from this research is that firms use internal markets opportunistically, particularly in response to distortions in local markets. This Research Spotlight summarizes this body of work.

Our research is based on work conducted at the U.S. Bureau of Economic Analysis (BEA) through a special program that provides access to the agency's rich store of confidential firm-level data on multinational companies for analytical purposes (see the box "BEA Program for Outside Researchers"). The firm-level data collected in BEA's surveys of international direct investment are used by BEA to produce aggregated tabular data on multinational-company operations for release to the general public. In its benchmark and annual surveys of U.S. direct investment abroad, BEA collects the most comprehensive and reliable available data on the activities of U.S. multinational firms.

Chapter 5 - Three key measures of the worldwide operations of nonbank U.S. multinational companies (MNCs)—value added, employment, and capital expenditures—continued to increase in 2007, according to preliminary results from the annual survey of U.S. direct investment abroad conducted by the Bureau of Economic Analysis (BEA).[1] The preliminary 2007 estimates in this article supersede the advance summary estimates of U.S. MNC employment, capital expenditures, and sales, which were released in April (see the box "Revisions").

In 2007, all three of these measures of U.S. MNC operations grew for the fourth consecutive year, but the rate of growth for two of them—value added and capital expenditures—decelerated from 2006. Both domestic and foreign operations continued to grow, but the growth in foreign operations was faster than the growth in domestic operations. The worldwide current-dollar value added of U.S. MNCs—the combined value added of U.S. parent companies and their majority-owned foreign affiliates ("foreign affiliates")—increased 4.8 percent; value added of parents increased 2.0 percent, while value added of foreign affiliates increased 11.6 percent (table 1). Value added measures the contribution of a company to the gross domestic product (GDP) of its country of location.

Chapter 6 - U.S. investors abroad receive a higher return on their assets than their counterparts that invest in the United States. I examine the degree to which excluding intangible assets from the measurement of foreign direct investment can account for this gap. Using a growth accounting framework, I estimate intangible capital stocks for foreign-owned affiliates and find that including unmeasured capital reduces the gap by up to two thirds. U.S. affiliates abroad hold a relatively large share of their assets as intangible capital since they are taxed at the relatively high U.S. corporate rate and intangible investment is expensed. Accounting for intangibles reduces a similar gap in British FDI returns by nearly half.

Chapter 7 - IN 2008, both the U.S. direct investment abroad and foreign direct investment in the United States positions, valued at historical-cost, grew 8 percent. This marked a slowdown in growth for both positions compared with 2007, when the U.S. direct investment abroad—or "outward"—position rose 18 percent and the foreign direct investment in the United States—or "inward"—position rose 15 percent.[1]

The much slower growth in the outward direct investment position reflected a drop in new investment activity abroad by U.S. parent companies.[2] The slowdown in growth in the inward direct investment position reflected the write-downs of financial assets, especially in banking and nonbank finance and insurance, as a result of unsettled conditions in financial markets.

In: Direct Investment Abroad
Editor: Caleb J. Blackwell

ISBN: 978-1-61668-857-8
© 2010 Nova Science Publishers, Inc.

Chapter 1

U.S. DIRECT INVESTMENT ABROAD: TRENDS AND CURRENT ISSUES*

James K. Jackson

SUMMARY

The United States is the largest investor abroad and the largest recipient of direct investment in the world. For some Americans, the national gains attributed to investing overseas are offset by such perceived losses as displaced U.S. workers and lower wages. Some observers believe U.S. firms invest abroad to avoid U.S. labor unions or high U.S. wages, however, 70% of U.S. foreign direct investment is concentrated in high income developed countries. Even more striking is the fact that the share of investment going to developing countries has fallen in recent years. Most economists conclude that direct investment abroad does not lead to fewer jobs or lower incomes overall for Americans and that the majority of jobs lost among U.S. manufacturing firms over the past decade reflect a broad restructuring of U.S. manufacturing industries.

RECENT INVESTMENTS

New spending by U.S. firms on businesses and real estate abroad, or U.S. direct investment abroad,[1] although substantial, fell slightly in 2008 compared to 2007. Net investments fell from $333 billion in 2007 to $318 billion in 2008, according to the Department of Commerce.[2] A drop in U.S. direct investment abroad that occurred in 2005 reflects actions by U.S. parent firms to reduce the amount of reinvested earnings going to their foreign affiliates for distribution to the U.S. parent firms in order to take advantage of one-time tax provisions in the American Jobs Creation Act of 2004 (P.L. 108-357).

---

* This is an edited, reformatted and augmented version of a CRS Report for Congress publication dated November 2009,

Generally, relative rates of growth between U.S. and foreign economies largely determine the direction and magnitude of direct investment flows. These flows also are affected by relative rates of inflation, interest rates, and expectations about the performance of national economies, which means they can be quite erratic at times. The drop in U.S. direct investment abroad in 2008 compared with 2007 reflected an increase in equity capital, a decrease in intercompany debt, an increase in reinvested earnings arising from an increase in distributed earnings, and a large currency devaluation.. The sharp drop in stock market valuations around the world in 2008 devalued U.S. direct investment abroad, measured at market value, by $2.2 trillion. During the same period, the market value of foreign firms operating in the United states experienced a loss of over $1.0 trillion in 2008.

Since the mid-1990s, the combination of strong growth and low inflation in the U.S. economy attracted foreign investors, as indicated in Figure 1. From 2002 to 2007, U.S. direct investment abroad averaged more than twice the amount foreigners invested in the U.S. economy, reflecting the period of slower growth in the economy from 2001-2003. Data for the first two quarters of 2009 indicate that U.S. direct investment abroad is about half the amount recorded in the comparable period in 2008. Such investments way well pick up in the second half of the year as the rate of economic growth improves. On the whole, U.S. firms are the most prolific overseas investors: a recent study by the United Nations indicates that U.S. firms are the largest foreign direct investors in the world and own as much abroad as the British and Germans combined, the next largest foreign direct investors.

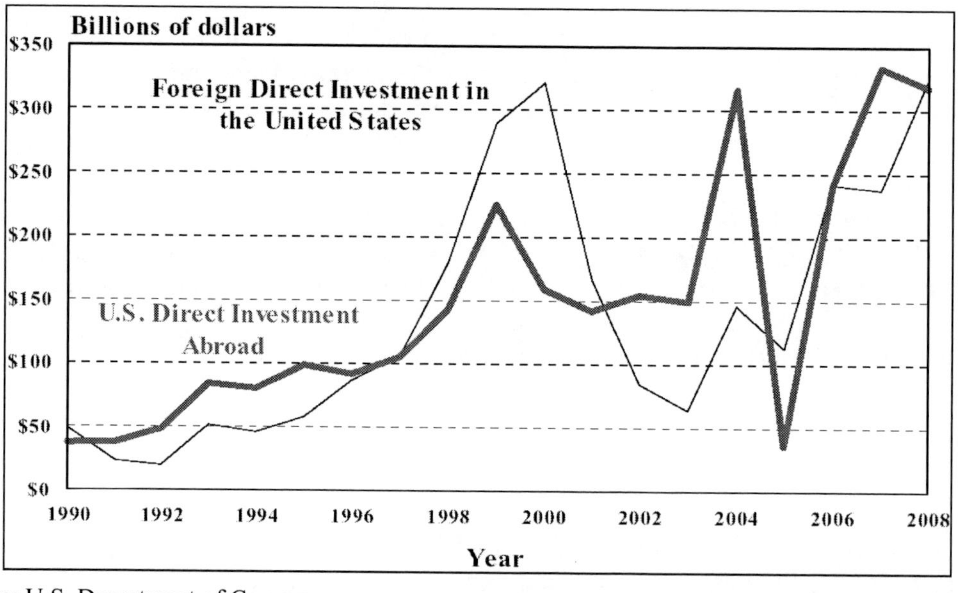

Source: U.S. Department of Commerce

Note: The drop in U.S. direct investment abroad in 2005 reflects actions by U.S. parent firms to reduce the amount of reinvested earnings going to their foreign affiliates for distribution to the U.S. parent firms in order to take advantage of one-time tax provisions in the American Jobs Creation Act of 2004 (P.L. 108-357).

Figure 1. Foreign Direct Investment in the United States and U.S. Direct Investment Abroad, Annual Flows, 1990-2008 (in billions of dollars)

Table 1. U.S. Direct Investment Position Abroad on a Historical-Cost Basisat Year-End 2008 (in millions of dollars)

	All industries	Manufacturing	Wholesale trade	Information	Banking	Finance	Services	Holding companies	Other
All	**3,162,021**	**512,293**	**178,213**	**121,864**	**141,557**	**634,046**	**81,242**	**1,128,538**	**212,409**
Canada	227,298	72,523	18,332	4,113	3,676	32,728	8,164	30,511	33,472
Europe	**1,809,876**	**259,844**	**99,980**	**80,971**	**80,823**	**328,307**	**53,845**	**750,883**	**116,716**
Belgium	65,054	20,058	6,234	-758	(D)	31,434	1,811	2,857	(D)
France	75,040	29,207	4,850	2,250	2,059	9,201	2,602	12,398	12,375
Germany	110,784	33,993	10,501	2,495	2,321	14,441	5,401	32,769	8,450
Ireland	146,194	19,051	1,249	15,723	10,227	24,235	(D)	27,596	26,588
Italy	28,653	11,684	3,153	1,967	412	3,071	1,160	1,925	5,221
Luxemb.	163,167	6,305	2,684	1,734	1,033	30,383	80	120,320	467
Netherl.	442,926	33,026	17,120	8,099	(D)	49,629	(D)	306,257	(D)
Spain	69,649	11,379	3,337	254	986	7,506	2,123	40,850	3,138
Sweden	43,391	3,286	736	749	(D)	15,618	546	19,862	(D)
Switzer.	123,358	8,996	21,423	2,649	7,240	4,844	632	70,100	7,284
Turkey	6,089	1,507	1,749	-42	2,703	65	20	-4	93
UK	420,873	56,685	17,689	42,867	19,727	122,854	13,913	101,062	37,060
LAmerica	**563,809**	**60,709**	**24,265**	**8,609**	**12,699**	**195,083**	**2,078**	**204,950**	**24,724**
Brazil	45,500	20,357	980	2,210	3,096	9,286	616	6,287	444
Chile	12,613	2,238	968	127	1,394	3,978	129	617	2,104
Venez’	17,332	3,951	263	81	(D)	3,057	206	7,610	(D)
Mexico	95,618	21,821	2,361	2,758	(D)	15,736	460	16,865	(D)

Table 1. (Continued)

	All industries	Manufacturing	Wholesale trade	Information	Banking	Finance	Services	Holding companies	Other
Bermuda	165,857	1,303	3,790	632	(D)	81,179	272	72,566	(D)
Dom. Republic	960	599	137	(D)	(D)	1	1	(*)	10
UK Car.	139,290	695	10,699	436	-16,963	(D)	98	(D)	1,716
Africa	**36,640**	**2,856**	**1,157**	**128**	**1,899**	**1,814**	**372**	**8,664**	**1,375**
Middle East	**32,488**	**11,763**	**2,145**	**1,447**	**720**	**569**	**933**	**7,594**	**799**
Asia	**491,910**	**104,598**	**32,334**	**26,596**	**41,740**	**75,544**	**15,850**	**125,935**	**35,324**
Austral.	88,549	12,743	3,856	13,100	2,285	11,275	3,762	13,875	7,310
China	45,695	21,428	3,219	223	(D)	1,895	773	1,556	(D)
HK	51,505	3,742	6,858	833	3,694	11,535	2,931	19,552	2,360
Japan	79,235	17,380	9,036	5,609	1,144	28,032	2,806	5,911	9,316
Korea	27,673	9,165	1,812	448	(D)	3,625	332	(D)	(D)
Sing.	106,529	16,544	3,322	2,130	(D)	6,782	1,329	71,250	(D)
Taiwan	16,604	3,816	2,018	310	(D)	7,141	295	102	(D)
OPEC	69,299	9,879	1,909	146	(D)	4,206	828	29,774	(D)

Source: Ibarra, Marilyn, and Jennifer Koncz, Direct Investment Positions for 2008: Country and Industry Detail. *Survey of Current Business*, July 2009. p.32.

Note: A (D) indicates that the data have been suppressed by the Department of Commerce to avoid disclosing the data of individual companies.

Table 1 indicates that the overseas direct investment position of U.S. firms on a historical-cost basis,[3] or the cumulative amount at book value, reached $3.2 trillion in 2008, the latest year for such investment position data.[4] More than 70% of these overseas investments are in developed countries: Europe alone accounts for over half of all U.S. direct investment abroad, or $1.8 trillion. Europe has been a prime target of U.S. investment since U.S. firms first invested abroad in the 1 860s. American firms began investing heavily in Europe following World War II as European countries rebuilt their economies and later when they formed an intra-European economic union.

Typically, U.S. firms have placed the largest share of their annual investments in developed countries, primarily in Western Europe, but this tendency has increased since the mid-1990s. In the last half of the 1990s, U.S. direct investment abroad experienced a dramatic shift from developing countries to the richest developed economies: the share of U.S. direct investment going to developing countries fell from 37% in 1996 to 21% in 2000. In 2008, U.S. firms focused a slightly greater percent of their investment funds in Europe and Latin America, while scaling down the share of their investment spending in Canada. Developed countries received 70% of the investment funds of U.S. multinational firms, while developing countries received 30%.

Patterns in U.S. direct investment abroad generally reflect fundamental changes that occur in the U.S. economy during the same period. As investment funds in the U.S. economy shifted from extractive, processing, and manufacturing industries toward high technology services and financial industries, U.S. investment abroad mirrored these changes. As a result, U.S. direct investment abroad focused less on the extractive, processing, and basic manufacturing industries in developing countries and more on high technology, finance, and services industries located in highly-developed countries with advanced infrastructure and communications systems. The total amount of U.S. direct investment abroad, or the position, during the 2000-2008 period more than doubled, rising from $920 billion to $2.4 trillion. Investments in the banking, finance, and insurance sectors all fell in 2008, reflecting the financial crisis. Generally, service-oriented sectors continued to grow through 2008. Within the manufacturing sector, the direct investment position fell in most sectors in 2008, reflecting the economic recession that had started earlier in that year.

U.S. MULTINATIONALS

Nations once hostile to American direct investment now compete aggressively by offering incentives to U.S. firms. A debate continues within the United States, however, over the relative merits of U.S. direct investment abroad. Some Americans believe that U.S. direct investment abroad, directly or indirectly, shifts some jobs to low wage countries. They argue that such shifts reduce employment in the United States and increase imports, thereby affecting negatively both U.S. employment and economic growth. Economists generally believe that firms invest abroad because those firms possess some special process or product knowledge or because they possess special managerial abilities which give them an advantage over other firms. On the whole, U.S. firms invest abroad to serve the foreign local market, rather than to produce goods to export to the United States, although some firms do establish overseas operations to replace U.S. exports or production, or to gain access to raw materials, cheap labor, or other markets. On average, about 8% of affiliate sales are to the U.S. parent companies.[5]

U.S. multinational corporations (MNCs) rank among the largest U.S. firms. According to data collected by the Commerce Department's Bureau of Economic Analysis (BEA), when American parent companies and their foreign affiliates are compared by the size structure of employment classes, 40% of the more than 2,000 U.S. parent companies employ more than 2,499 persons. These large parent firms account for 95% of the total number of people employed by U.S. MNCs. Employment abroad is even more concentrated among the largest foreign affiliates of U.S. parent firms: the largest 2% of the affiliates account for 90% of affiliate employment.[6]

While U.S. MNCs used their economic strengths to expand abroad between the 1980s and early 2000s, the U.S.-based parent firms lost market positions at home, in large part due to corporate downsizing efforts to improve profits. U.S. MNC parent companies' share of all U.S. business gross domestic product (GDP)—the broadest measure of economic activity—declined from 32% to 25% from 1977 to 1989.[7] In 2007 (the latest year for which estimates are available), U.S. parent companies accounted for about 21% of total U.S. business activity. These MNC parent companies accounted for about 41% of total U.S. manufacturing activity, down from 46% in 2000.

As U.S. MNC parent companies were losing their relative market positions at home, their cumulative amount of direct investment abroad doubled. This increase did spur a shift in some economic activity among the U.S. MNCs from the U.S. parent companies to the foreign affiliates. During the period from 2000 to 2007, the foreign affiliates increased their share of the total economic activity within U.S. MNCs—the combined economic output of the U.S. parent and the foreign affiliates—from 22% to 30%.[8]

EMPLOYMENT

One of the most commonly expressed concerns about U.S. direct investment abroad is that U.S. parent companies invest abroad in order to send low-wage jobs overseas. Such effects are difficult to measure because they are small compared with much larger changes occurring within the U.S. economy. In addition, a cursory examination of the data seems to indicate that employment losses among parent firms occurred simultaneously with gains in foreign subsidiaries, thereby giving the impression that jobs are being shifted abroad. Employment among U.S. parent companies fell during the early 1980s, but increased in the 1992-2000 period, from 17.5 million to 23.9 million. From 2000 to 2003, however, employment among U.S. parent companies fell by 12% to 21.1 million, before rising after 2003 to reach 22 million in 2007 as U.S. economic growth picked up. Employment among foreign affiliates also rose in 2007 by 4.0% to 10.0 million, from 9.6 million in 2006.

After employment losses in the early 1980s, employment at both the parent firms and the foreign affiliates increased after 1992, although at different rates and in different industries. Both the U.S. parent companies and the foreign affiliates lost employment during the first part of the 2000s as the U.S. economy recovered from a period of slow growth. During such downturns, U.S. parent firms and their foreign affiliates often lose or gain employment in many of the same industries. Both the parent firms and the affiliates lost employment in the petroleum and finance sectors, although both gained employment in the services and wholesale trade sectors. Furthermore, employment gains and losses among MNCs more likely reflect fundamental shifts within the U.S. economy, than any formal or informal efforts to shift employment abroad.

Some observers also contend that U.S. direct investment abroad supplants U.S. exports, thereby worsening the U.S. trade deficit and eliminating some U.S. jobs. Most analyses indicate, however, that intra-company trade, or trade between the U.S. parent company and its foreign subsidiaries, represents a large share of U.S. trade and that foreign investment typically boosts U.S. exports more than it contributes to a rise in imports or to a loss of exports. For instance, American multinational corporations account for over 60% of U.S. exports and 40% of U.S. imports, indicating that U.S. parent firms tend to be a more important source of supply to their affiliates than the affiliates are to their parent companies.

CONCLUSIONS

American direct investment abroad has grown sharply since the mid-1990s, raising questions for many observers about the effects of such investment on the U.S. economy. These questions seem pertinent since American multinational corporations lost shares of U.S. GDP over the last decade and their domestic employment had declined until the mid-1990s. Increased economic activity abroad relative to that in the United States increased overseas affiliate employment in some industries, including manufacturing. Most of this affiliate activity, however, is geared toward supplying the local markets in which they are located. In 2004, 9.5% of the sales of the foreign affiliates of U.S. firms was accounted for by exports back to the United States,[9] although this share is nonetheless substantial.

Some observers believe U.S. direct investment abroad is harmful to U.S. workers because it shifts jobs abroad. There is no conclusive evidence in the data collected to date to indicate that current investment trends are substantially different from those of previous periods or that jobs are moving offshore at a rate that is significantly different from previous periods.[10] There are instances when firms shift activities abroad to take advantage of lower labor costs. However, it is clear from the data that the majority of U.S. direct investment abroad is in developed countries where wages, markets, industries, and consumers' tastes are similar to those in the United States. U.S. direct investment in these developed countries is oriented toward serving the markets where the affiliates are located and they tend, in the aggregate, to boost exports from the United States. In addition, foreign firms have been pouring record amounts of money into the United States to acquire existing U.S. firms, to expand existing subsidiaries, or to establish "greenfield" or new investments.

End Notes

[1] The United States defines direct investment abroad as the ownership or control, directly or indirectly, by one person (individual, branch, partnership, association, government, etc.) of 10% or more of the voting securities of an incorporated business enterprise or an equivalent interest in an unincorporated business enterprise. 15 CFR § 806.15 (a)(1).

[2] Weinberg, Douglas B., Erin M. Whitaker, and Gregory A. Tenentes, U.S. International Transactions: Fourth quarter and Year 2008. *Survey of Current Business*, April 2009, p. 28. Direct investment data reported in the

balance of payments differ from capital flow data reported elsewhere, because the balance of payments data have not been adjusted for current cost adjustments to earnings.

[3] The position, or stock, is the net book value of U.S. parent company's equity in, and outstanding loans to, their affiliates abroad. A change in the position in a given year consists of three components: equity and intercompany inflows, reinvested earnings of incorporated affiliates, and valuation adjustments to account for changes in the value of financial assets. The Commerce Department also publishes data on the U.S. direct investment position valued on a current-cost and market value bases. These estimates indicate that U.S. direct investment abroad measured at current cost increased by $247 billion, but fell when measured by market value by $2.2 trillion in 2008, to reach $3.7 and $3.1 trillion, respectively.

[4] Ibarra, Marilyn, and Jennifer Koncz, Direct Investment Positions for 2008: Country and Industry Detail, *Survey of Current Business*, July, 2009. p. 32.

[5] *U.S. Direct Investment Abroad: Operations of U.S. Parent Companies and Their Foreign Affiliates, Preliminary 2004 Estimates*, October 2006. Table III. F. 1.

[6] Mataloni, Raymond J. Jr. U.S. Multinational Companies: Operations in 1998. *Survey of Current Business*, July 2000. pp. 24-45.

[7] Mataloni, Raymond J. Jr. U.S. Multinational Companies: Operations in 2003. *Survey of Current Business*, July 2005. p. 15.

[8] Ibid., p. 31.

[9] Mataloni, Operations of U.S. Multinational Companies. p. 41.

[10] CRS Report RL32461, *Outsourcing and Insourcing Jobs in the U.S. Economy: Evidence Based on Foreign Investment Data*, by James K. Jackson.

Chapter 2

THE OVERSEAS PRIVATE INVESTMENT CORPORATION: BACKGROUND AND LEGISLATIVE ISSUES*

Shayerah Ilias

SUMMARY

The Overseas Private Investment Corporation (OPIC) was established in 1969 and began operations in 1971 as a development agency to promote and assist U.S. business investment in developing nations. Today, OPIC is a U.S. government agency that provides project financing, investment insurance, and other services for U.S. businesses in over 150 developing nations and emerging economies. To date, OPIC has funded, guaranteed, or insured over $180 billion in investments.

OPIC's activities are guided by U.S. foreign policy objectives. Geographical priority areas for OPIC-supported activities are sub-Saharan Africa, the Broader Middle East and North Africa, and Asia. Sectoral priorities for the agency are renewable energy and access to credit for micro-, small-, and medium-sized enterprises. OPIC-supported projects must not have negative economic effects on U.S. employment and industry and must fulfill other statutory requirements.

OPIC's budget is fully self-sustaining from its own revenues. Congress, as part of its oversight activities, annually provides OPIC with the authority to cover its administrative expenses and credit subsidy funding from user fees and its own income. The Omnibus Appropriations Act of 2009 (P.L. 111-8) extended OPIC's authority through September 30, 2009. The Act provided $50.6 million for OPIC's administrative expenses and authorized a transfer of $29 million from OPIC's noncredit account to conduct its credit and insurance programs. Legislation to extend OPIC reauthorization until September 30, 2013 (S. 705) has been introduced in the 111th Congress.

---

* This is an edited, reformatted and augmented version of a CRS Report for Congress publication dated December 2009,

Background

The Overseas Private Investment Corporation (OP IC) is a U.S. government agency that provides project financing, investment insurance, and other services for U.S. businesses in over 150 developing nations and emerging economies.[1] Structured like a private corporation, OPIC operates on a self-sustaining basis to mobilize and facilitate private capital investment in developing countries. The agency has recorded a positive net income for every year of operation, with reserves (comprised of U.S. Treasury securities) totaling about $5 billion.[2]

Created under the Foreign Assistance Act of 1961 (P.L. 87-195) as amended, OPIC was established in 1969 and began operations in 1971 as a development agency amid an atmosphere of congressional disillusionment overall with U.S. aid programs, especially large infrastructure projects. In his first message to Congress on aid, President Nixon recommended the creation of OPIC to assume the investment guaranty and promotion functions that were being conducted by the U.S. Agency for International Development (AID). President Nixon also directed that OPIC would provide "businesslike management of investment incentives" to contribute to the economic and social progress of developing nations.[3]

In creating OPIC, the Nixon Administration indicated that it was not attempting to end official U.S. foreign assistance, because "private capital and technical assistance cannot substitute for government assistance programs," a combination that can provide, "official aid on the one hand, and private investment and technical assistance on the other." Private investment activities, however, were meant to complement the official assistance programs and, thereby, multiply the benefits of both. In addition, market-oriented private investment was viewed as an antidote to the government-oriented aid projects that were considered by some to be costly and inefficient. OPIC was created as a first step in the eventual overhaul of the entire U.S. aid program. In 1973, this overhaul was completed as the United States largely abandoned infrastructure building and other large capital projects in favor of humanitarian aid to meet basic human needs.

At present, OPIC is directed to "mobilize and facilitate the participation of United States private capital and skills in the economic and social development of less developed countries and areas, and countries in transition from nonmarket to market economies... under the policy guidance of the Secretary of State."[4] OPIC's programs are intended to promote U.S. private investment in less developed countries by mitigating risks, such as political risks (including currency inconvertibility, expropriation, political violence, and terrorism), for U.S. firms making qualified investment overseas. To accomplish these goals, OPIC is authorized to finance U.S. investment through loans and guarantees, insure against political risk, and provide various investor services. OPIC's authority to guaranty and insure U.S. investments abroad is backed by the full faith and credit of the U.S. government and OPIC's own financial resources.

In addition to their development objectives, OPIC's activities are intended to assist U.S. firms and small businesses' foreign operations. For instance, Congress directed OPIC to focus on projects that have "positive trade benefits for the United States." OPIC is required to decline its services, however, if it determines an overseas investment may reduce employment in the United States, either because a U.S. firm shifts part of its production abroad, or because output from an overseas investment will be shipped to the United States and "reduce substantially the positive trade benefits" of the investment.[5] OPIC also is generally barred by its enabling legislation from participating in projects that pose an "unreasonable or major environmental health, or safety, hazard," or participating in countries that do not "extend internationally recognized workers rights," or that impose domestic content requirements.

PROGRAMS

OPIC operates in over 150 countries and areas worldwide. As OPIC's activities are guided by U.S. foreign policy objectives, OPIC has identified three priority regions—sub-Saharan Africa, the Broader Middle East and North Africa, and Asia—where it believes that OPIC-supported private investment could advance U.S. foreign policy goals. In recent years, OPIC also has identified sectoral priorities for its activities, including renewable energy and access to credit for micro-, small-, and medium-sized enterprises. To date, OPIC has funded, guaranteed, or insured over $180 billion in investments.[6] Although OPIC offers U.S. firms an array of services, its activities can be grouped into three categories: finance, insurance, and support for private equity funds.

Finance

OPIC's finance program operates like an investment bank, customizing and structuring a complete package for individual projects in countries where conventional financing institutions often are unwilling or unable to lend on a reasonable basis. The finance program is carried out through two departments, one that focuses on projects involving small- and medium-sized enterprises and the other that focuses on larger infrastructure and financial services projects involving larger U.S. businesses.

To obtain OPIC financing, the venture must be commercially and financially sound and have some portion of U.S. ownership. Projects may be wholly owned by U.S. companies, foreign subsidiaries of U.S. companies, or joint ventures involving local companies and U.S. sponsored firms. In the case of a joint venture involving existing firms, the U.S. investor generally is expected to own at least 25% of the equity of the project. For new ventures, financing may be equal to 50% of the total project cost; a larger share is possible for plant expansions.

The amount of OPIC's participation may vary taking into consideration financial risks and benefits. In general, OPIC will not support more than 75% of the total investment. OPIC provides financing to investors through two major programs: direct loans and loan guarantees. Direct loans generally range between $100,000 and $10 million, although they can be more in certain cases. Direct loans are available only for ventures sponsored by, or significantly involving, U.S. small- and medium-sized businesses or cooperatives (such as joint ventures).

Loan guarantees typically are used for larger projects, ranging in size from $10 million to $250 million, but in certain cases can be as high as $400 million. OPIC's guarantees are issued to financial institutions that are more than 50%-owned by U.S. citizens, corporations, or partnerships. Rates and conditions on loans and guarantees depend on financial market conditions at the time and on OPIC's assessment of the financial and political risks involved.

Consistent with commercial lending practices, OPIC charges up-front, commitment, and cancellation fees, and reimbursement is required for project-related expenses.

As part of its thrust toward U.S. small business investors, OPIC established the Enterprise Development Network (EDN) in June 2007. Under the EDN, OPIC collaborates with participating financial intermediaries to expand access of small businesses to OPIC-supported products and services. OPIC recently announced the selection of several financial consulting firms to serve as loan originators in the EDN.[7]

Insurance

OPIC political risk insurance is available to U.S. citizens, U.S. firms, or to the foreign subsidiaries of U.S. firms as long as the foreign subsidiary is at least 95%-owned by a U.S. citizen. According to OPIC, such insurance is available for investments in new ventures or in expansions of existing enterprises, and can cover equity investments, parent company and third party loans and loan guarantees, technical assistance agreements, cross-border leases, assigned inventory or equipment, and other forms of investment. This insurance covers three broad areas of political risk: currency inconvertibility, expropriation, and political violence. **Currency inconvertibility** coverage compensates investors if new currency restrictions are imposed which prevent the conversion and transfer of remittances from insured investments, but it does not protect against currency devaluation.

Expropriation coverage protects U.S. firms against the nationalization, confiscation, or expropriation of an enterprise, including actions by foreign governments that deprive an investor of fundamental rights or financial interests in a project for a period of at least six months. This coverage excludes losses that may arise from lawful regulatory or revenue actions by a foreign government and actions instigated or provoked by the investor of foreign firm.

Political violence coverage compensates U.S. citizens and firms for property and income losses directly caused by various kinds of violence, including declared or undeclared wars, hostile actions by national or international forces, civil war, revolution, insurrection, and civil strife (including politically motivated terrorism and sabotage). Income loss insurance protects the investor's share of income from losses that result from damage to the insured property caused by political violence. Assets coverage compensates U.S. citizens and firms for losses of or damage to tangible property caused by political violence. OPIC also has a number of special programs that protect U.S. banks from political violence. This type of insurance reduces risks for banks and other institutional investors, which allows them to play a more active role in financing projects in developing countries. Specialized types of insurance coverage also is available for U.S. investors involved with certain contracting, exporting, licensing, or leasing transactions that are undertaken in a developing country.

Investment Development

OPIC also supports and mobilizes risk capital by providing debt capital for the creation of privately-owned and privately-managed equity **investment funds**. These funds make direct equity and equity-related investments in new, expanding or privatizing emerging market economies. In most instances, OPIC provides up to one-third of the fund's total capital, and receives debt returns on its investment. OPIC supports these funds in situations where U.S. firms either cannot allocate or cannot raise sufficient capital to start or expand their businesses overseas. OPIC uses a competitive selection process in order to select fund managers with venture capital investment capability and experience. Since the initiation of its investment funds program in 1987, OPIC has committed $3.6 billion in funding to more than 50 private equity funds. These funds subsequently have invested $4.6 billion in over 470 privately owned and privately managed companies, mainly in small- and medium-sized enterprises, in regions eligible for OPIC support.

By geographical area, nearly half (47%) of all of OPIC-supported investment funds are located in Africa. For example, as part of OPIC's initiative to broaden and deepen capital markets in Sub- Saharan Africa, OPIC's Board of Directors has approved a number of investment funds, including the Africa Catalyst Fund, Atlantic Coast Regional Fund, and Millennium Global Africa Opportunities. For each fund, OPIC will provide around $100 million in financing.[8] Other regions where OPIC-supported investment funds are concentrated include Central/Eastern Europe (15%), Latin America/Caribbean (15%), and Asian (1 2%).[9]

OPIC supports investment funds in a range of economic sectors. Projects in the technology/media/telecommunications area and in financial services account for about one-fifth of all of OPIC-supported investment funds. In line with OPIC's sectoral focus on renewable energy, OPIC's Board of Directors has approved $505 million in financing for several new private equity funds established to invest in clean and renewable energy projects in developing markets. These funds include the Middle East & Asia Capital Partners Clean Energy Fund II, South Asia Clean Energy Fund, FE Global Clean Energy Services Fund IV, and US Renewable Group Emerging Market Fund. [10]

In addition, OPIC offers limited pre-investment services to aid U.S. investors. For instance, OPIC sponsors periodic investment conferences to inform U.S. businesses about investment opportunities. As part of these activities, OPIC has sponsored a series of regional outreach workshops to provide women- and minority-owned businesses with information and contacts for investing in overseas markets.[11]

OPIC's Budget

OPIC's budget is fully self-funded from its own revenues. Each year, however, Congress provides through the appropriations process authority for OPIC to pay its administrative expenses and credit subsidy funding from user fees and other income. This fulfills OPIC's statutory mandate to conduct its operations on a "self-sustaining basis." These funds are not actually provided to OPIC, because OPIC relies on its own resources. Congress follows this procedure in order to exercise its oversight role and to set limits on the extent to which OPIC can obligate U.S. government resources.

Table 1. OPIC's Budget Summary (in millions of dollars)

	FY04 Actual	FY05 Actual	FY06 Actual	FY07 Actual	FY08 Actual	FY09 Est.	FY10 Est.
NON CREDIT ACCOUNT							
Operating Expenses	$41	$43	$42	$43	$48	$50	$52
Noncredit administrative expenses	16	17	17	18	29	20	21
Credit administrative expenses [a]	25	26	25	25	19	30	31
Other Noncredit Expenses	53	4	120	45	28	24	23
Insurance claim payments/provisions	—	—	118	33	25	10	20
Adjustments to accounts	3	2	2	4	3	5	3
Iraq Middle Market Development Foundation	50	2	—	8	—	9	—
Subtotal, Budget authority (gross)	81	51	172	112	83	201	182
Subtotal, Outlays (gross)	180	-10	46	52	49	55	70
Offsetting collections	-316	-257	-323	-292	-295	-260	-242
Federal sources	-50	-26	-25	-34	-39	-30	-31
Interest on U.S. securities	-222	-203	-200	-206	-212	-210	-191
Non-Federal sources	-44	-28	-22	-24	-18	-20	-20
	FY04 Actual	**FY05 Actual**	**FY06 Actual**	**FY07 Actual**	**FY08 Actual**	**FY09 Est.**	**FY10 Est.**
Budget authority (net)	-229	-201	-153	-185	-208	-59	-60
Outlays (net)	-135	-267	-277	-240	-246	-205	-172
Budget authority:							
Transferred to other accounts [b]	48	49	45	45	52	59	60
CREDIT ACCOUNT							
Total New Program Obligations [c]	198	180	167	177	110	144	72
Direct loan subsidy	6	22	7	16	6	7	13
Guaranteed loan subsidy	33	11	1	20	5	14	19
Program cost re-estimates	134	121	134	116	70	89	—
Credit administrative expenses [a]	25	26	25	25	29	29	31
Budget Authority (net)	182	174	179	161	123	148	60
Appropriations [d]	134	120	134	116	71	89	—
From other accounts [c]	48	49	45	45	52	59	60

Source: *Budget of the United States Government*, various years. U.S. Government Printing Office, Washington.

Notes:

a Credit administrative expenses originate from noncredit account balances and are transferred to the program account where they are returned to the noncredit account as collection. In this way, the program account reflects the cost of the credit program.

b Budget authority transferred to other accounts, including OPIC's credit account.

c These funds include transfers from OPIC's noncredit account (see footnote 'a') and from the Export-Import Bank and AID for OPIC guarantees to Newly Independent States (NIS) countries.

d OPIC does not receive an appropriation for the initial funding of its credit program subsidy. In accordance with the Federal Credit Reform Act, OPIC receives an appropriation for the funding of the upward subsidy re-estimates.

Prior to FY1992, OPIC relied exclusively on non-appropriated resources (fees and interest on Treasury securities) to fund its operations. With federal government credit reform, however, OPIC was required to receive an appropriation based on an estimate of its credit programs (direct loans and guarantees). From 1992 to 1994, OPIC returned to the General Fund of the U.S. Treasury an amount equal to its direct appropriation. For FY1998 and beyond, OPIC's appropriations language provides OPIC with the authority to spend from its own income.

OPIC's budget is composed of noncredit and credit accounts, in conformity with the standards set out in the Federal Credit Reform Act of 1990 (see **Table 1**). The noncredit portion of OPIC's budget relates to OPIC's political risk insurance program; its credit program accounts are comprised of OPIC's direct and guaranteed loans. OPIC has accumulated $4.7 billion in assets in its noncredit account, which it uses to fund losses it may experience in its guarantees and insurance coverage. [12] OPIC uses premium income and the interest it accrues from the assets in its noncredit account to fund the direct and indirect expenses in its noncredit and its credit accounts.

In FY2008, the maximum exposure of OPIC's insurance and finance programs stood at $11.3 billion. Of this amount, OPIC's maximum insurance exposure stood at $2.9 billion. The agency's direct loan exposure was $1.2 billion, of which $766 million was outstanding. OPIC had $7.2 billion in exposure for its investment guarantees, of which $4.8 billion was outstanding. Although the agency's total maximum exposure in FY2007 and FY2008 was about the same, OPIC's insurance liability decreased and investment guarantees liability increased from FY2007 to FY2008.

OPIC regularly returns "surplus" funds to the U.S. Treasury. These funds represent a reserve fund against losses that OPIC may accrue from losses through its financing and insurance programs. The transfer of these funds to the Treasury essentially is a transaction in the accounting ledger between the Treasury and OPIC, rather than a cash transfer of funds. Currently, OPIC has accumulated about $5 billion in reserves (comprised of U.S. Treasury securities). [13]

RECENT DEVELOPMENTS

With the advent of the current international financial crisis,[14] OPIC has reported that the risks associated with its investment projects have increased. Private sponsors of OPIC-supported investment projects have faced challenges obtaining private equity and debt financing for projects scheduled to be conducted in the future. Businesses financed and insured by OPIC also have been affected by the global decline in demand. OPIC notes that it has taken measures to monitor current and potential projects in view of the current economic climate.[15]

According to OPIC, the challenges posed by the financial crisis have heightened the need for OPIC's services by U.S. business companies. The international financial crisis has spurred liquidity problems for the U.S. financial sector, leading to a contraction of credit and insurance available in private markets. U.S. companies that are interested in investing in developing countries may turn to OPIC loans, guarantees, and political risk insurance to fill the gap in commercial capacity. OPIC reports that it has experienced an increase in inquiries for its services as a result of tightening of private credit sources. [16]

In other developments, in February 2009, a settlement was reached in an environmental lawsuit brought by Friends of the Earth, Greenpeace, and four cities (Boulder, Colorado and the cities of Arcata, Santa Monica, and Oakland in California) against OPIC and another U.S. government agency, the Export-Import Bank (Ex-Im Bank), in 2002.[17] In the lawsuit, the environmental groups and cities alleged that OPIC and the Ex-Im Bank provided more than $32 billion in financing and insurance from 1990 to 2003, without assessing the extent to which the projects contributed to climate change in the United States as required by the National Environmental Policy Act (NEPA, P.L. 91-190).

Under the settlement, OPIC is able to continue funding such projects, but must take several measures. Among the settlement provisions, OPIC agreed to subject "Category A" projects, those resulting in emissions of more than 100,000 tons of carbon dioxide equivalents, to a NEPAequivalency Environmental Impact Analysis; to make public its determinations about the environmental impact of such projects on its agency website and to provide opportunity for comment; and, on an annual basis, to publicly report greenhouse gas emissions from projects in its active portfolio that emit more than 100,000 tons of carbon dioxide equivalents a year. Consistent with OPIC's ongoing commitment to support renewable energy projects, OPIC also agreed to provide at least $250 million for investment funds to give priority and preferential financing terms to renewable energy projects and to encourage applicants seeking OPIC support to explore opportunities to employ renewable energy sources in project designs. In addition, OPIC has agreed to reduce by 20% over the next ten years the greenhouse gas emissions associated with Category A projects. This is in line with an initiative previously adopted by OPIC in June 2007.[18]

OPIC has taken a series of actions to increase transparency and accountability and to facilitate receipt of information from the public in the project review process. In 2004, OPIC created an Office of Accountability to assess and review complaints about OPIC-supported projects. OPIC also posts on its website public summaries of OPIC-supported projects approved by the OPIC Board of Directors and those delegated by the OPIC Board of Directors to be approved by OPIC management. Recently, OPIC announced several new transparency initiatives, including the posting of detailed project summaries prior to all Board of Directors meetings and the revision of its Environmental Handbook for the first time since 2004 (to be renamed the OPIC Environmental and Social Policy Statement).[19]

LEGISLATIVE ISSUES

Congress does not approve individual OPIC projects, but has a number of oversight responsibilities related to the agency and its activities. The Senate confirms Presidential appointments to OPIC's Board of Directors and to the agency positions of President and Executive Vice President.[20] Congress authorizes OPIC's ability to conduct its credit and insurance programs for a period of time chosen by Congress. In addition, Congress approves an annual appropriation for OPIC that sets an upper limit on the agency's administrative expenses to conduct its programs. Congress also can amend or change OPIC's governing legislation, the Foreign Assistance Act of 1961 (P.L. 87-195) as amended.

The Omnibus Appropriations Act of 2009 (P.L. 111-8) extended OPIC's operating authority through September 30, 2009. The Act provided self-funding for OPIC; it set a limit of $50.6 million for OPIC's administrative expenses and authorized a transfer of $29 million from OPIC's noncredit account to conduct its credit and insurance programs. For FY20 10, the State-Foreign Operations Appropriations bills (H.R. 3081, S. 1434) would set a limit of $52.31 million to fund OPIC's administrative expenses and would authorize a transfer of $29 million for its credit and insurance programs to be funded by a transfer from OPIC's noncredit account.

On March 25, 2009, the Senate introduced S. 705 to reauthorize OPIC until September 30, 2013. The bill directs OPIC to ensure transparency and accountability of its investments funds through the use of competitive, open procedures in the selection of its investment fund managers and through annual reporting requirements. The bill also requires OPIC to provide more information to the public on the methodology used to evaluate the impacts of OPIC projects and to provide more opportunity for public input on OPIC projects. In addition, the legislation directs OPIC to ensure that extractive industry projects conform to Extractive Industry Transparency Initiative (EITI) standards and principles and to give preference to projects in which eligible investors have agreed to implement the transparency standards and principles. The bill also extends OPIC's authority to conduct projects in Iraq. Among other provisions, the bill strengthens statutory provisions on workers' rights overseas and prohibits OPIC assistance to entities with investments of $20 million or more in countries that are state sponsors of terrorism.

OPIC's authorization has lapsed periodically. When OPIC's authorization lapses, OPIC is able to continue operating; the agency is able to disburse funds for already committed projects, but is unable to sign contracts for new projects. OPIC's Small and Mid-Size Enterprise Finance Division reportedly developed a large backlog of unapproved transactions during the lapse in reauthorization. Expiration of reauthorization also reportedly affects OPIC's capacity for longterm planning and ability to provide assurances to investors about OPIC programs.[21] From an operational standpoint, some argue that OPIC would benefit from multi-year authorizations. Others argue that frequent reauthorizations allow for more opportunity for congressional oversight of OPIC's activities.

Previous reauthorization bills introduced in the 110th Congress (H.R. 2798, S. 3297) included new directives for OPIC, such as to promote the use of clean energy technology and reduce greenhouse gas emissions associated with OPIC-supported projects. The Senate did not act on S. 3297 because some Members were reportedly opposed to the provisions on clean energy technology. The OPIC reauthorization bill introduced in the 111th Congress (S. 705) does not include any such directives for OPIC.

Other legislation pertaining to OPIC was introduced in the 110th Congress. The Energy Independence and Security Act of 2007, P.L. 110-140, expressed the sense of Congress that OPIC should promote greater investment in clean energy technologies and includes a reporting requirement. The Caribbean Coral Reef Protection Act, H.R. 1679, would have prohibited OPIC from providing its services to any person who has made investments contributing to the development of petroleum resources off Cuba's coast. H.R. 1886 would have prohibited OPIC from supporting any oil or gas project. The Currency Reform for Fair Trade Act of 2007, H.R. 2942, would have prohibited OPIC from supporting projects in designated countries that issue fundamentally misaligned currencies.

ECONOMIC AND POLICY ISSUES

Economists generally oppose the use of subsidized credits to promote trade or investment abroad. They believe such subsidies tend to distort the flow of capital and resources away from the most efficient uses. They also believe that by promoting investment abroad, OPIC may be crowding out, and thereby reducing, some domestic investment. As long as OPIC's non-federal collections—or the fees it charges the public for its services—are sufficient to cover all of its credit and noncredit activities (as indicated by some estimates), it may not have a negative impact on the federal government's budget. OPIC's impact on U.S. capital and resource markets, however, may well be negative due to the distorting effects of subsidized credits. Some supporters argue that, with a total finance and insurance portfolio of $11.3 billion, OPIC is not large enough to affect the cost of capital in the United States. They also argue that OPIC screens proposed investments to ensure that they would not affect U.S. employees negatively or displace U.S. production domestically or in overseas markets.

OPIC was established as part of the Foreign Assistance Act of 1961, as amended. As such, much of the rationale for OPIC relates to U.S. foreign policy goals, a premise that is being questioned by some Members of Congress. Initially, OPIC was established to enhance U.S. aid policy during a period when policymakers were dissatisfied with the focus of U.S. aid programs on officially supported capital intensive projects. OPIC was designed to assist U.S. private firms to take the lead in developing projects that not only would enhance economic development but be economically viable as well. In this role, OPIC's programs may serve to rectify certain "market failures" that dissuade U.S. firms from investing in developing countries. In many of these countries, labor, goods, and capital markets are not well established, and information about the economy often is difficult to obtain. Given this lack of information, individual firms may well attach more risk to investing in developing economies than is warranted. Until the firms gain greater experience or information, or otherwise change their assessments of the risks and rewards of investing in developing countries, they may be overly reluctant to commit resources to investments in the least developed countries without OPIC's guarantees. While critics argue that many countries may no longer need OPIC support due to the successful transformation of their markets, supporters maintain that there are numerous countries around the world, including those in Latin America, Africa, and the Middle East, experiencing economic transformations that require the type of private sector-oriented support provided by OPIC.

End Notes

[1] For additional information, see OPIC's website: http://www.opic.gov/.

[2] Estimated at fair value. OPIC, *OPIC 2008 Annual Report*, p. 34.

[3] *Public Papers of the Presidents: Richard Nixon*. Washington, U.S. Government Printing Office, 1969. p. 412.

[4] 22 U.S.C. Section 2191.

[5] 22 U.S.C. Section 2191, 3(k)(1).

[6] OPIC, annual reports, various years. OPIC, *Budget Request of the Overseas Private Investment Corporation, Fiscal Year 2009*, Congressional Budget Justification, February 2008, pp. 9-16. Telephone conversation with OPIC official, April 14, 2009.

[7] OPIC, "OPIC Selects Global Export Finance, LLC as Originator in Enterprise Development Network ," press release, November 20, 2009. OPIC, "OPIC Selects Alliant Emerging Markets as Originator in Enterprise Development Network ," press release, November 20, 2009. OPIC, "OPIC Selects Ignite Corporate Financial Solutions as Originator in Enterprise Development Network ," press release, November 20, 2009. OPIC, "OPIC Selects Saltus, LLC as Originator in Enterprise Development Network," press release, November 20, 2009. OPIC, "OPIC Selects Global Business Advisory Services, LLC as Originator in Enterprise Development Network ," press release, November 20, 2009.

[8] OPIC, *Budget Request of the Overseas Private Investment Corporation, Fiscal Year 2009*, Congressional Budget Justification, February 2008, pp. 20-21. OPIC, "OPIC: Making Difference in Africa's Capital Markets," *OPIC News*, Winter 2008, p. 4.

[9] OPIC website, http://www.opic.gov/investment-funds/participating-funds.

[10] OPIC, "OPIC Board Approves Over $500 Million for New Renewable Energy Funds," *OPIC News*, Fall 2008, pp. 1-2.

[11] OPIC, "OPIC Workshops Help U.S. Minority and Women-Owned Business Go Global," *OPIC News*, Winter 2008, p. 1. OPIC, "OPIC Workshop for Minority and Women-Owned Businesses Draws 120," press release, October 22, 2009.

[12] OPIC, *Budget Request of the Overseas Private Investment Corporation: Fiscal Year 2009*, Congressional Budget Justification.

[13] Estimated at fair value. OPIC, *OPIC 2008 Annual Report*, p. 34.

[14] For a thorough background and analysis of the international financial crisis, see CRS Report RL34742, *The Global Financial Crisis: Analysis and Policy Implications*, coordinated by Dick K. Nanto.

[15] OPIC, *Budget Request of the Overseas Private Investment Corporation: Fiscal Year 2009*, Congressional Budget Justification, p. iii.

[16] Ibid.

[17] Friends of the Earth v. Mosbacher, 488 F. Supp. 2d 889 (N.D. Cal. 2007).

[18] "Lawsuit Forces U.S. Financing Agencies to Account for Climate," *Environment News Service*, February 7, 2009. Gerald Karey, "ExIm Bank, OPIC agree to provide $500 mil for renewable energy," *Platts Commodity News*, February 6, 2009. Meeting with Export-Import Bank officials, March 9, 2009. Overseas Private Investment Corporation, "OPIC Announces Greenhouse Gas Initiative Capping Emissions on New Projects, Shifting Emphasis to Renewable Energy," press release, June 14, 2007.

[19] OPIC, "OPIC to Disclose Detailed Project Information in New Commitment to Transparency," press release, April 8, 2009, http://www.opic.gov/news/pressreleases/2007/pr040809.asp.

[20] Telephone conversation with OPIC congressional liaison, February 10, 2009.

[21] Small Business Exporters Association, "Congress Restores Authority for Key Small Business International Trade Agency," press release, October 1, 2008, http://www.nsba.biz/content/2018.shtml. OPIC, *Budget Request of the Overseas Private Investment Corporation: Fiscal Year 2009*, Congressional Budget Justification, p. iii.

In: Direct Investment Abroad
Editor: Caleb J. Blackwell

ISBN: 978-1-61668-857-8
© 2010 Nova Science Publishers, Inc.

Chapter 3

FOREIGN INVESTMENT: LAWS AND POLICIES REGULATING FOREIGN INVESTMENT IN 10 COUNTRIES*

United States Government Accountability Office

WHY GAO DID THIS STUDY

Foreign acquisitions of U.S. companies can pose a significant challenge for the U.S. government because of the need to balance the benefits of foreign investment with national security concerns. The Exon-Florio amendment to the Defense Production Act authorizes the President to suspend or prohibit foreign acquisitions of U.S. companies that may harm national security.

To better understand how other countries deal with similar challenges, GAO was asked to identify how other countries address the issues that Exon-Florio is intended to address. Specifically, this chapter describes selected countries' (1) laws and policies enacted to regulate foreign investment to protect their national security interests and (2) implementation of those laws and policies.

This chapter updates a 1996 GAO report that describes how four major foreign investors in the United States—France, Germany, Japan, and the United Kingdom— monitored foreign investment in their own countries to protect national security interests. It also examines foreign investment in six additional countries: Canada, China, India, the Netherlands, Russia, and the United Arab Emirates (UAE). GAO reviewed selected laws and regulations and interviewed foreign government officials and others concerning their implementation and any planned changes to their foreign investment laws, regulations, and policies.

To view the full product, including the scope and methodology, click on GAO-08-320. For more information, contact Ann CalvaresiBarr at (202) 512-4841 or calvaresibarra @gao.gov.

---

* This is an edited, reformatted and augmented version of an U. S. Government Accountability Office publication dated February 2008.

What GAO Found

As is the case in the United States, the countries we reviewed have enacted laws and instituted policies regulating foreign investment, often to address national security concerns. However, each of the 10 countries has its own concept of national security that influences which particular investments may be restricted. As a result of the differing concepts, restrictions range from requiring approval of investments in a narrowly defined defense sector to broad restrictions on the basis of economic security and cultural policy. In addition, some countries have recently made changes to their laws and policies to more explicitly identify national security as an area of concern, in some cases as the result of controversial investments. Several countries have also introduced lists of strategic sectors in which foreign investment requires government review and approval.

While there are many unique characteristics of the systems employed by the 10 countries to regulate foreign investment, in many ways the systems are similar to each other, and to the U.S. process under Exon-Florio. Eight countries use a formal review process—usually conducted by a government economic body with input from government security bodies—to review a transaction. Generally, national security is a primary factor or one of several factors considered in evaluating transactions. While the concepts of national security vary from country to country, all countries share concerns about a core set of issues. These include, for example, the defense industrial base, and more recently, investment in the energy sector and investment by state-owned enterprises and sovereign wealth funds. Most countries have established time frames for the review and can place conditions on transactions prior to approval. For example, a country may place national citizenship requirements on company board members.

However, unlike the voluntary notification under Exon-Florio, most countries' reviews are mandatory if the investment reaches certain dollar thresholds or if the buyer will obtain a controlling or blocking share in the acquired company. Further, unlike the United States, five countries allow decisions to be appealed through administrative means or in court.

Two countries do not have a formal review process. The Netherlands restricts entry into certain sectors such as public utilities, and the UAE restricts the extent of ownership allowed in all sectors without a review. In addition to the formal mechanisms, there are unofficial factors that may influence investment in each of the 10 countries. For example, in some countries an informal government preapproval for sensitive transactions may be needed.

In commenting on a draft of this chapter, the Department of the Treasury emphasized the United States' commitment to an open investment policy.

Abbreviations

CFIUS	Committee on Foreign Investment in the United States
DBERR	Department of Business, Enterprise, and Regulatory Reform
DIPP	Department of Industrial Policy and Promotion
EC	European Community
ECJ	European Court of Justice
EU	European Union

FAS	Federal Anti-Monopoly Service
FDI	foreign direct investment
FEFTA	Foreign Exchange and Foreign Trade Act
FEMA	Foreign Exchange Management Act
FERA	Foreign Exchange Regulation Act
FINSA	Foreign Investment and National Security Act
FIPB	Foreign Investment Promotion Board
FTZ	free trade zone
GDP	gross domestic product
ICA	Investment Canada Act
IMF	International Monetary Fund
IPO	initial public offering
METI	Ministry for Economy, Trade, and Industry
MOFCOM	Ministry of Commerce
NAFTA	North American Free Trade Agreement
NDRC	National Development and Reform Commission
NSEA	National Security Exception Act
OECD	Organization for Economic Co-operation and Development
OFT	Office of Fair Trading
SAIC	State Administration for Industry and Commerce
SASC	State-owned Assets Supervision and Administration Commission
SOE	state-owned enterprise
UAE	United Arab Emirates
UK	United Kingdom
UNCTAD	United Nations Conference on Trade and Development
WTO	World Trade Organization

February 28, 2008
The Honorable Richard Shelby Ranking Member
Committee on Banking, Housing, and Urban Affairs
United States Senate

U.S. investment policy is anchored in the belief that global investment is beneficial and necessary to bring economic prosperity worldwide. The United Nations reported that between 2000 and 2006, annual foreign direct investment in the United States averaged $144 billion, which is 16 percent of the world's total during that period. The Deputy Secretary of the Treasury testified in 2005 that there is an inherent link between our national security interests and a strong U.S. economy that facilitates free and fair trade.[1] However, foreign acquisitions of U.S. companies can pose a significant challenge for the U.S. government because of the need to balance the benefits of foreign investment with national security concerns. The Exon-Florio amendment to the Defense Production Act authorizes the President to suspend or prohibit transactions that could result in foreign control of U.S. companies[2] if the transaction threatens to impair national security.[3] The review of individual transactions has been delegated to an interagency committee, the Committee on Foreign Investment in the United States (CFIUS). In July 2007, the Foreign Investment and National Security Act of 2007[4] amended Exon-Florio to, among other things, expand the factors to be considered in deciding what could affect national security and bring greater transparency to the CFIUS review process.[5]

To better understand how other countries deal with similar challenges, you asked us to identify other countries' approaches for addressing the issues that Exon-Florio is intended to address. Specifically, this chapter describes selected countries' (1) laws and policies enacted to regulate foreign investment to protect their national security interests and (2) implementation of those laws and policies.

The Government Accountability Office has reported on the implementation of Exon-Florio dating back to the 1990s.[6] In addition, in 1996 we issued a report that describes how four major investors in the United States---France, Germany, Japan, and the United Kingdom---- monitored foreign investment in their own countries to protect national security-related interests.[7] This chapter updates the 1996 report and also expands it by describing foreign direct investment policies and processes in six additional countries: Canada, China, India, the Netherlands, Russia, and the United Arab Emirates (UAE). Appendixes IV–XIII contain country- specific information for each of the 10 countries. Our selection of the countries was based on a number of factors: We chose countries with which the United States has a large reciprocal investment relationship, countries with diverse investment controls, countries chosen for regional diversity, and those selected in prior GAO work. We obtained and reviewed copies of relevant laws and regulations and interviewed foreign government officials concerning their implementation and any planned changes to their foreign investment laws, regulations, and policies. The information on foreign laws and regulations in this chapter does not reflect our independent legal analysis, but is based on interviews and secondary sources such as analysis by foreign law specialists at the U.S. Library of Congress and our review of the laws in the original language, or translated copies of the various foreign laws obtained from foreign government officials, foreign government Web sites, or U.S. State Department sources. We also interviewed law firms and companies that had been involved in merger and acquisition activities in the countries in our sample. For a complete description of our scope and methodology, see appendix I.

We conducted this performance audit from December 2006 to February 2008 in accordance with generally accepted government auditing standards. Those standards require that we plan and perform the audit to obtain sufficient, appropriate evidence to provide a reasonable basis for our findings and conclusions based on our audit objectives. We believe that the evidence obtained provides a reasonable basis for our findings and conclusions based on our audit objectives.

RESULTS IN BRIEF

As is the case in the United States, the countries we reviewed have enacted laws and instituted policies regulating foreign investment, often to address national security concerns. However, each of the 10 countries has its own concept of national security that influences which particular investments may be restricted. As a result of the differing concepts, restrictions range from requiring approval of investments in a narrowly defined defense sector to broad restrictions on the basis of economic security and cultural policy. In addition, some countries have recently made changes to their laws and policies to more explicitly emphasize national security concerns, in some cases as the result of controversial investments. Several countries have also introduced lists of strategic sectors in which foreign investment requires government review and approval.

While there are many unique characteristics of the systems employed by the 10 countries to regulate foreign investment, in many ways the systems are similar to each other, and in several ways similar to the U.S. process under Exon-Florio. Eight countries use a formal review process— usually conducted by a government economic body with input from government security bodies—to review a transaction. Generally, national security is a primary factor or one of several factors considered in evaluating transactions. While the concepts of national security vary from country to country, all countries share concerns about a core set of national security issues. These include, for example, the defense industrial base, and more recently, investment in the energy sector and investment by state-owned enterprises and sovereign wealth funds.[8] Most countries have established time frames for the review and can place conditions on selected transactions prior to approval. For example, a country may place national citizenship requirements on company board members. However, unlike the voluntary notification under Exon-Florio, most countries' reviews are mandatory if the investment reaches certain dollar thresholds or if the buyer will obtain a controlling or blocking share in the acquired company. Further, unlike in the U.S. process, five countries allow decisions to be appealed in court or through administrative means. Two countries do not have a formal review process. The Netherlands restricts entry into certain sectors such as public utilities, and the UAE restricts the extent of ownership allowed in all sectors without a review. In addition to the formal mechanisms, there are unofficial factors that may influence investment in each of the 10 countries. For example, in some countries it may be necessary to obtain an informal government preapproval for sensitive transactions.

The Department of the Treasury (Treasury) provided written comments on a draft of this chapter. Treasury emphasized the commitment of the United States to an open investment policy and stated that countries' general investment policies and the relationship of foreign investment reviews to those policies are important in understanding investment review regimes. Agency comments are included in their entirety in appendix II of this chapter.

BACKGROUND

The United States is the main source of foreign direct investment and also the leading host country for foreign direct investment (FDI).[9] The top three destinations for U.S. foreign direct investment, cumulatively as of 2006, were the United Kingdom, Canada, and the Netherlands. The top three foreign direct investors into the United States, cumulatively as of 2006, were the United Kingdom, Japan, and Germany. Figure 1 shows the amount of foreign direct investment from the United States into the countries we reviewed and the amount of worldwide investment into these countries, cumulatively as of 2006.

Foreign direct investment is defined as the purchase of real assets abroad for the purpose of acquiring a lasting interest in an enterprise and exerting a degree of influence on that enterprise's operations.[10] There are several different kinds of foreign direct investment, including the following:

Greenfield investments: A greenfield investment is the investment in a physical structure in an area where no corporate facilities previously existed. It normally entails complete ownership and therefore full control over management.

Strategic partnerships: A strategic partnership is a formal alliance (joint venture, licensing agreement, distributorship, or agency contract) between two commercial enterprises, usually formalized by one or more business contracts, where they mutually participate in certain activities (advertising, branding, product development, etc.).

Mergers and acquisitions: A merger is a business event wherein two or more companies decide to pool their assets to form a single new company. In the course of this transaction, one of the previously existing companies ceases to exist. An acquisition does not necessarily constitute a merger if the preexisting companies continue to exist. Both of these business transactions can result in a foreign entity gaining a portion of a domestic entity.

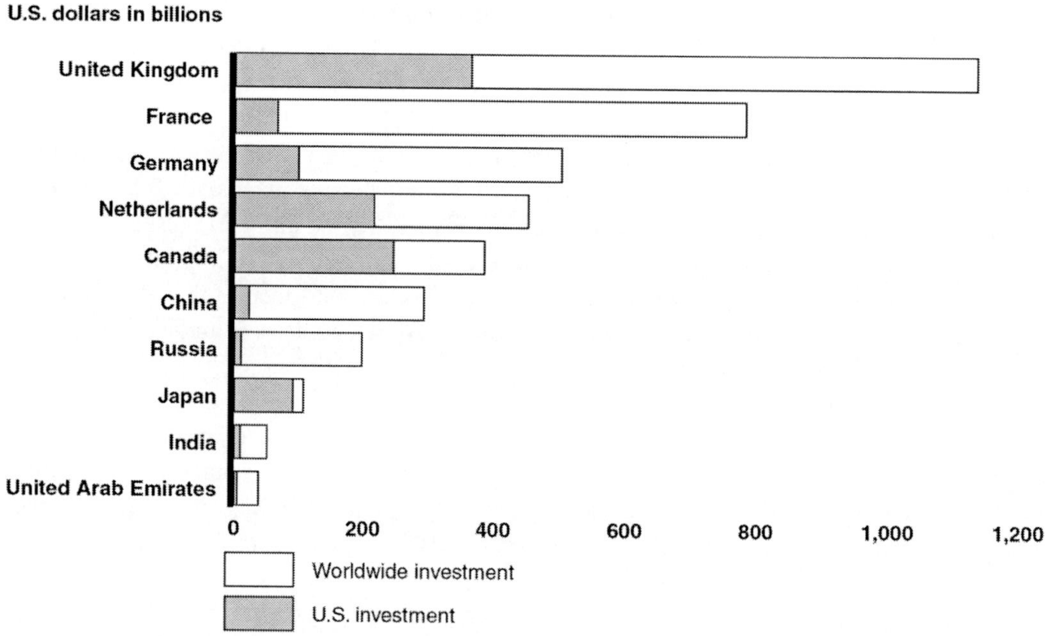

Source: U.S. Department of Commerce, Bureau of Economic Analysis (U.S. investment); and United Nations Conference on Trade and Development (worldwide investment).

Figure 1. U.S. and Worldwide Foreign Direct Investment Stocks in the 10 Selected Countries as of 2006

The Committee on Foreign Investment in the United States

The Exon-Florio amendment authorizes the President to suspend or prohibit foreign acquisitions of U.S. companies if they are determined to pose a threat to national security. The President delegated the authority to investigate individual transactions to an interagency committee, the Committee on Foreign Investment in the United States.[11] While application to CFIUS for review is voluntary, firms subject to an Exon-Florio review that do not notify

CFIUS remain indefinitely subject to Exon-Florio and appropriate actions by the President. However, Exon-Florio applies only when a transaction is related to national security, which is the case in a small percentage of the overall number of foreign direct investments in the United States. According to the Treasury Department, historically less than 10 percent of foreign direct investments in U.S. companies were reviewed by CFIUS. For example, in 2006, there were approximately 1,730 transactions of foreign companies acquiring U.S. companies. In the same year, CFIUS received 113 notices, or 6.5 percent of the total transactions for 2006. Seven of those notices proceeded to a 45-day investigation and none of them were prohibited. In 2007, CFIUS received 147 notices. Of these 147 notices, 6 proceeded to a 45-day investigation and none were prohibited.[12]

Particular transactions may be approved by CFIUS without conditions, or may be approved on the condition that the investor adheres to certain mitigation agreements. The President can, based on the advice of the committee, exercise his authority under the Exon-Florio provision to suspend or prohibit a foreign acquisition of a U.S. company only if he finds that there is credible evidence that the foreign entity exercising control might take action that threatens national security, and that laws, other than Exon-Florio and the International Emergency Economic Powers Act, do not provide adequate and appropriate authority to protect national security.[13] On July 26, 2007, the Foreign Investment and National Security Act of 2007 was passed, amending Exon-Florio. The act addressed some of the issues related to the protection of national security interests. See appendix III for a summary of the changes.

Foreign Investment Laws, Policies, and Processes Address National Security Concerns

As is the case in the United States, each of the countries we reviewed has enacted laws and instituted policies regulating foreign investment—often to address national security concerns. History and each country's experience with foreign investment have influenced its concept of national security, which in turn influences restrictions placed on investments. For example, foreign investment policies can be affected by the specific legal system under which the country operates, and the length of time the country has adhered to a market-based economic system. Restrictions range from requiring approval of investments in a narrowly defined defense sector to broad restrictions on the basis of economic security and cultural policy. Recent and proposed changes in the countries' laws and policies have more explicitly identified national security as an area of concern, in some cases as the result of controversial investments.

Various Legal Means Exist to Regulate Foreign Direct Investment

Similar to the United States, the countries we studied generally have laws and regulations that restrict foreign investment based on national security, though the scope of that authority varies significantly. See table 1 for the relevant laws by country and the stated reasons for the restrictions.

Table 1. Selected Laws and Regulations Addressing Foreign Investment Restrictions

Country	Laws and regulations	Reasons for review or restrictions
Canada	Investment Canada Act, 1985	To ensure net benefit to Canada
China	2006 Regulations for Mergers and Acquisitions of Domestic Enterprises by Foreign Investors, Catalog for the Guidance of Foreign Investment Industries	National economic security, protection of critical industries, purchase of famous trademarks or traditional Chinese brands
France	Law 2004-1343, Decree 2005-1739	Public order, public safety, national defense
Germany	2004 Amendment to 1961 Foreign Trade and Payments Act	Ensure essential security interests, prevent disturbance of peaceful international coexistence or foreign relations
India	Foreign Exchange Management Act, 1999	National security and domestic, cultural, and economic concerns
Japan	1991 Amendment to the Foreign Exchange and Foreign Trade Act of 1949	National security, public order, public safety, or the economy
The Netherlands	Financial Supervision Act of 2006	Competition, financial market oversight
Russia	1999 Federal Law on Foreign Investments	Protection of foundations of the constitutional order, national defense and state security, anti-monopoly
United Arab Emirates	Agencies Law of 1981, Companies Law of 1984	Economic and demographic concerns
United Kingdom	Enterprise Act of 2002	Public interest, control of classified and sensitive technology
United States	Exon-Florio Amendment to the Defense Production Act of 1950, as amended	National security

Source: GAO summary and analysis of laws and information obtained as described in our scope and methodology. See appendix I.

The two countries without a review process, the Netherlands and the UAE, restrict entry into certain sectors or restrict the extent of ownership allowed in a sector. However, their investment policies are significantly different. The Dutch law does not restrict foreign investment for national security. Other than the Dutch Central Bank's capability through the Financial Supervision Act to block financial sector acquisitions, the country has few restrictions on foreign investment. The UAE maintains an ownership limit of 49 percent on foreign investment in every sector through its Companies Law. According to U.S. and UAE government officials, the restrictions were primarily designed to ensure that UAE citizens are beneficiaries of the country's economic growth, since a majority of residents and private sector employees are not UAE citizens. These restrictions can also be used to protect the country's national security interests.

Historical Factors Affect a Country's Receptiveness to Foreign Investment

The approach to foreign investment that each country in our review has taken is based in part on the structure of its legal system, its history, and economy. For example, the laws regulating investment in countries that operate under a common law system tended to be less specific and less detailed than the laws and policies of countries that operate under a civil law system. More specifically, in a common law system, case law determines the scope and intent of a given law. In contrast, civil law systems are, in general, based on a systematic codification of the law. In civil law systems, case law formally plays a minor role compared to the status of the civil code. Finally, some countries' laws do not fit into the single category of civil or common law system. Instead, these countries' utilize more than one legal system, and therefore can be described as mixed. Table 2 categorizes the different legal systems under which the selected countries operate.

In addition to the impact of various legal systems, in the late 20th century, several countries began to transition from centrally controlled to market- based economies. As this occurred, previously state-owned enterprises have been privatized. A country's experience with privatization can affect its view of foreign investment.

Table 2. Legal Systems of Selected Countries

Country	Type of system
Canada	Mixed: primarily common law and some civil law
China	Mixed: civil law, communist legal system, and traditional Chinese law
France	Civil law
Germany	Civil law
India	Common law
Japan	Civil law
The Netherlands	Civil law
Russia	Civil law
United Arab Emirates	Mixed: Islamic and civil law
United Kingdom	Common law

Source: U.S. Library of Congress.

Recent Changes More Explicitly Emphasize National Security Concerns

Recent changes to foreign investment laws and policies have in some cases subjected foreign investment to greater scrutiny. Specifically, each country has changed or considered changing its foreign investment laws, policies, or processes in the last 4 years; many of the changes demonstrate an increased emphasis on national security concerns. In some cases, specific transactions were catalysts in the reconsideration of policies and the development of new ones. However, according to government officials in several countries, these changes simply codified and made more transparent prevailing practices.

Canada

The Investment Canada Act provides for a transparent foreign investment review process.[14] All transactions above designated dollar thresholds are to be reviewed and approved by either the Minister of Industry or the Minister of Canadian Heritage. The act currently does not require a review based on national security. Instead, the review process considers economic factors and cultural policy objectives. In June 2005, the Canadian government introduced a bill to amend the foreign investment review process that included provisions to allow the government to review foreign investment based on national security concerns.[15] However, the 38th Parliament was dissolved at the end of 2005 to prepare for the 2006 election, and the bill was never passed.

In July 2007, the Canadian government created a Competition Policy Review Panel to review key elements of Canada's competition and investment policies, including the Investment Canada Act, which will be updated as a result of the panel's review. The panel is expected to provide its recommendations to the Minister of Industry by the end of June 2008. The government of Canada is also examining the need for a mechanism to screen foreign investment on the basis of national security.

China

The Chinese political-legal system exerts a wide range of controls over foreign direct investment and restricts or prohibits foreign investment in targeted industries via an ad hoc and opaque system of laws, regulations, and policies, according to the U.S. Library of Congress and officials familiar with foreign investment in China. In 2005, a U.S. private equity firm's attempt to purchase 85 percent ownership of a Chinese state-owned company that manufactured construction equipment led to a public outcry against foreign acquisitions in China. Beginning in 2006, China revised its foreign investment regulations to introduce a new "national economic security" screening requirement for cross-border mergers and acquisitions. The Chinese government also introduced a list of seven specific sectors deemed critical to the national economy,[16] a new 5-year plan for utilizing foreign investment that promised a fundamental shift from "quantity" to "quality" in foreign investment, and new provisions on the acquisition of domestic enterprises by foreign investors. The new regulations were released by six government agencies, led by the Ministry of Commerce.

France

In 2000, the European Court of Justice ruled that France had contravened European Community law by prohibiting an investment in France. The European Court of Justice ruled that France should clarify its investment restrictions. As a result, France enacted Law 2004-1343 in 2004, reforming the foreign investment review process. An accompanying Ministerial Decree, issued in 2005, identifies 11 sectors of the economy that require the prior approval of the French Ministry of Economy, Finance, and Employment when foreign investors seek to obtain a controlling share or a specified portion of a French company.[17] In October 2006, the European Commission formally asked France to amend its regulations. As of February 2008, France has made proposals to address the European Commission concerns, and discussions are ongoing.

Germany

The German Foreign Trade and Payments Act, which regulates foreign investment, was amended in 2004 after a U.S. company bought a controlling share of a German submarine manufacturer. The amendments tightened regulations regarding the foreign ownership of defense-related enterprises. Under the new regulations, the acquisition of more than 25 percent of the voting rights of a German company producing armaments, ammunition, cryptographic equipment, or engines and gear systems for tanks or other armored military tracked vehicles is subject to review. Germany is currently considering further changes to the law to address the national security implications of investments by sovereign wealth funds because of concerns that they may be driven by political rather than economic reasons.

India

In India, foreign investment in some sectors, including retail and atomic energy, are prohibited. Foreign investment in other sectors, including defense, insurance, and print media, is limited. Investments in specified industries including aerospace and explosives must receive an industrial license and approval from the Foreign Investment Promotion Board. Frequent changes to restrictions in individual sectors are common. Recent changes in Indian investment policy have focused on liberalizing the limits on the percentage of foreign ownership. For example, in April 2007, India finalized changes to restrictions on foreign investment in the telecommunications sector, raising the ownership cap from 49 percent to 74 percent. In January 2008, the government approved additional changes in other sectors, increasing the limit on foreign investment in petroleum refining, some parts of the civil aviation sector, and several other sectors. However, according to an Indian government official, the liberalization and privatization of domestic investment have had a bigger impact on the Indian economy than foreign investment. In addition to making changes to various sector-specific foreign investment restrictions, the Indian government has also recently considered implementing a national security-based review process. The National Security Council Secretariat suggested a new law—-the National Security Exception Act—-that would have established a process for assessing security threats related to foreign investment, similar to the process used by CFIUS. Although the act met resistance from the Ministries of Commerce and Finance and was subsequently abandoned, India is still debating the need for a national security review of foreign investment.

Japan

Under the Japanese Foreign Exchange and Foreign Trade Act, a foreign investor is required to notify the government in advance if it intends to invest in sensitive industries, including those related to national security. The transaction is then reviewed to determine whether it might imperil national security, disturb public order or public safety, or adversely affect the Japanese economy. In September 2007, the government instituted changes to foreign investment policies in Japan. The primary change is that foreign investment in industries with dual use technologies is now subject to prior notification and a government review. This change is intended to prevent the outflow of technology, with a focus on items that have a high probability of conversion to use in weapons of mass destruction and items that are used to maintain the defense production and technology infrastructure. The revisions include a list of all specific industries and items that fall under the new prior notification requirements, including accessories, components, and equipment related to weapons manufacturing.

Russia

The 1999 Federal Law on Foreign Investments in the Russian Federation specifically allows the government to regulate foreign investment for the defense of the country or the security of the state. However, implementing regulations were never issued. According to Russian government officials, two transactions, one an acquisition by a U.S. company of Russian facilities that produced parts for the Russian military, revealed the need for a formal process to address national security concerns. The government has since drafted a new law to introduce a formal review of foreign investment, similar to reviews by CFIUS. The proposed law was submitted to the Russian Duma in July 2007; however a revised version was announced by the government in February 2008. According to the U.S. State Department, the revised law is more restrictive. As of February 26, 2008, the legislation had not been passed and is therefore subject to change. If the most recent version of the Strategic Sectors Law is enacted, foreign investors will need government authorization to acquire a controlling stake in a Russian company in any of 40 strategic sectors. The new version also restricts foreign investment to 10 percent in companies utilizing strategic subsoil assets, including oil, gas, gold, and copper. In addition, the Russian government is in the process of drafting amendments to the Russian Federation Law on Subsoil. (See app. XI for more information on the draft Strategic Sectors Law and draft amendments to the Subsoil Law.)

United Arab Emirates

The UAE does not have a process for reviewing foreign direct investment or a law that restricts foreign investment specifically for national security purposes. However, the UAE's regulatory and legal framework favors domestic over foreign investment. For example, the UAE's Companies Law and the Agencies Law limit foreign ownership to 49 percent and mandate that trade must be conducted through an Emirati agent. The UAE does not allow foreign majority ownership of any business outside of designated Free Trade Zones, and restricts foreign ownership of land. Although no UAE law restricts foreign investment specifically for national security, protection of the UAE's oil and natural gas deposits is effectively a national security issue. According to both U.S. and UAE officials, the UAE government plans to liberalize the Companies Law and the Agencies Law. However, this probably will happen in stages on a sector-by-sector basis.

The United Kingdom and the Netherlands

The United Kingdom and the Netherlands maintain the most open economies of all the countries we reviewed. However, changes to regulations affecting foreign investment have been discussed in these countries. For example, as a result of a potential foreign investment in the energy sector, the United Kingdom considered whether changes to its existing foreign investment laws or review process were required. The British government decided against making any changes to its current laws. Similarly, members of the Dutch Parliament have discussed the possibility of changes to their merger and acquisition regulations as a result of a recent transaction.

Table 3. Common Elements

	Relevant FDI laws	Formal review	National security review	Reviewing body	Sectors requiring review	Reasons for review/ restrictions	Review time frames	Appeal	Approval conditions or mitigation agreements
Canada	Investment Canada Act, 1985	Yes	No	Industry Canada and Canadian Heritage	Specified	To ensure net benefit to Canada	45 days, with a possible 30-day extension	No	Yes
China	2006 Regulations for Mergers and Acquisitions of Domestic Enterprises by Foreign Investors Catalog for the Guidance of Foreign Investment Industries	Yes	Yes	Ministry of Commerce	Specified	National economic security, protection of critical industries, purchase of famous trademarks or traditional Chinese brands	Not specified	No	Yes
France	Law 2004-1343 Decree 2005-1739	Yes	Yes	Ministry of Economy, Finance, and Employment	Specified	Public order, public safety, national defense	60 days	Yes	Yes
Germany	2004 Amendment to 1961 Foreign Trade and Payments Act	Yes	Yes	Federal Ministry of Economics and Technology	Specified	Essential security interests, disturbance of peaceful international coexistence, disturbance of foreign relations	30 days	Yes	No
India	Foreign Exchange Management Act, 1999	Yes	Yes	Foreign Investment Promotion Board	Specified	National security, domestic, cultural and economic concerns	30 days, in practice 3 months	Yes	No
Japan	1991 Amendment to the ForeignEx-change and Foreign Trade Act of 1949	Yes	Yes	Ministry of Finance	Specified	National security, public order, public safety, or the economy	30 days, ministries can extend to 5 months	Yes	Yes
The Netherlands	Financial Super-vision Act of 2006	No	No	N/A	N/A	Competition, financial market oversight	N/A	N/A	N/A

Table 3. (Continued)

	Relevant FDI laws	Formal review	National security review	Reviewing body	Sectors requiring review	Reasons for review/ restrictions	Review time frames	Appeal	Approval conditions or mitigation agreements
Russia	1999 Federal Law on Foreign Investments	Yes	Yes	Federal Anti-Monopoly Service	Not currently specified	Protection of foundations of the constitutional order, national defense and state security, anti- monopoly	30 days for anti-monopoly review (No specified time frames for national security review)	Yes	Yes
United Arab Emirates	Agencies Law of 1981 Companies Law of 1984	No	No	N/A	N/A	Economic and demographic concerns	N/A	N/A	N/A
United Kingdom	Enterprise Act of 2002	Yes	Yes	Office of Fair Trading	Not officially specified	Public interest, control of classified and sensitive technology	6 months, in practice 30 days	No	Yes
United States	Exon-Florio Amendment to the Defense Production Act of 1950, as amended	Yes	Yes	Committee on Foreign Investment in the United States	Not officially specified	National security	30 days, with a possible 45-day investigation	No	Yes

Source: GAO analysis of country data.

Note: N/A means "not applicable.

Foreign Investment Review Implementation Has Many Similarities in Different Countries

While there are many unique characteristics to the systems employed by the 10 countries to regulate foreign investment, in many ways the systems are similar to each other, and in several ways similar to the CFIUS process in the United States. See table 3 for a comparison of selected elements of the countries' foreign investment review processes.

Eight of the 10 countries use a formal review process to approve or deny a transaction. Generally, this review is conducted by a government economic body with input from government security bodies, and national security is a primary factor or one of several factors considered in evaluating transactions. Although the concepts of national security vary from country to country, all countries share similar concerns about national security-related issues. These concerns include, for example, their defense industrial base, and more recently, investments in energy sectors and investments of state-owned enterprises and sovereign wealth funds; the latter because of concerns that political rather than economic motivation may be behind the investment.

As in the United States, most countries have established time frames for the review ranging from 30 days to 6 months, and a majority of the governments can require that certain conditions be met prior to approving a transaction. For example, a country may place national citizenship requirements on company board members. Unlike the U.S. system, most countries' reviews are mandatory if the investment reaches certain dollar thresholds or if the buyer will obtain a controlling or blocking share in the acquired company. Finally, unlike in the U.S. process, five countries allow review process decisions to be challenged in court or through administrative means. In addition to the formal mechanisms, there are unofficial factors that may influence investment in each of the 10 countries. For example, in some countries, it may be necessary to vet sensitive transactions through a political process before the formal legal or administrative process is initiated.

Most Countries Use a Formal Review Process to Regulate Foreign Investment

Eight of the 10 countries we examined rely primarily on a review process through which the government grants or denies approval for transactions, usually above a specified threshold or within specified economic sectors. Canada reviews investments above specified monetary thresholds to determine if they would provide a net benefit to Canada. China maintains a decentralized review process split between central and local government authorities and retains the power to restrict or block any foreign investment that may have a significant impact on national economic security. In France, prior government authorization is required for foreign investments in 11 sensitive sectors. Germany reviews foreign investments specifically for national security purposes, but limits those reviews to investments in the German defense industry. Although foreign investment in India is primarily regulated through sector-based ownership restrictions, India also uses a review process. Japan reviews transactions in sectors potentially affecting national security, public order, public safety, and the smooth management of the economy. Any foreign investment over 10 percent in a company listed on the Japanese stock exchange and any investment in an unlisted company that falls into the specified sectors must provide prior notification and is reviewed. Investment in all other sectors must provide notification after the investment is made, but those investments are not reviewed. In Russia the anti-monopoly review has been used to review foreign investment transactions for national security purposes. The government of the United Kingdom has the authority to review and block transactions that may have an adverse effect on competition and the public interest. The United Kingdom also can intervene when confidential defense-related information is involved. This latter intervention is separate from the formal competition review.

Besides a formal review process for foreign investment, every country reviewed had companies and sectors that are fully or partially government owned or controlled. For example, in India, foreign investment in the state-owned atomic energy is prohibited. In the Netherlands, as well as other countries, there are restrictions in areas such as transportation and public utilities. In the UAE and China, there are significant restrictions in a number of areas.

Some countries have companies that are fully or partially owned or controlled by the government that may allow domestic private investment, but restrict foreign investment. An example of this type of barrier to investment includes golden shares. Golden shares are special rights given to governments in private companies. Such rights allow the government to maintain a certain degree of control over such companies. For example, a government may maintain control over the percentage of foreign-owned shares, or approval requirements for the dissolution or disposal of any strategic assets. The European Court of Justice ruled against governments utilizing golden shares in 2002 and 2003 because these shares restrict the free movement of capital within the European Union (EU), and determined that the use of golden shares is acceptable only in specific circumstances.

Reviews are Normally Conducted by an Economic Body within the Government

All 8 of the countries with a review process have formally designated an economic-related ministry or body within the government to conduct the review. This body generally coordinates as needed with government security bodies. For example, similar to several countries we reviewed, France's Ministry of Economy, Finance, and Employment is the focal point of the review, and this ministry confers with the Ministry of Defense and other relevant ministries, depending on the sector of the proposed investment. In China, the Ministry of Commerce has primary responsibility for reviewing and supervising foreign investment transactions. In Japan, foreign investors must provide notification to the Ministry of Finance and the ministry with industry area jurisdiction. Russia and the United Kingdom both maintain the legal process to block investments based on national security concerns. Investments that must be reviewed for national security reasons are routed through their competition review process. None of the countries we studied, however, maintain a formal interagency review committee such as CFIUS.

As is the case in the United States, in other countries, such as France, India, and Russia, bureaucratic tension exists between economic government bodies and generally more conservative, security-focused bodies within the government such as the defense ministry. This natural tension serves to balance economic and security concerns both when laws and policies are being developed and when decisions are made on individual applications in the review process.

Countries Share Similar Concerns about Foreign Investment

Many of the countries have concerns about national security-related issues. National security, as viewed by each of the countries, is a primary factor to be considered in evaluating transactions in seven of the eight countries with a review process. It is Germany's sole factor for review of investments. However, there is diversity among the countries as to what is considered essential to national interests and when it is necessary for the government to protect certain sectors from foreign investment or control. This diversity is reflected in each country's foreign investment regulatory regime. Factors considered during the review of foreign investment in other countries include public safety, public order, economic concerns, and cultural policies. Some countries do not specifically use the term "national security" in their laws, and most countries do not define what is covered under the term "national security," or similar terms such as "public interest," "public order," or "essential security."

Most countries have provisions that limit the sale of defense companies to foreign investors or provide for a review of those investments. The Chinese *Catalog for the Guidance of Foreign Investment Industries* states that foreigners are prohibited from investing in Chinese companies that manufacture weapons and ammunition. India requires official approval and limits foreign ownership in the defense industry to 26 percent. In the UAE, foreign investment in military production is clearly, if not explicitly, off limits, according to a UAE official. Japan requires prior notification and approval for foreign investment in defense-related industries, including companies producing dual use items. France and Germany require reviews for foreign investment in companies with sensitive or classified technologies or contracts, while Russia and the United Kingdom also normally review these investments. The other two countries we reviewed are less restrictive. Canada's review process does not address foreign investment in the defense sector beyond the thresholds for review that apply to all foreign investments. The Netherlands has no restrictions on foreign investment in the defense industry other than those that are derived from international agreements.

All countries, with the exception of Germany, have specific restrictions or review requirements that apply to investments in companies involved in the production or distribution of energy. This issue of energy security, especially with regard to the foreign acquisition of energy infrastructure, has been raised by the European Union. For example, in September 2007, the European Commission put forth a proposal to establish a European energy policy. One aspect of this energy policy proposal would be a prohibition on non-EU companies acquiring control of a European Community energy transmission system or transmission system operator, unless it is specifically permitted by an agreement between the EU and the foreign company. The stated goal of this proposal is to promote competition, but the effect would also be to block foreign companies, state-owned enterprises, sovereign wealth funds, and others from being able to acquire certain energy assets in an EU country.

Some countries review or restrict foreign investment based on economic security or cultural nationalism. Canada, China, and Japan formally indicate economic reasons as part of the criteria for the review of foreign investment. For example, China reviews the acquisition of traditional Chinese brands, and Canada restricts foreign investment specifically to protect Canada's cultural heritage. The UAE also has in place investment restrictions focused on ensuring UAE citizen involvement in the country's economy. India maintains restrictions on investments in the financial sector, defense industry, real estate, infrastructure, telecommunications, print media, and single-brand product retail, among other sectors.

Government officials in six countries have expressed specific concerns about investments by foreign state-owned enterprises or sovereign wealth funds. Because sovereign wealth funds are government owned, there are concerns that they may be guided by political objectives rather than profit maximization or that their financial decisions may be motivated by support for certain "national champion" companies. A sovereign wealth fund is a fund owned by a government and is composed of financial assets such as stocks, bonds, property, or other financial instruments. Sovereign wealth funds are generally composed of government fiscal surpluses, or from official foreign exchange reserves at central banks. Because of the unknown potential for sovereign wealth funds to be motivated by political instead of economic considerations, countries may seek to limit such investments.

On February 27, 2008, the European Commission released a document entitled *A Common European Approach to Sovereign Wealth Funds* proposing that EU leaders endorse a common EU approach to increasing the transparency, predictability, and accountability of sovereign wealth funds. The International Monetary Fund (IMF) is also developing best practices on how to manage sovereign wealth funds.[18] According to the IMF, sovereign wealth funds have existed since the 1950s, but their total size worldwide has increased significantly in the last 10 to 15 years. The IMF estimates that as of September 2007, total holdings of sovereign wealth funds were between $2 trillion and $3 trillion, and may reach $10 trillion by 2012.[19]

China, Russia, and the UAE all maintain sovereign wealth funds whose worth is estimated in the billions of dollars. Japan has also proposed establishing its own sovereign wealth fund, according to a private sector representative. In Germany and France, specific concerns have been raised about sovereign wealth funds investing in the two countries. In a joint letter, the German Chancellor and the French President wrote to the current President of the European Union Council in September 2007 to request that attention be paid by the European Union to the manner in which sovereign wealth funds can distort competition, as well as to call for a code of conduct to be developed for hedge funds investing in Europe. The letter emphasized that financial market transparency and appropriate regulation and supervision of investors is necessary to avoid potential negative results. Further, the German government is considering whether to develop measures to address concerns about the implications of sovereign wealth funds acquiring German companies.

Russian government officials told us that under the July 2007 version of the proposed Strategic Sectors Law, state-owned enterprises and sovereign wealth funds would require government approval and will not be able to obtain a controlling share in certain strategic sectors. The U.S. State Department has indicated that in the February 2008 version of the draft, entities partially owned by a foreign government would face a 5 percent limit on unsupervised ownership. In December 2007, the Canadian government issued new guidelines to clarify how the Investment Canada Act applies to state-owned enterprises, including sovereign wealth funds. Entities within the United Kingdom and the Netherlands have also expressed concerns about foreign government-controlled investments, but the governments do not currently have plans to revise their foreign investment policies to address those concerns.

Most Countries Specify Review Time Frames, Can Set Conditions on Approval, Specify Thresholds for Review, and Allow Appeals

Every country except China specifies time frames in which the review is to be completed. Time frames tend to be between 30 and 60 days, and in some cases the review may be extended up to 6 months. In Germany, a transaction is automatically approved unless it is denied within 30 days of application. In Japan, the time frame for review is also 30 days, but can be extended up to 5 months. France's review is required to be completed within 2 months. In Canada, the review should be completed within 45 days, with the possibility of a 30-day extension. In India, approval should be given within 30 days. However, a government official stated that, in practice, the review usually takes 3 months. In Russia, the current antimonopoly review time frame is 30 days, but national security reviews have no set time frames.[20] Reviews in the United Kingdom must be completed within 6 months, although many are completed in 30 days. In several countries, including Canada, France, and Germany, the review time frame does not start until the reviewing body considers the application package complete. As a result, the period from the initial application to the official approval can be longer than the stated review period.

The requirement of an investor to meet certain conditions prior to official approval of a transaction is common among six of the countries we reviewed. These conditions, also referred to as undertakings, contingencies, or mitigation agreements, were generally similar in each of the countries. For example, a country may place national citizenship requirements on an acquired company's board members, or a company may be required to maintain its defense contracts after an acquisition. Examples of conditions imposed by the French government include (1) guaranteed continuation of the activities of the company, (2) protection of the companies' research and development capabilities, and (3) guarantees that the company will meet its obligations under its current procurement contracts. In the United Kingdom, when foreign investors have acquired companies that produced items for the military, those investors have been required to agree to conditions related to the maintenance of strategic capabilities. For example, when a U.S. defense company acquired a defense company in the United Kingdom, the British government required the acquiring company to agree to certain conditions related to the protection of classified technology and information. We also found that similar conditions have been required in Canada and Russia. Further, some countries have required annual reporting by the investing companies to ensure adherence to the mitigation agreements, and may require divestment if the company does not adhere to the agreements.

Of the eight countries with a review process, six maintain official thresholds for review, either dollar thresholds or a controlling or blocking stake, which may be defined differently in each country. China reviews all transactions at some government level. India requires government notification for all investments, and does not specify monetary thresholds for review. In Germany, an investor's failure to comply with the notification requirement may generate civil and criminal penalties. Countries generally rely on the fear of reprisal, fines, or mandatory divestment to encourage application and adherence to their review process, rather than actively pursuing companies that do not file.

Unlike the United States, five countries allow judicial appeal of decisions or have an administrative procedure to ask for reconsideration of a decision made as a result of the review process. However, the appeals processes are rarely used, primarily because the review processes rarely result in a formal denial.

Foreign Investment is Affected by Factorsoutside Formal Processes

In practice, there are often informal or unofficial factors that may influence the success or failure of a potential foreign investment. Certain foreign investments may be considered sensitive by the host government; therefore, a firm may informally contact the host government to discuss the transaction prior to formal application for review. This was a common practice in several of the selected countries. Seeking unofficial preapproval can enable the potential investor to assuage any concerns the host government may have about the pending transaction. Likewise, if a host government is unlikely to approve a transaction, this can be communicated to the investor prior to the formal application process. In such a case, the investor may never apply for review because of unofficial feedback from government officials concerning the likelihood of approval. In other circumstances, a firm may withdraw its application for a review if it receives unofficial feedback from the government that the transaction is unlikely to be approved.

Although the laws and policies that regulate the review of foreign investment are generally designed to be apolitical, for example, by basing the review mechanism in an administrative component of the host government, political influence in the public sphere may negatively affect the outcome of an attempted investment. Regardless of the official policy of the country, domestic politics play an important role in the review and approval of foreign investment. This can add a measure of uncertainty to the review process. According to the Organization for Economic Cooperation and Development (OECD), political pressure often occurs in areas of policy that are loosely defined, such as protecting national and cultural interests. Political figures may be able to block an investment on these grounds.

While most governments support foreign direct investment in their economy, in some instances the perceived economic impact of a particular investment may still be a cause for concern. According to the OECD, countries may attempt to mask this by citing national security considerations or other legitimate national interests to block a foreign investment transaction. The European Commission has reported to the OECD that these reasons have been cited in several instances by European Union member states to disguise economic or protectionist actions.[21] In some cases, host governments may seek to protect certain companies, "national champions," from external takeover or competition. National champions may be protected from foreign acquisition through, among other means, the public comments of political figures or the provision of government assistance to aid a company in seeking an alternative domestic merger partner.

The public may also react negatively to foreign investment. For example, the 2006 Chinese mergers and acquisitions regulations allow competing domestic firms to request that the Chinese government review a foreign merger or acquisition for anti-trust concerns, a procedure that provides Chinese companies a legal process to become involved in decisions about foreign investment reviews of their competitors. Further, the public may react negatively to the sale of local companies to foreign firms because such sales may place a local region's economy in the control of a foreign entity. Local employees and residents may fear that foreign investment will increase the likelihood of layoffs and other reductions in force. The practice of foreign private equity firms purchasing a company to obtain its assets, and then laying off or significantly restructuring the local workforce so as to reap rapid profits through resale of the company, is a concern, and has been referred to as "vulture" and "locust" capitalism in Japan and Germany.

APPENDIX I: SCOPE AND METHODOLOGY

This chapter expands and updates a 1996 GAO report that compared the laws and processes governing foreign investment in Japan, France, Germany, and the United Kingdom.[22]

To identify the relevant laws and policies for regulating foreign investment in foreign countries, we selected a nongeneralizable sample of 10 countries based on the following criteria: the size of the reciprocal investment relationship with the United States, a variety of investment controls, regional diversity, prior GAO work in the subject area, and congressional interest. We held in-country interviews in 5 of the countries and collected basic information from officials in Washington, D.C., on the remaining 5 countries.

We held in-country interviews with officials in

- Canada,
- China,
- France,
- Germany, and
- Russia.

We collected basic information from officials in Washington, D.C., on

- India,
- Japan,
- the Netherlands,
- the United Arab Emirates, and
- the United Kingdom.

The information on foreign laws and regulations in this chapter does not reflect our independent legal analysis, but is based on interviews and secondary sources such as analysis by the U.S. Library of Congress and our review of the laws in the original language, or translated copies of the various foreign laws obtained from foreign government officials, foreign government Web sites, or U.S. State Department sources. The U.S. Library of Congress compiled a summary of the laws and policies relevant to the regulation of foreign investment for each of the selected countries at our request. We also interviewed and obtained information from U.S. government officials from the Departments of the Treasury, Commerce, State, and Defense; the Office of the U.S. Trade Representative; and the Intelligence Community Acquisition Risk Center under the office of the Director of National Intelligence. In addition to Washington, D.C., based sources, we interviewed U.S. embassy representatives in Canada, China, France, Germany, and Russia as well as the U.S. Mission to the European Union. We also obtained information from U.S. embassy officials in India, Japan, the Netherlands, the United Kingdom, and the United Arab Emirates.

We interviewed or obtained information from foreign government officials at each of the 10 embassies in Washington, D.C. For 5 of the countries--- Canada, China, France, Germany, and Russia--- we met with representatives in various foreign government offices and discussed how foreign investment is regulated.

We interviewed representatives from the European Commission in Belgium and the Organization for Economic Co-operation and Development (OECD) in France. We reviewed reports from the OECD, the United Nations Conference on Trade and Development (UNCTAD), the International Monetary Fund (IMF), and the Eurasia Group, among others, to obtain information about foreign investment review processes, laws, and policies, as well as basic figures for comparing foreign investment inflows.

To identify how countries implement foreign investment regulations, we interviewed a broad range of representatives for each of the selected countries, including think tanks and other nongovernmental organizations, business and trade associations, chambers of commerce, law firms, and industry representatives that have invested in the selected countries, all of whom possessed expert knowledge about foreign investment. In Canada, China, France, Germany, and Russia, we interviewed representatives for these organizations that were based in-country as well as in the United States, while for India, Japan, the Netherlands, the United Kingdom, and the United Arab Emirates, we only interviewed organizations, firms, and businesses that had offices in the United States.

While our observations provide a cross section of various types of foreign investment regimes, such observations are not representative of how all countries regulate foreign investment. Further, as reporting standards for foreign direct investment figures vary from country to country, we were unable to obtain comparable country- and sector-specific foreign direct investment-related data. We did obtain information and data available through UNCTAD, IMF, and OECD. Finally, it is impossible to know the full extent to which informal factors influence investment, and specifically the process for reviewing foreign direct investment. Although there has been significant cross-border investment, it is unknown how many potential foreign investments were forgone or never pursued because of the burden imposed by the regulations that were in place in a given country. Official figures for denials and approvals were not available for some of the countries we reviewed, and the figures that are available do not necessarily represent the extent to which foreign investment restrictions or barriers affect investment. Likewise, data do not exist to determine the number of transactions initially pursued that were withdrawn prior to receiving government approval.

We conducted this performance audit from December 2006 to February 2008 in accordance with generally accepted government auditing standards. Those standards require that we plan and perform the audit to obtain sufficient, appropriate evidence to provide a reasonable basis for our findings and conclusions based on our audit objectives. We believe that the evidence obtained provides a reasonable basis for our findings and conclusions based on our audit objectives.

APPENDIX II: COMMENTS FROM THE OF DEPARTMENT OF TREASURY

DEPARTMENT OF THE TREASURY
WASHINGTON, D.C. 20220

February 28, 2008

Ms. Ann Calvaresi-Barr
Director
Acquisition and Sourcing Management
U.S. Government Accountability Office
Washington, DC 20548

Dear Ms. Calvaresi-Barr:

Thank you for providing the Department of the Treasury with the opportunity to review and comment on the draft of Government Accountability Office (GAO) report GAO-08-320, "Foreign Investment: Laws and Policies Regulating Foreign Investment in 10 Countries." We believe that the report is a useful summary and analysis of the foreign investment restrictions of the countries covered by the report, and we appreciate the significant research that went into the report.

We offer the following comments that we believe would make the report even more useful to Congress, as well as to our international outreach efforts on these topics.

The Committee on Foreign Investment in the United States (CFIUS) conducts national security reviews of certain foreign investments in U.S. businesses within the context of the long-standing U.S. commitment to open investment. President Bush reiterated this commitment in his Statement on Open Economies in May 2007, as well as in the executive order he issued on January 23, 2008, instituting certain reforms to the CFIUS process to implement the Foreign Investment and National Security Act of 2007 (FINSA). The legislative history of FINSA also makes clear Congress's intention to maintain CFIUS' open investment orientation.

FINSA, the new executive order, and our internal reforms to the CFIUS process demonstrate that it is possible to safeguard the national security while continuing to welcome foreign investment. These reforms ensure that CFIUS is able to conduct robust reviews to address national security concerns in each of its cases. Consistent with the U.S. open investment policy, the reforms also ensure that CFIUS will focus only on genuine national security concerns, not on broader economic or policy goals, including industrial policy.

In his Statement on Open Economies, President Bush also stated that the United States is equally committed to securing fair, equitable, and nondiscriminatory treatment for U.S. investors abroad. Accordingly, Treasury is engaged with other countries, both bilaterally and multilaterally, to encourage them to ensure that any foreign investment review processes they may have or be considering are designed and conducted consistent with open investment principles. We will be placing special emphasis on this point in the coming months, during and after the issuance process for revised CFIUS regulations to implement FINSA.

The general investment policies of the United States and the countries covered by the report, and the relationship of foreign investment reviews to those policies, are important to consider in order to understand and compare CFIUS and other countries' investment review regimes.

We hope you will find these comments helpful. Please feel free to contact me if you would like to discuss any of our comments or have any other questions.

Sincerely,

Nova Daly
Deputy Assistant Secretary
for Investment Security and Policy

APPENDIX III: HIGHLIGHTS OF RECENT CHANGES TO EXON-FLORIO

On July 26, 2007, the President signed the Foreign Investment and National Security Act of 2007 (FINSA) into law.23 FINSA amends section 721 of the Defense Production Act of 1950, also known as the Exon-Florio amendment.24 The following provides a summary of some of the more significant changes to Exon-Florio, which became effective on October 24, 2007. FINSA provides that implementing regulations shall become effective no later than April 21, 2008.

The Committee on Foreign Investment in the United States

Prior to FINSA, Exon-Florio gave the President the authority to investigate the impact of foreign acquisitions of U.S. companies on national security, and by executive order the President delegated that authority to the interagency Committee on Foreign Investment in the United States (CFIUS).[25] FINSA statutorily establishes CFIUS to carry out reviews and investigations as well as other responsibilities assigned to it in the act or delegated by the President. FINSA also defines the membership of CFIUS, but allows the President to add the heads of other executive departments, agencies, or offices. Table 4 shows pre- and post-FINSA membership of CFIUS.

Table 4. Changes in CFIUS Membership

Established by executive order prior to FINSA	Established by FINSA and Amendment of Executive Order 11858, issued January 23, 2008
Secretary of the Treasury (chair)	Secretary of the Treasury (chair)
Secretary of Commerce	Secretary of Commerce
Secretary of Defense	Secretary of Defense
Secretary of Homeland Security	Secretary of Homeland Security
Secretary of State	Secretary of State
Attorney General of the United States	Attorney General of the United States
Chairman of the Council of Economic Advisors	*Chairman of the Council of Economic Advisors*
Director of the Office of Management and	*Director of the Office of Management and*
Budget	*Budget*
Director of the Office of Science and Technology Policy	*Director of the Office of Science and Technology Policy*
The U.S. Trade Representative	*The U.S. Trade Representative*
Assistant to the President for Economic Policy (National Economic Council)	*Assistant to the President for Economic Policy (National Economic Council)*
Assistant to the President for National Security Affairs (National Security Council)	*Assistant to the President for National Security Affairs (National Security Council)*
	Assistant to the President for Homeland Security and Counterterrorism
Established by executive order prior to FINSA	**Established by FINSA and Amendment of Executive Order 11858, issued January 23, 2008**
	Secretary of Energy
	Secretary of Labor (nonvoting, ex officio)
	Director of National Intelligence (nonvoting, ex officio)
	The heads of any other executive department, agency, or office, as the President or the Secretary of the Treasury determines appropriate, on a case-by-case basis

Sources: Exec. Order No. 11858, as amended, and Pub. L. No. 110-49.

Note: New members added by FINSA are in bold. Members added by the Amendment to the Executive Order are in italics.

Critical Infrastructure

Although transactions involving U.S. critical infrastructure were reviewed and investigated by CFIUS in the past, Exon-Florio did not explicitly provide for reviews or investigations of critical infrastructure. FINSA specifically identifies critical infrastructure as an area of concern. For example, FINSA explicitly requires CFIUS to investigate transactions that involve critical infrastructure if the transaction could impair the national security of the

United States and the impairment has not been mitigated.[26] Also, FINSA specifically identifies the effect of a transaction on United States critical infrastructure as a factor that must be considered by CFIUS in conducting a national security review.

Investigations

Prior to FINSA, Exon-Florio provided for a 45-day investigation to determine the effects of a transaction on the national security of the United States, and for a mandatory investigation in those cases in which the acquiring company is controlled by or acting on behalf of a foreign government and the transaction could affect the national security of the United States. FINSA specifically provides for a 45-day investigation when

- the lead agency responsible for negotiating mitigation agreements and other conditions and for monitoring compliance with mitigation agreements recommends an investigation and CFIUS agrees, or
- whenever a review results in a determination that
    - the transaction threatens national security and the threat has not been mitigated;
    - the transaction is a foreign government-controlled transaction; or
    - the transaction would result in control of critical infrastructure, CFIUS determines that the transaction could impair national security, and the impairment has not been mitigated.

However, FINSA also provides that an investigation is not required for foreign government-controlled transactions or transactions involving critical infrastructure if the Secretary of the Treasury and the lead agency jointly determine that the transaction will not impair the national security of the United States.

Factors to Be Considered

FINSA has expanded the number of factors for CFIUS and the President to consider in conducting reviews and investigations and making determinations of whether a transaction poses a threat to national security. Under FINSA, CFIUS and the President must consider, as appropriate, the following additional factors:[27]

- the potential national security-related effects on U. S. critical infrastructure, including major energy assets;
- the potential national security-related effects on U.S. critical technologies;
- whether the transaction is a foreign government-controlled transaction;
- as appropriate, and particularly with respect to transactions requiring an investigation, a review of the current assessment of
    - the acquiring country's adherence to nonproliferation regimes;
    - the relationship of the acquiring country with the United States, specifically on its record on cooperating in counterterrorism efforts; and

   - the potential for transshipment or diversion of technologies with military applications, including an analysis of national export control laws and regulations;
- the long-term projection of U.S. requirements for sources of energy and other critical resources and material; and
- the potential effects of the transaction on sales of military goods, equipment, or technology to any country identified by the Secretary of Defense as posing a potential regional military threat to the interests of the United States.

Mitigation Agreements

Prior to FINSA, neither Exon-Florio nor its implementing regulations addressed the issue of mitigation agreements---agreements between CFIUS or a member agency and the parties to the acquisition that are intended to mitigate national security concerns. FINSA explicitly permits CFIUS or a lead agency, as designated by the Treasury Department, to negotiate, enter into, impose, and enforce any agreement or condition with any party to the transaction to mitigate any threat to U.S. national security that arises as a result of the transaction. FINSA also provides that a lead agency shall monitor and enforce, on behalf of CFIUS, any mitigation agreement.

Tracking Withdrawn Notices

Prior to FINSA, Exon-Florio contained no provisions for actions to be taken in the event companies withdrew an official notification to CFIUS, although the implementing regulations provided procedures to companies on how to request a withdrawal. FINSA specifically provides for CFIUS to establish, as appropriate

- interim protections to address concerns raised during the review or investigation,
- time frames for the companies to resubmit notification to CFIUS, and
- a process for tracking any actions the companies may take before the companies resubmit the notification.

Reporting to Congress

FINSA has expanded Exon-Florio's requirement for reports to Congress. Prior to FINSA, Exon-Florio required the President to submit a report to Congress only when the President made a determination whether or not to take action to block or suspend an acquisition using the authority of ExonFlorio. The report was required to address only the acquisition that was the subject of the presidential determination. FINSA requires annual reporting to specific congressional committees on all reviews and investigations completed by CFIUS during the preceding 12-month period, as well as a certified report on the results of any investigation shortly after CFIUS concludes the investigation, unless the transaction under investigation is sent to the President for a decision.[28] FINSA also provides for CFIUS to provide briefings to specific Members of Congress on any transaction that has been concluded.

Appendix IV: Canada

- Canada ranked sixth in terms of the average value of foreign direct investment (FDI) inflows worldwide between 2000 and 2006.
- In 2006, FDI in Canada totaled $385.2 billion, an increase of 81 percent over FDI stock in 2000.
- FDI stock in Canada as a proportion of gross domestic product (GDP) was 30.4 percent in 2006.
- Canada was the second most popular destination for U.S. FDI, behind the United Kingdom as of 2006.

Background

Canada became a self-governing dominion in 1867 while retaining ties to the British crown. Canada is a constitutional monarchy with a federal system, a parliamentary government, and democratic traditions. Criminal law, based largely on British law, is uniform throughout the nation and is under federal jurisdiction. Civil law is also based on the English common law, except in Quebec, which has retained its own civil code patterned after that of France. Justice is administered by federal, provincial, and municipal courts.

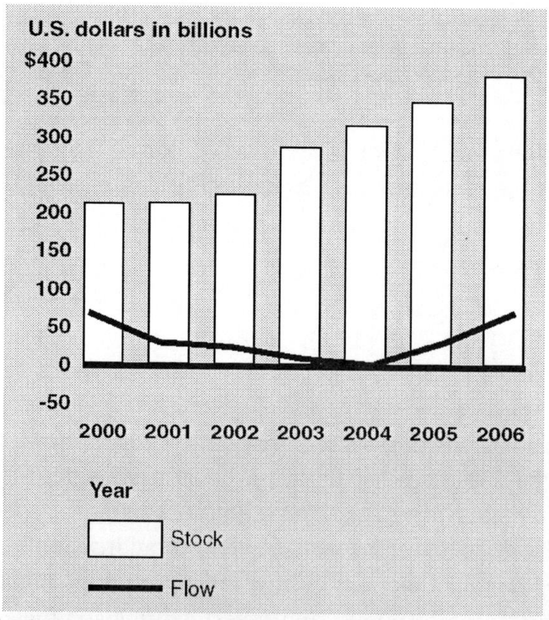

Source: United Nations (data).

Foreign investment in Canada (stocks and flows 2000–2006)

For decades, foreign investment has been significant to Canada's market economy. The United States, the United Kingdom, France, and the Netherlands are Canada's largest foreign investors. At the end of 2006, the stock of U.S. investment in Canada was $241 billion, about 61 percent of total foreign investment in Canada. Economic sectors with a relatively high foreign presence include manufacturing, oil and gas, wholesale trade, transportation and warehousing, and finance and insurance. Recently, merger and acquisition activity has been the largest part of foreign investment flows into Canada, accounting for 71 percent of inward foreign investment in 2005 and 2006, according to the Canadian government.

Canada is signatory to the World Trade Organization (WTO) Agreement and the North American Free Trade Agreement (NAFTA). Under WTO and NAFTA, Canada is generally required to provide national treatment and most favored nation status so that foreign investors are treated no less favorably than domestic investors with respect to the establishment, acquisition, management, and sale of investments.

Foreign InvestmentLaws and Policies

The Canadian government, through the Investment Canada Act (ICA), provides for a foreign investment review process in order to ensure that the investment is likely to be of "net benefit" to Canada.[29] Under the ICA, Canada's investment review process is managed by Industry Canada and led by the Minister of Industry. According to a Canadian government official, in the late 1990s, the review of cultural investments was shifted to Canadian Heritage under the direction of the Minister of Canadian Heritage. Ministry officials review all cases and identify other government ministries that need to be involved. For example, Industry Canada would consult with Natural Resources Canada for an acquisition dealing with oil or gas. All non-Canadians must file a notification with either Industry Canada or Canadian Heritage when they begin a new business in Canada or acquire an existing Canadian business. However, only transactions whose asset value reaches certain thresholds require a review.[30] The relevant Minister of either Industry Canada or Canadian Heritage makes the final decision on transactions.

Sensitive Sectors and Criteria for Review

National security is not currently a part of Canada's foreign investment review process. Instead, the review considers a series of economic factors, as well as national cultural policy objectives. While Canadian officials told us that the ICA is not driven by national security, a number of laws, regulations, and policies allow Canada to deal with national security concerns stemming from foreign investments in certain sectors. Canada requires government review and approval in uranium production, financial services, transportation services (including pipelines), and cultural businesses.[31] However, there is no specific exemption for the petroleum industry in the act. The financial sector is subject to ownership restrictions, and foreigners are limited to 25 percent ownership of air carriers, and 33 percent ownership in telecommunications companies. The Department of Canadian Heritage reviews investments in businesses that affect Canada's cultural heritage, including the publication of books, magazines, and newspapers as well as film and music production.

The factors assessed in the ICA review are (1) the effect of the investment on the level and nature of economic activity in Canada, including employment, resource processing, domestic sourcing, and exports; (2) the degree and significance of Canadian participation in the business enterprise and in the industry sector to which the enterprise belong; (3) the effect on productivity, industrial efficiency, technological development, innovation, and product variety in Canada; (4) the effect on competition in Canada; (5) the impact of the investment on Canada's ability to compete in world markets; and (6) the compatibility of the investment with national industrial, economic, and cultural policies, taking into consideration industrial, economic, and cultural policy objectives of any province likely to be significantly affected by the investment.

New Developments

On June 20, 2005, the Canadian government introduced a bill to amend its foreign investment review process. According to U.S. and Canadian government officials, the proposed bill included provisions to allow the government to review foreign investment based on national security concerns.[32] The proposed law did not define national security and would have required the responsible minister to recommend a review, according to Canadian government officials. In addition, a transaction would have been reviewed only if it came to the attention of the intelligence or defense communities and they determined that it needed to be reviewed. According to U.S. government officials, this bill was partially driven by concerns about recent attempts by Chinese firms to acquire Canadian natural resource assets. However, the Canadian Parliament was dissolved at the end of 2005 prior to the 2006 election, and the bill was never passed.

In 2006, the Department of Finance Canada issued *Advantage Canada*, an economic planning document stating that the Canadian government would review its foreign investment policy framework, including the Investment Canada Act, with the goal of maximizing the benefits of foreign investment for Canadians while retaining its ability to protect national interests. The Canadian government has stated that there may be rare occasions where a particular foreign investment might damage Canada's long-term interests. For example, foreign investment by state-owned enterprises with noncommercial objectives and unclear corporate governance may not be beneficial to Canadians. Further, the Minister of Industry stated in October 2007 that the Canadian government's concern is to ensure that state-owned enterprises in Canada are operating under the same standards as any other commercial enterprise in Canada, including those related to transparency, good governance, and free market principles. In December 2007, the Canadian government issued new guidelines to clarify how the Investment Canada Act applies to state-owned enterprises, including sovereign wealth funds.

In July 2007, a Competition Policy Review Panel was created by the Canadian government to review key elements of Canada's competition and investment policies. The panel is to consider whether or not the government should develop new rules to protect Canada's national interests. The panel is expected to report to the Minister of Industry by

June 30, 2008 with recommendations. The government of Canada is also separately examining the need for a mechanism to screen foreign investment on the basis of national security. According to a paper issued in October 2007 by the Competition Policy Review Panel, while Canadians have always been concerned about foreign influence on the Canadian economy, this concern has been exacerbated by a recent series of significant takeovers of a number of prominent Canadian firms by foreign investors, including mining companies like Falconbridge and Inco.[33]

Review Process

The ICA review process begins when a company submits an application. The application must be filed at any time prior to the implementation of the investment. The application requires information about the investor, the investment, the Canadian business to be acquired, its assets, and the investor's plan for the Canadian business. In the application, companies also can take the opportunity to give their reasons why the minister should approve the transaction, according to Canadian government officials and private industry representatives. The ICA includes confidentiality provisions to protect the privileged information provided by the businesses through the course of the application process. Once the application is found to be complete, the Canadian government has 45 days to determine whether or not to approve a particular transaction. If the government does not send a notice to the applicant within 45 days, the application is considered approved. The Ministers of Industry and Heritage each have the option of extending the review by 30 days. Further extensions are permitted by agreement between the investor and the minister. According to the Canadian government, over the period from 2003 to 2007, the average length of an Industry Canada review was 52 days. The average Canadian Heritage review will usually take at least 75 days to complete.

The review includes the following steps:

1. Government officials verify the application is complete.
2. Case officers share certain information with relevant government offices, both federal and provincial, and with the Competition Bureau.
3. Industry Canada and/or Canadian Heritage discuss the results of the review with the investor.

Conditions for Approval

To be granted approval for a transaction, investors must demonstrate that their investment will likely be of net benefit to Canada through their business plans and the conditions for approval, also called undertakings, which they negotiate with the Canadian government. The conditions for approval generally focus on future plans for the business following the completion of the transaction. According to the Canadian government, there has been a shift over time toward conditions related to productivity, technology transfer, and efficiency, and away from a focus on employment. Common conditions for approval might include the following:

- Canadian participation on the acquired company's board, usually 25 percent;

- Canadian participation in the acquired company's management;
- research and development expenditures;
- employment levels;
- productivity improvements; and
- exploration expenditures for transactions involving mining.

APPENDIX V: CHINA

- China is the third largest recipient of FDI in the world, ranking behind the United States and the United Kingdom in terms of the average value of FDI inflows between 2000 and 2006.
- In 2006, FDI in China totaled $292.6 billion, an increase of 51 percent since 2000.
- FDI stock in China as a proportion of GDP was 11.1 percent in 2006.

Background

Over the last several decades, China's economy has moved from a centrally planned system that was largely closed to international trade to a more market-oriented system. Since 1978 China's GDP has increased more than 1,000 percent. According to U.S. State Department officials, the development of Chinese investment regulations has not kept pace with the development of its markets, and the complexity of the foreign investment review process reflects vestiges of China's past as a planned economy. Since the period of economic reform began, China has continued to review inward investment to ensure proposed projects conform to China's industrial policy and national interests. Foreign investment in China typically began in the form of equity joint ventures in the manufacturing sector and, according to industry officials, has progressed to the point where foreigners can merge with or acquire entire Chinese companies.

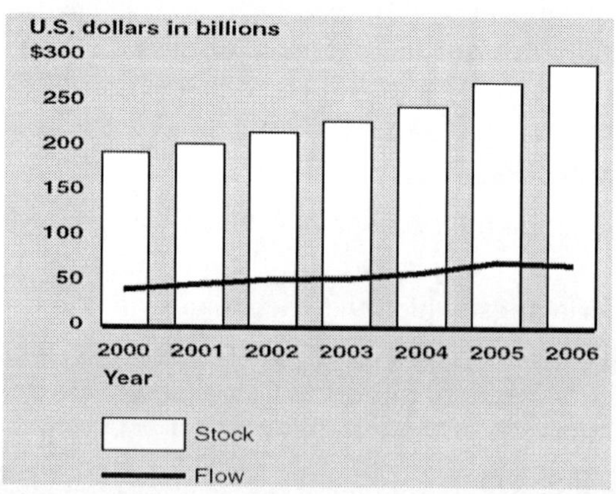

Source: United Nations (data).

Foreign investment in China (stocks and flows 2000–2006)

Several Chinese government entities are involved in the review of foreign investment, including the following:

- *State Council:* The State Council is China's chief executive and administrative authority. Members include the Premier, as the head of government; a variable number of vice premiers; 22 ministers; and 4 State Council commission directors.

- *National Development and Reform Commission (NDRC):* The NDRC is the State Council's economic policy planning arm. According to U.S. and industry officials, it is a powerful macroeconomic management agency with broad planning control over the Chinese economy, and specific control over heavy industry. U.S. and industry officials have stated that the NDRC is deeply involved in the review of foreign investment transactions.

- *Ministry of Commerce (MOFCOM):* MOFCOM is under the State Council and is charged with managing China's external economic relations. Its duties include formulating trade policy, regulating foreign participation in markets, implementing import and export quotas, implementing trade and economic cooperation policies, and guiding foreign investment.

- *State-owned Assets Supervision and Administration Commission (SASAC):* SASAC is a commission under the State Council that represents the central government's ownership interests in 159 state- owned enterprises (SOE). As part of its duties, SASAC guides SOE reform, drafts laws and regulations on SOE management, and supervises the preservation of SOE value.

- *State Administration for Industry and Commerce (SAIC):* SAIC is a State Council ministry in charge of supervising market competition, investigating illegal trade, regulating contract performance, and handling trademark registration and administration.

Foreign Investment Laws and Policies

According to Chinese officials, China's system of written law can be broken into different categories according to their level. Chinese laws that are broad and general form the highest level. They are passed by the Chinese legislative body, the National People's Congress, during its annual meeting in Beijing. At the next level are regulations that are issued by individual state ministries and are intended to interpret and characterize laws. Below that are guiding opinions. According to Chinese officials, opinions are not binding and are used as planning documents. However, according to one U.S. official, they are assumed to carry the weight of law. According to Chinese officials, since Chinese laws are broad and general, regulations and guiding opinions provide the real substance of the Chinese legal system.

In 2006, China began to adopt laws and regulations to describe the procedures it uses to review, and potentially block, proposed foreign acquisitions that it deems are not in China's national interest. According to Chinese officials, two regulations provide the primary framework for China's foreign investment review. First, the 2006 Provisions for Merger and Acquisition of Domestic Enterprises by Foreign Investors (the 2006 regulations)[34] are the most important rules for managing foreign investment. According to the Organization for Economic Co-operation and Development, these regulations bring China closer to international norms for foreign investment reviews and increase regulatory transparency.

The 2006 regulations establish the need for government approval of foreign investment if the transaction

- affects national economic security,
- involves a major industry, or
- results in the transfer of famous trademarks or traditional Chinese brands.

If foreign investors fail to apply for approval, the Chinese government has the legal authority to force divestiture if a transaction causes or may cause significant impact on China's economic security.

Second, the Chinese *Catalog for the Guidance of Foreign Investment Industries* (the Catalog) restricts foreign investment in specified sectors. A revised version of the Catalog was issued by the NDRC in November 2007. According to Chinese officials, the Catalog is a reflection of industrial policy and is intended as a guide for foreign investors. It assigns industry sectors to one of three categories: "encouraged," "restricted," and "prohibited." Investment in unlisted sectors is automatically considered "permitted."

According to the U.S. Investment Climate Statement on China, the Catalog prohibits foreign investment in sectors that China views as key to its national security. However, the Catalog does not prohibit investment for stated reasons, or define national security, although some industries clearly fall into that category, including weapons and ammunition manufacturing, mining and processing of radioactive materials and rare earth metals, and construction and operation of power networks. Other sectors are prohibited based on a broader definition of national security, including film, television, book publishing, and other media production. Other prohibited sectors appear completely unrelated to national security, including processing special Chinese teas, preparation of traditional Chinese medicines, and production of enamel products and rice paper. According to U.S. and Chinese government officials, foreign investment in certain sectors may be encouraged if the investment would bring advanced technology into China that would benefit China's future economic development. Further, according to a U.S. State Department official, industry representatives have stated that China intends to restrict or ban foreign investment in sectors deemed strategic or sensitive to economic security.

Additional Foreign Investment Laws and Policies

Other Chinese laws, regulations, and opinions also regulate foreign investment. However, only the Anti-Monopoly Law does so explicitly for national security.

- The State Council's Opinions on Revitalizing the Industrial Machinery Industry: Suggests that "large, key and backbone equipment manufacturers" obtain government approval when transferring a "controlling stake" to foreign investors. It also calls for China to expand the market share of domestic companies in 16 equipment- manufacturing fields.
- The Guiding Opinion Concerning the Advancement of Adjustments of State Capital and the Restructuring of State-Owned Enterprises: Lists seven sectors the government deems critical to the national economy, which must be kept under government control, including defense, power generation and distribution, oil and petrochemicals, telecommunications, coal, aviation, and shipping.
- The Anti-Monopoly Law: Adopted in August 2007, and becomes effective in August 2008. The law creates an antitrust review of foreign and domestic mergers and acquisitions and also orders the government to create a process to review inward investment for national security concerns. As of January 2008, implementing regulations for the law had not been released.
- Three overarching laws guide foreign investment: The Equity Joint Ventures Law, the Foreign Contractor Joint Ventures Law, and the Foreign Capital Enterprises Law. However, since Chinese laws are very general, the implementing regulations associated with each of these laws are more important for understanding foreign investment controls.
- According to Chinese officials, China has other industry- and sector- specific laws to control foreign investment; for example, in telecommunications or financial services. In total, China has more than 200 laws and regulations that involve foreign investment.

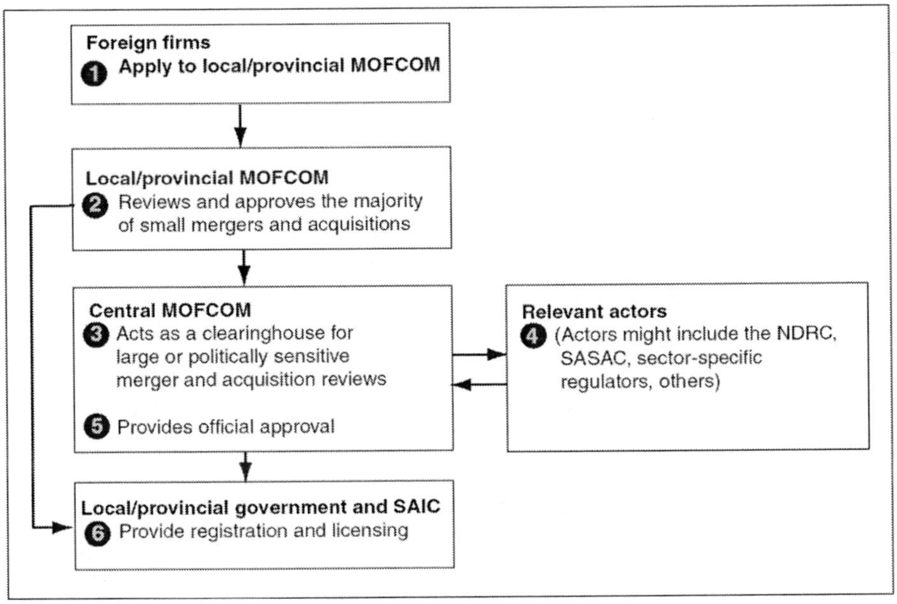

Source: GAO analysis of information from Chinese Government officials.

Note: Steps 3 and 4 may occur simultaneously; Step 4 is sometimes omitted.

Figure 2. Nominal Foreign Investment Review Process.

Review Process

China has a nominal process for reviewing all foreign mergers and acquisitions. The standards that China uses to conduct reviews of foreign investment are opaque, and have resulted in a system that is not fully transparent. However, it is clear that in addition to national security concerns, they also include an assessment of whether a given investment conforms to China's economic development plan. Various factors make China's foreign investment review process unpredictable in practice. Factors affecting the review process include (1) competitor firms generating negative public attention that may influence relevant officials, (2) bureaucratic infighting, (3) differences in priorities between the local and central level Chinese government related to their motivations for the approval of foreign investment, (4) the Chinese political calendar, and (5) regulatory ambiguity and lack of procedural transparency. All five factors can affect the outcome of a particular review, resulting in an application process that is unpredictable for investors. In addition, China's foreign investment regulations are considered complex, in transition, and lack definitions for key terms, making the review process ambiguous.

According to Chinese officials, there is one review process with many facets, and all transactions must go through the Ministry of Commerce.

Step 1: All foreign investors must apply to the local or provincial-level Ministry of Commerce when attempting to merge with or acquire a Chinese firm.

Step 2: Most small transactions are reviewed and approved by the local- level Ministry of Commerce and then go to the local- or provincial-level government for registration and licensing. (Step 6.) If the local MOFCOM does not submit the review to the national-level MOFCOM, then it will distribute the application to the local subsidiaries of NDRC and SASAC, etc. These local subsidiaries may then forward the review to their national- level representatives if they find something of concern. (Step 4.)

Step 3: The central-level Ministry of Commerce reviews large or politically sensitive transactions. Factors affecting political sensitivity might include the size of the transaction, whether a state-owned enterprise is involved, whether the sector itself is sensitive, and whether actors involved in the transaction are connected to the State Council. At this point, the central- level Ministry of Commerce acts as the administrative coordinator for the review.

Step 4: Other relevant actors provide "preapproval." This step generally determines whether or not a transaction will be approved. The NDRC plays an important role in the review as the lead economic planning agency, as does SASAC in cases involving Chinese state-owned enterprises.

Step 5: The central-level Ministry of Commerce reviews the application and provides the official approval or denial. If another governmental entity has jurisdiction, the Ministry of Commerce will rely on it to determine approval or denial. Within 6 months of a transaction being approved, the Ministry of Commerce issues a certificate of foreign investment.

Step 6: Once the central-level Ministry of Commerce issues a certificate of foreign investment, the foreign company has 1 month to obtain a business license and register the business with the State Administration of Industry and Commerce.

China's foreign investment review process is unpredictable. While the great majority of transactions are cleared without incident, the review's multiple layers and ambiguous standards allow intervention by parties opposed to a transaction, according to U.S. State Department officials. For example, the 2006 regulations state that domestic competitors of the Chinese firm being acquired can request that the Chinese government review a transaction for anti-trust concerns. According to U.S. and industry officials, domestic competitors can also indirectly affect transactions by generating negative public attention around a deal that could then affect decision makers. For example, when a U.S. private equity firm attempted to purchase 85 percent ownership of a construction machinery company, the chief executive officer of a rival Chinese firm stated that selling the company to a foreign firm was not in China's interest, and he reportedly worked to derail the transaction. Recently this type of interference has become more common.

A second factor that can slow approvals is bureaucratic infighting. According to U.S. and industry officials, a number of Chinese bureaucracies have overlapping jurisdictions and competing interests, which can affect the outcome of a particular review. For example, Chinese officials in the Ministry of Commerce and the State Administration of Industry and Commerce both suggested they conducted anti-trust reviews, but, according to U.S. State Department officials, there appears to be little coordination of their efforts. This overlapping claim is indicative of the lack of clarity regarding what governmental bodies are involved in a given review.

A third factor that can affect approvals is the difference in incentives between the local and central level Chinese government when approving foreign mergers and acquisitions. According to U.S. government officials, there is a split between the central government, which is concerned about implementing social policies, and the local governments, which are more concerned with economic growth, providing jobs, and attracting investment. Since local governments have a large degree of influence in the approval process, they are one of the major forces counteracting protectionist tendencies in China.

A fourth factor is the Chinese political calendar. According to U.S. and industry officials, foreign firms can have increased difficulty getting government approval for mergers and acquisitions in the year preceding a Chinese Communist Party congress. The Chinese Communist Party convenes a party congress approximately every 5 years. At these events, the party decides its future policy positions and selects new leadership. According to U.S. and industry officials, the atmosphere preceding a party congress is politically charged. Since the appearance of appeasing foreigners can have negative political repercussions in the Chinese political system, many Chinese officials are apprehensive about approving any foreign investments during this time. In particular, since most top executives at state-owned enterprises are party members, investments that affect powerful vested interests, particularly in state-dominated sectors, or those that risk being viewed as contrary to central government policies, are more likely to face political interference according to the U.S. State Department.

In addition to those factors, according to U.S. officials and industry representatives, the relationships among various laws and regulations are complex and unclear. This lack of clarity lessens the ability of foreign firms to predict the likelihood of government approval of an investment. For example, Chinese officials stated that the 2006 regulations and the Catalog provide the primary regulatory framework for reviewing and regulating foreign investment. However, they could not articulate the relationship between the two other than to say that the Catalog is one of many factors considered in the review process. Moreover, according to a U.S. government official, Chinese laws tend to be vaguely worded and general in nature. This allows implementing ministries leeway in interpreting these measures. Implementing rules sometimes offer clarification. Further, according to the Organization for Economic Co-operation and Development, the 2006 regulations appear to create a new layer of review, in addition to the examination and approval process based on the Catalog.

In another example, the State Council Opinion on Revitalizing the Industrial Machinery Industry calls for China to expand the domestic market share in 16 equipment-manufacturing fields. The Guiding Opinion Concerning the Advancement of Adjustments of State Capital and the Restructuring of State-Owned Enterprises lists seven sectors the government deems critical to the national economy, which must be kept in the state's hands. However, it is unclear how these opinions are related to the review process. A Chinese official from the commission that promulgated the list stated that it would be more difficult for a foreign firm to purchase a Chinese company in one of those sectors. However, another Chinese official did not view the list as important because it is nonbinding.

The Chinese government has not defined key terms in the 2006 regulations, contributing to a lack of transparency in the review process. The updated regulations add a screening requirement if the foreign investment transaction affects "national economic security," involves a "major industry," or results in the transfer of "famous trademarks" or "traditional" Chinese brands. However, the regulations do not define these terms, making it difficult for businesses to determine when screening is required and when it is not.

According to U.S. government and industry officials, the definition of "national economic security" is particularly unclear. In fact, according to an industry official, the Ministry of Commerce has not publicly used national economic security as a reason for preventing a foreign merger or acquisition. According to the U.S. State Department, some Chinese scholars affiliated with more protectionist factions of the government use national economic security to refer to self-sufficient economic growth. Thus, investment that would lead China to become dependent on foreign participation in the economy to sustain economic growth should be restricted. Other Chinese scholars believe national economic security refers to economic development that promotes stability, such as a continued increase in living standards, progress on environmental protection, and the creation of jobs. Since China's leaders see economic development as key to maintaining internal stability, national security and national economic security are treated as equally important, according to Chinese and U.S. officials. In practice, the sectors China considers important to national security are listed as forbidden in the Catalog.

Confusion over new regulations is common. According to industry representatives, the Chinese government sometimes promulgates a regulation that many, including those in the government charged with implementing the regulations, do not understand. Implementing regulations are key to spelling out the details of a law, but may be released after the law takes effect. When this occurs, the business community attempts to determine the parameters of the law or regulation through trial and error. Over time, the regulation will take shape. Accordingly, a U.S. State Department official said the lack of definitions and transparency in the 2006 regulations could be indicative of disagreements within the Chinese government regarding how to regulate foreign investment. Conversely, other U.S. and industry officials stated that the updated regulations are intended to allow the government discretion to restrict foreign investment when it is in its interest to do so.

Recent Developments

According to U.S. and industry officials, several factors may have contributed to a slowdown in foreign investment approvals and activity starting in mid-2006. These factors include pragmatic concerns by the Chinese government about the appropriate level of foreign investment and protectionist concerns commonly characterized as economic nationalism. As the Chinese government has promulgated new regulations, industry uncertainty has grown regarding China's review process. However, according to U.S. officials, it is impossible to know whether the current slowdown in approvals will continue or if it is merely associated with temporary political conditions. Nevertheless, according to U.S. and industry officials, the long-term trend toward improved regulatory transparency and efficiency remains positive.

Factors cited as affecting the review process and foreign investment activity include the following:

- *Rapid rise in foreign investment:* Foreign mergers and acquisitions increased from 4 percent of foreign investment in 2002 to over 11 percent in 2005. According to U.S. and industry officials, some Chinese government officials are concerned about increased foreign control over China's economy.

- *Historical antecedents:* Large-scale foreign ownership of Chinese companies can appear to the Chinese as foreign encroachment, drawing on historical fears of foreigners taking control of their country.

- *Populist perceptions of foreign investment:* According to U.S. and industry officials, many people in China believe their country has sold vital state-owned enterprises and traditional Chinese brands to foreigners at below-market value. They fear China will lose its best companies to foreigners. In addition, they perceive that many foreign countries would not sell similar assets to Chinese companies.

- *High-profile transactions:* The U.S. State Department has reported that senior Chinese officials frequently point to the failure of China National Offshore Oil Corporation's (CNOOC) attempt to purchase the U.S. oil company Unocal as justification for China's new investment screening mechanisms. Later, a U.S.-based company's attempted purchase of a Chinese machinery company led to a public outcry against foreign acquisitions in China.

- *Competitor's interventions*: Chinese businesses are becoming more adept in using domestic media to generate opposition to inward investment that threatens their businesses.

- *Desire to build world-class companies:* According to Chinese and U.S. officials, the Chinese government wants to develop world-class companies that can compete internationally. This includes developing famous Chinese brands so that Chinese firms can retain a larger share of the profits from products they manufacture. The government would likely oppose foreign takeovers of these companies.

- *New regulations:* In June 2006 the State Council released an opinion defining machinery and capital equipment as pillar industries, and stating that selling key enterprises to foreigners will require its approval. In December 2006 SASAC released its list of seven sectors the government deems critical to the national economy. In August 2007 the National People's Congress promulgated the Anti-Monopoly Law, adding a national security examination to China's review process.

- *Change in industrial policy*: In November 2006 the Chinese government released its 11th 5-year plan on foreign capital utilization, wherein it emphasized a shift from "quantity" to "quality" of foreign investment, including plans to restrict environmentally damaging and energy inefficient investments. Chinese Vice Premier Wu Yi said the shift in emphasis had also occurred because China had rectified its capital deficiency.

- *Macroeconomic controls:* Investment contributes an unusually large proportion of China's economic growth. Overcapacity may be building in some sectors, and the government is seeking to slow investment generally, according to U.S. State Department officials.

- *Currency stability*: Chinese government concerns exist about excessive foreign exchange inflows that could affect the appreciation of Chinese currency and money supply growth.

- *Political season:* In October 2007 the Chinese Communist Party held its Party Congress. According to U.S. and industry officials, government officials were hesitant to approve foreign mergers or acquisitions during the months leading up to the Party Congress. Large or politically sensitive deals were especially subject to being delayed, according to U.S. officials and industry representatives.

- *Other factors*: The equalization of tax rates for foreign and domestic enterprises, the impact of rising labor costs, and the influence of regulatory issues such as the new labor contract law.

APPENDIX VI: FRANCE

- France ranked fifth in terms of the average value of FDI inflows worldwide between 2000 and 2006.
- In 2006, FDI stock in France totaled $782.8 billion, an increase of approximately $523 billion since 2000.

- FDI stock in France as a proportion of GDP in France was 35 percent in 2006.
- The United States is the leading investor in France, followed by Germany and the United Kingdom.

Background

France, as a member of the European Union, is subject to the articles of the European Community Treaty (EC Treaty). The articles relevant to foreign investment include the requirement that EU member states allow the free movement of capital, as well as allow investors from other countries to conduct business within the member state unencumbered.[35] However, under the EC Treaty, EU member states retain the right to impose restrictions on foreign investment based on public security considerations, as long as those restrictions do not result in arbitrary discrimination or a disguised restriction on trade.[36]

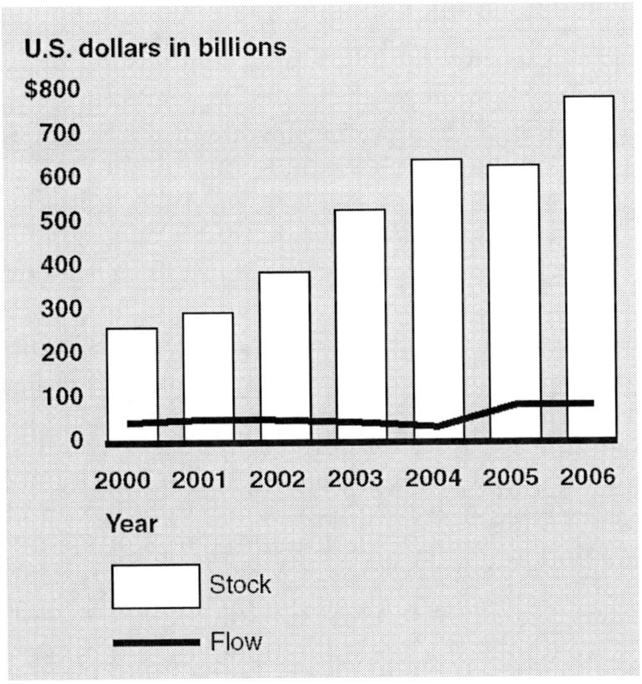

Source : United Nations (data).

Foreign investment in France(stocks and flows 2000–2006)

Foreign Investment Laws and Policies

France regulates foreign direct investment for national security considerations through Decree No. 2005-1739, which implements Article L. 151 of the French Monetary and Financial Code. The 2005 Decree lists 11 specific sectors subject to foreign investment regulation on the grounds of defending France's public order, public safety, or national defense interests, as well as introduces a distinction between EU investors and non-EU investors, with a less restrictive regime applicable to the former.

According to the French Monetary and Financial Code, financial dealings between France and foreign countries are unrestricted.[37] However, certain exceptions to this general policy relate to the regulation of foreign investment for national security considerations. The code states that the French government may require a range of foreign exchange transactions, which includes mergers, acquisitions, and other types of foreign investment, to be subject to prior approval by the French government if they may jeopardize public order, public safety, or national defense interests. [38] In addition, foreign investment in the research, production, and marketing of arms, munitions, or explosives is also subject to prior approval. Approval may be granted by the government based on conditions. Failure on the part of the investor to agree to these conditions may result in approval for the investment being denied.[39]

European Court of Justice Ruling in 2000 Led to Current Regulations

In 2000, in a case brought before the European Court of Justice (ECJ), the ECJ ruled that France had violated the EC Treaty provisions on the free movement of capital.[40] France had restricted the transfer of funds from abroad to the French Church of Scientology, on the grounds that French public security interests were at stake. At the time, French law required an advance authorization for any foreign investment that might present a threat to public security—a requirement the ECJ found to be overly broad.[41] As a result, France promulgated Decree No. 2005-1739, which implements Article L. 151-3 of the French Monetary and Financial Code, in December 2005.

The French decision to include gambling/casinos as one of the specified sectors subject to review, as well as the distinctions made between EU and non-EU investors, has caused further tension between France and the European Commission.[42] The European Commission began infringement proceedings, and in October 2006, formally asked France to amend its regulations.[43] As of February 2008, France had made proposals to address the European Commission concerns, and discussions are ongoing.

Review Process

France's Ministry of Economy, Finance, and Employment leads the foreign investment review process. This ministry seeks input from various other ministries, including the Ministry of Defense, and issues an approval or denial based on the input of all government reviewers. Failure to apply for a national security review when required can result in criminal and civil penalties. If investors are unsure whether the proposed investment is subject to review they may request an opinion from the Ministry of Economy, Finance, and Employment. The ministry has 2 months to respond to the investor. However, the decree notes that a lack of response on the part of the ministry within the specified time frame does not release the investor from the review requirement.

The decree states that a review of an investment within a sensitive sector must be conducted if the investor will

- acquire "control" of a firm whose corporate headquarters are located in France,[44]
- acquire a branch of a firm whose corporate headquarters are located in France, or
- acquire more than one-third of the capital or voting rights of a firm whose corporate headquarters are located in France.

These conditions apply to investment from a non-EU company. Investment from a company that is based in the EU is subject to review when investing within a sensitive sector in France only when meeting one of the first two conditions above for the last four sectors listed below, and only when meeting the second condition for the first seven sectors of the list.

The decree defines the following sectors/activities as sensitive for purposes of a national security review:

1. gambling and casinos;
2. private security;
3. research, development, or production of means to stem the unlawful use, in terrorist activities, of pathogens or toxins;
4. equipment designed to intercept correspondence and monitor conversations;
5. testing and certification of the security of information technology products and systems;
6. production of goods or supply or services to ensure the security of the information systems;
7. dual-use items and technologies;[45]
8. cryptology equipment and services;
9. activities carried out by firms entrusted with national defense secrets, in particular under the terms of national defense contracts or of security clauses;
10. research, production, or trade in weapons, ammunitions, powders, and explosives intended for military purposes or war materials;
11. activities carried out by firms holding a contract for the design or supply of equipment for the Ministry of Defense, either directly or as subcontractors, to produce an item or supply a service for one of the sectors referred to in points 7 through 10 above.

Companies based in an EU member state are subject to the same scope of sectors/activities for 8 through 11 above as a non-EU state, but a more refined scope for sectors/activities 1 through 7 above.

The investor is asked to provide

- the location where the investor is a legal entity;
- details on the individuals and public legal entities that have ultimate control over the investing organization;
- the identity of the primary known shareholders holding more than 5 percent of the capital or voting rights;
- the board members' names and addresses;
- if the investor is an investment fund, the identity of the fund manager(s);

- the investment target's business activity;
- the investment target's last fiscal year revenues; and
- the shareholder structure before and after the contemplated deal.

If the Ministry of Economy, Finance, and Employment does not complete its review and respond within 2 months, then the transaction is considered to be automatically approved. However, the 2-month time frame only begins once a complete application is submitted. If more information from the investor is needed, the review period can be extended. According to French government officials, the Ministry of Economy, Finance, and Employment maintains an open dialogue with the investor so that the ministries reviewing a transaction can be assured of a complete understanding of the proposal. According to French government officials, during the approval procedure, informal consultations between the investor and the French government may take place. During this informal consultation, the investor may revise the proposal to obtain approval.

The decree states that the Ministry of Economy, Finance, and Employment may determine whether security concerns can be mitigated by attaching one or more conditions to the approval of a transaction. For example, according to French officials, the government might require that the investor commit to fulfill ongoing contracts or obligations of the target firm, particular sensitive technologies be kept within France, or aspects of a company's business that require the use of classified information be limited to French citizens. Half of the cases reviewed in 2006 included mitigation agreements. According to government officials, it is common to require the investor to submit an annual report to the government confirming adherence to the agreement. Depending on the sector involved, the ministry with industry jurisdiction oversees the enforcement of commitments by the investor.

In the event that the Ministry of Economy, Finance, and Employment does not approve the transaction, the investor has the right under French law to appeal the decision in the French administrative courts. If the investor can demonstrate that the ministry failed to apply French law correctly, the negative decision may be overturned. In addition, the investor could challenge the decision before the European Court of Justice if EC Treaty provisions are thought to have been violated. According to French government officials, there has never been a denial, and consequently, there have been no appeals under the decree since it was promulgated in December 2005.

According to lawyers experienced with foreign investment policies in France, an important part of the application process for businesses is regularly following up with the Ministry of Economy, Finance, and Employment to check on the status of the application as it works its way through the review process. In a particularly sensitive deal, the investor is likely to hire advisers to contact the government to determine the likelihood of approval even before submitting an application for review. Lawyers and French government officials both stated that as a result of the explicitness of the decree, the French system is deemed to be relatively predictable and transparent for businesses because it is clear in the decree what is subject to review. U.S. government officials told us that they have not received any major complaints from U.S. businesses about French foreign investment policies or review procedures.

Other Foreign Investment Laws and Policies

In addition to the decree's requirements, France has a number of single- sector restrictions. For example, non-EU media companies are restricted from acquiring more than a 20 percent stake in French-language audiovisual communications and media companies, and foreign investment in the French banking and insurance sector requires approval from French banking and insurance regulators. The French government also reserves the right to restrict foreign-controlled enterprises in the aerospace sector. Finally, a number of public monopolies exist in France that are not open to investment, including atomic energy, railway passenger transport, coal mines, gunpowder and explosives, and certain postal services.

Recent Developments

According to a senior French government official, France is not philosophically opposed to foreign investment by foreign state-owned enterprises. However, it is informally considered in the investment review process. For example, the percentage of the investor that is owned by a foreign government would be taken into consideration. However, France does not have any laws or policies that specifically restrict state-owned enterprises or sovereign wealth funds from investing in France.

A growing concern in France is related to energy infrastructure security. For example, in June 2007 the French Parliament issued a report stating that the French government should consider whether energy should be added to the list of sectors in the decree that require government review and approval. As of February 2008, there was no legislation being discussed that provides for such an addition to the decree. A senior French government official also noted that while the use of French government golden shares is not targeted at foreign investors, the French government could use such a share to oppose any measure that might jeopardize the security of energy supplies---potentially including the purchase of French energy infrastructure by foreign state-owned enterprises, private hedge funds, or sovereign wealth funds.

Appendix VII: Germany

- Germany ranked fourth in terms of the average value of FDI inflows worldwide between 2000 and 2006.
- In 2006, FDI in Germany totaled $502.4 billion, an increase of 85 percent over FDI stock in Germany in 2000.
- FDI stock in Germany as a proportion of GDP was 17.4 percent in 2006.
- The United States is the third largest investor in Germany.

Background

Germany, as a member of the European Union, is subject to the European Community Treaty, including the requirement that EU member states allow the free movement of capital.

EU members must also allow investors from other countries to conduct business within the member state unencumbered.[46] However, under the EC Treaty, EU member states retain the right to impose restrictions on the free movement of capital based on public security considerations, but these restrictions must not result in arbitrary discrimination or a disguised restriction in trade.[47]

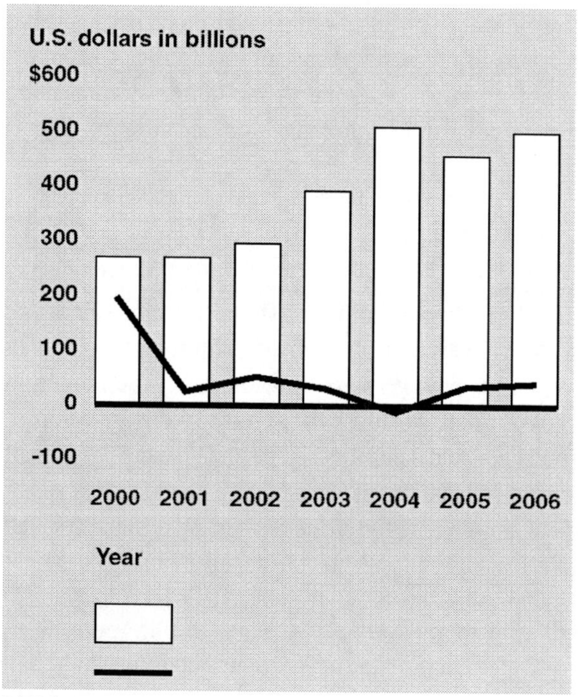

Source: United Nations (data).

Foreign investment in Germany(stocks and flows 2000–2006)

Foreign Investment Laws and Policies

In Germany, as a general rule, foreign investment is not restricted by the government. However, in 2004 Germany enacted Section 7 of the German Foreign Trade and Payments Act, which established exceptions to the free movement of foreign investment into Germany for the "protection of security and external interests." Specifically, foreign investment may be restricted to guarantee the essential security interests of the Federal Republic of Germany,[48] prevent a disturbance of the peaceful coexistence between nations, or prevent a major disruption of the foreign relations of the Federal Republic of Germany.[49] The act specifies that foreign investment transactions are subject to review if the transaction involves a German company that produces or develops war weapons and other military equipment, or produces cryptographic systems for the transmission of classified information.

German government officials told us that the catalyst for the 2004 amendments was the 2003 purchase of a majority stake in a German submarine manufacturer by a U.S. private equity investment firm.[50] According to these officials, there was uncertainty whether existing

German export control laws were adequate to protect German national security interests, and the government did not posses the legal means to block such transactions. For example, the German government feared that a foreign company could purchase a German company possessing sensitive technologies, after which the investor could take the sensitive technology out of Germany and out of the purview of German export control laws.

After passage of the 2004 amendments to the act, the Federal Ministry of Economics and Technology issued implementing regulations specifying which transactions were subject to review. These included the acquisition of German companies, or the direct participation in such companies, that produce or develop items specified in Germany's War Weapons Control Act, such as

- missiles and rockets;
- combat aircraft and helicopters;
- vessels of war and special naval equipment;
- combat vehicles;
- barrel weapons (guns, cannons, howitzers, mortars, etc.);
- light anti-tank weapons, military flame throwers, mine laying and throwing devices;
- torpedoes, mines, bombs, explosives, etc.;
- related accessory and ancillary items; and
- laser weapons.

Acquisitions of companies that produce certain cryptographic systems are also subject to review under the implementing regulations of Section 7 of the act. Further, in September 2005, the German government added acquisitions of specialized engine and gear manufacturers to the list.[51] According to lawyers experienced with foreign investment policies in Germany, this change occurred in response to the proposed sale of a German defense firm.

Review Process

The review of foreign investment in Germany is conducted by the Federal Ministry of Economics and Technology, which obtains input from the Ministry of Defense and the Ministry of Foreign Affairs, among others, on whether there are national security concerns. If the transaction involves a cryptography company, for example, the Ministry of the Interior and German intelligence services would also be involved with the review. The ministry may prohibit a given acquisition if the reviewing officials determine that there would be an essential security interest at stake if the transaction were to be allowed. According to German government officials, in general, approval is a consensus decision.

Non-German companies, as well as German companies in which a foreigner holds at least 25 percent of the voting rights, are subject to review if they are seeking to invest in one of the specified sectors and they are seeking to acquire a 25 percent or greater stake in the German company. If these criteria are met, the investor should report the transaction to the Federal Ministry of Economics and Technology. The investor submits a range of information about both the investor and the target company, including the following:

- proof of the businesses' legal domicile;
- whether the target company has classified information;
- a description of the business operations that fall under the War Weapons List, or cryptographic products;
- the companies' financial statements for the prior 3 years;
- the number of shares held, directly or indirectly, in the target company;
- a description of stakeholders in the companies who hold more than a 25 percent stake;
- a listing of the major suppliers and customers of the target company for the prior 3 years; and
- a breakdown of the companies' market share in war weapons in the German market, in the EU market, and when known in the markets of non-EU countries.

Reporting foreign investment transactions to the German government is required. An investor's failure to notify the government may generate a fine and may be considered a criminal offense. German government officials noted that it is possible that a foreign investor could invest in Germany without obtaining ministry approval by not reporting the transaction. However, according to German government officials, companies commonly approach the Federal Ministry of Economics and Technology prior to formal application to gauge whether a given transaction is likely to be approved.

Under the act, the German government has 1 month to reach a decision after submission of a complete application to the Federal Ministry of Economics and Technology. Absent a decision, the transaction is automatically valid after the 1-month period. According to German government officials, they have not had problems completing a review within 1 month. Since the end of July 2004, when the new rules under the Foreign Trade and Payments Act for reviewing foreign investment came into effect, a total of 11 acquisitions have been reported for review.

The regulations do not permit government-imposed conditions on approval. However, according to German government officials, during the review process the ministry stays in contact with the applicant regarding any concerns or issues. If such issues are identified, the applicant can agree to make changes to the business arrangements outlined in its notification materials to facilitate an approval.

If the Federal Ministry of Economics and Technology were to deny an application, the decision can be appealed through an administrative process within the German legal system. To date, there have been no denials and, consequently, no appeals.

According to German government officials, about 50 companies constitute the core of the German defense industrial base. If an acquisition were attempted in relation to these companies, the investor would apply to the ministry to obtain approval. These officials estimated that roughly 800 companies in Germany could require approval for a foreign merger or acquisition on national security grounds if the German government were to extend the review requirement to all defense-related companies. The law currently does not include dual use items.

Other Foreign Investment Laws and Policies

In addition to Section 7 of the act, Germany has a number of single-sector restrictions. For example, ownership control provisions apply in the private television broadcasting sector. In addition, the German Banking Act requires an acquisition to be reviewed by regulators if an investor is interested in purchasing a controlling stake in a bank in Germany. Finally, a limited number of public monopolies exist in Germany, including inland waterways, employment services, and the lottery.

APPENDIX VIII: INDIA

- India ranked 25th in terms of the average value of FDI inflows worldwide between 2000 and 2006.
- In 2006, FDI in India totaled $50.7 billion, an increase of $33.2 billion over FDI stock in India in 2000.
- FDI stock in India as a proportion of GDP was 5.7 percent in 2006.
- India posted an average growth rate of more than 7 percent in the decade between 1996 and 2006.

Background

When India gained independence from British rule in 1947, the country welcomed foreign investment to establish a technology base as well as skills in entrepreneurship. In 1973, the Foreign Exchange Regulation Act (FERA) imposed a ceiling of 40 percent in foreign investment equity in Indian companies, leading to a flight of foreign investors. In the mid-1980s, India reversed course and began liberalizing its economy, including removing various restrictions on foreign investment. Further liberalization followed the announcement of a new Industrial Policy in July 1991.

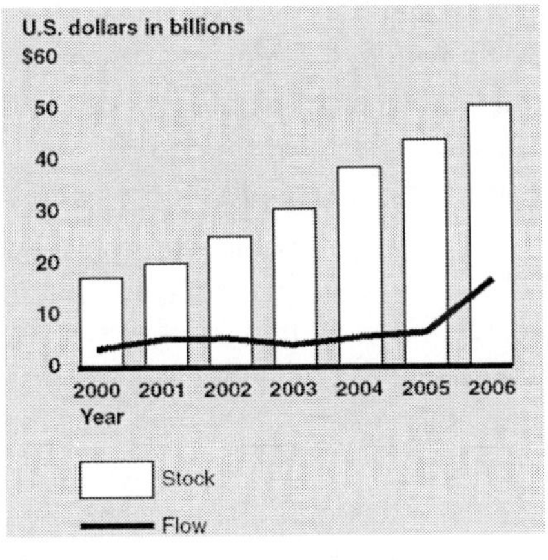

Source: United Nations (data).

Foreign investment in India (stocks and flows 2000–2006)

The Reserve Bank of India automatically approved foreign investment in industries designated by the government as priority recipients of investment. The Foreign Exchange Management Act of 1999 replaced FERA and removed restrictions on foreign corporations. Further, policies on licensing were liberalized.

While India has liberalized its foreign investment policy substantially since 1991, according to an Indian government official, the most important liberalization has occurred in domestic investment brought on by the privatization of the Indian economy. As the government continues to privatize state-owned sectors such as ports and energy production, India would like to attract both domestic and foreign private investment.

Foreign Investment Laws and Policies

The Foreign Exchange Management Act (FEMA) is one of the primary laws regulating foreign investment in India.[52] FEMA broadly regulates the foreign exchange market and provides the Indian government the legal authority to restrict foreign investment. Because FEMA does not include implementing regulations, Indian foreign investment policy is primarily established through a series of public notices or "Press Notes" issued separately for each sector. Press Notes are usually approved by the government cabinet and released by the Department of Industrial Policy and Promotion (DIPP), a department within the Ministry of Commerce and Industry. DIPP makes all Press Notes publicly available and has published a comprehensive summary of the individual Press Notes.

The Press Notes establish, among other things, whether investments in each individual sector must receive government approval or whether investments fall under the "automatic route," which does not require government approval. The Foreign Investment Promotion Board (FIPB) is an interagency body with the authority to approve investment transactions. Any proposed investment that requires government approval must receive approval from the FIPB before the transaction can be completed. In addition to investments in sectors specifically listed as requiring approval by the Press Notes, an investment must receive government approval if (1) the activity requires an industrial license, (2) the investment is in the financial sector or is subject to the Securities and Exchange Board, (3) the investor has an existing joint venture in India in the same field, or (4) the investment falls outside of ownership caps or in sectors in which foreign investment is prohibited. Investment that receives FIPB approval is granted the general permission of the Reserve Bank of India, which administers FEMA, without a separate approval process.

The Press Notes also establish the percentage of a company that can be owned by a foreign investor in each sector. Foreign ownership caps are usually set at one of the following levels: zero percent (prohibited), 26 percent (allowing the foreign investor a sufficient share to block major decisions), 49 percent (maintaining that a majority of shares are held by Indian nationals), 74 percent (maintaining that Indian nationals hold a sufficient share to block major decisions), or 100 percent (completely open). The reasons for the limits on foreign ownership vary from sector to sector. However, according to an Indian government official, domestic and economic concerns, such as the effect on Indian businesses, contribute to the restrictions. In some industries with primarily domestic concerns, such as retail trade, foreign investment is prohibited. However, it is allowed, within limits, in the defense industry, which is commonly associated with national security concerns.

The following are examples of sector-based ownership caps on foreign investment in India.[53]

Foreign investment is prohibited in:

- retail trades (except single-brand retail),
- atomic energy,
- lotteries,
- gambling and betting,
- housing and real-estate business,[54]
- certain types of agriculture.

Limited to 26 percent in (among others):

- defense industries,
- print media,
- insurance.

Limited to 49 percent in (among others):

- broadcasting,
- domestic airlines,
- infrastructure/service sectors.

Limited to 74 percent in (among others):

- establishment and operation of satellites,
- atomic minerals,
- exploration and mining of coal.

Allowed up to 100 percent in other sectors, including:

- development of airports,
- private oil refineries,
- nonatomic electricity generation,
- roads and highways.

Ownership caps are independent of government approval requirements. For example, a sector open to 100 percent foreign ownership may still require government approval, while a sector capped at 49 percent may be open through the automatic route. There are no stated monetary thresholds that trigger a review of foreign investment, except for certain currency transactions, which must be reviewed by the Reserve Bank of India at various thresholds.

Foreign investors under the automatic route are only required to notify the Reserve Bank of India within 30 days of completing the transaction. According to a government official, the notification information is primarily for statistical purposes. All foreign investment transactions require notification, regardless of value or equity percentage, although according to a government official, there are no measures in place to ensure compliance with the notification requirement. According to an Indian government official, potentially harsh penalties for noncompliance deter investors from avoiding requirements.

Some sectors have additional restrictions and approvals. The Industries (Development and Regulation) Act of 1951 currently requires industrial licenses for several sectors, including alcoholic drinks, tobacco, electronic aerospace and defense equipment, industrial explosives, and hazardous chemicals. An industrial license was also required for a manufacturing plant with capital of more than 10 million rupees (roughly $250,000) to produce any of the 114 items that are reserved for "small scale" producers (under 10 million rupees) as well as for any industrial project within 25 kilometers of any city with a population of 1 million or more as of the 1991 census. According to the U.S. State Department, the government of India recently reduced the number of small scale reservations from 114 to 35, part of an incremental reduction that is expected to continue. Investments in these sectors must receive an industrial license in addition to approval from the FIPB.

In addition to the required FIPB review and approval for foreign investment, investment in the financial sector is subject to approval by the Reserve Bank of India. Guidelines for FIPB reviews state that for private sector banks, FIPB approval would be granted only after permission had been obtained, in principle, from the Reserve Bank. These guidelines are included in a document entitled *Investing in India: a Comprehensive Manual for Foreign Direct Investment-Policy and Procedures,* published by the Indian government.

Foreign institutional investors such as mutual funds are regulated by the Securities and Exchange Board of India Act as well as under FEMA. While foreign nationals are not allowed to invest directly in the Indian stock market, foreign institutions that are regulated in their home country are allowed to invest, subject to certain rules, according to the Indian government. For example, no single foreign institutional investor can acquire more than 10 percent of an Indian company, and all foreign institutional investment cannot exceed 24 percent of the capital of the Indian company. Foreign institutional investors must also receive approval from the Reserve Bank in some instances, such as non-stock exchange sales and purchases. According to a law firm familiar with foreign investment policies in India, the Securities and Exchange Board of India regulations are much less demanding than those under the FIPB approval process. In 2006, India amended the Securities and Exchange Board of India regulations, expanding the list of entities considered foreign institutional investors, which are allowed to invest in the Indian stock market, to include governmental agencies such as sovereign wealth funds.

Review Process

For those transactions that do not qualify for the automatic route, the FIPB has the authority to reject an investment transaction, and judges each proposal on a case-by-case basis. FIPB can reject a transaction based upon "special circumstances" or on factors it considers relevant, according to FIPB guidelines. While the guidelines emphasize FIPB's flexibility, they also offer nonbinding factors that FIPB should consider in a review. For example, FIPB should consider whether an investment has any strategic or defense-related considerations. However, the FIPB guidelines do not specify what would constitute a strategic or defense related consideration. An Indian government official stated that while an FIPB review could consider other factors, the primary focus of a review is to determine whether the proposed investment is compliant with Indian policy, such as sector equity caps, joint venture approval requirements, and industrial licensing requirements. According to an Indian government official, in most cases, FIPB denies approval only if a transaction is not compliant with Indian foreign investment policy requirements.

The FIPB is composed of the Secretaries of the Department of Economic Affairs (the Chair), the Department of Industrial Policy and Promotion, the Department of Commerce, the Division of Economic Relations within the Ministry of External Affairs; and the Ministry of Overseas Indian Affairs. According to an Indian government official, the ministry with industry jurisdiction for each case contributes to the FIPB decisions. Guidelines suggest that applications submitted to specific ministries should be brought before the FIPB within 15 days of submission, and that government approval or rejection should be communicated within 30 days. However, according to an Indian government official, an investor should plan on a 3-month review and approval process. Investors may file grievances or complaints to the Grievances Officer-cum-Joint Secretary within the DIPP or to the Business Ombudsman within the Ministry of Commerce and Industry. Once an investor has received approval through the FIPB, he or she is automatically granted the general permission of the Reserve Bank without additional review; however, the companies must notify the Reserve Bank within 30 days of receipt of inward remittances and within 30 days of the issue of shares to the foreign investors.

According to a lawyer familiar with investment in India, FIPB approval is usually a legal formality, and FIPB denials are rare. FIPB does not place conditions upon approval. However, according to a U.S. State Department official, if the investment application requires modification, an investor is permitted to resubmit an amended investment application to the FIPB for approval. Proposals can also be deferred or referred to a different regulatory body.

Government ministries can exert influence on investment transactions prior to the transaction entering the formal FIPB process. According to a U.S. State Department official, the Indian government has intervened in a number of cases where investors from countries of concern have attempted to invest in sectors deemed sensitive, such as the telecommunications sector, often through involvement from the ministry with industry jurisdiction on an ad hoc basis rather than through the formal process. Negotiations and informal discussions with the ministries occur before an investor submits an application to the FIPB, according to the U.S. State Department. Furthermore, some investment applications to the FIPB from investors in countries of concern have sat for over a year without approval or denial, according to a U.S. State Department official.

New Developments

Indian foreign investment policy in individual sectors changes frequently. Each year, the Indian Cabinet reviews foreign investment policy and announces a series of sector-based changes as part of a government-wide FDI review, according to the U.S. State Department. In January 2008 the Indian government approved several changes to its FDI policy. The limit on foreign investment in state-owned petroleum refineries was increased from 26 to 49 percent. The limits in some parts of the civil aviation sector, including cargo airlines, were increased from 49 to 74 percent, although investment in passenger airlines is still limited to 49 percent. Additional liberalization of foreign investment rules was approved for construction development projects, commodity exchanges, credit information companies, industrial parks, and titanium mining. According to the U.S. State Department, the cabinet-approved policy, which was delayed several months, dropped the most controversial proposals to expand FDI in retail and other areas. Changes to individual sectors also can occur outside the annual foreign investment policy review, according to the U.S. State Department. For example, in April 2007, the government announced changes to the conditions of ownership in the telecommunications sector as a follow-up to changes made in March of 2005 that increased the telecommunications sector ownership cap from 49 percent to 74 percent. The 2007 changes introduced additional specific security conditions for the telecommunications industry, which, according to business association representatives, are intended to offset potential security concerns associated with increased foreign ownership in the sector.

According to business representatives that have had experience investing in India, there have been no recent significant changes that have tightened controls on foreign investment or increased ownership restrictions. Indian government officials as well as representatives from a law firm with Indian investment experience stated that the trend of liberalization will continue in India. Despite a likely trend of liberalization in the long term, one of the most controversial areas for liberalization has been in the retail sector, where foreign investment is seen as a threat to small Indian retail businesses. According to the U.S. State Department, The Ministry of Commerce and Industry announced in October 2007 that liberalization in the retail sector would not occur as part of the ongoing foreign investment policy review.

The Indian government has also recently considered implementing a security-based review process. According to the U.S. State Department, the Indian National Security Council Secretariat suggested creating a National Security Exception Act (NSEA), which would have established a process for assessing security threats related to foreign investment, similar to the U.S. CFIUS process. The idea met resistance from the Ministry of Commerce and Industry and the Ministry of Finance and was subsequently abandoned. The debate over the changes represents the institutional differences between agencies. The National Security Council Secretariat and the Ministry of Home Affairs would prefer to make security controls an explicit part of the formal process, while the Ministry of Commerce and Industry and the Ministry of Finance are concerned about the effect on investment that further review requirements might have, according to the U.S State Department. Since the initial proposal was abandoned, U.S. State Department officials have reported that Indian government agencies are still debating the need for a national security review of foreign investment.

APPENDIX IX: JAPAN

- Japan ranked 37th in terms of the average value of FDI inflows worldwide between 2000 and 2006.
- In 2006, FDI in Japan totaled $107.6 billion, an increase of $57.3 billion over FDI stock in Japan in 2000.

- Japan is ranked 21st in the world in terms of FDI stock as of 2006.
- FDI stock in Japan as a proportion of GDP was 2.5 percent in 2006.

Background

Japan possesses the third largest economy in the world. However, foreign investment is significantly less in Japan than for other large economies. In 2003, the Japanese government set a national goal of doubling the nation's stock of foreign investment from its 2001 level by the end of 2006. In March 2006, the Japanese government set an updated goal that has been officially adopted by the cabinet to increase foreign investment in Japan to 5 percent of the country's GDP by 2010.

Trends of foreign investment in the Japanese economy are best understood within the historical context of the Japanese recovery after World War II, according to an academic familiar with the Japanese economy. Whereas countries such as West Germany and France emerged from the war and took measures to attract foreign capital to rebuild, Japan has historically had a surplus of capital and therefore little need to attract foreign investment, according to a consultant on Japanese financial and trade-related issues. Japan enacted the Foreign Exchange and Foreign Trade Act (FEFTA) in 1949, which, according to an academic, barred foreign companies from repatriating profits from Japan, effectively prohibiting all but a few cases of foreign investment. This continued until 1967, at which time Japan was required to open its economy to foreign investment to become a member of the OECD. Japan further changed its laws in 1991, by amending the Foreign Exchange and Foreign Trade Act, which today remains the primary law relevant to FDI. However, despite changes in the law, foreign investment did not increase substantially until the economic downturn in the late 1990s; this increase in foreign investment is the result of bankrupt companies seeking foreign investors in order to stay afloat, according to U.S. State Department officials and representatives from the private sector and academia.

Officials also offered multiple explanations for why foreign investment in Japan has been low. One explanation is that foreign acquisitions of Japanese companies face barriers caused by business practices such as cross-shareholding—the practice of companies holding shares of each other's stock—and *keiretsu* relationships—groups of affiliated companies that hold each other's shares and may also have financial (such as bank loans) or manufacturer-supplier ties or distributor relationships. Cross- shareholding and *keiretsu* relationships lessen the amount of shares available on the stock market. In addition, cross-shareholding may prevent a foreign company from taking management control of a company, even if the foreign company is the largest individual shareholder. The Japanese government notes that *keiretsu* relationships and cross-shareholding have become less common than they were in the past. Another explanation is that Japanese businesses are averse to foreign investment. One reason for that is because Japan possesses a system of guaranteed lifetime employment, which has led Japanese business managers to place a greater value on internal corporate loyalty than shareholder returns, according to the U.S. State Department. Many Japanese companies believe that foreign investors, especially private equity firms, will harm a Japanese company's long-term business interests solely to increase short-term profits, according to an academic and private sector representatives.

In addition to a business environment generally averse to foreign investment, companies have increasingly instituted corporate defensive measures to prevent hostile takeovers by both foreign and domestic companies as a response to revisions of Japan's Corporate Code that expanded the types of merger and acquisition transactions allowable in Japan. Defensive measures such as “poison pills” allow a corporation to prevent a hostile takeover at the cost of diluting the value of all shareholders' holdings. In May 2005, the Japanese government released guidance on how to appropriately implement defensive measures. As of May 2007, about 340 companies in Japan had instituted such defensive measures. In at least one case, the Japanese courts have upheld the right of a Japanese firm to prevent a foreign acquisition using defensive measures, according to industry association representatives.

Since the 1990s, acceptance of foreign investment has increased, although high-profile cases have fueled a fear of foreign investment, according to U.S. government officials. In the economic recession in the 1990s, Japanese companies in financial distress needed foreign investors to prevent bankruptcy, according to an academic. In fact, foreign investment mergers and acquisitions in Japan have typically occurred only when the Japanese company is in financial distress, according to a business association representative. While there have been successful transactions that have benefited the investor and the Japanese company, some foreign investment transactions have been viewed as harmful to Japan, according to an academic familiar with the Japanese economy. One such case involves a foreign private equity firm's acquisition of a bank and subsequent large initial public offering (IPO) for the private equity firm. This company forced another Japanese company to declare bankruptcy while producing a large profit for itself, a fact that contributed to the view that foreign firms do not share Japanese interests.

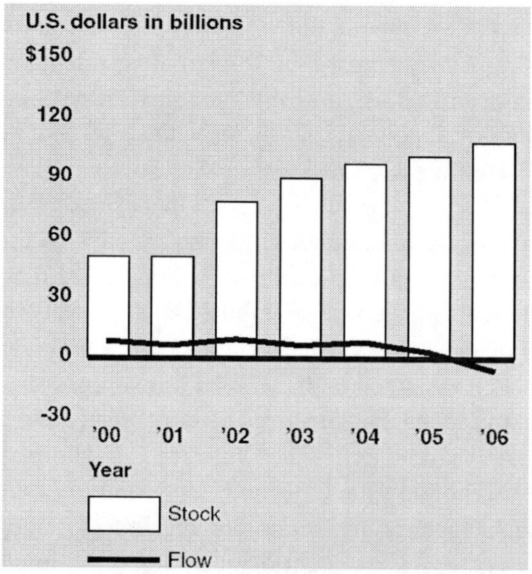

Source: United Nations (data).

Foreign investment in Japan stocks and flows 2000–2006)

Foreign Investment Laws and Policies

Japan's primary law concerning foreign investment, is the Foreign Exchange and Foreign Trade Act.55 The law provides that government ministries may prohibit or place conditions on a proposed foreign investment if they determine that it may harm national security, public order, public safety, or the smooth management of the economy. However, the Japanese government has not used this authority since FEFTA was amended in 1991, according to the Japanese government.

The Japanese regulatory scheme established under FEFTA treats foreign investment differently based upon the sector in which the investment is taking place, among other criteria. Foreign investment in a sector that is determined to be sensitive requires prior notification and government approval, while investment in other sectors only requires an after-the-fact notification to the government. Foreign investment in all industries requires notification through one of these routes. A government notice provides tables that specify the sectors and the individual industries that require prior and after-the-fact notification. Industries not listed in either table must submit prior notification. Failure to notify, among other violations under FEFTA, can result in criminal penalties including jail for up to 3 years and/or a fine of three times the investment amount or 1 million yen, whichever is larger.

According to the Japanese government, prior notification of a foreign investment is required for

- national security: aircraft, weapons, nuclear power, spacecraft, and gunpowder;
- public order: electricity, gas, heat supply, communications, broadcasting, water, railroads, passenger transport;
- public safety: biological chemicals, guard services; and
- smooth management of the economy: primary industries relating to agriculture, forestry and fisheries, oil, leather and leather products manufacturing, air transport, and maritime transport. (These areas are reserved under Article 2 of the OECD Code of Liberalization of Capital Movements.)

Prior notification is also required in additional circumstances. The Japanese government requires prior notification for investments from countries with which Japan has not completed a reciprocal investment agreement 56 and if the foreign investment involves certain capital transactions subject to permission by the Finance Minister.57 If there is doubt as to whether a company is subject to prior notification, administrative agencies will provide an advance consultation outside of the formal review process.

On September 28, 2007, a Japanese Cabinet Ordinance came into effect, requiring that industries for dual use items and items used for the maintenance of the defense industrial base provide prior notification for foreign investment. These changes were based on recommendations of a study group convened by the Ministry for Economy, Trade, and Industry (METI), according to the Japanese government. The change was intended to prevent the outflow of technology, especially that which has a high probability of conversion to use in weapons of mass destruction, and maintain the domestic defense industrial base. The revisions include a list of all specific industries and items that fall under the new prior notification requirements, including industries involved in making accessories or components related to the manufacture of arms, aircraft, satellites, and nuclear reactors. Additionally, manufacturers making testing equipment, repair equipment, and certain types of software usable in weapons and airplanes will fall under prior notification requirements.

According to the Japanese government, the review of foreign investment regulations was initiated because of the changed security environment surrounding Japan and trends in international investment activity. This was the first review of foreign investment regulations in 16 years, since FEFTA was amended in 1991. While there was no single triggering event for these changes, there were several controversial investments, both domestic and foreign, that have raised public concern with mergers and acquisitions over time, according to U.S. State Department and industry association representatives.

A foreign investor in sectors that require after the fact reporting must file a report with the Ministry of Finance and the ministry with jurisdiction over the industry through the Bank of Japan within 15 days after a transaction occurs. In previous interviews with Japanese government officials, GAO was told that this chaptering was for statistical purposes and in case of an emergency, such as a financial crisis or war.58

FEFTA broadly defines "foreign investment" as the (1) acquisition of at least 10 percent foreign ownership of shares in a company listed on a Japanese stock exchange; (2) acquisition of any shares in an unlisted company; (3) establishment of a branch, factory, or other business office in Japan; (4) consent given to change the corporate objectives of a domestic company with one-third or more foreign ownership; or (5) loan of certain types and amounts of money to domestic companies.

In addition to adding industries subject to prior notification and review, the September 2007 Cabinet Ordinance made several other changes. It expanded the scope of FEFTA to include investment in a parent company when a subsidiary falls under a sector that is subject to review and provided clarification on the percentages of foreign ownership that fall under the regulations. If more than 50 percent of a company is controlled by foreigners, but no single foreign investor owns more than a 10 percent share, that investment will not fall under FEFTA regulations. However, if 10 percent of the company is owned among separate investors that have agreed to collectively exercise their voting rights, the investment will be subject to FEFTA regulations. Also, the ministries can request detailed information from the foreign investors and the target company; under previous regulations, such information was available only if the investor supplied it voluntarily.

In addition to the review process implemented under FEFTA, there are specific restrictions to other sectors. According to OECD, foreigners or foreign-controlled enterprises are not granted licenses in the broadcasting sector (except cable television and broadcast on telecommunications services) under the Radio Law and Broadcast Law, which were both passed in 1950. Similarly, the 1984 Law Concerning Nippon Telegraph and Telephone Corporation requires that board members and auditors of the Nippon Telegraph and Telephone Corporation have Japanese nationality. Also, the Japanese government is obligated to hold stocks in Japan Tobacco Inc.

Review Process

FEFTA authorizes the Ministry of Finance and the ministry with industry area jurisdiction to review investments that are required to provide prior notification. The notification form requires information on the percentage of shares to be acquired, the business plan of the investing company, and the reason for the transaction. However, the ministries may also consider information related to foreign control, such as the number of foreign board members and the foreign company's reputation, according to Japanese government officials. The ministries review investments on a case-by-case basis. While threats to national security, public order, public safety, or the economy are factors considered in a review, specific criteria used to determine when an investment poses a significant threat are not published.

The ministries have 30 days to review a proposed investment after a foreign company has notified the ministries of its intent to invest. If the investor has not received a response within that time, the transaction is automatically approved, according to METI officials. The ministries may extend the review period up to 4 months if they believe further inquiry is necessary. A Committee on Foreign Exchange and Other Transactions also may extend the review period an additional month. However, the Japanese government noted that reviews can be, and frequently are, shortened to 14 days. Japanese law provides for a public hearing if an investor wishes to contest the result of the ministerial review. After the public hearing, an investor may submit an administrative appeal to overturn the decision and if the appeal is rejected, an investor can then request the court to overturn the decision.

Appendix X: The Netherlands

- The Netherlands ranked eighth in terms of the average value of FDI inflows worldwide between 2000 and 2006.
- In 2006, FDI in the Netherlands totaled $451.5 billion, an increase of 85 percent over FDI stock in 2000.
- FDI stock in the Netherlands as a proportion of GDP was 68.2 percent in 2006.

Background

The Netherlands' trade and investment policies are among the most liberal in the world. As a founding member of the EU and the home of the International Court of Justice, the Netherlands has historically emphasized the development of international institutions and maintains an economy with a strong international focus. The Netherlands Constitution is one of only two constitutions in the world to include a provision requiring the government to further international institutions and the rule of law.59 According to lawyers familiar with foreign investment policies in the Netherlands, there were a series of significant changes in Dutch corporate law in the 1980s that favored corporate shareholders. The changes were largely reactions to the broad social policies of the 1960s and 1970s. These revisions to the law, combined with the fact that the Netherlands has a highly educated population, have made the country a prime target of investment over the past several decades. Foreign companies established in the Netherlands account for roughly one-third of industrial production and employment.

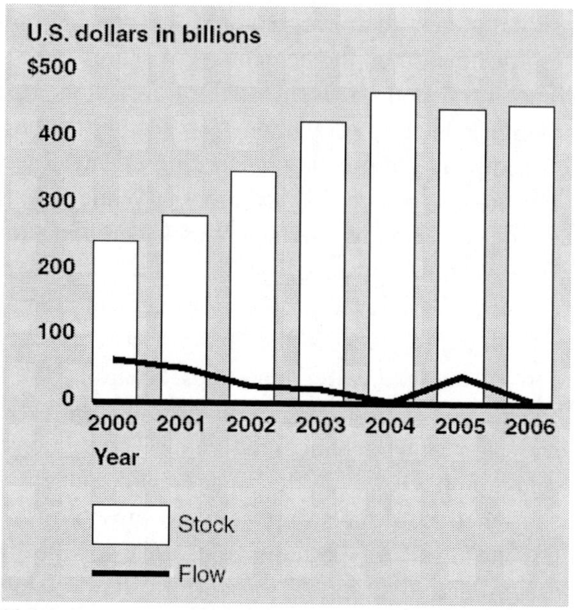

Source: United Nations (data).

Foreign investment in Netherlands (stocks and flows 2000–2006)

Foreign Investment Laws and Policies

The Netherlands possesses no review process for foreign investment, and according to Dutch government officials, the Netherlands lacks the general authority to block investment. Foreign and domestic companies are treated equally under Dutch law, and regulations for mergers and acquisitions apply to domestic as well as foreign investment, according to Dutch government officials.60 Foreign investment, like domestic investment, must go through an anti-trust review. However, these reviews do not provide the Dutch government the authority to block investment upon national security grounds, according to government officials. The one exception is in the financial sector, in which the Netherlands Central Bank, and in some cases the Finance Minister, can block mergers and acquisitions.

The Financial Supervision Act establishes the authority for the Netherlands Central Bank to review and grant approval to all mergers and acquisitions involving Dutch companies in the financial sector, including banks, management companies for collective investments, investment firms, and insurance companies. For a transaction involving one of the five largest banks in the Netherlands, the transaction must receive approval from the Ministry of Finance. When a company acquires at least 10 percent ownership of a Dutch company, the investor must apply to the Netherlands Central Bank to receive a “declaration of no objection.” According to Dutch government officials, this application can be submitted after a transaction has been completed. The Netherlands Central Bank performs a review of the transaction and decides whether or not to issue a declaration of no objection. In the case of the five largest banks, the Netherlands Central Bank makes a recommendation to the Finance Minister, who has the authority to issue the declaration of no objection. The Netherlands Central Bank or the Finance Minister can effectively block a transaction by refusing to issue this declaration. The Bank or Finance Minister has 3 months from the date of application to render a decision.

The review and approval process in the financial sector is primarily intended to determine whether any financial mergers or takeovers would lead to undesirable developments in the Dutch financial sector. According to Dutch government officials, the process is not generally treated as a review or approval process at all; rather, it is a contractual agreement whereby acceptable conditions of the merger are established. However, the Financial Supervision Act states that the government of the Netherlands has the authority to provide "prudential supervision" of mergers, and according to a Dutch law firm with experience facilitating investment in the Netherlands, this review provides a general discretionary authority to deny transactions so long as a decision is supported on reasonable grounds. According to the law firm, if there is a threat to national security, the Netherlands Central Bank or the Finance Minister could block a transaction using this authority. According to Dutch government officials, a situation in which foreign transactions could be blocked would be if there was spillover from U.S. sanctions. For example, investment from businesses in countries such as Venezuela and Iran may be determined to harm the functioning of the Dutch market and could thus be blocked.

Restricted Sectors

Certain sectors are publicly owned and controlled, and are therefore closed to foreign investment. According to a Dutch government official, public monopolies exist in the following instances:

- A state-owned enterprise owns and administers the national high-voltage electricity grid. However, electricity production and distribution are open to foreign investment.
- Water grids are locally held monopolies. While some water grids have been privatized to foreign entities, new legislation passed in 2004 prevents further privatization. According to Dutch government officials, water is maintained by the government primarily due to health concerns.
- Railway passenger services are controlled by a state-owned enterprise and are effectively closed to investment.
- The national airport is currently closed to investment. While privatization has been discussed for years, the current government has decided not to privatize the airport.
- The Netherlands Central Bank is a monopoly and is closed to investment.
- Postal service below 50 grams per letter is closed to investment. This monopoly is still in place, but is slated to be abolished by December 31, 2010, as part of a decision to abolish this monopoly in most of the European Union nations.
- Public bus transport is generally open to foreign investment, although within some cities, the bus lines are owned by the local government.

Dutch government officials generally cited maintaining a competitive market as a reason why these sectors are closed to investment. Dutch government officials noted that privatizing sectors where there is a monopoly would present a threat to open competition in the market. However, Dutch government officials also cited other reasons for the government maintaining control of sectors, such as the fact that the water grids could present a health issue if not properly maintained. All of the listed restrictions fall under the transportation, water supply, energy, or banking sectors, which are considered part of "critical infrastructure" by U.S. government sources. According to a U.S. State Department official, one reason these sectors are protected in the Netherlands is that they are perceived by the Dutch to be vital to their security interests.

The Netherlands has imposed nationality requirements in the air transport industry. European Union law requires that an airline registered and licensed in the Netherlands must be majority owned and controlled by EU nationals. In 2004, an airline from another EU member state acquired the Dutch national airline and maintains a majority share in the combined company. Despite the fact that the partner investor is another European airline, the Netherlands recently renewed the right to dilute shares to acquire 50.1 percent of voting rights in the case that another nation terminates or restricts an international route because the airline is not effectively controlled by Dutch nationals.

New Developments

The Netherlands currently has no plans to change its laws for managing foreign investment, according to U.S. State Department officials. However, some members of the Dutch government have argued that changes should be made. High-profile transactions have raised concerns with foreign investment among certain factions in the Netherlands. According to U.S. State Department officials, the debate about whether the Netherlands should institute stricter controls on foreign investment was first raised with the acquisition of the Dutch national airline in 2004. Some people believed that certain traditionally Dutch companies should stay in control of Dutch nationals, according to U.S. State Department officials.

The negotiations involving the acquisition of a Dutch bank by foreign investors has reopened the debate concerning the protection of Dutch companies from foreign acquisitions. The terms of the acquisition of the bank by foreign investors were approved by the Ministry of Finance and were recently finalized. However, some members of Parliament have expressed concern about the transaction and announced a desire to debate both the specific transaction as well as potential changes to the entire regulatory scheme for granting approvals. While the Parliament has not intervened in the regulatory process, the Finance Committee within the Dutch Parliament planned to debate the bank transaction on October 17, 2007, and again on November 8, 2007. According to U.S. State Department officials, one change suggested by Dutch government officials has been to increase the role of the financial supervisor, effectively delegating a body within the government to oversee mergers and acquisitions. Another suggestion has been to reintroduce golden shares in certain domestic companies. Golden shares would grant the government veto rights over substantial changes to particular companies that have been determined to serve the public interest. The Netherlands divested its golden share in the national postal firm in 2006 after the European Court of Justice ruled that the golden share unduly restricted the free movement of capital.[61]

The bank transaction also raised concerns about state-owned enterprises and sovereign wealth funds. A failed bidder for the Dutch bank was partially owned by a state-owned bank from China and a sovereign wealth fund from Singapore. Had the transaction been completed, a minority share of the Dutch bank would be indirectly owned by the Chinese and Singaporean governments. This fact, according to a Dutch law firm familiar with the transaction, concerned members of the Dutch Parliament and was one reason for calls for debate over the bank transaction. However, the Netherlands has typically not been opposed to investment from government-controlled investors, and according to Dutch government officials, there are already state-owned enterprises that have invested in companies in the Netherlands.

APPENDIX XI: RUSSIA

- Russia ranked 18th in terms of the average value of FDI inflows worldwide between 2000 and 2006.
- In 2006, FDI in Russia totaled $197.7 billion, an increase of more than $165.5 billion over FDI stock in 2000.
- FDI stock in Russia as a proportion of GDP was 20.2 percent in 2006.

Background

In 1991, Russia began its transition from a centralized command economy to a market-based economy and thus has less than two decades of experience with foreign investment. Roughly three-quarters of the Russian economy has been privatized, although the state continues to hold blocks of shares in many privatized enterprises. According to U.S. business representatives and lawyers in Russia, business ventures have become more complex since the earliest days of the opening of the country to foreign investment. According to the U.S. State Department, while the Russian economy has begun to diversify and institute economic reforms, the government budget and economy continue to be dependent on oil and gas revenues. About 40 percent of investment in Russia is in the energy sector. Other sectors receiving foreign investment are transportation, real estate, services, machinery, banking, and retail. The Russian government recognizes the need to promote new investment in aging infrastructure and believes it can do this through controlling strategic enterprises, state-sponsored investment funds, special economic zones, and limiting foreign investment in key strategic sectors.

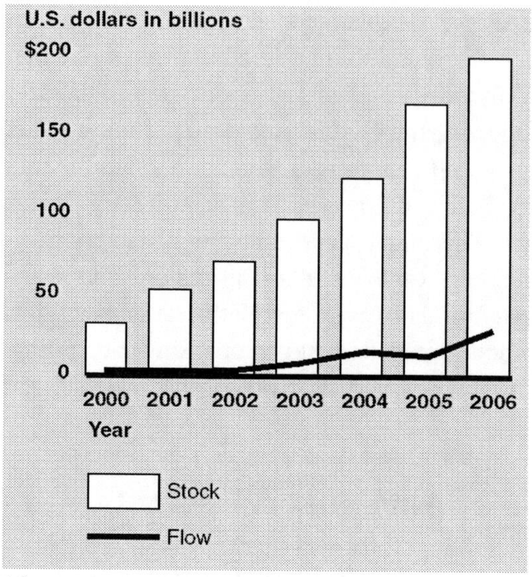

Source: United Nations (data).

Foreign investment in Russia (stocks and flows 2000–2006)

Foreign Investment Laws and Policies

Under the 1999 Federal Law on Foreign Investments, the Russian government may block foreign investment to ensure the defense of the country and the security of the state. However, according to Russian government officials, no regulation or process was put in place to implement that section of the law. Two transactions with national security implications were attempted in 2004 and 2005. The Russian government reviewed the transactions using an ad hoc process in which the Federal Anti-Monopoly Service (FAS) received the investors' applications for an anti-monopoly review and then coordinated a review through the Russian government's security ministries. One transaction was eventually approved and one was not. As a result of these attempted investments, the Russian President's 2005 State of the Russian Federation speech called for legislation to formalize a process to protect Russia's interests by reviewing foreign investment in sensitive economic sectors, according to Russian government officials.

In response, according to Russian government officials, the Ministry of Economic Development and Trade and the Ministry of Industry and Energy, in conjunction with the Russian presidential administration and the Russian security services, developed the proposed Strategic Sectors Law—which, according to a senior Russian government official, resembles certain aspects of the U.S. CFIUS process. Several versions of the legislation have been drafted; one version went to the Russian Duma for approval in July of 2007. According to the U.S. State Department, a more restrictive version of the Strategic Sectors Law and relevant amendments to the Subsoil Law were announced by the Russian government on February 21, 2008. As of February 26, 2008, the Strategic Sectors Law had not been passed, and is subject to change. The new draft of the Strategic Sectors Law and the Subsoil Law amendments could be considered by the Duma in the spring of 2008.

The Russian legal system is based on civil, not common, law. As a result, according to a senior Russian government official, Russian laws are more detailed than might be the case under a common law system. This official noted that this characteristic of civil law systems partially explains the degree of detail that is found in the proposed Strategic Sectors Law. In addition, Russia's basis in civil law also helps illuminate why the lack of implementation procedures in the 1999 Federal Law on Foreign Investments in Russia was particularly problematic.

Review Process

According to Russian government officials, under the current system, the Federal Anti-Monopoly Service is the only government entity with explicit authority to approve foreign investment transactions. The current process requires investors to submit applications for anti-monopoly review to the FAS. The FAS determines whether the investment may cause a national security concern, in addition to its primary role of determining anti-monopoly considerations. The FAS solicits input from other members of the Russian federal government on whether the proposed transaction should be approved or blocked, and delivers the decision to the investor. According to Russian government officials, this ad hoc process was developed out of necessity, it is not a process intentionally crafted to most effectively protect Russian national interests, and it is a painful process for foreign investors because of the lack of transparency.

Thresholds for Mandatory Review

Under the 1999 Federal Law on Foreign Investments, application for FAS review of foreign investment is mandatory when a proposed transaction meets certain thresholds. For example, if the aggregate value of the assets of the merged or acquired entities exceeds 3 billion rubles, if the aggregate revenues of the entities will exceed 6 billion rubles, if the entities control more than 35 percent of the market, or if the investor seeks to obtain more than one-third of the shares in a company, then prior approval of the investment by the FAS is required. According to U.S. industry officials in Russia, in cases where the thresholds are not met, the investor may need to notify the FAS of the transaction, but not necessarily obtain prior approval.

Standard Review Time Frames

Under the current FAS anti-monopoly review, the standard time frame for review, upon receipt of the complete investor application, is up to 30 days. These 30 days are for conducting the FAS review, and do not incorporate a standard time frame for conducting national security reviews. Because national security reviews under the current process are ad hoc, they have no set time frames. For example, according to an industry official, in one case, which did ultimately receive approval, it took over 7 months for a final decision to be reached. During this period, the investor provided the Russian government with supplemental materials to the FAS review packet, in addition to holding meetings with Russian government entities.

Use of Mitigation Agreements

While the current FAS anti-monopoly review process is not technically designed to mitigate potential concerns that arise during the ad hoc national security review of foreign investment, in practice the signing of mitigation agreements has occurred between the Russian government and the applicant investor to enable the approval of a transaction.

Judicial Appeal of Review Decisions

According to lawyers experienced in foreign investment in Russia, a denial issued by the FAS under the current anti-monopoly review process can technically be appealed through the Russian judicial system. However, these lawyers do not believe that an appeal attempt is likely to be successful, unless the investor presents information that was not included in the original application.

New Developments

The Russian government's Ministry of Economic Development and Trade and the Ministry of Industry and Energy, in conjunction with the presidential administration and the security services, developed a new Strategic Sectors Law. The new draft of the law could be considered by the Duma in the spring of 2008, according to the U.S. State Department. If passed, the law will create an interagency review process for foreign investment. The July 2007 version of the proposed Strategic Sectors Law specified 39 sectors that are considered sensitive. Among other changes, the February 2008 version of the draft combined some sectors and added four strategic sectors to the list.

Under the proposed law, investors would still apply to the FAS for an anti-monopoly review, but would also be subject to a separate review if the proposed investment falls within a covered sector. According to the July 2007 draft of the Strategic Sectors Law, the review will occur within an interagency body representing a range of Russian government economic and security ministries, potentially headed by the Prime Minister's office. The interagency body may include

- the Federal Anti-Monopoly Service,
- the Ministry of Economic Development and Trade,
- the Ministry of Industry and Energy,
- the Ministry of Defense, and
- the Federal Security Service.

However, according to Russian government officials, the Russian government has not decided which government entity will receive applications for review. Further, according to the U.S. State Department, as of February 2008, the government had not reached agreement on which agency will lead the interagency group in reviewing investments, which has vital implications for the potential implementation of the proposed law. It is clear, however, that the February 2008 version of the draft reflects additional input from Russian security ministries, including the Federal Security Service.

Under the most recent version of the proposed Strategic Sectors Law, foreign companies seeking to obtain greater than 50 percent or a controlling stake, as defined by the law, in a Russian company will need to obtain Russian government approval if the target company is in a listed sector. These are

- pathogens;
- nuclear devices and radiation sources;
- coding/cryptographic equipment;
- explosives, weapons, and military machinery;
- aviation security and machinery (except civil aviation);
- any activities related to space;
- natural monopolies (e.g., oil and gas extraction); and
- metals and alloys having special properties.

The February 21, 2008, version of the Strategic Sectors Law adds four sectors to those that were included in the July 2007 draft. The additional sectors are

- telecommunications,
- radio,
- television, and
- fishing.

In addition, the February version of the Strategic Sectors Law further limits unsupervised foreign acquisition of Russian companies that own licenses to develop "strategic subsoil assets" to 10 percent, according to the U.S. State Department. Further, entities partly owned by foreign governments would be subject to a 5 percent limit on unsupervised ownership, according to the most recent draft. Foreign entities seeking a greater share of relevant Russian companies would need Russian government approval from a special commission.

The government approval includes both the mandatory anti-monopoly review and the national security review of the proposed investment. If a foreign investor does not seek a controlling stake, then only the standard FAS review is required. According to Russian government officials, the determination of what sector a proposed transaction falls within will be based on the acquired company's government-issued business license. According to Russian government officials and lawyers experienced with foreign investment in Russia, the proposed Strategic Sectors Law, like the current FAS review process, identifies the specific documents and materials that must be submitted for the review to be completed. Under the current FAS review process, the FAS can ask for supplemental documentation from the investor if it deems it necessary, which may delay the application process somewhat. However, according to the lawyers, this additional documentation is not normally difficult to provide or time-consuming.

According to Russian government officials, the proposed Strategic Sectors Law identifies specific criteria against which the proposed transaction will be judged by the interagency review body that is designated to determine whether a national security consideration merits denying an application. Decision criteria include, for example, whether the company to be invested in

- possesses state secrets,
- produces products subject to export controls,
- produces military goods, or
- deals with natural monopolies (e.g., oil, gas).

Under the proposed Strategic Sectors Law, the standard time frame for governmental review of foreign investment will be up to 90 days. In the event that the government determines that it needs additional time to complete its review, the initial 90-day review period can be extended by an additional 90 days, for a total of 180 days, or 6 months. According to the U.S. State Department, the Russian government has not decided whether the anti-monopoly review and the national security review will occur concurrently or consecutively. If held concurrently, the total review time frame would be 90 days, or 180 days in exceptional cases. If held consecutively, the total review time frame would expand to 120 days, or 210 days in exceptional cases.

If a proposed transaction meets the criteria for possible denial, but the threat to Russian national interests can be mitigated, then, according to a Russian government official, the deal will be approved if the investor accepts certain required conditions. The proposed Strategic Sectors Law provides for a range of possible mitigation conditions that may be enacted. These may include

- a commitment to protect state secrets, including potential access limitations for the investor;
- a commitment to continue deliveries of products, performance of work, and rendering of services under existing military contracts;
- a commitment to maintain the acquired firm's mobilization capacity;
- a commitment to work in accordance with tariffs subject to Russian Federation legislation on natural monopolies;
- a commitment to the fulfillment of business plans for further development;
- a commitment to measures to be taken aimed at preventing a threat to national security if martial law or a state of emergency is imposed; or
- a commitment to avoid staff layoffs for a designated period.

For example, according to a Russian government official, the Russian law on state secrets governs and limits who can lead an organizational unit of a company that possesses Russian state secrets. If a Russian company were purchased by a foreign entity, based on signed mitigation conditions, the unit within the company holding state secrets may be required to be run by Russian nationals with security clearances. According to a Russian government official, it has not yet been decided which Russian governmental entity will be responsible for ensuring that signed mitigation conditions are adhered to by the foreign investor.

The proposed Strategic Sectors Law provides for a judicial appeals process if the Russian government fails to issue a decision within 90 days or within the designated extended time frame.

The current 1999 Federal Law on Foreign Investment does not differentiate between foreign state-owned enterprises and others that seek to invest in Russia. According to Russian government officials, under the proposed Strategic Sectors Law, special rules will apply to foreign state-owned enterprises. Such entities will be barred from acquiring a controlling stake in Russian companies that are subject to the proposed Strategic Sectors Law, and in addition, foreign state-owned enterprises will have to seek Russian government approval to acquire a noncontrolling 25 to 49 percent stake in a Russian company.

While reviews of foreign investment fall under the provisions of the 1999 Federal Law on Foreign Investment as applied through the FAS anti-monopoly review process, the extraction of subsoil resources, for example, oil and natural gas, is subject to a range of requirements under the Russian Federation Law on Subsoil. The current standard has allowed foreign investment in certain projects above the 50 percent threshold. The Russian government is currently in the process of drafting amendments to the Subsoil Law that would implement a number of changes.62 The July 2007 draft of the amendments allowed foreign investment in strategic subsoil resources up to 50 percent of the total stake in the given reserve. In addition, according to a Russian government official, under the proposed amendments, the required licenses for operations will only be given to domestic extractors. Foreign investors will have to enter into joint ventures with Russian oil and gas companies to invest in these areas.

Another important proposed change to the Subsoil Law would be the designation of certain reserves of subsoil resources (e.g., oil, natural gas, gold, and copper), that are larger than specified thresholds, to be “of federal significance” to the Russian Federation. The amendments would define "strategic field" as any oil field with extractable reserves of more than 70 million tons, gas fields with more than 50 billion cubic meters, and all offshore fields. Companies in which the Russian government is a majority owner would be exempt from limitations of foreign ownership.

Other Foreign Investment Laws and Policies

In addition to the 1999 Federal Law on Foreign Investment, other laws and policies in Russia affect foreign investment. For example, based on a Presidential Decree, certain Russian state-owned enterprises (SOE) and companies are not open to foreign investment. This listing of over 1,000 SOEs and companies that are off limits to foreign investment includes scientific, defense, and military factories and institutes; media companies; ports; airports; and shipping companies. According to a Russian government official, the Presidential Decree list and the companies in the sectors identified in the proposed Strategic Sectors Law may overlap.

In addition to the listing of specific SOEs and companies that are off limits to foreign investment, certain individual sectors within the Russian economy also have investment limitations. For example, according to a Russian government official, foreign investment in the aviation sector in Russia cannot currently exceed 50 percent control of the target company, and foreign investors must seek approval for obtaining a 25 to 50 percent stake.

Appendix XII: United Arab Emirates

- The United Arab Emirates (UAE) ranked 32nd in terms of the average value of FDI inflows worldwide between 2000 and 2006.

- The UAE was the 50th largest recipient of FDI in the world in 2006.
- In 2006, FDI in the UAE totaled $37.1 billion, an increase of more than $36 billion over FDI stock in the UAE in 2000.
- FDI stock in the UAE as a proportion of GDP was 22 percent in 2006.

Background

The UAE is a loose federation of seven emirates, each with its own ruler. The UAE constitution established a government that includes a President, Vice President, Council of Ministers, Federal Supreme Council, and a 40- member Federal National Council. The Federal Supreme Council is the highest constitutional authority and is composed of the seven emirate rulers.

According to U.S. State Department officials, the UAE has one of the most open economies in the Middle East. In 2005, foreign investment in the UAE was approximately $10 billion, accounting for nearly 34 percent of total foreign capital in the Arab world that year. Oil and natural gas production generated approximately 36 percent of the country's GDP in 2005. In addition, the UAE controls almost 10 percent of the world's oil reserves.[63] However, only 15 to 20 percent of the UAE's 4.4 million residents are UAE citizens. According to a UAE official, over 90 percent of private sector output comes from non-UAE residents.

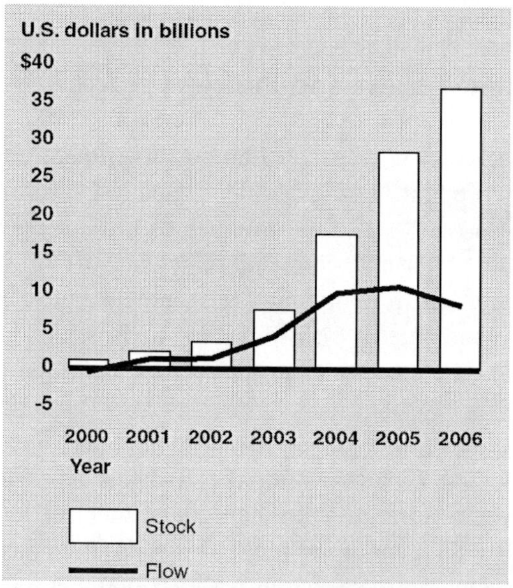

Source: United Nations (data).

Foreign investment in the United Arab Emirates (stocks and flows 2000–2006)

According to U.S. officials and oil industry representatives, there are important relationship components to doing business in Arab cultures. For example, foreign investment and joint ventures in the UAE's oil and natural gas industries are based on decades-long relationships between the government of the UAE and western business partners.

Laws and Policies

According to U.S. and UAE officials, the Companies Law and the Agencies Law[64] represent the largest legal barriers to foreign direct investment in the UAE. The Companies Law states that foreigners and foreign companies are prohibited from owning more than 49 percent of a company established in the UAE. The Agencies Law states that foreign importers must operate through an agent to bring goods into the UAE. This agent must be either a UAE national or a company that is wholly owned by a UAE national.

According to U.S. and UAE officials, the Companies Law and the Agencies Law were implemented to ensure the country's economic growth would benefit its small citizen population by drawing UAE citizens into the workforce. However, according to a UAE official, since most private sector output comes from non-UAE citizens, these laws were particularly intended to draw UAE citizens from the government workforce into the private sector. Together, these efforts are sometimes referred to as the Emiratisation policy. According to a UAE official, these efforts reflect a constant tension between maintaining openness to the world and avoiding the social and political strife that can accompany efforts to modernize.

Related Restrictions to Foreign Investment

The Government Tenders Law and the Federal Industry Law also restrict foreign investment in the UAE. The Government Tenders Law states government suppliers and contractors must be UAE citizens or companies at least 51 percent owned by UAE citizens. In addition, according to an official from the Office of the U.S. Trade Representative, each emirate has its own rules on government procurement. The Federal Industry Law states that industrial projects must be 51 percent owned by UAE citizens, and that projects must be managed by a UAE citizen or have a board of directors that has a majority of UAE citizens.

In addition to the above restrictions, the UAE limits foreign ownership of land, with rules varying from emirate to emirate. The UAE also has sector- by-sector limits on foreign ownership. Some sectors, like insurance, telecommunications, and travel agencies, are still mostly closed to foreigners. Traditionally, foreign investment in the UAE's oil and natural gas sectors has been limited to 40 percent, divided among several foreign joint venture partners. Emirate-level governments retain control of the other 60 percent, according to U.S. and oil industry officials.

Exceptions Exist to the UAE's Foreign Investment Restrictions

According to U.S. officials, the UAE has exceptions to the Agencies Law and the Companies Law, including 32 free trade zones (FTZ), which are special administrative areas governed by individual emirates, and country- specific exemptions. According to UAE officials, FTZs are not subject to any federal laws except criminal. Consequently, FTZs are exempt from the Companies, Agencies, Government Tenders, and Industry Laws. According to U.S. officials, FTZs usually have lower labor and tax requirements, and allow foreign companies to own 100 percent of an enterprise in any FTZ. This makes them attractive locations for foreigners to invest. However, according to U.S. officials, a foreign company invested in an FTZ that attempts to invest in non-FTZ areas would be subject to the UAE's foreign investment laws and regulations. According to one of these officials, this has created two separate and distinct economies in the UAE—the FTZ economy and the regular UAE economy.

According to U.S. officials, many of the barriers associated with foreign direct investment do not apply to citizens of other Gulf Cooperation Council countries, including Saudi Arabia, Qatar, Bahrain, Oman, and Kuwait. U.S. officials said the result is that the UAE has three levels of access for investors, whereby UAE nationals receive the most investment access, Gulf Cooperation Council nationals receive slightly less access, and non-Gulf Cooperation Council nationals receive the least access to investment opportunities in the UAE.

Practices

While the UAE does not have a formal foreign investment review process, according to U.S. and UAE officials, foreign investors are informally notified of sensitivities associated with attempted investments. According a UAE official, some sectors, like military production, contain sensitive technologies and are clearly, if not explicitly, off limits to foreign investors. Moreover, other sectors, like oil and natural gas, contain sensitive technologies, but foreigners are allowed to invest in them. Further, since these prohibitions are not codified, if a foreigner to invest in an area deemed to be unacceptable, the investor will be privately redirected.

According to U.S. and UAE officials, this practice is informal for several reasons. First, the UAE's reputation for having an open business environment is very important to its economic success. Consequently, the UAE government is hesitant to say publicly that a given sector is closed. Second, since business deals in the UAE are based on personal relationships, the UAE government generally believes it is better to handle rejections quietly. Third, the UAE and individual emirates try to direct foreign investment into sectors where they see a development need. Fourth, since the UAE has only existed as a nation since 1971, its informal practices are not yet institutionalized.

The UAE has several national security concerns that, while not publicly stated, the government may consider when assessing foreign investment. For example, according to U.S. officials, the UAE treats oil and natural gas production as a national security issue since these industries represent a major portion of the country's GDP. U.S. officials told us that, as a consequence, the UAE government strictly controls investment in those areas, although restrictions are not made public. The UAE's labor market is another unstated national security concern, since the vast majority of private sector workers are foreigners. Water and power generation are considered strategic as well.

New Developments

According to U.S. and UAE officials, the UAE is in the process of relaxing its investment laws. However, according to U.S. officials, this is difficult due to opposition from Emeriti citizens who benefit from the current laws. According to U.S. and UAE officials, current laws limiting foreign investment in the UAE are incongruent with the UAE's efforts to attract foreign investment. However, according to the U.S. State Department, the UAE's current laws have created interest groups in the UAE that depend on the benefits these rules provide. U.S. officials told us that opening investment outside the FTZs involves overcoming entrenched opposition from local constituencies, particularly those with agency agreements, making further liberalization of investment policies a slow process.

According to U.S. and UAE officials, the UAE government plans to liberalize the Companies Law and the Agencies Law. For example, according to UAE officials, the UAE has modified the Agencies Law to allow companies to break contracts with nonperforming agents. These officials told us that companies can now petition the Ministry of the Economy to dissolve such contracts. However, according to a U.S. official, while foreign companies technically have legal recourse, in reality the process of dissolving a contract with a nonperforming agent is still extremely difficult.

According to a UAE official, the central government intends eventually to dissolve the Companies Law and the Agencies Law. However, this probably will happen in stages. According to the same official, the current 49 percent cap on foreign ownership in the Companies Law likely will be raised to 75 percent, and then 100 percent. Moreover, this liberalization probably will happen on a sector-by-sector basis.

Appendix XIII: United Kingdom

- The United Kingdom (UK) ranked second in terms of the average value of FDI inflows worldwide between 2000 and 2006.
- In 2006, FDI stock in the UK totaled $1,135 billion, an increase of $696.6 billion over FDI stock in 2000.
- FDI stock in the UK as a proportion of GDP was 47.8 percent in 2006.

Background

The UK has historically maintained a liberal investment policy with an economy based on trade and is the second largest single recipient of inbound foreign investment in the world. The UK generally makes no policy distinction between domestic and foreign investment. The primary exception is for investments affecting national security. More than 25 percent of businesses located in London are currently under foreign ownership.

Foreign Investment Laws and Policies

The UK has no legal framework specifically designed to monitor foreign direct investment for national security reasons. However, the government has the authority under multiple laws to block specific transactions that are determined to be against the national interests of the United Kingdom. Since the UK is subject to European Union law, the European Union Merger Regulation, established in 1990, has shaped its policy on foreign investment because the regulation details the criteria under which a government can intervene in mergers and acquisitions. The Industry Act of 1975 provides the British government with the authority to intervene when the takeover of important manufacturing concerns by nonresidents is used the authority provided under this act. The Enterprise Act of 2002 provides the government the authority to intervene to block or place conditions on the approval of mergers and acquisitions involving British companies if the transaction is considered to be against the public interest. The authority under the act has been designated to the Secretary of State for the Department of Business, Enterprise, and Regulatory Reform (DBERR— previously the Department of Trade and Industry).[66] The Enterprise Act overhauled the framework for regulating mergers in the UK, updating the Fair Trading Act of 1973.

According to British government officials, the Enterprise Act is primarily intended as a review of competition or anti-trust concerns associated with mergers. However, the law allows for a "special intervention" when the Secretary of State determines that a transaction may harm the public interest. This allows the government to intervene if a foreign investment poses a threat to public security.[67] The act, as amended, specifies that foreign investment involving national security, the media, or water is subject to a public interest intervention by the Secretary of State. The Enterprise Act provides specified considerations that are relevant to the United Kingdom's national security. However, the Secretary of State has broad authority to intervene due to considerations that, while not specified by the law, "in the opinion of the Secretary of State, ought to be so specified." Similarly, the Secretary of State has the authority to issue an order that effectively modifies the relevant section of the Enterprise Act so that considerations that have not been specified are effectively added to the law. The Enterprise Act also specifies that the Secretary of State has the authority to intervene in mergers involving a UK government contractor that possesses information "relating to defense and of a confidential nature."

Transactions in which (1) sales exceed £17 million annually or (2) the relevant market share exceeds 25 percent may require a review by the British Office of Fair Trading. Additionally, the UK may intervene in a foreign investment of any size in the areas of national security or the media if the government deems it is in the public interest to do so and the Secretary of State issues a special intervention.

Since the Enterprise Act merger provisions came into effect in 2003, the Secretary of State has issued an intervention notice six times on national security grounds; only one of these notices was issued when there was not also an accompanying anti-monopoly review. All six of these cases involve the protection of sensitive information associated with military programs. The Secretary of State approved each proposed transaction under the condition that the acquiring company accepts a series of undertakings to mitigate the security risk associated with the investment. According to business representatives familiar with the intervention and review process, one of the companies eventually did not complete the proposed approved deal. A seventh public interest intervention was initiated because of a merger in the media field. The Secretary of State issued an intervention notice for the acquisition of a minority share in a television broadcasting company in February 2007. The case was reviewed by the Competition Commission, one of the reviewing bodies under the Enterprise Act. The Competition Commission made recommendations to the Secretary of State, and in January 2008, the Secretary made an adverse public interest finding in the case and will require a partial divestment of shares.

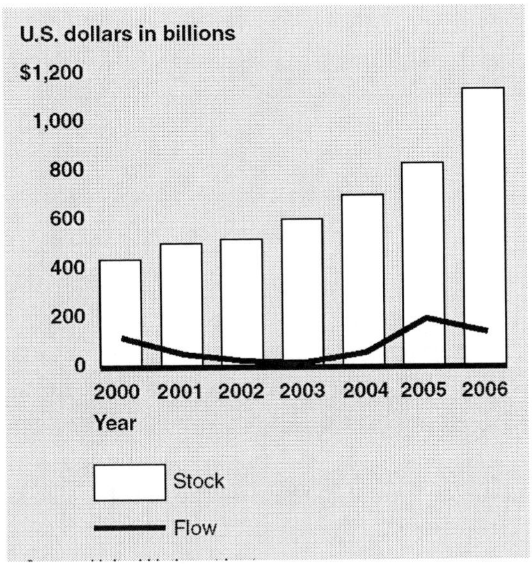

Source: United Nations (data).

Foreign investment in the United Kingdom (stocks and flows 2000–2006)

Related Restrictions to Foreign Investment

The British government restricts foreign investment in specific companies that it considers important to the national security of the UK. Through government ownership of a golden share established in the articles of association of each company, the UK has various rights related to citizenship requirements for the companies' boards of directors, control over the percentages of foreign-owned shares, or approval requirements for the dissolution or disposal of any strategic assets. This share does not give the government control over the companies' routine business activities, investment decisions, or appointments. The use of golden shares faced a number of adverse decisions from the European Court of Justice in 2002 and 2003, which ruled that the use of golden shares is acceptable only in specific circumstances and with strict conditions. However, the UK continues to use golden shares on the grounds of national security, and does not intend to dispose of these shares in certain strategic areas.

Some prominent company specific limitations established in golden shares include the following:

- BAE Systems limits foreign ownership of voting stocks to 15 percent.
- Rolls-Royce limits foreign ownership of voting stocks to 15 percent. The British government's consent is required for the disposal of the company's nuclear business or the group as a whole.
- British Energy requires the consent of the government to allow a purchase of more than 15 percent of its issued shares.
- Other companies in which the government holds a golden share are Rosyth Royal Dockyard Limited, Davenport Royal Dockyard Limited, BAES (Marine) Limited, the Atomic Weapons Establishment, and QinetiQ. Each company's articles of association grant the government various rights, including the ability to impose certain restrictions and oversee major company decisions.

Review Process

Government reviews of foreign investment are conducted by the Office of Fair Trading (OFT). If the OFT determines that there is potential for anticompetitive consequences from the transaction, it refers the transaction to the Competition Commission for further review. The Competition Commission may consult with the parties to the transaction and normally issues decisions in 30 days, although it is allowed 6 months to complete the review. The Competition Commission can negotiate undertakings with the investor as conditions for approval of the transaction. Once a transaction is approved, the decision is final. It cannot be reopened, modified, or reversed.

Prior to an official review, companies generally meet informally with the relevant agency to discuss the potential transaction. For example, the parties to a proposed transaction in the defense sector would normally consult in advance with the UK Ministry of Defense and negotiate acceptable undertakings so that Secretary of State would not need to issue a notice of intervention. During the informal review process, the relevant government offices consult with the investor and agree on undertakings. According to a lawyer familiar with the UK review process, the formal process primarily serves to provide a public comment period for the decisions that have already been made as part of the informal process. There is no requirement to notify the government of an investment before a transaction is completed. The government has 4 months after a transaction is completed to decide if it is necessary to intervene.

New Developments

According to British government officials, no changes are currently being considered to the United Kingdom's policies regarding foreign investment. It is possible that changes or additions to European Union policies in this area could affect the United Kingdom. In 2006, the potential takeover of a major oil company in the United Kingdom by a foreign state-owned oil company caused public controversy. However, British government officials discussed the potential transaction and decided that despite the possible threat to the United

Kingdom's energy supply, the British government would not intervene in the transaction on public security grounds.

The United Kingdom's Chancellor of the Exchequer outlined British policy toward sovereign wealth funds investing in the United Kingdom in his first speech as Chancellor. He stated that the United Kingdom welcomes foreign investment, including that of state-owned enterprises. To exemplify this openness, British government officials pointed out that all of the United Kingdom's ports are owned by Dubai Ports World.

END NOTES

[1] Testimony of Deputy Secretary Robert M. Kimmitt, U.S. Department of the Treasury, before the U.S. Senate Committee on Banking, Housing, and Urban Affairs, October 20, 2005.

[2] By "U. S. companies" we mean companies engaged in interstate commerce in the United States.

[3] Omnibus Trade and Competitiveness Act of 1988 § 5021, Pub. L. No. 100-418, 102 Stat. 1107 (1988) (codified at 50 U.S.C. App. § 2170).

[4] Pub. L. No. 110-49 (2007).

[5] The Foreign Investment and National Security Act of 2007 became effective on October 24, 2007.

[6] GAO, *Defense Trade: Enhancements to the Implementation of Exon-Florio Could Strengthen the Law's Effectiveness,* GAO-05-686 (Washington, D.C.: Sept. 28, 2005); *Defense Trade: Mitigating National Security Concerns under Exon-Florio Could Be Improved,* GAO-02-736 (Washington, D.C.: Sept. 12, 2002); *Defense Trade: Identifying Foreign Acquisitions Affecting National Security Can Be Improved,* GAO/NSIAD-00-144 (Washington, D.C.: June 29, 2000).

[7] GAO, *Foreign Investment: Foreign Laws and Policies Addressing National Security Concerns,* GAO/NSIAD-96-61 (Washington, D.C.: Apr. 2, 1996).

[8] Sovereign wealth funds are entities that can manage national savings for the purposes of investment. These funds may be similar in their investment behavior to other forms of investment funds, such as private equity funds. However, they fundamentally differ in that they are not privately owned.

[9] In this chapter, we use the term "foreign investment" to refer to foreign direct investment, specifically mergers and acquisitions, because Exon-Florio governs foreign direct investment via mergers, acquisitions, and takeovers in the United States, and this law is the basis of our work.

[10] Foreign direct investment is measured in both stocks and flows. Foreign direct investment stocks are data showing an economy's cumulative direct investment assets and liabilities at a given point in time. The stock of foreign direct investment results from an accumulation of flows. Foreign direct investment flows are transactions between an investor in one economy and an enterprise in another economy that occurred during a specific time period.

[11] Subsequently the Foreign Investment and National Security Act of 2007 statutorily established CFIUS and its membership.

[12] The number of notices received by CFIUS in 2006 and 2007 slightly exceeded the number of distinct transactions reviewed because several cases were terminated prior to completion of a review, either because of withdrawal or dismissal for lack of jurisdiction.

[13] The International Emergency Economic Powers Act allows the President to declare a national emergency to deal with extraordinary threats to national security or the economy. 50 U.S.C. §§ 1701–1706.

[14] Investment Canada Act, June, 20, 1985.

[15] Bill C-59, an Act to Amend the Investment Canada Act, First Reading, June 20, 2005.

[16] The seven sectors identified as critical are defense, power generation and distribution, oil and petrochemical, telecommunications, coal, aviation, and shipping. In addition, sectors have been identified in which the government should maintain control: equipment manufacturing, automotive, electronic information, construction, iron and steel, nonferrous metal, chemical, survey and design, and science and technology.

[17] See appendix VI for a list of the 11 sectors.

[18] The Organization for Economic Co-operation and Development has also issued guidance on the corporate governance of state-owned enterprises.

[19] The IMF has encouraged exporters of nonrenewable resources to build up sovereign wealth funds in preparation for when the price of these resources fall, or when they are no longer able to rely on the export of such resources.

[20] Under the proposed Strategic Sectors Law, the review time frame is 90 days, with the possibility of a 90-day extension.

[21] Article 21 (4) of the European Commission Merger Regulation provides the possibility for member states to take measures to protect their legitimate interests, other than defending against competition, if they are compatible with the general principles and other provisions of European Community law. Public security, plurality of the media, and prudential rules are generally acknowledged as legitimate interests. If national governments adopt incompatible measures, the European Commission is entitled to adopt a decision declaring them illegal and requiring their withdrawal.

[22] GAO, *Foreign Investment: Foreign Laws and Policies Addressing National Security Concerns.* GAO/NSIAD-96-61 (Washington, D.C.: Apr. 2, 1996).

[23] Pub. L. No. 110-49 (2007).

[24] 50 U.S.C. App. § 2170 (2006).

[25] Exec. Order No. 11,858, 3 C.F.R. 990 (1971-1975), as amended by Exec. Order No. 12,188, 3 C.F.R. 131 (1981); Exec. Order No. 12,661, 3 C.F.R. 618 (1989); Exec. Order No. 12,860, 3 C.F.R. 629 (1994); and Exec. Order No. 13,286, 3 C.F.R. 166 (2004).

[26] In section 721 (b)(2)(D)FINSA also provides that an investigation is not required for transactions involving critical infrastructure if the Secretary of the Treasury and the lead agency jointly determine that the transaction will not impair the national security of the United States.

[27] The original factors include (1) domestic production needed for projected national defense requirements; (2) the capability and capacity of domestic industries to meet national defense requirements, including the availability of human resources, products, technology, materials, and other supplies and services; (3) the control of domestic industries and commercial activity by foreign citizens as it affects the capability and capacity of the United States to meet the requirements of national security; (4) the potential effects of the transaction on sales of military goods, equipment, or technology to any country identified under applicable law as (a) supporting terrorism or (b) a country of concern for missile proliferation or the proliferation of chemical and biological weapons; and (5) the potential effects of the transaction on U.S. international technological leadership in areas affecting national security. 51 U.S.C. App. § 2170(f) (2006).

[28] We reported in September 2005 that, in some instances, the parties to a transaction withdrew their notification to CFIUS during the 45-day investigation and refiled notifications, thus avoiding a presidential decision and the resultant report to Congress. See GAO, *Defense Trade: Enhancements to the Implementation of Exon-Florio Could Strengthen the Law's Effectiveness*, GAO-05-686 (Washington, D.C.: Sept. 28, 2005), 17.

[29] Investment Canada Act, June, 20, 1985.

[30] The 2008 threshold for any direct acquisition of a Canadian business by an investor from a WTO country is Can$295 million. For investments from non-WTO member countries and investments in certain sectors (cultural businesses, transportation, financial services, or the production of uranium) the threshold is Can$5 million for direct investments and Can$50 million for indirect transactions. Except for transaction exempted from the act, all transactions above these designated dollar thresholds are required to be reviewed.

[31] Transactions in these sectors have a Can$5 million threshold for review.

[32] Bill C-59, an Act to Amend the Investment Canada Act, First Reading, June 20, 2005.

[33] Government of Canada, *Sharpening Canada's Competitive Edge.* Ottawa, Oct. 30, 2007.

[34] These regulations update a version promulgated in 2003.

[35] Articles 43, 48, 56, and 57 of the EC Treaty.

[36] More explicitly, the EC Treaty allows member states to "take any necessary measures for the protection of the essential interests of their security which are connected with the production of or trade in arms, munitions, and war material."

[37] Article L. 151-1.

[38] Article L. 151-2.

[39] Article L. 151-3.

[40] C-54/99 (Eglise de Scientologie).

[41] According to the ECJ opinion, the requirements of public security must be interpreted strictly, and public security may be relied on only if there is a genuine and sufficiently serious threat to a fundamental interest of society.

[42] According to French government officials, gambling and casinos are used to launder money, which the French seek to prevent.

[43] The EC asked France to amend its regulations in part because France's regulations allowed for restrictions on investments by companies that are legally established in the European Union and have shareholders in non-EU countries, as indirect investments are subject to review under the French regime.

[44] According to French law 233-3, a company is deemed to "control" another company

- when it directly or indirectly holds a fraction of the capital that gives it a majority of the voting rights at that company's general meetings;
- when it alone holds a majority of the voting rights in that company by virtue of an agreement entered into with other partners or shareholders and this is not contrary to the company's interests;
- when it effectively determines the decisions taken at that company's general meetings through the voting rights it holds;

• when it is a partner in, or shareholder of, that company and has the power to appoint or dismiss the majority of the members of that company's administrative, management, or supervisory structures.

Further it is presumed to exercise such control when it directly or indirectly holds a fraction of the voting rights above 40 percent and no other partner or shareholder directly or indirectly holds a fraction larger than its own.

[45] As listed in Annex IV of European Council Regulation No. 1334/2000 of June 22, 2000.

[46] Articles 43, 48, 56, and 57 of the EC Treaty.

[47] Article 296.

[48] What constitutes the essential security interests of Germany is not defined within Article 296.

[49] Foreign Trade and Payments Act of the Federal Republic of Germany, April 28, 1961.

[50] The firm subsequently sold its stake in 2004.

[51] Specifically, companies that produce or develop motors or gear systems for combat tanks or other armored military tracked vehicles are subject to review.

[52] The other primary law relating to foreign investment is the Industries (Development and Regulation) Act of 1951, which is discussed later in this appendix.

[53] With FIPB approval, investment can exceed the sector ownership caps in specific instances.

[54] Foreign investment is allowed in "integrated townships" including housing, commercial units, resorts and hotels. Foreign institutional investors can also invest in real estate Initial Public Offerings.

[55] The law has been referred to by GAO in a past report as the Foreign Exchange and Foreign Trade Control Law (FECL). GAO is currently using the translation of the law released by the Office of the Cabinet Secretariat of the Japanese government.

[56] Specific countries that have conducted reciprocal investment agreements are listed in the ordinance implementing FEFTA.

[57] Specifically, FEFTA requires prior notification for capital transactions that (1) may disturb fulfillment of an international agreement or contribution to international peace by Japan; (2) might make the maintenance of Japan's balance of international payments difficult; (3) might result in the drastic fluctuation of Japan's foreign exchange rates; or (4) transfers funds between Japan and foreign countries in a large volume, and thereby might adversely affect Japan's financial or capital market.

[58] GAO, *Foreign Investment: Foreign Laws and Policies Addressing National Security Concerns,* GAO/NSIAD-96-61 (Washington D.C.: Apr. 2, 1996).

[59] The second constitution that includes this provision is the Constitution of Surinam.

[60] The only Dutch exception to the principle of national treatment is in air transport. As in the United States, bilateral and multilateral agreements provide nationality and ownership requirements for Dutch airlines.

[61] The European Community Treaty allows for countries to restrict the free movement of capital in cases determined to be justified on public policy or public security grounds.

[62] According to Russian government officials, the Subsoil Law Amendments were originally to be included in the proposed Strategic Sectors Law. However, it was later determined that the Subsoil Law Amendments should be separated from the proposed Strategic Sectors Law.

[63] Most of these reserves are located in the Emirate of Abu Dhabi.

[64] The Commercial Companies Law No. 8 of 1984 is commonly referred to as the "Companies Law." Federal Act No. 18 of 1981 Concerning Organizing Trade Agencies is commonly referred to as the "Agencies Law."

[65] The law does not define the term "important." However, manufacturing industries are defined under the Standard Industrial Classification Orders and include defense-related sectors such as ordnance and aerospace equipment manufacturing.

[66] The Department of Business, Enterprise, and Regulatory Reform is charged with recommending intervention on the basis of public interest when necessary. If intervention is recommended, the UK Secretary of State at DBERR issues a special intervention and refers the matter to the Office of Fair Trading and the Competition Commission for further review.

[67] The authority can be invoked regardless of the domicile of the involved parties; hence, a transaction could involve only British nationals.

Chapter 4

THE INTERNATIONAL MARKETS OF MULTINATIONAL FIRMS*

Mihir A. Desai, C. Fritz Foley and James R. Hines, Jr.

The rising economic importance of multinational firms has been accompanied by significant changes in their structure and functioning. Multinational firms, historically characterized as webs of autonomous subsidiaries spread across countries, now represent globally integrated production systems serving worldwide customers. These changes are manifest in the rising significance of intrafirm trade and financial flows for these firms. While there is extensive analysis of aggregate patterns in intrafirm flows of goods and capital, few firm-based studies examine the workings of the internal markets of multinational firms, largely because of the difficulty in accessing the necessary data.

A number of our recent projects investigated the internal markets of U.S. multinational firms. Our research demonstrates that internal market operations represent a critical aspect of firm responses to costly external finance, capital controls, and currency fluctuations. Our research also shows that the changing nature of internal markets has influenced how firms operate and finance themselves around the world. An important insight emerging from this research is that firms use internal markets opportunistically, particularly in response to distortions in local markets. This Research Spotlight summarizes this body of work.

Our research is based on work conducted at the U.S. Bureau of Economic Analysis (BEA) through a special program that provides access to the agency's rich store of confidential firm-level data on multinational companies for analytical purposes (see the box "BEA Program for Outside Researchers"). The firm-level data collected in BEA's surveys of international direct investment are used by BEA to produce aggregated tabular data on multinational-company operations for release to the general public. In its benchmark and annual surveys of U.S. direct investment abroad, BEA collects the most comprehensive and reliable available data on the activities of U.S. multinational firms.[1]

---

* This is an edited, reformatted and augmented version of a U. S. Bureau of Economic Analysis publication dated March 2007.

Mihir A. Desai is an Associate Professor at Harvard Business School, C. Fritz Foley is an Assistant Professor at Harvard Business School, and James R. Hines Jr. is a Professor of Economics at the University of Michigan. Statistical work for the studies described here was performed at BEA under a special program for outside researchers. (See the box "BEA Program for Outside Researchers.") The opinions expressed in this article represent the views of the authors.

Several notable features of BEA's direct investment abroad surveys distinguish them from other data sources. First, BEA's firm-level data include balance sheets and income statements for all of a multinational firm's affiliates, offering considerably finer firm-level detail than the aggregated geographic or industry segment data available through public financial records. Also, aggregation in public financial statements and the differential reporting standards of firms in different countries can hinder comparisons across firms. Second, the BEA filings provide details on intrafirm transactions, such as intrafirm borrowing, intrafirm dividends, and intrafirm trade. Without access to such detailed information, previous studies were forced to infer aspects of intrafirm transactions (such as capital reallocations across divisions) from observed outcomes. The variety of operating information for parent companies and their affiliates also allows for analysis that controls for a variety of potentially confounding factors.

This rich data source creates two distinct research opportunities. First, new insights regarding financing and operating decisions can be obtained by analyzing decisionmaking in different institutional settings. Second, examining the internal markets of multinational firms promises to generate new insights into how firms structure their worldwide operations and how policies can impact those decisions. The remainder of this article summarizes our research on the internal markets of multinational firms in the following areas:

- Ownership decisions
- Weak investor protection and shallow capital markets
- Dividend policies
- Capital controls
- Currency depreciations

OWNERSHIP DECISIONS

One of the most fundamental decisions firms face when expanding abroad is whether to organize foreign operations as joint ventures or as wholly owned affiliates. Multinational firms frequently have the option to own 100 percent, majority, or minority shares of foreign entities. It is widely believed that the forces of globalization make the use of joint ventures particularly attractive, but this presumption rests on aspects of the ownership decisions of American multinational firms that, until recently, were not rigorously examined.

"The Costs of Shared Ownership: Evidence From International Joint Ventures" provides a comprehensive review of U.S. overseas affiliate activity from 1982 to 1997, offering evidence that over time American multinational firms have become less inclined to organize their foreign operations as joint ventures. In 1982–97, the share of all affiliates that were wholly owned increased from 72 percent to 80 percent, and the share of minority-owned affiliates fell from 18 percent to 11 percent. Whole ownership affords the parent company the ability to control the operation and destiny of a foreign affiliate. The growing use of whole ownership suggests an increased appetite for control by multinational parents, one that appears to be related to rising costs of employing the joint venture organizational form.

BEA PROGRAM FOR OUTSIDE RESEARCHERS

Recognizing that some research requires data at a more detailed level than that provided in its publicly disseminated tabulations, the Bureau of Economic Analysis maintains a program that permits outside researchers to work on site as unpaid special sworn employees of BEA for the purpose of conducting analytical and statistical studies using the microdata that it collects under the International Investment and Trade in Services Survey Act.

This work is conducted under strict guidelines and procedures that protect the confidentiality of company-specific data, as required by law. Because the program exists for the express purpose of advancing scientific knowledge and because of legal requirements that limit the use of the data to analytical and statistical purposes, appointment to special-swornemployee status under this program is limited to researchers. Appointments are not extended to persons affiliated with organizations that collect taxes, enforce regulations, or make policy.

We identify three sources of rising costs to joint ventures by analyzing the factors that influence ownership shares. First, joint ventures limit a firm's ability to structure its worldwide operations in a tax-efficient manner. This is the inevitable byproduct of divided interests, as joint venture partners are concerned with local profits while multinational parents are concerned with the profits of their global operations. Second, the attractiveness of transferring intellectual property to overseas operations is reduced by the prospect of potential appropriation of that technology by joint venture partners. Third, the desire to decentralize worldwide production through greater intrafirm trade creates the potential for conflict with local partners over sourcing decisions and transfer pricing. Because multinational firms increasingly rely on worldwide tax planning, global technology transfer, and production decentralization, they face growing incentives to avoid sharing ownership with local partners.

Wholly owned foreign affiliates of U.S. companies have considerably greater financial and commercial ties to their U.S. parent companies than do partially owned foreign affiliates. However, this cross-sectional evidence that whole ownership is associated with close coordination of parent and affiliate activity does not prove that ownership decisions are functions of coordination costs. Another possibility is that both ownership and operational decisions are responses to other unmeasured factors. In distinguishing these two interpretations of the same evidence, we identify exogenous changes in ownership levels and trace their effects on intrafirm transactions. By principles of symmetry (implied by the theory of the firm), any effects of ownership on intrafirm transactions should be mirrored by equal effects of intrafirm transactions on ownership decisions. Our analysis examines two changes in government policy that affected the relative costs of sharing ownership—the liberalization of foreign ownership restrictions and tax penalties on joint ventures featured in the U.S. Tax

Reform Act of 1986. Our results indicate that affiliates operating in liberalizing countries and firms whose joint ventures would be subject to tax penalties after 1986 both engaged in greater intrafirm transactions after the reforms.

These reactions imply that the increased desire to coordinate parent and affiliate trade, technology transfers, and tax planning that has been evident over the last 20 years contributed to the rising appetite for control over worldwide operations. Our estimates imply that between one-fifth and three-fifths of the decline in the use of partial ownership by multinational firms over the sample period is attributable to the increased importance of intrafirm transactions. These findings indicate that the forces of globalization have diminished rather than accelerated the use of shared ownership.

Weak Investor Protection and Shallow Capital Markets

Capital market conditions differ markedly around the world. Some countries offer legal protections and supportive regulation that produce liquid capital markets of the type found in the United States, whereas others have legal structures or regulatory policies that produce extremely shallow capital markets. These differences influence the capital structure choices that firms make. Empirical attempts to study these issues face significant challenges. Recent efforts using cross-country samples of local firms exploit the rich variation that international comparisons offer, but these efforts have faced problems associated with nonstandardized measurement across countries and limited statistical power because of small sample sizes. An alternative approach is to analyze the financing choices of local affiliates of multinational firms. This approach affords the prospect of comparing the financing decisions of affiliates of the same multinational firm operating in different institutional settings. Furthermore, an analysis of multinational firm responses to capital market conditions illuminates the workings of internal capital markets, as multinational firms may be able to substitute internal capital reallocations for external financing when it is most costly.

In "A Multinational Perspective on Capital Structure Choice and Internal Capital Markets," we study BEA's firm-level data and find that both the level and the composition of leverage of multinational affiliates are strongly influenced by capital market conditions. Analysis of these data illuminates the mechanisms by which weak capital markets affect external and internal financing choices. Our findings indicate that interest rates paid by U.S.-owned affiliates are significantly higher in countries with underdeveloped credit markets and weak creditor rights. This interest-rate difference very likely reflects the default premium that lenders demand in countries where legal institutions make it difficult or costly to use bankruptcy procedures to recover unpaid loans and the price premium paid for capital in countries with thin capital markets. In addition, the difference between the costs of bor rowing from external lenders and parent companies is larger for affiliates in these weaker institutional environments. In response to these differences, multinational firms borrow less from external sources and more from internal sources in settings with weak credit markets. These differences are manifest in a simple comparison of the internal and external borrowing decisions of affiliates in countries where creditor rights are very weak and very strong (chart 1). Regression analysis indicates that greater internal borrowing offsets approximately three-quarters of the reduction in external borrowing arising from adverse local credit market conditions.

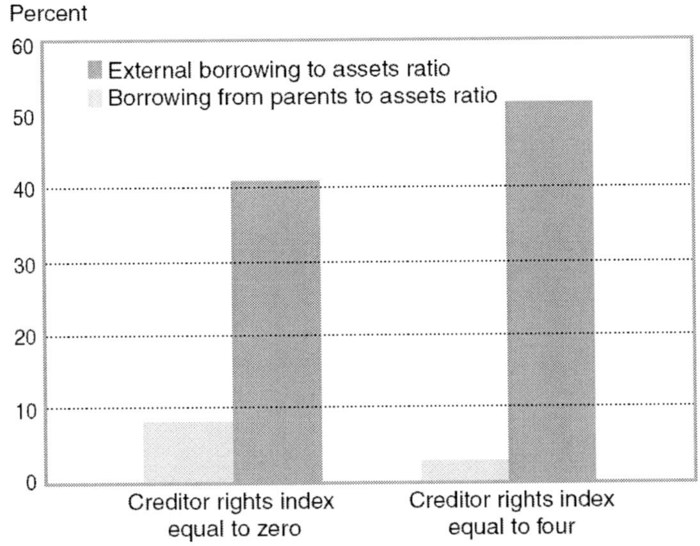

Note. This chart presents the median debt ratios for affiliates in countries with a creditor rights index of zero or four. The ratio of borrowing from U.S. parents to assets is the ratio of net current liabilities and long-term debt borrowed from U.S. parents to total assets, as measured in the 1994 benchmark survey. External borrowing to assets is the ratio of current liabilities and long-term debt borrowed from nonparent sources to total assets, as measured in the 1994 benchmark survey. The creditor rights index is from Rafael La Porta, Florencio Lopez-de-Silanes, Andrei Shleifer, and Robert Vishny, "Law and Finance," Journal of Political Economy 106 (1998): 1,113–1,155.

Chart 1. Relationship Between Creditor Rights and Types of Affiliate Borrowing, 1994

The tests in our paper control for other determinants of financing choices, including political risk, inflation, and tax rates. Greater political risk is associated with higher affiliate leverage. Higher inflation is associated with more external borrowing and less internal borrowing. Finally, higher corporate tax rates are associated with higher leverage. The analysis also reveals that borrowing from parent companies responds more sharply to tax rate differences than borrowing from external sources, suggesting that firms are better able to exploit internal capital markets than external capital markets when structuring optimal financing in response to tax differences.

In general, we found that firms use internal capital markets opportunistically when external finance is costly and when there are tax planning opportunities.

The results suggest that internal capital markets may give multinational firms an advantage over local firms in countries with poorly developed credit markets. Local firms that borrow from external sources face high costs of debt in countries with shallow capital markets or weak creditor rights. Although weak credit markets also reduce external borrowing by multinational firms, these firms can draw on resources from internal capital markets to obtain needed financing.

DIVIDEND POLICIES

Dividend payments from U.S.-owned foreign affiliates to U.S. parent companies represent sizable financial flows. In 1999, public U.S. corporations had after-tax earnings of \$516 billion and paid \$198 billion in dividends to common shareholders.[2] In the same year, foreign affiliates of U.S. multinational firms had after-tax earnings of \$182 billion and paid \$97 billion to the their parents as dividends. Indeed, the partial tax holiday featured in the 2004 American Jobs Creation Act was motivated by the prospect that large dividend payments from the foreign affiliates of U.S.-owned multinational firms would have favorable macroeconomic consequences for the U.S. economy.[3] "Dividend Policy Inside the Multinational Firm" identifies three main determinants of dividend policy within the multinational firm: The taxation of dividend income, domestic financing and investment needs, and agency problems inside firms.

Dividends include payments to multinational parent firms declared out of the income of foreign subsidiaries, but they do not include flows related to invested equity. Tax considerations alone would suggest that dividend payments inside the firm would be irregular and lumpy, since the tax implications of dividend payments often differ sharply between years, reflecting a firm's changing tax situation. However, dividend payments from the foreign affiliates of U.S. multinational firms are regular and can be characterized by a process of partial adjustment that was first described by John Lintner.[4] Multinational firms behave as though they select target payouts for their foreign affiliates, gradually adjusting payouts over time in response to changes in affiliate earnings. Dividends paid by affiliates rise by roughly \$0.40 for every additional dollar of their after- tax profits. Our regression evidence indicates that this pattern of persistent payouts is not an artifact of other regularized investment or financing decisions at the affiliate level.

Further analysis presented in our paper provides additional evidence that tax minimization only partially explains observed dividend policies; incorporated and unincorporated foreign affiliates, which face sharply differing tax consequences of paying dividends, nonetheless exhibit only modest differences in their dividend policies. Similarly, some firms simultaneously pay dividends and invest new equity in the same affiliate, a practice that is hard to reconcile with tax minimization.

Circumstances may lead parent companies to seek cash dividends from their foreign affiliates to satisfy domestic financing and investment needs. A simple comparison of multinational firms illustrates such a motivation for dividend policies within multinational firms. Chart 2 displays shares of parent companies receiving dividend payments from their foreign affiliates, where parent companies are grouped according to their ratios of dividend payouts to external shareholders (as a fraction of after-tax earnings). The heights of the bars in chart 2 measure fractions of parent companies receiving dividends from their affiliates. Parent companies with the highest external dividend payout ratios are the most likely to receive dividends from their foreign affiliates. This simple association also appears in a regression analysis that controls for various confounding factors. Parent companies require cash to pay dividends to external shareholders and foreign affiliates often represent ready sources of cash, ones that are particularly attractive to firms that would face high costs of raising funds externally. The analysis also reveals that financially constrained parents in industries with attractive investment opportunities are particularly likely to receive dividends from foreign affiliates. Hence, it seems that dividend payments from foreign affiliates are often used to satisfy parent company cash needs.

Finally, dividend payments from foreign affiliates appear to play a role in monitoring the activities of foreign managers. Regular dividend payments can restrict the financial discretion of foreign managers, mitigating whatever agency problems may exist within firms. Conflicts of interest between managers of foreign affiliates and managers of parent companies are likely to be most pronounced when the parent company owns only a fractional share of the affiliate, as other owners may be tempted to transact with the affiliate at non- market prices. Consequently, parent companies have incentives to require steady flows of dividend payments in order to limit the scope of potential malfeasance by foreign affiliates. Indeed, the evidence indicates that regularized dividend payments are most common when affiliates are partially owned, even when such payments are explicitly tax penalized. This finding suggests that at least some of the regularization of dividend repatriations is a consequence of control considerations inside the firm.

The foreign affiliates of U.S. multinational corporations follow well-defined repatriation policies featuring gradual adjustment of payouts to target ratios that depend on current earnings and the tax costs of repatriating dividends. In addition to taxation, costly external finance and agency problems—motivations that are typically emphasized with respect to arm's-length financing decisions—also appear to influence the internal capital markets of multinational firms.

CAPITAL CONTROLS

Countries concerned about the economic instability that may be associated with exposure to world capital markets are often tempted to impose controls on short-term international capital movements. These controls can take many forms, and their effect on economic growth and firm performance is hotly debated.

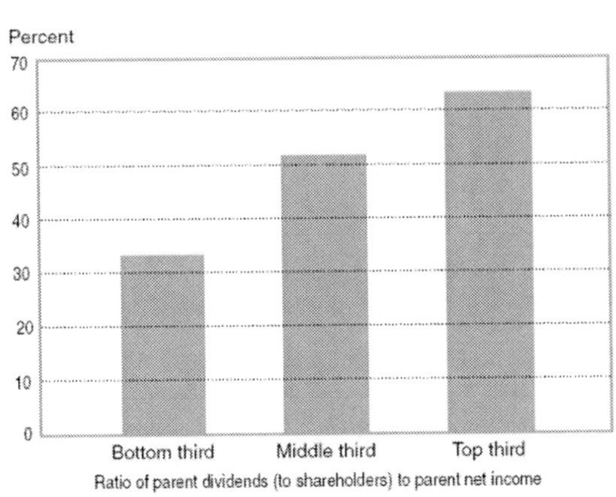

Note. This chart presents the share of U.S. parents receiving dividends from their foreign affiliates grouped on the basis of their dividend payout ratio (dividends paid to common shareholders divided by net income).

Chart 2. Share of Parents Receiving Dividends from Affiliates

Countries imposing capital controls are typically also eager to attract foreign direct investment, but the potential inconsistency of attempting to control capital movements while also attracting inbound foreign direct investment has hitherto received limited attention.

"Capital Controls, Liberalizations, and Foreign Direct Investment" analyzes the effects of capital controls on the operations of the foreign affiliates of U.S. multinational firms. Evidence indicates that foreign affiliates located in countries imposing capital controls face borrowing rates that average 5.25 percentage points more than those faced by other affiliates of the same multinational parent companies.

Multinational firms operating in countries with capital controls have incentives to use their internal product and capital markets to mitigate the effects of capital controls by limiting local profits that are subject to such controls. Similar incentives are created by high tax rates, and it is possible to compare the effects of capital controls with the effects of high income tax rates. Our results indicate that multinational firms distort their reported profitability and their dividend repatriations in order to mitigate the impact of capital controls. Affiliates in countries imposing capital controls have 5.2-percent lower reported profit rates than comparable affiliates in countries without capital controls, reflecting in part trade and financing practices that reallocate income within a firm. The distortions to reported profitability are comparable with those that stem from a 27-percent difference in corporate tax rates. Dividend repatriations are also regularized to facilitate the extraction of profits from countries imposing capital controls.

Evidence of the impact of removing capital controls is consistent with the comparisons of foreign affiliates located in countries with and without capital controls. U.S.-owned foreign affiliates in countries with capital controls experience 6.9-percent faster annual growth of property, plant, and equipment investment after the liberalization of controls, indicating that capital controls impose significant burdens on foreign investors. There is, however, no discernible effect of the imposition or removal of capital controls on the volatility of affiliate profitability or the volatility of affiliate growth rates. Hence, it appears that capital controls are responsible for slow growth of U.S.-owned affiliates, and local reported profit rates significantly below those reported elsewhere.

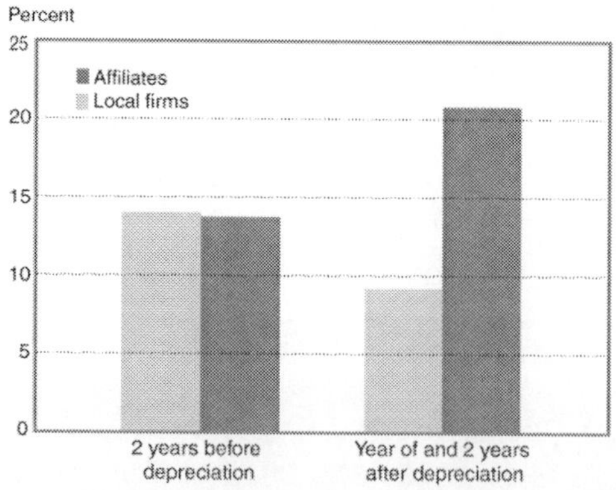

Note. The two bars represent the average of the annual median asset growth rates for local firms and multinational affiliates. The first pair of bars are averages for the 2 years prior to a currency crisis. The second pair of bars are averages for the year of, the year after, and 2 years following a crisis.

Chart 3. Asset Growth of Local Firms and Affiliates of Multinationals After Currency Crises

CURRENCY DEPRECIATIONS

Settings where investment opportunities and financial constraints move in identifiable ways provide valuable opportunities to study the impact of financial constraints on firm growth. Because firms typically incur some costs in local currency terms, currency depreciations are hypothesized to provide improved investment opportunities. Firms differ, however, in their access to financial resources at the time of the depreciation. A comparison of the investment responses to currency depreciations by firms with differential access to financial resources can illustrate the degree to which financial constraints can limit growth. This comparison, given its setting, can also help explain why hypothesized benefits of depreciations are often not manifest.

In the paper "Financial Constraints and Growth: Multinational and Local Firm Responses to Currency Depreciations," the effects of sharp currency depreciations on the behavior of U.S.-owned affiliates and local firms in the tradable sectors of emerging markets are compared.[5] The differential response of local firms and multinational affiliates is manifest in the simple comparison provided in chart 3. In this chart, the bars represent annual growth rates in assets in the year prior to a sharp depreciation and subsequent years for local firms and multinational affiliates. This basic difference between local firms and multinational affiliates is robust. Regression analysis demonstrates that U.S.- owned affiliates increase sales 5.4 percent, and assets 7.5 percent, more than local firms after currency depreciations. The improved relative performance of U.S.-owned affiliates is even more striking in investment. Capital expenditures are 34.5 percent higher for U.S.-owned firms than for local firms in the aftermath of large currency depreciations. Our analysis investigates the sources of this distinctive performance, with particular emphasis on the possible role of differential operating exposures and financing capabilities.

Differential changes in investment opportunities could give rise to distinctive investment opportunities for local firms and multinational affiliates. For example, multinational affiliates may export more of their output to countries with undepreciated currencies. In order to consider this possibility, we compared multinational and local firms with similar product and input market exposures. We also computed measures of the operating exposures of firms in order to investigate whether differences in operating exposures explain differences in the behavior of U.S.-owned affiliates and local firms.

Our tests offered little evidence that the relative growth of multinational affiliates after sharp currency depreciations can be traced to differential investment opportunities. Multinational affiliates that are more reliant on exports prior to depreciations increase investment by larger amounts, but affiliates that exclusively serve the local market increase investment by considerably more than local firms. Large differences in the investment responses of affiliates and local firms persist after including measures of operating exposure as controls.

Given the evidence on the opportunistic use of internal capital markets by multinational firms discussed above, it is possible that a superior ability to overcome financing constraints is the reason for the better post- depreciation performance of U.S.-owned affiliates. Tests reveal that financing constraints play a decisive role in explaining the differential investment response of multinational affiliates and local firms. Following currency depreciations, the leverage of local firms increases more than the leverage of multinational affiliates, in part reflecting the tendency of local firms to borrow in foreign currency terms. Local firms with the most leverage and with the shortest term debt reduce investment the most. The examination of the internal capital markets of multinationals shows that multinational parents provide additional financing in response to sharp currency depreciations. These results indicate that multinational firms overcome the negative consequences of large depreciations by avoiding the financial constraints that handicap local firms.

In addition to offering a test of how financial constraints influence investment, this evidence illustrates an effect of foreign direct investment not previously emphasized. The internal capital markets of multinational firms allow their affiliates to expand output after severe currency depreciations, precisely when economies are fragile and prone to severe economic contrac tions. As a consequence, multinational affiliates may be able to mitigate some of the aggregate effects of currency crises. This analysis does not consider the long- run distributional consequences of the differential impact of currency crises on multinational affiliates. Increased multinational activity during crises may help support local firms through spillover effects, such as increased demand for local inputs or improved access to technology or trade credit. However, multinationals could also use crises to expand at the expense of local firms with potentially persistent effects. While the internal capital markets of multinational firms appear to mitigate the contractionary output effects of severe currency depreciations, the longer term effects on local firms remain an open question.

CONCLUSION

The data collected by BEA in its surveys of international direct investment provide a unique window on the internal markets of U.S. multinational firms.

Our analyses of BEA's firm-level data reveal that the increased importance of internal capital markets has reduced the use of joint ventures; that multinational firms respond opportunistically to cross-country differences in capital markets, capital controls, and taxes; that the set of factors that influence dividend payouts by U.S.-owned foreign affiliates are similar to those that influence dividends paid to external shareholders; and that multinationals access their internal capital markets to overcome financial constraints associated with currency depreciations.

As more firms expand their global activities, BEA's work in collecting these data will become even more critical to policymakers, business leaders, and others seeking to make informed policy decisions and business choices.

REFERENCES

Mihir A. Desai, C. Fritz Foley and Kristen J. Forbes. "Financial Constraints and Growth: Multinational and Local Firm Responses to Currency Depreciations" *Review of Financial Studies* (forthcoming).

Mihir A. Desai, C. Fritz Foley and James R. Hines Jr. "Capital Controls, Liberalizations, and Foreign Direct Investment," *Review of Financial Studies 19*, no. 4 (Winter 2006): 1,433–1,464.

———. "The Costs of Shared Ownership: Evidence From International Joint Ventures," *Journal of Financial Economics* 73, no. 2 (August 2004): 323–374.

———. "Dividend Policy Inside the Multinational Firm," *Financial Management* (forthcoming).

———. "A Multinational Perspective on Capital Structure Choice and Internal Capital Markets," *Journal of Finance 59,* no. 6 (December 2004): 2,451–2,488.

End Notes

1 For a discussion of the most recent data collected, see Raymond J. Mataloni Jr. and Daniel R. Yorgason, "Operations of U.S. Multinational Companies: Preliminary Results From the 2004 Benchmark Survey," SURVEY OF CURRENT BUSINESS 86 (November 2006): 37–68. For general information on the statistics that are available on U.S. multinational firms, see Raymond J. Mataloni Jr., "A Guide to BEA Statistics on U.S. Multinational Companies," SURVEY 65 (March 1995): 38–55.

2 Gustavo Grullon and Roni Michaely, "Dividends, Share Repurchases, and the Substitution Hypothesis," *Journal of Finance* 57 (2002): 1,649–1,684.

3 For an assessment of the effects of this act on affiliate dividend payments, see Ralph Kozlow and Patricia Abaroa, "U.S. Multinational Firms, Dividends, and Taxes" (paper presented at the International Association for Official Statistics, Ottawa, September 6–8, 2006).

4 John Lintner, "Distribution of Incomes of Corporations Among Dividends, Retained Earnings, and Taxes," *American Economic Review* 61 (1956): 97–113.

5 Unlike the other papers described in this spotlight, this paper was written by Mihir A. Desai, C. Fritz Foley, and Kristin J. Forbes. The other papers were written by Mihir A. Desai, C. Fritz Foley, and James R. Hines Jr. See the references.

In: Direct Investment Abroad
Editor: Caleb J. Blackwell

ISBN: 978-1-61668-857-8
© 2010 Nova Science Publishers, Inc.

Chapter 5

U.S. MULTINATIONAL COMPANIES: OPERATIONS IN THE UNITED STATES AND ABROAD IN 2007*

Kevin B. Barefoot, Raymond J. Mataloni, Jr.

Three key measures of the worldwide operations of nonbank U.S. multinational companies (MNCs)—value added, employment, and capital expenditures—continued to increase in 2007, according to preliminary results from the annual survey of U.S. direct investment abroad conducted by the Bureau of Economic Analysis (BEA).[1] The preliminary 2007 estimates in this article supersede the advance summary estimates of U.S. MNC employment, capital expenditures, and sales, which were released in April (see the box "Revisions").

In 2007, all three of these measures of U.S. MNC operations grew for the fourth consecutive year, but the rate of growth for two of them—value added and capital expenditures—decelerated from 2006. Both domestic and foreign operations continued to grow, but the growth in foreign operations was faster than the growth in domestic operations. The worldwide current-dollar value added of U.S. MNCs—the combined value added of U.S. parent companies and their majority-owned foreign affiliates ("foreign affiliates")—increased 4.8 percent; value added of parents increased 2.0 percent, while value added of foreign affiliates increased 11.6 percent (table 1). Value added measures the contribution of a company to the gross domestic product (GDP) of its country of location.

REVISIONS

The estimates of MNC operations in 2007 are preliminary. The estimates of employment, capital expenditures, and sales supersede the advance summary estimates that were released on April 17, 2009. From the advance estimates to the preliminary estimates, the estimate of employment was revised up 0.2 percent, the estimate of capital

* This is an edited, reformatted and augmented version of a U. S. Bureau of Economic Analysis publication dated August 2009.

expenditures was revised up 0.9 percent, and the estimate of sales was revised down 0.3 percent.

The final estimates of MNC operations in 2006 are also presented. The final estimates of employment, capital expenditures, and sales supersede the summary estimates in the April news release and the preliminary estimates that were published in the November 2008 SURVEY OF CURRENT BUSINESS.[1] From the summary estimates to the final estimates, the estimate of employment was revised up 0.5 percent, the estimate of capital expenditures was revised up 0.4 percent, and the estimate of sales was revised up 0.2 percent. From the preliminary estimates to the final estimates, the estimate of employment was revised down less than 0.1 percent, the estimate of capital expenditures was revised up 0.8 percent, and the estimate of sales was revised down 0.1 percent.

In addition to the estimates of the levels of U.S. MNC employment, capital expenditures, and sales, the April news release included estimates of 2006–2007 growth rates. The revisions to the levels of the 2006 and 2007 estimates discussed above resulted in revisions to the growth rates; employment growth was revised down 0.4 percentage point, capital expenditures growth was revised up 0.5 percentage point, and sales growth was revised up 0.6 percentage point.

[1] See Raymond J. Mataloni Jr., "U.S. Multinational Companies: Operations in 2006," SURVEY 88 (November 2008): 26–47.

Worldwide employment by U.S. MNCs increased 2.5 percent in 2007. Employment by U.S. parents increased 1.8 percent, and employment by foreign affiliates increased 4.2 percent. Worldwide capital expenditures by U.S. MNCs increased 8.5 percent. Expenditures by parents increased 8.4 percent, and expenditures by foreign affiliates increased 9.0 percent.

The value added of U.S. MNCs expanded in 2007 at a slower rate, compared with worldwide GDP growth: value-added growth of their U.S. operations (2.0 percent) trailed current-dollar U.S. GDP growth (4.8 percent), and value-added growth of their foreign operations (11.6 percent) trailed worldwide current- dollar GDP growth excluding the United States (14.6 percent).[2]

Increases in MNC value added were widespread by industry and geographic area. By industry, the sharpest increases were in "other industries" (mainly retail trade) and in finance (except banks) and insurance.[3] The largest dollar increases were in manufacturing and in "other industries" (mainly retail trade). By geographic area, the sharpest increases were in the Middle East and Latin America and Other Western Hemisphere, mainly in Brazil (chart 1). The largest dollar increases were in the United States and in Europe.

The following are additional highlights of MNC operations in 2007:

- The operations of U.S. MNCs remained concentrated in the United States: U.S. parents accounted for roughly 70 percent, and foreign affiliates for roughly 30 percent, of their combined value added of $3,706.4 billion, capital expenditures of $651.6 billion, and employment of 32.0 million. However, the parent shares of value added and employment had declined about 10 percentage points over the preceding two decades.
- Most foreign affiliates continued to be located in high-income countries. In 2007, affiliates in these countries accounted for over three-fourths of the value added by all

affiliates and for nearly two- thirds of the value added by affiliates that were newly acquired or established. However, the highincome-country share of value added by all affiliates in 2007 had declined about 6 percentage points over the preceding two decades. The fall in the high- income country share reflected rapid growth in value added by affiliates in several middle-income countries, such as Brazil, China, Mexico, and Poland.

- U.S. MNCs continued to account for a large share of the U.S. trade in goods in 2007. Trade associated with U.S. parents or their foreign affiliates accounted for nearly half, or $558.6 billion, of total U.S. exports of goods and for over a third, or $728.4 billion, of total U.S. imports of goods.
- U.S. MNCs' expenditures for research and development (R&D) totaled $235.4 billion in 2007. U.S.parents accounted for over 80 percent of the total; however, R&D expenditures by foreign affiliates grew strongly in 2007, particularly in China.

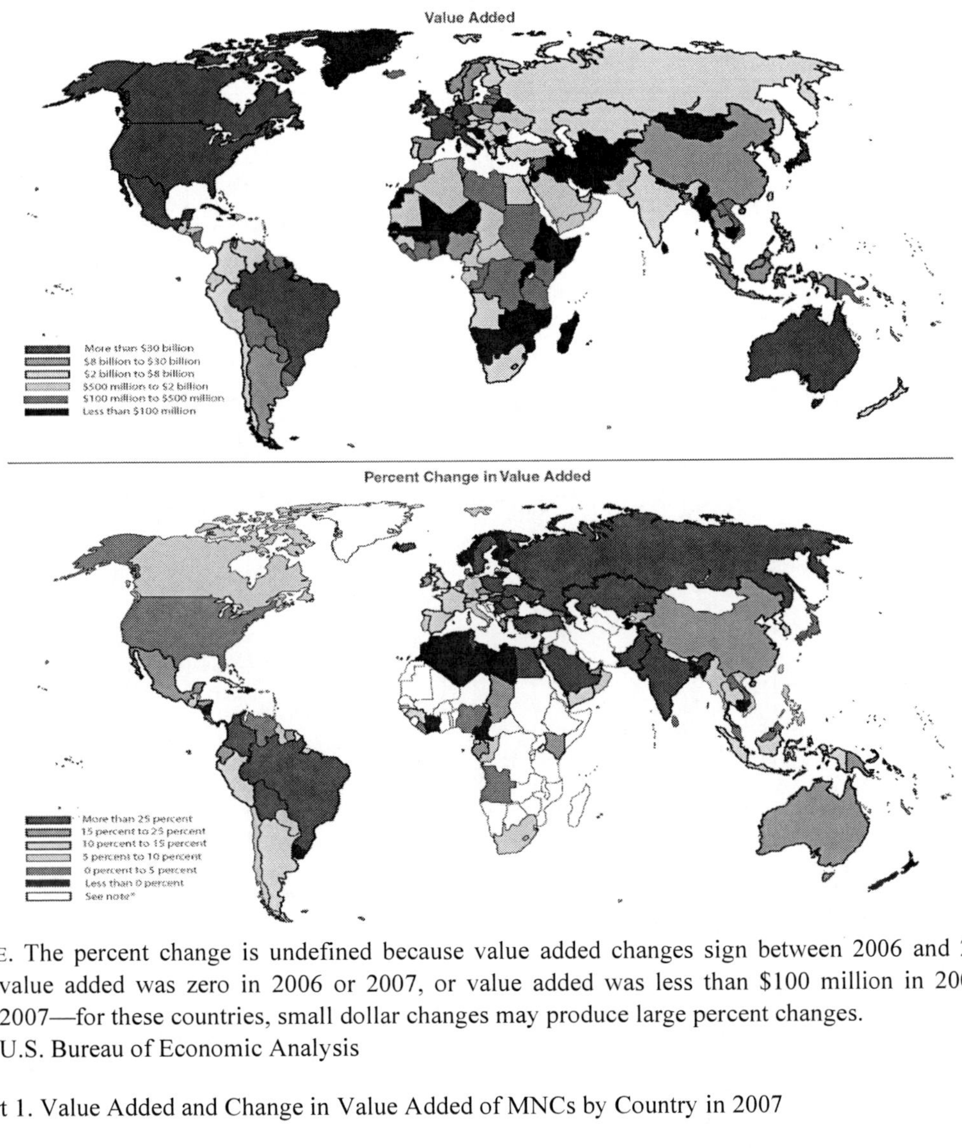

NOTE. The percent change is undefined because value added changes sign between 2006 and 2007, value added was zero in 2006 or 2007, or value added was less than $100 million in 2006 or 2007—for these countries, small dollar changes may produce large percent changes.
U.S. Bureau of Economic Analysis

Chart 1. Value Added and Change in Value Added of MNCs by Country in 2007

Table 1. Selected Statistics for Nonbank U.S. Multinational Companies, U.S. Parents, and Foreign Affiliates, 1982–2007

	U.S. MNCs			Affiliates		
	Parents and all affiliates	Parents and MOFAs	Parents	Total	MOFAs	Other
Value added Millions of dollars						
1982	n.a.	1,019,734	796,017	n.a.	223,717	n.a.
1983	n.a.	n.a.	n.a.	n.a.	216,683	n.a.
1984	n.a.	n.a.	n.a.	n.a.	220,331	n.a.
1985	n.a.	n.a.	n.a.	n.a.	220,074	n.a.
1986	n.a.	n.a.	n.a.	n.a.	231,644	n.a.
1987	n.a.	n.a.	n.a.	n.a.	269,734	n.a.
1988	n.a.	n.a.	n.a.	n.a.	297,556	n.a.
1989	n.a.	1,364,878	1,044,884	n.a.	319,994	n.a.
1990	n.a.	n.a.	n.a.	n.a.	356,033	n.a.
1991	n.a.	n.a.	n.a.	n.a.	355,963	n.a.
1992	n.a.	n.a.	n.a.	n.a.	361,524	n.a.
1993	n.a.	n.a.	n.a.	n.a.	359,179	n.a.
1994	n.a.	1,717,488	1,313,792	n.a.	403,696	n.a.
1995	n.a.	1,831,046	1,365,470	n.a.	465,576	n.a.
1996	n.a.	1,978,948	1,480,638	n.a.	498,310	n.a.
1997	n.a.	2,094,318	1,573,451	n.a.	520,867	n.a.
1998	n.a.	2,100,773	1,594,504	n.a.	506,269	n.a.
1999 [1]	n.a.	2,480,739	1,914,343	n.a.	566,396	n.a.
2000	n.a.	2,748,106	2,141,480	n.a.	606,626	n.a.
2001	n.a.	2,478,056	1,892,399	n.a.	585,657	n.a.
2002	n.a.	2,460,411	1,858,805	n.a.	601,606	n.a.
2003	n.a.	2,655,903	1,958,125	n.a.	697,778	n.a.
2004	n.a.	2,991,723	2,173,467	n.a.	818,256	n.a.
2005	n.a.	3,232,582	2,321,092	n.a.	911,490	n.a.

	U.S. MNCs			Affiliates		
	Parents and all affiliates	Parents and MOFAs	Parents	Total	MOFAs	Other
1995	25,921.1	24,499.7	18,576.2	7,344.9	5,923.5	1,421.4
1996	26,334.0	24,867.0	18,790.0	7,544.0	6,077.0	1,467.0
1997	27,851.0	26,358.0	19,878.0	7,973.0	6,480.0	1,493.0
1998	28,003.6	26,592.9	19,819.8	8,183.8	6,773.1	1,410.7
1999 [1]	32,227.0	30,772.6	23,006.8	9,220.2	7,765.8	1,454.4
2000	33,598.2	32,056.6	23,885.2	9,713.0	8,171.4	1,541.6
2001	32,538.7	30,929.2	22,735.1	9,803.6	8,194.1	1,609.5
2002	31,893.6	30,373.2	22,117.6	9,776.0	8,255.6	1,520.4
2003	30,762.3	29,347.0	21,104.8	9,657.5	8,242.2	1,415.3
2004	31,244.9	29,843.2	21,176.5	10,068.4	8,666.7	1,401.7
2005	32,093.7	30,573.3	21,472.0	10,621.7	9,101.3	1,520.4
2006 [r]	32,765.7	31,233.2	21,615.8	11,149.9	9,617.4	1,532.5
2007 [p]	33,740.6	32,019.7	22,003.1	11,737.5	10,016.6	1,720.9
Percent change at annual rates:						
1999–2006	0.2	0.2	–0.9	2.8	3.1	0.8
2006–2007	3.0	2.5	1.8	5.3	4.2	12.3
Capital expenditures Millions of dollars						
1982	248,262	233,078	188,266	59,996	44,812	15,184
1983	n.a.	197,534	160,656	n.a.	36,878	n.a.
1984	n.a.	203,791	168,692	n.a.	35,099	n.a.
1985	n.a.	221,509	185,027	n.a.	36,482	n.a.
1986	n.a.	203,809	169,131	n.a.	34,678	n.a.
1987	n.a.	199,171	162,139	n.a.	37,032	n.a.
1988	n.a.	223,814	177,203	n.a.	46,611	n.a.
1989	276,790	260,488	201,808	74,982	58,680	16,302
1990	n.a.	274,614	213,079	n.a.	61,535	n.a.

	U.S. MNCs			Affiliates				U.S. MNCs			Affiliates		
	Parents and all affiliates	Parents and MOFAs	Parents	Total	MOFAs	Other		Parents and all affiliates	Parents and MOFAs	Parents	Total	MOFAs	Other
2006[r]	n.a.	3,538,079	2,536,873	n.a.	1,001,206	n.a.	1991	n.a.	269,221	206,290	n.a.	62,931	n.a.
2007[p]	n.a.	3,706,396	2,588,811	n.a.	1,117,585	n.a.	1992	n.a.	272,049	208,834	n.a.	63,215	n.a.
Percent change at annual rates:							1993	n.a.	271,661	207,437	n.a.	64,224	n.a.
1999–2006	n.a.	5.2	4.1	n.a.	8.5	n.a.	1994	328,240	303,364	231,917	96,323	71,447	24,876
2006–2007	n.a.	4.8	2.0	n.a.	11.6	n.a.	1995	n.a.	323,616	248,017	n.a.	75,599	n.a.
							1996	n.a.	340,510	260,048	n.a.	80,462	n.a.
							1997	n.a.	398,037	309,247	n.a.	88,790	n.a.
Number of employees Thousands							1998	n.a.	411,155	317,184	n.a.	93,971	n.a.
1982	25,344.8	23,727.0	18,704.6	6,640.2	5,022.4	1,617.8	1999[1]	550,205	519,199	405,895	144,310	113,304	31,006
1983	24,782.6	23,253.1	18,399.5	6,383.1	4,853.6	1,529.5	2000	n.a.	548,212	437,575	n.a.	110,637	n.a.
1984	24,548.4	22,972.6	18,130.9	6,417.5	4,841.7	1,575.8	2001	n.a.	560,779	450,021	n.a.	110,758	n.a.
1985	24,531.9	22,923.0	18,112.6	6,419.3	4,810.4	1,608.9	2002	n.a.	477,709	367,434	n.a.	110,275	n.a.
1986	24,082.0	22,543.1	17,831.8	6,250.2	4,711.3	1,538.9	2003	n.a.	444,339	334,751	n.a.	109,588	n.a.
1987	24,255.4	22,650.0	17,985.8	6,269.6	4,664.2	1,605.4	2004	486,548	462,898	339,419	147,129	123,479	23,650
1988	24,141.1	22,498.1	17,737.6	6,403.5	4,760.5	1,643.0	2005	n.a.	507,322	377,182	n.a.	130,140	n.a.
1989	25,387.5	23,879.4	18,765.4	6,622.1	5,114.0	1,508.1	2006[r]	n.a.	600,373	445,295	n.a.	155,078	n.a.
1990	25,263.6	23,785.7	18,429.7	6,833.9	5,356.0	1,477.9	2007[p]	n.a.	651,566	482,492	n.a.	169,074	n.a.
1991	24,837.1	23,345.4	17,958.9	6,878.2	5,386.5	1,491.7	**Percent change at annual rates:**						
1992	24,189.7	22,812.0	17,529.6	6,660.1	5,282.4	1,377.7							
1993	24,221.5	22,760.2	17,536.9	6,684.6	5,223.3	1,461.3	1999–2006	n.a.	2.1	1.3	n.a.	4.6	n.a.
1994	25,670.0	24,272.5	18,565.4	7,104.6	5,707.1	1,397.5	2006–2007	n.a.	8.5	8.4	n.a.	9.0	n.a.

p Preliminary

r Revised

1. Break in series. Beginning with 1999, BEA expanded its estimates to include data for “very small” foreign affiliates and for parents that had only “very small” foreign affiliates. For details, see thetechnical note on page

121 of the December 2002 SURVEY OF CURRENT BUSINESS. MNCs Multinational companies MOFAs Majority-owned foreign affiliates n.a. Not available

A major improvement that starts with the 2007 survey is the annual collection of data for U.S. parents that are banks, for their bank and nonbank foreign affiliates, and for bank affiliates of nonbank U.S. parents. Previously, data for these parents and affiliates were collected only in benchmark surveys, which are generally conducted every 5 years. The inclusion of these parents and affiliates closed a significant gap that had existed in the industry coverage of the annual surveys (see the box "New Data on U.S. Bank Multinational Companies"). Most of the following discussion, however, addresses only the operations of nonbank U.S. MNCs, because the focus is on the 2007 change, and bank data are not available for 2006.

The remainder of this article examines worldwide operations of U.S. MNCs, operations of U.S. parents, and operations of their foreign affiliates.

NEW DATA ON U.S. BANK MULTINATIONAL COMPANIES

The 2007 annual survey of U.S. direct investment abroad is the first annual survey to collect data for U.S. parents and foreign affiliates in depository credit intermediation (banking). The inclusion of these parents and affiliates closed a significant gap that had existed in the industry coverage of the annual surveys. Starting with the 2007 survey, the data items for bank affiliates collected on the annual surveys are reported on a special form and include balance sheets and income statements as well as information on the destination of sales, employment, interest income and interest expense, and the information needed to compute value added.[1] The data for U.S. bank parents are collected on the same form as those for U.S. parents in other industries, and parents in all industries are required to report at the same level of detail. This new annual survey coverage for bank affiliates and bank parents represents an expansion in the detail available on the operations of bank MNCs to a level greater than that provided by previous benchmark surveys of U.S. direct investment abroad.

Highlights of the 2007 data on bank MNCs include the following:

- U.S. parents in banking employed 1.3 million workers and had value added of $122.5 billion; majority-owned foreign affiliates in banking employed 420,000 workers and had value added of $32.4 billion (see table A).
- Value added by U.S. parents in banking accounted for roughly a quarter of total U.S. value added in banking—a share that is similar to the overall parent share of private U.S. gross domestic product.
- The foreign banking activities of U.S. MNCs were concen- trated in a small number of countries. Affiliates in a single country—the United Kingdom—accounted for 49.0 percent of the assets, 16.7 percent of the employment, and 8.5 percent of the value added of all affiliates in banking. When combined with the operations of banking affiliates in six other countries—the Netherlands, Switzerland, Bermuda, the "United Kingdom Islands Caribbean," Hong Kong, and Singapore—the group accounted for 68.2 percent of the assets, 23.4 percent of the employment, and 39.4 percent of the value added of all affiliates in banking.

Table A. Selected Statistics for U.S. Multinational Companies in Banking, 2007 [Millions of dollars or thousands of employees]

	Assets	Sales	Employment	Value added
U.S. parents	8,628,285	632,414	1,334.4	122,548
	Majority-owned foreign affiliates			
All countries	5,058,158	267,174	420.2	32,421
Of which:				
Bermuda	49,396	2,309	0.5	200
Hong Kong	164,336	12,844	13.7	3,886
Netherlands	59,516	3,000	0.6	482
Singapore	146,325	8,901	7.7	2,845
Switzerland	38,268	2,601	3.6	932
United Kingdom	2,476,637	103,753	70.2	2,756
United Kingdom Islands, Caribbean	513,668	11,121	2.0	1,680

[1] The information on interest income and interest expense will be used to estimate services supplied through bank affiliates without explicit charge. For details, see Maria Borga, "Improved Measures of U.S. International Services: The Cases of Insurance, Wholesale and Retail Trade, and Financial Services" in International Trade in Services and Intangibles in the Era of Globalization, ed. Marshall Reinsdorf and Matthew J. Slaughter (Chicago: The University of Chicago Press, 2009): 98–101. The estimates will be published in the article on U.S. international services in the October SURVEY.

Worldwide Operations of U.S. MNCs

This section examines the 2007 worldwide operations of U.S. MNCs in all industries as well as the 2007 change in three aspects of the worldwide operations of nonbank U.S. MNCs: value added, employment, and U.S. trade in goods. It also examines the distribution of worldwide R&D between U.S. parents and foreign affiliates.

U.S. MNCs in all industries

The value added of U.S. MNCs in all bank and non- bank industries was $3,861.4 billion, compared with $3,706.4 billion for nonbank MNCs, and employment for all U.S. MNCs was 33.8 million workers, compared with 32.0 million workers for nonbank MNCs.

Nonbank U.S. MNCs

Value added

In current dollars, the value added of nonbank U.S. MNCs increased 4.8 percent in 2007 to $3,706.4 billion (table 2). The value added of U.S. parents increased 2.0 percent to $2,588.8 billion. And the value added of foreign affiliates in U.S. dollars increased 11.6 percent to $1,117.6 billion.

Table 2. Value Added of Nonbank U.S. Multinational Companies by Industry of Parent, 2006 and 2007 [Millions of dollars]

	2006	2007	Change	Percent change
All industries	3,538,079	3,706,396	168,317	4.8
Mining	103,929	95,295	–8,634	–8.3
Utilities	85,245	90,058	4,813	5.6
Manufacturing	1,721,692	1,800,208	78,516	4.6
Of which:				
Food	100,123	114,033	13,910	13.9
Petroleum and coal products	362,298	370,760	8,462	2.3
Chemicals	297,118	313,861	16,743	5.6
Primary and fabricated metals	76,650	73,137	–3,513	–4.6
Machinery	84,705	91,963	7,258	8.6
Computers and electronic products	172,328	185,783	13,455	7.8
Electrical equipment, appliances, and components	38,105	42,231	4,126	10.8
Transportation equipment	278,662	305,609	26,947	9.7
Wholesale trade	176,006	183,571	7,565	4.3
Information	357,961	374,835	16,874	4.7
Finance (except depository institutions) and insurance	267,287	284,341	17,054	6.4
Professional, scientific, and technical services	203,947	215,142	11,195	5.5
Other industries	622,013	662,945	40,932	6.6

The available evidence on changes in prices and exchange rates suggests that in real terms, the value added of U.S. parents decreased, and the value added of foreign affiliates increased. For U.S. parents, the 2.0 percent increase in current-dollar value added did not keep pace with the 2.7 percent rate of inflation (as measured by the implicit price deflator for U.S. GDP). For foreign affiliates, the 11.6 percent increase in value added exceeded the increase in current-dollar values that could be attributed to the combined effects of the 1.9 percent average rate of inflation in host countries and the 6.9 percent depreciation of the dollar against major foreign currencies.[4] The increase for foreign affiliates was concentrated in nonmanufacturing industries. Estimates presented later in this article indicate that the real value added of foreign affiliates in manufacturing decreased 1.5 percent in 2007.

Employment

In 2007, employment by nonbank U.S. MNCs increased 2.5 percent to 32.0 million workers. The employment by U.S. parents increased 1.8 percent to 22.0 million; the largest increases were in "other industries," information, and "professional, scientific, and technical services." The increases in "other industries" (mainly retail trade, miscellaneous services, and accommodation and food services) fully accounted for the growth in employment by U.S. parents. The 1.8 percent growth in parent employment, which mainly reflected growth by companies that were parents in both 2006 and 2007, was greater than the 1.0 percent growth in employment in all U.S. domestic private industries.

DATA AVAILABILITY

The final statistics on the worldwide operations of U.S. multinational companies (MNCs) for 2006 and the preliminary statistics for 2007 are presented in this article. The statistics are based on the 2006 and 2007 annual surveys of U.S. direct investment abroad. More detailed statistics are posted on BEA's Web site.

The final statistics on U.S. MNC operations for 1977 and for 1982–2005 are available in publications or in files that can be downloaded free of charge from our Web site at www.bea.gov.

For more information about these products and how to obtain them, go to www.bea.gov/scb/ account_articles/international/iidguide.htm.

The Bureau has a free service on its Web site that allows users to interactively access detailed statistics on the operations of U.S. MNCs, on the operations of foreign-owned companies in the United States, and on other aspects of U.S. direct investment abroad and foreign direct investment in the United States. For an introductory guide to this service, see Ned G. Howenstine, "Primer: Accessing BEA Direct Investment Data Interactively," SURVEY 86 (May 2006): 61–64.

Employment by foreign affiliates increased 4.2 percent to 10.0 million. By area, the largest increases were in Asia and Pacific and Latin America and Other Western Hemisphere. By industry, the largest increases were in "other industries" (mainly employment services and retail trade), "professional, scientific, and technical services," and manufacturing.

Table 3. U.S. Trade in Goods Associated with Nonbank U.S. Multinational Companies, 2006 and 2007 [Millions of dollars]

	2006	2007
MNC-associated U.S. exports, total	**532,576**	**558,624**
Intra-MNC trade	200,237	214,470
Shipped by U.S. parents to their MOFAs	191,317	205,839
Shipped by U.S. parents to their other foreign affiliates [1]	8,920	8,631
MNC trade with others	332,339	344,154
Shipped by U.S. parents to foreigners other than their own affiliates of which:	294,410	300,964
Shipped by U.S. parents to their foreign parent groups [2]	41,871	42,335
Shipped to foreign affiliates by U.S. persons other than their own parents	37,929	43,190
To MOFAs	37,929	41,803
To other foreign affiliates [3]	n.a.	1,387
MNC-associated U.S. imports, total	**694,518**	**728,412**
Intra-MNC trade	249,608	272,041
Shipped by MOFAs to their U.S. parents	237,583	259,561
Shipped by other foreign affiliates to their U.S. parents [1]	12,025	12,480
MNC trade with others	444,910	456,371

Table 3. (Continued)

	2006	2007
Shipped to U.S. parents by foreigners other than their own affiliates of which:	387,352	396,478
Shipped to U.S. parents by their foreign parent groups [2]	106,103	94,447
Shipped by foreign affiliates to U.S. persons other than their own parents	57,558	59,893
By MOFAs	48,048	52,844
By other foreign affiliates [3]	9,510	7,049
Addenda:		
All U.S. exports of goods	1,025,967	1,148,199
U.S.-MNC-associated U.S. exports as a percentage of total	52	49
Intra-U.S.-MNC exports as a percentage of total	20	19
All U.S. imports of goods	1,853,938	1,956,962
U.S.-MNC-associated U.S. imports as a percentage of total	37	37
Intra-U.S.-MNC imports as a percentage of total	13	14

1. This number is calculated as total exports (imports) between U.S. parents and all of their foreign affiliates (as reported for U.S. parents) less exports (imports) between U.S. parents and MOFAs (as reported for MOFAs).
2. Pertains to U.S. parents that are, in turn, owned 10 percent or more by a foreign person. The foreign parent group consists of (1) the foreign parent of the U.S. parent, (2) any foreign person, proceeding up the foreign parent's ownership chain, that person, proceeding down the ownership chain(s) of each of these members, that is owned more than 50 percent by the person above it.
3. This number is calculated as total exports (imports) associated with "other" (that is, minority-owned and 50-percent owned) foreign affiliates (as reported for affiliates) less the estimate of exports (imports) between U.S. parents and "other" foreign affiliates that are calculated as described in footnote 1. However, these esti mates may be imprecise because of differences in the coverage of the data reported for U.S. parents and for foreign affiliates. No estimate of exports can be made for 2006 because the difference was especially large in that year. MNCs Multinational companies

MOFAs Majority-owned foreign affiliates

n.a. Not available

U.S. trade in goods

In 2007, U.S. exports of goods that involved nonbank U.S. parents or their majority-owned or minority- owned nonbank foreign affiliates—MNC-associated exports—increased 4.9 percent to $558.6 billion (table 3). This increase was noticeably less than that for ex percent in 2007. The MNC-associated share of total U.S. exports of goods has been declining in recent years, falling 15 percentage points over the last decade.

MNC-associated imports of goods increased 4.9 percent to $728.4 billion in 2007. The increase nearly kept pace with the increase in total U.S. imports of goods (5.6 percent). As a result, the MNC-associated share of total U.S. imports of goods remained relatively unchanged, at 37.2 percent, in 2007. Over the last decade, the MNC-associated share of total U.S. imports of goods has decreased slightly, falling 3 percentage points.

The increase in MNC-associated exports of goods in 2007 reflected increases in both trade between U.S. parents and their foreign affiliates (intra-MNC trade) and trade between U.S. MNCs and "others" (trade between U.S. parent companies and foreigners other than their own affiliates and trade between foreign affiliates and U.S. residents other than their own parents). Exports by U.S. parents to their foreign affiliates increased 7.1 percent to $214.5 billion (chart 2), and U.S. exports between U.S. MNCs and others increased 3.6 percent to $344.2 billion. By industry of foreign affiliate, the largest increase in intra-MNC exports was to affiliates in wholesale trade, specifically drugs and druggists' sundries. By industry of U.S. parent, the largest increases in exports between U.S. MNCs and others were by parents in food, chemical, and petroleum and coal products manufacturing.

The increase in MNC-associated imports of goods reflected increases in both imports shipped by foreign affiliates to their U.S. parents (intra-MNC trade) and U.S. MNC trade with others. Imports by U.S. parents from their foreign affiliates increased 9.0 percent to $272.0 billion, and U.S. imports between U.S. MNCs and others increased 2.6 percent to $456.4 billion. By industry of foreign affiliate, the largest increases in intra-MNC U.S. imports were shipped by affiliates in computers and electronic products manufacturing and wholesale trade, specifically petroleum and petroleum products. By industry of U.S. parent, the largest increase in imports between U.S. MNCs and others was to parents in retail trade and petroleum and coal products manufacturing.

Research and development

Expenditures for R&D performed by nonbank U.S. MNCs increased 10.0 percent to $235.4 billion in 2007 (table 4). U.S. parents accounted for $200.4 billion, or 85.1 percent of the worldwide total, and foreign affiliates accounted for $35.0 billion, or 14.9 percent of the worldwide total.

Table 4. Research and Development Performed by Nonbank U.S. Multinational Companies by Industry of U.S. Parent, 2007 [Millions of dollars or percent]

	U.S. MNCs	Parents	MOFAs	MOFA share
All industries	235,416	200,397	35,019	14.9
Mining	(D)	637	(D)	(D)
Utilities	27	24	3	11.1
Manufacturing *Of which:*	185,402	157,231	28,171	15.2
Food	2,369	1,852	517	21.8
Chemicals	58,712	50,449	8,263	14.1
Primary and fabricated metals	1,368	1,016	352	25.7
Machinery	7,630	6,360	1,270	16.6
Computers and electronic products	45,326	39,852	5,474	12.1
Electrical equipment, appliances, and components	3,482	2,925	557	16.0
Transportation equipment	53,453	43,698	9,755	18.2
Wholesale trade	7,057	5,686	1,371	19.4
Information	20,354	18,797	1,557	7.6
Finance (except depository institutions) and insurance	(D)	237	(D)	(D)
Professional, scientific, and technical services	19,595	15,810	3,785	19.3
Other industries	2,059	1,975	84	4.1

D Suppressed to avoid disclosure of data of individual companies.
MNCs Multinational companies
MOFAs Majority-owned foreign affiliates

The concentration of the R&D activities of U.S. MNCs in the United States reflects a number of factors. First, the United States is relatively well endowed with the scientific and technological infrastructure—institutions, facilities, and personnel—needed to develop new products and processes. Second, U.S. MNCs may wish to concentrate R&D activity where the bulk of their output is sold and where they can most easily receive and respond to feedback from their consumers. Third, due to economies of scale in knowledge generation, it may be more efficient for MNCs to concentrate their global R&D activities in a single country and then distribute the results of the R&D to affiliates, which can often be done at little or no additional cost; as a location for doing this, the United States offers the advantage of being the country of origin and the country of headquarters for the MNC. Finally, U.S. MNCs may conduct most of their R&D in their U.S. headquarters to reduce the risk of diffusion of their proprietary technologies to competitors.[5]

Although the tendency to concentrate global R&D at home is pervasive, the foreign-affiliate share of MNC global R&D varies by industry. Among the five industries and industry sectors shown in table 4 in which MNC global R&D exceeded $10 billion, the foreign affiliate share was relatively low in information (7.6 percent) and computers and electronic products (12.1 percent), and it was relatively high in "professional, scientific, and technical services" (19.3 percent) and in transportation equipment manufacturing (18.2 percent). The high foreign-affiliate share in transportation equipment partly reflects the competitive advantage that certain countries, such as Germany, possess in automotive technology. A source of this competitive advantage is presence of industrial agglomeration (or clustering) in places such as Stuttgart and Bavaria in Germany and the West Midlands in the United Kingdom. Innovation can be heightened when competing firms operate in geographic clusters that attract pools of highly skilled labor and that increase rivalry among firms.[6] The high foreign-affiliate share in transportation equipment also reflects the need to customize automobiles for the tastes of local consumers and to comply with local laws and regulations. The low foreign-affiliate share in information partly reflects the dominance of the United States in the global software industry and possibly the difficulties in protecting intellectual property in this industry.

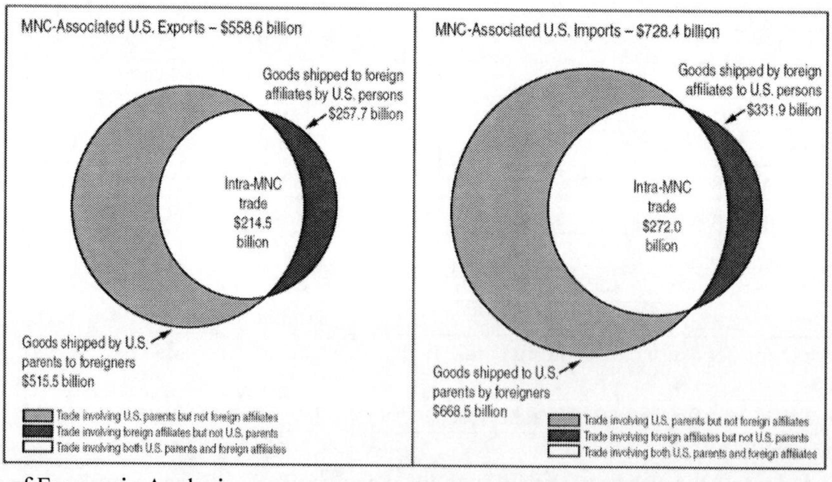

U.S. Bureau of Economic Analysis

Chart 2. Distribution of U.S. Trade in Goods Associated with Nonbank U.S. MNCs in 2007

U.S. PARENTS' OPERATIONS

This section examines the 2007 operations of U.S. parents in all industries as well as the 2007 change in two aspects of the operations of nonbank U.S. parent companies: value added and R&D.

U.S. Parents in all Industries

The value added of U.S. parents in all industries was $2,711.2 billion, compared with $2,588.8 billion for nonbank parents, and employment for all U.S. parents was 23.3 million workers, compared with 22.0 million workers for nonbank parents.

Nonbank U.S. Parents

Value added

Current-dollar value added of nonbank U.S. parents increased 2.0 percent in 2007 to $2,588.8 billion after increasing at the much faster rate of 9.3 percent in 2006. Almost 60 percent of the 2007 increase reflected increased production by ongoing parents (table 5, line 4). There was also an increase related to unallocated changes (line 6), and a small increase related to the addition of new parents to the U.S. MNC universe (line 3). These increases were partly offset by a small decrease related to the departure of U.S. parents that sold or liquidated their last foreign affiliate (line 5).

Table 5. Sources of Change in the Value Added of Nonbank U.S. Parent Companies, 2006–2007 [Millions of dollars]

1	**2006 level**	**2,536,873**
2	Total change	51,938
3	New parents[1]	383
4	Changes for ongoing parents[2]	30,813
5	Parents departing the universe [3]	– 4,132
6	Other changes[4]	24,874
7	**2007 level**	**2,588,811**

1. Parents that established or acquired their first foreign affiliate in 2007.
2. Businesses that were parents in both 2006 and 2007. It consists of changes in their existing operations and changes from parents acquiring, establishing, selling, or liquidating parts of their consolidated operations. BEA generally requires survey respondents to fully consolidate their U.S.-parent operations.
3. Parents that sold or liquidated their last foreign affiliate and those that went out of business in 2007.
4. Equals the change in the value added of parents not accounted for in lines 3–5, such as changes resulting from the addition to the survey universe of parents that were required to report in earlier years but did not. Line 6 will also capture any measurement error in the items on the other lines, because it is calculated as the d iffer-ence between line 2 and the sum of lines 3, 4, and 5.

ACKNOWLEDGMENTS

The 2007 annual survey was conducted under the direction of David H. Galler, Patricia C. Walker, and Barbara K. Hubbard. James Y. Shin supervised the editing and processing of the reports. The following staff contributed to the processing and editing of the survey or to the related computer programming: Catherine E. Ama, Helen Bai, Gregory L. Brace, Christina D. Briseno, Tonia Courtney, James J. Crim, Ian P. Dusenberry, Andre Garber, Brian C. Goddard, Mark D. Goddard, David L. Grayton, Carole J. Henry, Jenni- fer A. Jones, Sarin Koerner, Sherry Lee, Neeta Kapoor, Marcia S. Miller, Amanda M. Petersen, Kevin J. Reagan, Robert L. Ruiz, Myriam B. Rullan, Aqeel A. Sahibzada, Gary E. Sowers, Nancy F. Steffen, Christopher J. Stein, and Stacy A. Young.

In 2007, growth in U.S. parents' value added slowed in several of the major industry groups, with the most noticeable slowdown being in finance (except banks) and insurance. This slowdown partly reflected the financial crisis stemming from difficulties in the U.S. subprime mortgage market in the second half of 2007, which led to deteriorating credit quality and tight interest margins that slowed growth in consumer credit.

Table 6. Value Added of Nonbank U.S. Parent Companies, by Major Industry, 2006 and 2007 [Millions of dollars]

	2006	2007	Change	Percent change
All industries	2,536,873	2,588,811	51,938	2.0
Mining	69,046	62,293	–6,753	–9.8
Utilities	76,832	83,883	7,051	9.2
Manufacturing *Of which:*	1,054,035	1,064,666	10,631	1.0
Food	66,895	75,080	8,185	12.2
Chemicals	185,338	180,227	–5,111	–2.8
Primary and fabricated metals	59,364	52,851	–6,513	–11.0
Machinery	55,833	60,136	4,303	7.7
Computers and electronic products	111,623	118,353	6,730	6.0
Electrical equipment, appliances, and components	28,084	29,843	1,759	6.3
Transportation equipment	192,575	204,360	11,785	6.1
Wholesale trade	136,825	137,904	1,079	0.8
Information	307,525	316,760	9,235	3.0
Finance (except depository institutions) and insurance	226,903	229,235	2,332	1.0
Professional, scientific, and technical services	146,091	153,575	7,484	5.1
Other industries	519,617	540,493	20,876	4.0

Value added by parents in "other industries" increased 4.0 percent or $20.9 billion in 2007 (table 6). The increase partly reflected an increase by parents in retail trade, largely due to a strong increase in sales by discount department stores.

Value added by parents in manufacturing increased 1.0 percent or $10.6 billion in 2007 and accounted for the largest share (41.1 percent) of value added. The overall increase in manufacturing was primarily due to strong growth by parents in transportation equipment, food, computers and electronic products, machinery, and "electrical equipment, appliances, and components." In transportation equipment, value added increased 6.1 percent or $11.8 billion, primarily reflecting aerospace-related spending. In food, value added increased 12.2 percent or $8.2 billion, partly reflecting strong revenues in both the meat and dairy products industries. In computers and electronic products, value added increased 6.0 percent or $6.7 billion, reflecting strong sales in the "navigational, measuring, and other instruments," "computers and peripheral equipment," and "semiconductors and other electronic components" industries. In machinery, value added increased 7.7 percent or $4.3 billion as a result of growth in both "agriculture, construction, and mining machinery" and industrial machinery and strong global markets for mining and energy development. In "electrical equipment, appliances, and components," value added increased 6.3 percent or $1.8 billion as a result of strong sales to foreign markets.

Value added by parents in information increased 3.0 percent or $9.2 billion. The increase reflected strong growth by parents in "internet, data processing, and other information services," which benefitted from increased demand for online advertising.

Value added by parents in "professional, scientific, and technical services" increased 5.1 percent or $7.5 billion. The increase partly reflected increased spending by pharmaceuticals and biotechnology companies and academic institutions for scientific services and rising sales of custom software and related support services to businesses.

Value added by parents in utilities experienced near double-digit growth in 2007, increasing 9.2 percent or $7.1 billion. The increase reflected higher revenues stemming from strong energy markets and increased power generation, particularly in the West and Southeast regions.

Research and development

In 2007, expenditures for R&D performed by nonbank U.S. parents increased 8.7 percent to $200.4 billion. U.S. parents accounted for 74.4 percent of total R&D performed by all U.S. businesses in 2007 (table 7). The parent share of all U.S. R&D is much higher than parents' shares of private industry value added, which was 24 percent, and of employment, which was 19 percent. Taken together, these shares suggest that production by U.S. parents is highly R&D intensive relative to Industry composition, with a high concentration of R&D being performed in the manufacturing and information sectors.

Expenditures for R&D performed by U.S. parents in manufacturing increased 7.4 percent to $157.2 billion (table 8). Both chemicals and transportation equipment experienced large upturns in 2007. Chemicals increased 12.5 percent and accounted for almost a third of expenditures for R&D performed by U.S. parents in manufacturing. Within chemicals, R&D spending expanded as a result of an increase in research for new drugs, a renewed focus on vaccine development, and preparatory moves for the more stringent regulation and safety standards required by the Food and Drug Administration Amendments Act of 2007. Transportation equipment increased 12.6 percent and accounted for more than a quarter of expenditures for R&D performed by U.S. parents in manufacturing. Within transportation equipment, most of the increase was in "other transportation equipment" and reflected an increase in aerospace-related spending.

Table 7. Research and Development Performed by Nonbank U.S. Parent Companies and by All U.S. Businesses, 1997–2007 [Millions of dollars]

	Performed by parents	Performed by all U.S. businesses [1]	R&D by parents as a percentage of R&D by all U.S. businesses
1997	106,800	157,739	67.7
1998	113,777	169,180	67.3
1999	126,291	182,711	69.1
2000	135,467	199,539	67.9
2001	143,017	198,505	72.0
2002	136,977	193,868	70.7
2003	139,884	200,724	69.7
2004	164,189	208,301	78.8
2005	177,598	226,159	78.5
2006	184,428	247,669	74.5
2007	200,397	269,267	74.4

Table 8. Research and Development Performed by Nonbank U.S. Parent Companies by Major Industry, 2006 and 2007 [Millions of dollars]

	2006	2007	Change	Percent change
All industries	184,428	200,397	15,969	8.7
Mining	538	637	99	18.4
Utilities	28	24	–4	–14.3
Manufacturing *Of which:*	146,435	157,231	10,796	7.4
Food	1,739	1,852	113	6.5
Chemicals	44,832	50,449	5,617	12.5
Primary and fabricated metals	1,082	1,016	–66	–6.1
Machinery	5,892	6,360	468	7.9
Computers and electronic products	40,124	39,852	–272	–0.7
Electrical equipment, appliances, and components	2,748	2,925	177	6.4
Transportation equipment	38,809	43,698	4,889	12.6
Wholesale trade	5,428	5,686	258	4.8
Information	15,047	18,797	3,750	24.9
Finance (except depository institutions) and insurance	260	237	–23	–8.8
Professional, scientific, and technical services	15,007	15,810	803	5.4
Other industries	1,684	1,975	291	17.3

Expenditures for R&D performed by U.S. parents in information grew rapidly, increasing 24.9 percent to $18.8 billion in 2007. Most of the growth was due to increased R&D expenditures by parents in telecommunications and in "internet, data processing, and other information services." This partly reflected the highly competitive nature of these growing industries, which has led to increased R&D spending by U.S. parents to help them to innovate and to deliver new products and services.

OPERATIONS OF FOREIGN AFFILIATES

This section examines the 2007 operations of foreign affiliates in all industries as well as the 2007 change in two aspects of the operations of nonbank foreign affiliates of nonbank U.S. parents: value added and research and development. For nonbank foreign affiliates of nonbank U.S. parents, it also examines the distribution by country and by industry of newly acquired or established affiliates and the affiliates' shares of host country GDP.

Foreign Affiliates in all Industries

The value added of foreign affiliates in all industries was $1,150.0 billion, compared with $1,117.6 billion for nonbank foreign affiliates of nonbank U.S. parents, and employment for all foreign affiliates was 10.4 million workers, compared with 10.0 million workers for nonbank foreign affiliates of nonbank U.S. parents.

Table 9. Sources of Change in Value Added of Nonbank Majority-Owned Foreign Affiliates, 2006–2007 [Millions of dollars]

1	**2006 level**	**1,001,206**
2	Total change	116,379
3	New foreign affiliates	12,071
4	Acquired by U.S. parents	7,048
5	Established by U.S. parents	5,023
6	Changes for ongoing affiliates[1]	111,923
7	Sales or liquidations of foreign affiliates	–20,631
8	Other changes[2]	13,016
9	**2007 level**	**1,117,585**

1. Covers businesses that were affiliates in both 2006 and 2007. It consists of changes in their existing oper- ations and changes from foreign affiliates acquiring, establishing, selling, or liquidating parts of their consolidated operations. BEA permits survey respondents to consolidate affiliate operations that are in the same country if the affiliates are also in the same industry or are integral parts of a single business operation.
2. Equals the change in the value added of foreign affiliates not accounted for in lines 3–7, such as changes resulting from the addition to the survey universe of affiliates that were exempt from reporting in earlier years and affiliates that were required to report in earlier years but did not. Line 8 will also capture any measurement error in the items on the other lines, because it is calculated as the difference between line 2 and the sum of lines 3, 6, and 7.

Nonbank Foreign Affiliates of Nonbank U.S. Parents

Value Added

Current-dollar value added of nonbank foreign affiliates of nonbank U.S. parents increased 11.6 percent to $1,117.6 billion in 2007. The increase largely reflected changes for ongoing affiliates (table 9, line 6); increases related to the addition of new affiliates to the U.S. MNC universe (line 3) or to unallocated changes (line 8) were not as large and were partly offset by a decrease related to the departure of affiliates that were sold or liquidated (line 7).

Table 10. Value Added of Majority-Owned Nonbank Foreign Affiliates by Major Area and by Major Industry of Affiliate, 2006 and 2007 [Millions of dollars]

	2006	2007	Change	Percent change
All areas, all industries	**1,001,206**	**1,117,585**	**116,379**	**11.6**
By area				
Canada	108,051	116,180	8,129	7.5
Europe *Of which:*	546,313	610,921	64,608	11.8
France	50,136	56,196	6,060	12.1
Germany	82,932	86,649	3,717	4.5
Netherlands	28,973	29,515	542	1.9
United Kingdom	154,997	172,310	17,313	11.2
Latin America and Other Western Hemisphere *Of which:*	107,121	123,544	16,423	15.3
Brazil	24,346	33,090	8,744	35.9
Mexico	28,273	31,327	3,054	10.8
Africa	42,332	43,269	937	2.2
Middle East	13,176	16,036	2,860	21.7
Asia and Pacific *Of which:*	184,213	207,635	23,422	12.7
Australia	37,821	44,088	6,267	16.6
China	18,489	22,429	3,940	21.3
Japan	38,328	38,954	626	1.6
By industry				
Mining	140,985	152,285	11,300	8.0
Utilities	11,788	11,145	–643	–5.5
Manufacturing *Of which:*	455,675	509,962	54,287	11.9
Food	28,519	30,403	1,884	6.6
Chemicals	86,816	107,519	20,703	23.8
Primary and fabricated metals	18,581	21,192	2,611	14.1
Machinery	28,180	32,404	4,224	15.0
Computers and electronic products	48,008	50,473	2,465	5.1
Electrical equipment, appliances, and components	12,505	13,085	580	4.6
Transportation equipment	62,539	71,208	8,669	13.9
Wholesale trade	139,494	151,964	12,470	8.9
Information	40,565	45,079	4,514	11.1
Finance (except depository institutions) and insurance	34,671	51,656	16,985	49.0
Professional, scientific, and technical services	57,154	61,383	4,229	7.4
Other industries	120,874	134,111	13,237	11.0

By area, the increases in value added of foreign affiliates were widespread, but the largest increases were in Europe, Asia and Pacific, and Latin America and Other Western Hemisphere (table 10). In Europe, the value added of affiliates increased $64.6 billion or 11.8 percent. The largest increases were in manufacturing and in finance (except banks) and insurance. The increases in manufacturing were widespread across countries, but they were largest in the United Kingdom and Switzerland. The increase in the United Kingdom partly reflected increased value added in the manufacture of motor vehicles. The increase in Switzerland mainly reflected increased value added in the manufacture of goods (such as pharmaceuticals and semiconductors) for export. The increase in finance was concentrated in the United Kingdom and partly reflected rising investment banking activity related to the rise in European merger and acquisition activity.

In Asia and Pacific, the value added of affiliates increased $23.4 billion or 12.7 percent. The largest increases were in manufacturing and "other industries" (mainly accommodation and food services). The increase in manufacturing was concentrated in China, Australia, and Singapore. The increase in China mainly reflected the expansion of existing affiliates and the establishment of new affiliates to serve the local market.[7] New Chinese manufacturing affiliates were engaged in producing both intermediate goods, such as electronic cables, and final goods, such as kitchen appliances and audio-visual equipment. The increases in Australia and Singapore were mainly in manufacturing. The increase in Australia was widespread across manufacturing industries and mainly reflected strong economic growth and rising consumer spending. The increase in Singapore mainly reflected increased value added in the manufacture of goods, such as pharmaceuticals, for export.

In Latin America and Other Western Hemisphere, the value added of affiliates increased $16.4 billion or 15.3 percent. The largest increases were in manufacturing and wholesale trade. Most of the increases occurred in Brazil and partly reflected strong economic growth and rising consumer spending. For example, value added of affiliates in transportation equipment manufacturing increased 40.1 percent, reflecting a 23.9 percent increase in total unit sales of motor vehicles in that country.

In Canada, the value added of affiliates increased $8.1 billion or 7.5 percent. The largest increases were in mining (mainly oil and gas extraction) and in "other accommodation and food services). The increases in oil and gas extraction partly reflected the expansion of production of natural gas and the extraction of oil from tar sands. The increases in retail trade and accommodations and food services partly reflected the opening of new locations of U.S. retail and restaurant chains.

In the Middle East, the value added of affiliates increased $2.9 billion or 21.7 percent. The increase was concentrated in mining (mainly oil and gas extraction) and in manufacturing. The increase in mining partly reflected the rise in petroleum prices, which both raised the value of a given level of output and encouraged expansion in output. The increase in manufacturing reflected increased value added in the manufacture of computer components and other high-technology products for export.

In Africa, the value added of affiliates increased $0.9 billion or 2.2 percent. The largest increase was in mining (mainly oil and gas extraction) and partly reflected the rise in petroleum prices.

By industry sector, increases were widespread but were largest in manufacturing and in finance (except banking) and insurance.

STATISTICS ON U.S. DIRECT INVESTMENT ABROAD

BEA collects two broad sets of data on U.S. direct investment abroad: (1) financial and operating data of U.S. multinational companies and (2) international transactions and direct investment position data. This article presents highlights of statistics derived from the first set of data; the statistics derived from the second set of data are usually published in the July and September issues of the SURVEY OF CURRENT BUSINESS.[1]

Financial and operating statistics. The financial and operating statistics provide a picture of the overall activities of foreign affiliates and U.S. parent companies, using a variety of indicators of their financial structure and operations. The statistics on foreign affiliates cover the entire operations of the affiliate, irrespective of the percentage of U.S. ownership. These statistics cover items that are needed in analyzing the characteristics, performance, and economic impact of multinational companies, such as sales, value added, employment and compensation of employees, capital expenditures, exports and imports, and research and development expenditures. Separate tabulations are available for all affiliates and for affiliates that are majority-owned by their U.S. parent(s).

International transactions and direct investment position statistics. The international transactions statistics cover a foreign parent(s), so these statistics deal with the U.S. share, or interest, in its affiliate rather than on the affiliate's tial to the compilation of the U.S. international transactions accounts (ITAs), the international investment position, and the national income and product accounts. The major items include capital flows (recorded in the financial account of the ITAs), which measure the funds that U.S. parents provide to their foreign affiliates, and income (recorded in the current account), which measures the return on those funds. Direct investment position statistics are stock (cumulative) measures, showing the total outstanding level of U.S. direct investment abroad at yearend. Estimates are provided both at historical cost and in terms of current- period prices. The historical-cost estimates are published by country and by industry.

[1] See Marilyn Ibarra and Jennifer Koncz, "Direct Investment Positions for 2008: Country and Industry Detail," SURVEY 89 (July 2009): 20–34 and Jeffrey H. Lowe, "Direct Investment, 2004–2007: Detailed Historical-Cost Positions and Related Capital and Income Flows," SURVEY 88 (September 2008).

Newly acquired or established affiliates. Although most of the increase in the value added of foreign affiliates in 2007 resulted from expansions in ongoing affiliates, the addition of affiliates that were newly acquired or established during the year also contributed. Data for these affiliates show where U.S. MNCs have been expanding their operations through new business enterprises and thus can provide some evidence of the countries and industries that have offered attractive investment opportunities to U.S. MNCs. In 2007, non- bank U.S. parents acquired or established 434 nonbank foreign affiliates, which had a combined value added of $12.1 billion and a combined employment of 143,600 workers (table 11).

By area, four countries accounted for more than half of the employment of all new affiliates in 2007; three of these countries—Canada, the United Kingdom and Germany—are high-income countries and one—China—is a middle-income country. These affiliates primarily serve local markets. The percent of total sales to local customers by new affiliates in these countries was 70.9 percent for the United Kingdom, 72.5 percent for Germany, 78.2 percent for Canada, and 90.3 percent for China.

By industry, manufacturing continued to be a leading industry for new affiliates in 2007. New manufacturing affiliates accounted for 30.9 percent of all new affiliates, for 53.3 percent of their value added, and for 44.2 percent of their employment.

Affiliate share of host-country GDP Value added of foreign affiliates represents these firms' contributions to their respective host countries' GDP. The share of host-country GDP accounted for by the value added of affiliates reflects the country's attractiveness to U.S. MNCs as a location for production, which includes the country's openness to foreign direct investment. Among the 51 host countries listed in table 12, the share of GDP accounted for by nonbank foreign affiliates of nonbank U.S. parents in 2007 ranged from 20.8 percent in Ireland to 0.1 percent in Saudi Arabia. In only 2 of the 51 host countries—Ireland and Singapore—did the value added of foreign affiliates of U.S. MNCs account for more than 10 percent of GDP.

The affiliate share of host-country GDP partly reflects characteristics of the host country, such as business infrastructure, macroeconomic conditions, the availability of natural resources, and governance aspects of host country. While each of these characteristics is important to the location of production by foreign affiliates, a strong relationship probably does not exist between any one of these characteristics and the affiliate share of host-country GDP, because some countries that score highly on one particular characteristic may not score as well on another characteristic. In addition, MNCs in different industries may not attach the same importance to a particular characteristic.

For example, MNCs in oil and gas extraction will attach a much higher importance to the presence of natural resources than affiliates in nonextractive industries. Nevertheless, each of these characteristics has some measurable impact on the location of foreign affiliates and the affiliate share of host-country GDP.

Governance of a host country refers to the "traditions and institutions by which authority in a country is exercised."[8] A study sponsored by the World Bank constructed indicators of the quality of host-country governance based on six governance characteristics that can affect the cost and risk of operating in a particular foreign country.[9] Countries that score favorably according to these indicators tend to attract more production by MOFAs than countries that score less favorably, suggesting that the quality of governance of the host country does in fact have an impact on the investment decisions by U.S. MNCs.

The value added of affiliates and therefore the affiliate share of host-country GDP also can be influenced by financial accounting strategies that some U.S. MNCs employ to reduce their tax liabilities.[10] For example, a U.S. company may locate the ownership rights to income-generating intellectual property in affiliates in countries with lower tax rates than the country in which the intellectual property was produced to reduce the tax liability on the income generated by this intellectual property.

Table 11. Newly Acquired or Established Nonbank Majority-Owned Foreign Affiliates by Major Area and Industry of Affiliate, 2006 and 2007

	2006					2007				
	Number of newly acquired or established affiliates			Value added (millions of dollars)	Number of employees (thousands)	Number of newly acquired or established affiliates			Value added (millions of dollars)	Number of employees (thousands)
	Total	Acquired	Established			Total	Acquired	Established		
Total	407	188	219	10,681	98.3	434	204	230	12,071	143.6
By area										
Canada	37	24	13	–332	10.2	42	22	20	1,315	19.7
Europe	239	119	120	3,861	56.9	244	129	115	6,130	70.1
Latin America and Other Western Hemisphere	43	13	30	1,319	5.8	69	19	50	(D)	(D)
Africa	14	6	8	84	1.1	3	1	2	(D)	(D)
Middle East	4	2	2	3,338	2.0	5	3	2	152	1.6
Asia and Pacific	70	24	46	2,411	22.4	71	30	41	2,136	39.5
High-income countries[1]	345	155	190	9,729	78.7	359	169	190	7,917	93.1
Upper-middle-income countries[1]	25	9	16	342	5.9	44	20	24	1,580	15.7
Lower-middle-income countries[1]	32	23	9	534	12.3	29	15	14	(D)	(D)
Low-income countries[1]	5	1	4	75	1.4	2	0	2	(D)	(D)
By industry										
Mining	27	22	5	4,808	3.1	18	11	7	2,246	5.1
Utilities	6	5	1	708	9.7	2	2	0	(D)	(D)
Manufacturing *Of which:*	104	61	43	2,231	43.1	134	103	31	6,432	63.4

	2006					2007				
	Number of newly acquired or established affiliates			Value added (millions of dollars)	Number of employees (thousands)	Number of newly acquired or established affiliates			Value added (millions of dollars)	Number of employees (thousands)
	Total	Acquired	Established			Total	Acquired	Established		
Food	3	2	1	33	0.8	7	2	5	276	5.0
Chemicals	14	8	6	375	6.7	55	52	3	649	18.8
Primary and fabricated metals	11	3	8	177	5.7	4	1	3	361	8.0
Machinery	15	11	4	471	7.2	4	2	2	65	1.6
Computers and electronic products	22	9	13	379	5.8	18	15	3	697	5.4
Electrical equipment, appliances, and components	3	3	0	15	0.7	4	4	0	87	3.5
Transportation equipment	6	5	1	144	4.2	7	6	1	1,335	8.9
Wholesale trade	32	20	12	480	5.1	29	21	8	770	8.9
Information	15	10	5	125	4.4	18	10	8	339	3.8
Finance (except depository institutions) and insurance	77	17	60	478	2.7	53	14	39	862	7.9
Professional, scientific, and technical services	11	8	3	139	1.7	9	7	2	(D)	(D)
Other industries *Of which:*	135	45	90	1,712	28.4	171	36	135	1,300	52.6
Holding companies	96	29	67	240	0.5	122	20	102	113	0.0

D Suppressed to avoid disclosure of data of individual companies. 1. As classified by the World Bank.

Note. The statistics in this table cover only newly acquired or established affiliates. They exclude data for consolidated units of existing affiliates that were acquired or established during the year.

Table 12. Value Added of Nonbank Majority-Owned Foreign Affiliates as a Percentage of GDP of Selected Host Countries, 2006 and 2007

	2006	2007
Ireland	21.3	20.8
Singapore	13.2	13.0
Canada	8.6	8.8
Nigeria	11.8	8.4
Switzerland	6.2	6.8
United Kingdom	6.6	6.2
Honduras	6.5	5.5
Australia	4.9	5.4
Hong Kong	5.4	5.3
Belgium	5.5	5.2
Costa Rica	5.7	5.1
Peru	4.6	4.6
Malaysia	5.3	4.4
Norway	5.4	4.3
Argentina	4.6	4.1
Thailand	4.2	4.0
Netherlands	4.4	3.9
Hungary	3.0	3.6
Mexico	3.4	3.1
Chile	3.3	3.0
Indonesia	3.2	3.0
Sweden	2.8	3.0
Israel	2.7	2.9
Philippines	3.4	2.9
Egypt	2.7	2.8
Germany	2.9	2.6
United Arab Emirates	2.3	2.6
Brazil	2.3	2.5
Colombia	2.8	2.5
Czech Republic	2.5	2.5
Venezuela	3.0	2.4
France	2.2	2.2
New Zealand	2.8	2.1
Poland	1.9	2.0
Portugal	2.2	2.0
South Africa	2.2	2.0
Denmark	2.2	1.9
Ecuador	1.7	1.8
Taiwan	1.6	1.8
Austria	1.7	1.6
Italy	1.6	1.5
Spain	1.4	1.4
Finland	1.5	1.3
Republic of Korea	1.2	1.3
Greece	1.2	1.1
Turkey	1.4	1.1
Japan	0.9	0.9

	2006	2007
China	0.7	0.7
India	0.6	0.6
Russia	0.4	0.5
Saudi Arabia	0.1	0.1
Weighted average of countries shown [1]	**2.9**	**2.8**

1. The average share of host-country GDP in these countries was derived as a weighted average in terms of host-country GDP.

Notes. The countries are sorted in descending order of their 2007 values. If two countries have the same 2007 value, they were sorted using unrounded values.

GDP data for host countries were obtained from the World Bank Web site.

GDP Gross domestic product

Real value added in manufacturing In addition to the current-dollar estimates of value added of foreign affiliates, BEA prepares estimates of the real value added of foreign affiliates in manufacturing that remove the effects of changes in prices and exchange rates. These estimates provide more meaningful comparisons of value added of foreign affiliates across countries and over time than the current-dollar estimates. Comparisons across countries are enhanced because the estimates in real terms are based on purchasing power parity (PPP) exchange rates rather than on market exchange rates.[11] Comparisons over time are enhanced because the estimates are denominated in chained (2005) dollars that account for both changes in prices and changes in the industry mix of production by manufacturing affiliates.[12] The real value added estimates are restricted to manufacturing because the required source data are not available for other industries.

The real value added of foreign affiliates in manufacturing decreased 1.5 percent to $391.2 billion in 2007 (table 13). The 27 countries for which estimates are separately available accounted for 68.8 percent of the total. The real value added of manufacturing affiliates in these countries decreased 8.8 percent to $269.0 billion, in contrast to a 2.6 percent increase in total manufacturing production in these countries (chart 3). The decrease partly reflected sales and liquidations of affiliates, which were especially pronounced in the automotive industry where some U.S. firms sold off foreign assets in an effort to raise cash to support domestic operations during a market downturn. The decreases were widespread across countries and were largest in Germany, the United Kingdom, and Canada. In the United Kingdom, real value added of foreign affiliates decreased $4.3 billion to $43.1 billion, mainly in "other manufacturing." In Germany, the real value added decreased $4.2 billion to $38.2 billion and largely reflected the complete or partial sales of parents' equity interest in foreign affiliates. In Canada, the real value added decreased $2.9 billion to $41.9 billion, mainly in transportation equipment manufacturing.

The real value added of foreign affiliates in the countries other than the 27 selected countries shown in table 13 increased 21.0 percent to $123.2 billion. Based on the market-exchange-rate-based estimates, the increase was most rapid in Latin America and Other Western Hemisphere.

By industry sector for all nonbank foreign affiliates, the largest increase was in manufacturing. The increase reflected large growth in both chemicals and transportation equipment, which increased $1.8 billion and $1.3 billion, respectively.

Table 13. Real Value Added by Majority-Owned Foreign Affiliates in Manufacturing by Country, 1999–2007

	Billions of chained (2005) dollars									Share of all-countries total (percent)								
	1999	2000	2001	2002	2003	2004	2005	2006	2007	1999	2000	2001	2002	2003	2004	2005	2006	2007
All countries	**363.3**	**371.2**	**363.0**	**368.4**	**367.6**	**395.4**	**388.0**	**397.0**	**391.2**	**100.0**	**100.0**	**100.0**	**100.0**	**100.0**	**100.0**	**100.0**	**100.0**	**100.0**
27 selected countries	**312.0**	**312.0**	**308.0**	**313.0**	**303.0**	**315.0**	**299.0**	**295.0**	**269.0**	**85.9**	**84.0**	**84.9**	**85.0**	**82.4**	**79.7**	**77.1**	**74.3**	**68.8**
Australia	9.5	10.5	10.7	9.7	9.7	10.5	10.4	11.9	10.4	2.6	2.8	2.9	2.6	2.6	2.7	2.7	3.0	2.7
Austria	1.8	1.8	1.8	1.6	1.4	1.7	1.8	2.0	1.8	0.5	0.5	0.5	0.4	0.4	0.4	0.5	0.5	0.5
Bulgaria	(*)	0.2	0.2	0.2	0.2	0.2	0.2	0.3	0.2	(*)	0.1	0.1	0.1	0.1	0.1	0.1	0.1	0.1
Canada	57.2	59.4	55.5	54.2	53.8	55.9	46.1	44.8	41.9	15.7	16.0	15.3	14.7	14.6	14.1	11.9	11.3	10.7
Czech Republic	2.1	2.2	2.7	2.7	2.6	3.4	3.5	3.3	2.9	0.6	0.6	0.7	0.7	0.7	0.9	0.9	0.8	0.7
Denmark	0.9	1.0	0.8	1.0	0.8	0.8	0.9	0.9	0.8	0.2	0.3	0.2	0.3	0.2	0.2	0.2	0.2	0.2
Finland	0.7	0.7	0.7	0.6	0.4	0.8	0.9	0.9	0.8	0.2	0.2	0.2	0.2	0.1	0.2	0.2	0.2	0.2
France	23.6	23.4	23.3	22.9	22.3	21.7	22.0	20.5	18.3	6.5	6.3	6.4	6.2	6.1	5.5	5.7	5.2	4.7
Germany	49.7	40.5	39.9	38.9	34.4	41.3	41.2	42.4	38.2	13.7	10.9	11.0	10.6	9.4	10.4	10.6	10.7	9.8
Greece	0.5	0.6	0.5	0.5	0.6	1.9	2.1	2.0	1.8	0.1	0.2	0.1	0.1	0.2	0.5	0.5	0.5	0.5
Hungary	2.0	2.1	1.9	2.5	2.0	1.7	2.2	2.6	2.2	0.6	0.6	0.5	0.7	0.5	0.4	0.6	0.7	0.6
Ireland	12.2	13.8	14.8	19.0	17.5	17.0	17.9	18.8	17.5	3.4	3.7	4.1	5.2	4.8	4.3	4.6	4.7	4.5
Italy	23.5	22.4	23.5	22.1	20.5	19.6	18.2	16.8	14.8	6.5	6.0	6.5	6.0	5.6	5.0	4.7	4.2	3.8
Japan	9.3	13.1	16.0	14.1	14.1	13.5	7.1	7.3	7.3	2.6	3.5	4.4	3.8	3.8	3.4	1.8	1.8	1.9
Lithuania	0.1	0.2	0.2	0.1	0.1	0.2	0.2	0.2	0.2	(*)	0.1	0.1	(*)	(*)	0.1	0.1	0.1	0.1
Mexico	23.4	24.4	24.6	25.5	26.0	24.0	23.0	24.0	23.0	6.4	6.6	6.8	6.9	7.1	6.1	5.9	6.0	5.9
Netherlands	13.8	14.0	13.7	14.0	13.1	13.6	15.3	13.0	11.5	3.8	3.8	3.8	3.8	3.6	3.4	3.9	3.3	2.9
Norway	1.9	1.7	1.9	1.9	1.7	1.7	1.9	1.4	1.3	0.5	0.5	0.5	0.5	0.5	0.4	0.5	0.4	0.3
Poland	1.9	3.5	3.9	4.3	5.0	5.9	6.0	6.7	5.7	0.5	0.9	1.1	1.2	1.4	1.5	1.5	1.7	1.5
Portugal	1.4	3.3	3.2	3.2	3.1	3.0	2.8	2.5	2.2	0.4	0.9	0.9	0.9	0.8	0.8	0.7	0.6	0.6
Slovak Republic	0.3	0.2	1.1	1.7	1.8	2.1	2.2	2.5	2.1	0.1	0.1	0.3	0.5	0.5	0.5	0.6	0.6	0.5
Slovenia	0.1	0.2	0.2	0.2	0.2	0.2	0.2	0.2	0.2	(*)	0.1	0.1	0.1	0.1	0.1	0.1	0.1	0.1
South Korea	2.2	3.2	2.9	4.0	4.0	4.9	5.6	6.4	6.1	0.6	0.9	0.8	1.1	1.1	1.2	1.4	1.6	1.6

Table 13. (Continued)

	Billions of chained (2005) dollars									Share of all-countries total (percent)								
	1999	2000	2001	2002	2003	2004	2005	2006	2007	1999	2000	2001	2002	2003	2004	2005	2006	2007
Spain	10.0	10.1	10.1	10.2	9.6	9.4	9.6	9.8	8.7	2.8	2.7	2.8	2.8	2.6	2.4	2.5	2.5	2.2
Sweden	2.7	3.4	3.2	3.4	4.4	5.0	4.1	4.5	4.1	0.7	0.9	0.9	0.9	1.2	1.3	1.1	1.1	1.0
Switzerland	2.6	3.1	1.8	2.0	2.2	2.8	3.2	4.1	3.9	0.7	0.8	0.5	0.5	0.6	0.7	0.8	1.0	1.0
United Kingdom	55.8	51.4	48.1	49.2	48.7	49.1	50.4	47.4	43.1	15.4	13.8	13.3	13.4	13.2	12.4	13.0	11.9	11.0
All other countries	52.8	60.0	55.8	57.0	64.8	80.9	89.0	101.8	123.2	14.5	16.2	15.4	15.5	17.6	20.5	22.9	25.7	31.5
Residual[1]	1.3	0.8	–0.1	1.7	2.6	2.6	0.0	–2.1	–3.0									

* Less than $500,000 or less than 0.05 percent.

1. Because the formula for the chain-type quantity indexes uses weights of more than one period, the corresponding chained-dollar estimates are usually not additive. The residual line is the difference between the first line and the sum of the most detailed lines.

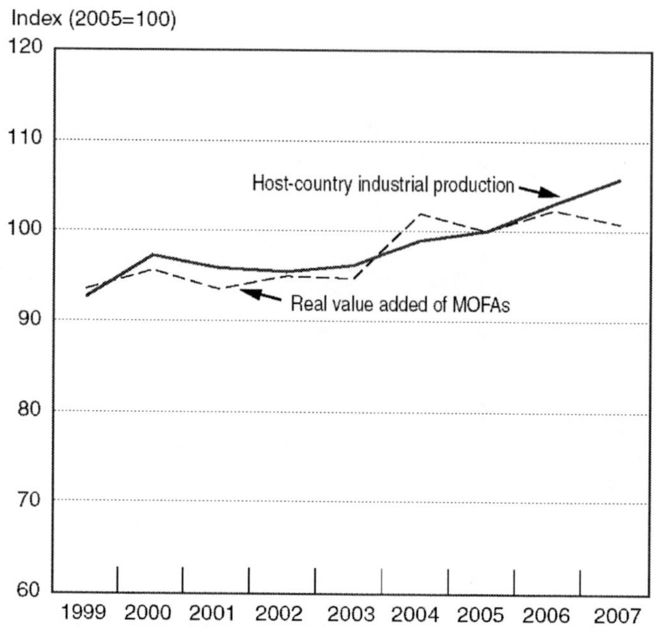

MOFAs Majority-owned foreign affiliates
Note. The 27 selected countries are listed below in Table 13.
The composite index of host-country industrial production was derived by weighting each country's index by the country's share in the dollar value of real value added of MOFAs in manufacturing. U.S. Bureau of Economic Analysis

Chart 3. Real Value Added of MOFAs in Manufacturing and Industrial Production in 27

Research and development

Expenditures for R&D performed by nonbank foreign affiliates of nonbank U.S. parents increased 18.4 percent or $5.4 billion to $35.0 billion in 2007 (table 14). R&D expenditures continued to be concentrated in a small number of host countries. The top two host countries—the United Kingdom and Germany—together accounted for over a third of the all-countries total change in R&D expenditures; however, there has been rapid growth in certain countries in Asia and Pacific—particularly in China—in recent years.

Chinese affiliates' R&D expenditures increased 50.3 percent or $0.4 billion, which was the third-highest change in R&D expenditures. By industry, a large portion of the Chinese R&D expenditures were in "computers and electronic products" and "electrical equipment, appliances, and components." Based on a recent academic study, the growth in R&D expenditures by Chinese affiliates appears primarily market- driven; reflecting the importance of the large Chinese population as customers in the marketing strategies of U.S. MNCs.[13] This is supported by the high share of sales to the local market. The growth in R&D expenditures by Chinese affiliates appears to be partly driven by the expanded capabilities for R&D in China. In recent years as China has focused on scientific education—with increased numbers of universities and research institutes—U.S. MNCs appear to have increasingly relied on their Chinese affiliates for innovations in products and processes while receiving additional advantages from strong industrial production and lower wages.

By industry sector for all nonbank foreign affiliates, the largest increase in R&D expenditures was in manufacturing. The increase reflected sizable growth in both chemicals and transportation equipment, which increased $1.8 billion and $1.3 billion, respectively.

KEY TERMS

The following key terms are used to describe U.S. multinational companies (MNCs) and their operations.[1]

U.S. MNCs

U.S. multinational company (U.S. MNC). The U.S. parent and its foreign affiliates. (In this article, an MNC is usually defined as the U.S. parent and its majority-owned foreign affiliates.)

U.S. parent. A person, resident in the United States, that owns or controls 10 percent or more of the voting securities, or the equivalent, of a foreign business enterprise. "Person" is broadly defined to include any indi- vidual, branch, partnership, associated group, association, estate, trust, corporation, or other organization (whether or not organized under the laws of any state), or any government entity. If incorporated, the U.S. parent is the fully consolidated U.S. enterprise consisting of (1) the U.S. corporation whose voting securities are not owned more than 50 percent by another U.S. corporation and (2) proceeding down each ownership chain from that U.S. corporation, any U.S. corporation whose voting securities are more than 50 percent owned by the U.S. corporation above it. A U.S. parent comprises the domestic operations of a U.S. MNC, covering operations in the 50 states, the District of Columbia, the Commonwealth of Puerto Rico, and all other U.S. areas.

U.S. direct investment abroad. The ownership or control, directly or indirectly, by one U.S. person of 10 percent or more of the voting securities of an incorporated foreign business enterprise or the equivalent interest in an unincorporated business enterprise.

Foreign affiliate. A foreign business enterprise in which there is U.S. direct investment, that is, in which a U.S. person owns or controls (directly or indirectly) 10 percent or more of the voting securities or the equivalent. Foreign affiliates comprise the foreign operations of a U.S. MNC over which the parent is presumed to have a degree of managerial influence. This article focuses on the operations of majority-owned foreign affiliates; for these affiliates, the combined ownership of all U.S. parents exceeds 50 percent. In 2007, these affiliates accounted for 85.3 percent of the employment of all foreign affiliates of U.S. MNCs.

Measures of Operations[2]

Value added. The portion of the goods and services sold or added to inventory or fixed investment by a firm that reflects the production of the firm itself. It represents the firm's country of residence, which is the value of goods and services produced by labor and property located in that country. Compared with sales, value added is a preferable measure of production because it indicates the extent to which a than from production that originates elsewhere, whereas sales data do not distinguish between these two sources of production. Value added can be measured as gross output minus intermediate inputs; alternatively, it can be measured as the sum of the costs incurred (except for intermediate inputs) and the profits earned in production. The value-added estimates presented in this article were prepared by summing the cost and profits data col- lected in the annual and benchmark surveys of U.S. direct investment abroad.[3]

Employment. The number of full-time and part-time employees on the payroll at yearend. If the employment of a parent or an affiliate was unusually high or low because of temporary factors (such as a strike) or large seasonal variations, the number that reflected normal operations or an average for the year was requested.

[1] For a comprehensive discussion of the terms and the concepts used, see Raymond J. Mataloni Jr., "A Guide to BEA Statistics on U.S. Multi- national Companies," SURVEY 75 (March 1995): 38–55.

[2] Statistics on the operations of U.S. MNCs cover the survey respondent's

[3] For the derivation of the current-dollar value-added estimates, see Raymond J. Mataloni Jr. and Lee Goldberg, "Gross Product of U.S. Multinational Companies, 1977–91," SURVEY 74 (February 1994): 57.

Table 14. Research and Development Performed by Majority-Owned Nonbank Foreign Affiliates by Major Area and by Major Industry of Affiliate, 2006 and 2007 [Millions of dollars]

	2006	2007	Change	Percent change
All areas, all industries	**29,583**	**35,019**	**5,436**	**18.4**
By area				
Canada	2,439	2,729	290	11.9
Europe *Of which:*	19,326	23,142	3,816	19.7
France	1,518	1,698	180	11.9
Germany	4,947	5,970	1,023	20.7
Netherlands	536	730	194	36.2
United Kingdom	5,551	6,522	971	17.5
Latin America and Other Western Hemisphere *Of which:*	1,046	1,151	105	10.0
Brazil	574	629	55	9.6
Mexico	(D)	316	(D)	(D)

Table 14. (Continued)

	2006	2007	Change	Percent change
Africa	67	65	–2	–3.0
Middle East	840	948	108	12.9
Asia and Pacific *of which:*	5,864	6,984	1,120	19.1
Australia	718	1,083	365	50.8
China	759	1,141	382	50.3
Japan	1,862	1,980	118	6.3
By industry				
Mining	23	48	25	108.7
Utilities	7	3	–4	–57.1
Manufacturing *Of which:*	24,172	28,171	3,999	16.5
Food	428	517	89	20.8
Chemicals	6,442	8,263	1,821	28.3
Primary and fabricated metals	327	352	25	7.6
Machinery	1,120	1,270	150	13.4
Computers and electronic products	4,954	5,474	520	10.5
Electrical equipment, appliances, and components..	652	557	–95	–14.6
Transportation equipment	8,505	9,755	1,250	14.7
Wholesale trade	1,131	1,371	240	21.2
Information	1,053	1,557	504	47.9
Finance (except depository institutions) and insurance	1	(*)		
Professional, scientific, and technical services	3,098	3,785	687	22.2
Other industries	98	84	–14	–14.3

* Less than $500,000.

D Suppressed to avoid disclosure of data of individual companies.

Table 15.1. Selected Statistics for Nonbank U.S. Parents by Industry of U.S. Parent, 2006

	Millions of dollars										Thousands of employees
	Total assets	Sales				Net income	Capital expenditures	Research and development expenditures	Value added	Compensation of employees	
		Total	Goods	Services	Investment income[1]						
All industries	**18,620,815**	**8,217,882**	**5,447,535**	**2,384,927**	**385,419**	**780,339**	**445,295**	**184,428**	**2,536,873**	**1,363,634**	**21,615.8**
Mining	**324,672**	**109,305**	**82,137**	**26,371**	**797**	**35,887**	**35,488**	**538**	**69,046**	**16,701**	**184.2**
Oil & gas extraction	190,344	50,592	(D)	(D)	113	19,382	24,326	8	37,063	3,602	30.7
Other	134,328	58,713	(D)	(D)	684	16,505	11,162	530	31,983	13,099	153.5
Utilities	**568,120**	**213,765**	**9,890**	**200,657**	**3,218**	**14,997**	**29,190**	**28**	**76,832**	**20,703**	**224.5**
Manufacturing	**4,965,393**	**3,786,625**	**3,548,728**	**169,231**	**68,666**	**344,825**	**168,790**	**146,435**	**1,054,035**	**570,706**	**7,457.9**
Food	293,807	295,413	294,027	1,377	9	22,740	7,986	1,739	66,895	35,808	631.7
Beverages and tobacco products	203,745	114,250	(D)	(D)	3,410	21,291	4,370	497	54,896	17,965	225.5
Textiles, apparel, and leather product	21,352	27,850	(D)	(D)	1	1,239	697	216	9,008	6,394	134.5
Wood products	36,194	27,908	(D)	(D)	384	680	1,153	121	8,558	4,729	69.8
Paper	105,029	78,720	(D)	(D)	47	7,548	3,384	1,596	31,749	17,827	220.1
Printing and related support activities	20,877	21,298	21,061	237	0	1,854	732	52	11,414	6,131	130.7
Petroleum and coal products	641,383	825,531	783,651	41,471	410	95,551	27,696	2,289	152,700	27,153	260.5
Chemicals	913,982	525,025	520,691	4,137	197	83,627	21,381	44,832	185,338	90,225	913.3
Basic chemicals	126,100	114,654	113,932	719	2	7,023	4,778	1,420	25,251	11,256	117.9
Resins and synthetic rubber, fibers and filaments	90,754	62,383	(D)	(D)	114	8,218	3,128	2,417	20,542	8,658	91.8
Pharmaceuticals and medicines	487,816	230,044	228,927	1,036	81	52,949	9,958	36,698	95,071	47,070	412.8
Soap, cleaning compounds, and toilet preparations	126,233	56,512	(D)	(D)	0	12,475	1,769	2,200	25,505	11,213	143.6
Other	83,079	61,433	60,149	1,284	0	2,962	1,748	2,097	18,969	12,027	147.3
Plastics and rubber products	86,904	82,213	79,742	2,471	0	3,137	2,639	1,287	26,006	17,316	280.4

Table 15.1 (Continued)

	Millions of dollars										Thousands of employees
	Total assets	Total	Sales Goods	Services	Investment income[1]	Net income	Capital expenditures	Research and development expenditures	Value added	Compensation of employees	
Nonmetallic mineral products	58,851	44,477	44,301	176	0	5,708	1,913	397	19,861	8,812	139.6
Primary and fabricated metals	171,651	185,694	181,361	4,190	143	17,187	5,704	1,082	59,364	34,112	521.9
Primary metals	113,555	128,395	126,136	2,116	143	13,473	4,331	444	38,011	19,839	284.2
Fabricated metal products	58,097	57,298	55,225	2,073	0	3,714	1,373	638	21,353	14,273	237.8
Machinery	240,882	184,070	175,992	4,744	3,334	17,841	6,071	5,892	55,833	35,475	545.5
Agriculture, construction, and mining machinery	128,239	76,548	71,987	(D)	(D)	7,743	3,119	2,359	17,935	12,301	155.9
Industrial machinery	41,286	34,087	32,357	1,730	0	5,383	1,291	2,024	13,787	6,744	104.7
Other	71,357	73,435	71,648	(D)	(D)	4,716	1,661	1,509	24,112	16,430	284.9
Computers and electronic products	535,275	318,592	293,195	25,378	19	45,412	15,757	40,124	111,623	70,181	851.6
Computers and peripheral equipment	123,860	88,442	(D)	(D)	0	9,296	2,766	8,081	17,928	13,219	179.6
Communications equipment	126,824	66,793	62,273	4,520	0	9,071	3,126	9,336	23,499	13,428	161.2
Plastics and rubber products	86,904	82,213	79,742	2,471	0	3,137	2,639	1,287	26,006	17,316	280.4
Semiconductors & other electronic components	172,722	91,733	(D)	(D)	1	17,805	8,332	16,748	42,414	23,700	234.7
Navigational, measuring, and other instruments	98,315	62,198	55,895	6,285	18	8,566	1,302	5,478	24,858	17,781	248.2
Magnetic and optical media	2,208	1,148	(D)	(D)	0	239	35	(D)	394	269	3.8
Electrical equipment, appliances, and components	99,680	95,722	88,760	6,963	0	4,944	2,600	2,748	28,084	19,096	299.0

Table 15.1 (Continued)

	Millions of dollars										Thousand of employees
	Total assets	Total	Sales Goods	Services	Investment income[1]	Net income	Capital expenditures	Research and development expenditures	Value added	Compensation of employees	
Transportation equipment	1,370,017	854,090	726,729	67,783	59,578	11,096	63,357	38,809	192,575	151,925	1,792.2
Motor vehicles, bodies and trailers, and parts	731,305	499,689	467,988	13,980	17,722	–16,755	48,526	14,840	65,339	65,251	870.1
Other	638,713	354,401	258,741	53,804	41,856	27,851	14,832	23,969	127,236	86,674	922.1
Furniture and related products	21,528	25,828	25,394	103	331	1,265	550	226	9,661	6,587	122.3
Miscellaneous manufacturing	144,235	79,946	71,627	7,514	805	3,706	2,799	4,528	30,469	20,968	319.4
Wholesale trade	**726,953**	**875,754**	**806,380**	**57,244**	**12,130**	**44,289**	**25,973**	**5,428**	**136,825**	**66,690**	**1,050.6**
Professional and commercial equip-ment and supplies	44,619	65,010	(D)	(D)	44	4,230	(D)	1,621	14,126	8,392	95.6
Petroleum and petroleum products	133,394	145,477	142,780	2,695	2	11,568	(D)	(D)	27,393	5,143	47.9
Drugs and druggists' sundries	53,874	172,962	(D)	(D)	0	2,230	656	(D)	8,402	3,912	84.0
Other	495,066	492,305	431,298	48,923	12,085	26,261	16,421	3,289	86,903	49,243	823.0
Information	**1,436,983**	**577,437**	**70,132**	**504,841**	**2,464**	**70,055**	**57,565**	**15,047**	**307,525**	**152,286**	**1,845.9**
Publishing industries	199,441	103,618	45,362	56,917	1,339	20,229	3,834	10,995	45,595	31,284	329.2
Motion picture and sound recording industries	39,382	14,934	6,426	8,508	0	105	509	(D)	3,797	2,768	50.7
Broadcasting and telecommunications	1,079,476	387,800	13,311	374,130	358	42,057	48,012	(D)	218,125	94,638	1,144.8
Broadcasting, cable networks and program distribution	309,387	118,805	11,809	106,929	66	17,236	5,106	(D)	50,571	19,363	266.5
Telecommunications	770,089	268,995	1,502	267,201	292	24,821	42,906	236	167,554	75,275	878.2

Table 15.1 (Continued)

	Millions of dollars										
	Total assets	Total	Sales Goods	Services	Investment income[1]	Net income	Capital expenditures	Research and development expenditures	Value added	Compensation of employees	Thousands of employees
Information services and data processing services	118,684	71,086	5,033	65,286	767	7,664	5,210	3,762	40,008	23,595	321.3
Finance (except depository institutions) and insurance.	**8,817,616**	**949,306**	**(D)**	**(D)**	**285,341**	**125,035**	**39,296**	**260**	**226,903**	**142,257**	**1,132.4**
Finance, except depository institutions	4,396,739	307,756	266	145,700	161,790	53,307	26,867	166	95,907	73,221	415.5
Securities, commodity contracts, and other											
intermediation	3,822,609	246,006	(D)	(D)	132,238	41,965	4,418	(D)	73,279	63,810	304.9
Other finance, except depository institutions	574,130	61,750	(D)	(D)	29,552	11,342	22,449	(D)	22,627	9,410	110.6
Insurance carriers and related activities	4,420,876	641,550	(D)	(D)	123,551	71,728	12,428	94	130,996	69,036	717.0
Professional, scientific, and technical services	**346,950**	**243,671**	**(D)**	**(D)**	**2,854**	**40,527**	**8,468**	**15,007**	**146,091**	**97,371**	**1,148.0**
Architectural, engineering, and related services	20,457	31,831	5,710	26,120	0	911	585	149	13,133	11,597	145.3
Computer systems design and related services	169,843	98,171	16,627	80,825	719	19,623	4,179	9,246	58,504	36,992	402.0
Management, scientific, and technical consulting	14,839	13,148	(D)	13,088	(D)	1,019	512	(D)	9,809	8,270	70.8
Advertising and related services	51,832	20,048	0	20,048	0	1,254	503	(D)	10,938	8,174	87.5
Other	89,980	80,473	992	(D)	(D)	17,720	2,688	5,537	53,708	32,338	442.3

Table 15.1 (Continued)

	Millions of dollars										
	Total assets	Total	Sales Goods	Services	Investment income[1]	Net income	Capital expenditures	Research and development expenditures	Value added	Compensation of employees	Thousands of employees
Other industries	**1,434,128**	**1,462,017**	**901,811**	**550,258**	**9,949**	**104,724**	**80,524**	**1,684**	**519,617**	**296,921**	**8,572.2**
Agriculture, forestry, fishing, and hunting	5,961	8,020	7,927	35	57	76	333	12	2,052	1,638	48.1
Construction	42,044	60,407	56,304	4,046	58	2,928	628	4	16,164	11,781	169.5
Retail trade	402,391	826,060	809,438	16,466	156	33,643	27,308	(D)	203,830	101,777	3,920.3
Transportation and warehousing	354,544	243,317	13,227	229,975	115	29,266	20,226	(D)	113,016	67,088	987.7
Real estate and rental and leasing	153,167	62,986	3,000	51,117	8,870	8,761	12,670	(D)	32,699	13,663	257.1
Real estate	62,440	16,841	(D)	8,520	(D)	4,828	3,204	0	9,084	4,049	44.3
Rental and leasing (except real estate)	90,727	46,145	(D)	42,597	(D)	3,933	9,466	(D)	23,615	9,615	212.8
Management of nonbank companies and enterprises	144,220	(D)	(*)	(D)	(D)	(D)	620	0	7,173	737	15.0
Administration, support, and waste management	111,007	96,560	(D)	(D)	220	5,951	4,810	(D)	54,410	41,940	1,210.0
Health care and social assistance	40,013	42,103	(D)	(D)	29	2,534	2,191	(D)	24,467	16,869	311.9
Accommodation and food services	95,321	71,155	(D)	(D)	436	8,271	6,196	(D)	40,629	25,886	1,200.2
Accommodation	44,794	19,602	(D)	(D)	1	2,238	3,043	0	11,090	6,379	263.7
Food services and drinking places	50,527	51,553	2,569	48,549	436	6,033	3,153	(D)	29,539	19,507	936.5
Miscellaneous services	85,459	(D)	(D)	45,361	(D)	(D)	5,542	248	25,175	15,540	452.3

* Less than $500,000 (+/–). , D Suppressed to avoid disclosure of data of individual companies.

1. Some parents and foreign affiliates primarily in finance and insurance include investment income in sales or gross operating revenues. Most other parents and affiliates consider investment income an incidental revenue source and include it in their income statements in an "other income" category rather than in sales. BEA collects data on investment income to ensure that—whe re it is included in total sales—it is not misclassi- fied as sales of services.

Table 15.2. Selected Statistics for Nonbank U.S. Parents by Industry of U.S. Parent, 2007

	Millions of dollars										
		Sales									
	Total assets	Total	Goods	Services	Investment income[1]	Net income	Capital expenditures	Research and development expenditures	Value added	Compensation of employees	Thousands of employees
All industries	**19,964,935**	**8,614,733**	**5,605,340**	**2,620,447**	**388,946**	**701,313**	**482,492**	**200,397**	**2,588,811**	**1,392,180**	**22,003.1**
Mining	**357,114**	**109,933**	**79,517**	**29,875**	**541**	**30,988**	**39,540**	**637**	**62,293**	**17,648**	**181.5**
Oil and gas extraction	216,314	54,958	52,562	(D)	(D)	19,870	27,567	14	32,544	4,043	32.4
Other	140,801	54,975	26,955	(D)	(D)	11,119	11,973	623	29,749	13,605	149.1
Utilities	**589,554**	**226,351**	**7,899**	**218,087**	**365**	**19,899**	**32,174**	**24**	**83,883**	**21,605**	**226.4**
Manufacturing	**5,239,985**	**3,904,730**	**3,667,896**	**166,065**	**70,769**	**337,040**	**173,447**	**157,231**	**1,064,666**	**569,987**	**7,292.2**
Food	343,007	340,951	(D)	(D)	(D)	25,144	8,480	1,852	75,080	40,002	665.9
Beverages and tobacco products	177,800	95,289	(D)	(D)	1,795	22,501	3,584	337	51,454	15,129	179.5
Textiles, apparel, and leather products	24,305	31,741	(D)	(D)	0	1,551	657	295	9,161	6,958	142.0
Wood products	34,018	25,694	24,968	(D)	(D)	1,158	1,024	114	6,387	4,030	62.4
Paper	111,755	78,375	77,761	599	15	8,202	3,886	1,406	30,422	16,838	207.2
Printing and related support activities	26,315	23,171	22,928	243	0	788	753	45	9,782	5,085	140.2
Petroleum and coal products	721,297	869,672	844,339	25,001	331	96,846	26,293	2,537	153,523	28,361	264.0
Chemicals	961,610	542,444	539,106	3,207	131	79,818	22,225	50,449	180,227	94,821	906.5
Basic chemicals	139,201	128,389	127,903	487	(*)	3,915	5,092	1,610	24,048	12,489	126.0
Resins and synthetic rubber, fibers and filaments	100,828	65,027	(D)	(D)	120	6,421	3,303	2,541	20,225	9,453	97.0
Pharmaceuticals and medicines	505,791	228,570	227,485	1,074	11	50,717	9,933	41,369	90,570	49,133	395.3
Soap, cleaning compounds, and toilet preparations .	130,140	58,185	(D)	(D)	0	13,126	1,741	2,780	25,859	11,785	147.7
Other	85,650	62,273	(D)	(D)	0	5,639	2,156	2,149	19,526	11,961	140.6
Plastics and rubber products	89,406	83,440	(D)	(D)	0	5,174	2,897	1,287	28,680	18,042	284.7
Nonmetallic mineral products	65,330	44,123	43,928	195	0	5,927	2,298	440	19,419	9,187	142.0
Primary and fabricated metals	187,746	178,382	174,472	3,794	116	13,449	6,054	1,016	52,851	31,483	480.8
Primary metals	124,113	118,931	117,377	1,438	116	9,618	4,618	447	32,471	16,802	244.8
Fabricated metal products	63,633	59,451	57,095	2,355	0	3,832	1,437	568	20,380	14,680	236.0
Machinery	263,211	197,929	188,932	5,823	3,174	20,523	6,924	6,360	60,136	37,007	549.5

Table 15.2 (Continued)

	Millions of dollars										
		Sales									
	Total assets	Total	Goods	Services	Investment income[1]	Net income	Capital expenditures	Research and development expenditures	Value added	Compensation of employees	Thousands of employees
Agriculture, construction, and mining machinery	137,708	83,581	78,558	(D)	(D)	8,332	3,723	2,429	19,968	12,847	160.9
Industrial machinery	42,627	35,979	34,257	1,722	0	6,969	1,290	2,153	15,310	7,244	109.2
Other	82,876	78,368	76,116	(D)	(D)	5,222	1,912	1,778	24,858	16,916	279.4
Computers and electronic products	603,914	343,401	316,439	26,946	16	42,680	18,751	39,852	118,353	70,138	858.9
Computers and peripheral equipment	131,069	92,002	(D)	(D)	0	11,396	3,446	8,066	19,967	13,185	179.2
Communications equipment	136,929	69,889	66,093	3,796	0	5,905	3,124	10,785	23,806	12,903	158.6
Audio and video equipment	(D)	8,111	(D)	(D)	0	–59	222	(D)	2,225	1,635	22.9
Semiconductors and other electronic components ...	208,193	99,580	(D)	(D)	(*)	16,472	10,486	15,213	44,121	23,282	242.1
Navigational, measuring, and other instruments	113,946	72,539	62,537	9,986	16	8,947	1,454	5,296	28,085	18,943	253.0
Magnetic and optical media	(D)	1,280	(D)	(D)	0	19	19	(D)	149	189	3.1
Electrical equipment, appliances, and components	107,288	102,591	95,641	6,950	0	7,236	2,743	2,925	29,843	19,785	298.3
Transportation equipment	1,375,798	858,046	712,630	81,532	63,884	778	63,819	43,698	204,360	150,315	1,751.1
Motor vehicles, bodies and trailers, and parts	697,700	482,497	447,930	16,104	18,463	–42,969	47,614	15,674	70,862	59,182	766.0
Other	678,098	375,549	264,700	65,428	45,421	43,747	16,205	28,024	133,498	91,133	985.1
Furniture and related products	20,561	24,623	24,191	110	322	1,187	559	233	9,050	6,390	116.7
Miscellaneous manufacturing	126,624	64,858	60,787	3,129	941	4,079	2,498	4,386	25,938	16,418	242.6
Wholesale trade	**840,823**	**951,837**	**869,026**	**72,841**	**9,970**	**42,990**	**28,217**	**5,686**	**137,904**	**73,223**	**1,074.3**
Professional and commercial equipment and supplies .	50,106	65,566	(D)	(D)	46	4,031	1,016	1,625	14,855	8,970	91.6
Petroleum and petroleum products	165,958	173,175	168,619	4,549	7	8,055	(D)	(D)	23,510	5,197	47.3
Drugs and druggists' 57,581 181,601 (D) sundries				(D)	0	3,431	(D)	(D)	9,948	4,717	82.3
Other	567,180	531,495	458,898	62,679	9,917	27,472	17,050	3,463	89,591	54,339	853.2
Information	**1,512,850**	**668,868**	**37,353**	**629,168**	**2,347**	**77,175**	**70,246**	**18,797**	**316,760**	**150,071**	**1,918.8**

Table 15.2 (Continued)

	Millions of dollars										
		Sales									
	Total assets	Total	Goods	Services	Investment income[1]	Net income	Capital expenditures	Research and development expenditures	Value added	Compensation of employees	Thousands of employees
Publishing industries	202,571	104,567	14,175	89,110	1,282	22,057	4,748	12,287	48,334	33,114	341.8
Motion picture and sound recording industries	47,754	16,016	4,788	11,228	0	272	411	(D)	5,119	2,899	52.9
Broadcasting and telecommunications	1,115,258	468,886	13,999	454,477	411	45,592	59,957	(D)	217,580	88,291	1,157.5
Broadcasting, cable networks, and program											
distribution	317,518	124,514	(D)	(D)	80	17,175	5,470	(D)	51,926	19,641	251.0
Telecommunications	797,741	344,373	(D)	(D)	331	28,417	54,487	1,254	165,653	68,650	906.5
Information services and data processing services	147,266	79,399	4,391	74,353	654	9,254	5,129	5,203	45,728	25,767	366.6
Finance (except depository institutions) and											
insurance	**9,496,868**	**987,882**	**5,581**	**687,187**	**295,115**	**60,955**	**40,882**	**237**	**229,235**	**146,537**	**1,129.1**
Finance, except depository institutions	4,587,803	330,428	(D)	178,837	(D)	277	27,945	(D)	95,340	74,841	393.2
Securities, commodity contracts, and other											
intermediation	4,000,843	264,830	3	134,115	130,712	–3,945	5,725	(D)	80,650	65,246	292.3
Other finance, except depository institutions	586,961	65,598	(D)	44,722	(D)	4,223	22,220	(D)	14,690	9,594	101.0
Insurance carriers and related activities	4,909,064	657,455	(D)	508,349	(D)	60,678	12,937	(D)	133,895	71,696	735.9
Professional, scientific, and technical services	**382,499**	**259,024**	**18,957**	**237,743**	**2,324**	**40,879**	**8,731**	**15,810**	**153,575**	**102,369**	**1,215.5**
Architectural, engineering, and related services	22,578	33,379	4,981	28,398	0	1,211	695	145	14,459	12,886	167.8
Computer systems design and related services	189,841	101,844	(D)	88,171	(D)	18,272	3,890	9,113	58,438	36,597	385.1
Management, scientific, and technical consulting	15,821	14,914	(D)	14,858	(D)	1,097	752	(D)	11,212	8,838	73.7
Advertising and related services	55,534	22,117	0	22,117	0	1,577	552	(D)	11,834	8,991	95.3

Table 15.2 (Continued)

	Millions of dollars										
		Sales									
	Total assets	Total	Goods	Services	Investment income[1]	Net income	Capital expenditures	Research and development expenditures	Value added	Compensation of employees	Thousands of employees
Other	98,725	86,770	1,629	84,199	942	18,722	2,843	6,468	57,633	35,057	493.6
Other industries	**1,545,241**	**1,506,109**	**919,112**	**579,481**	**7,516**	**91,385**	**89,256**	**1,975**	**540,493**	**310,740**	**8,965.3**
Agriculture, forestry, fishing, and hunting	6,924	9,257	9,180	38	40	129	276	5	2,446	2,015	64.1
Construction	37,237	50,263	45,916	4,316	31	–474	674	(D)	11,081	12,323	161.9
Retail trade	423,400	854,363	838,236	15,973	154	32,794	28,813	(D)	207,474	101,582	4,144.5
Transportation and warehousing	376,928	244,343	7,381	236,946	16	15,468	22,314	(D)	113,777	74,547	1,011.5
Real estate and rental and leasing	123,724	52,893	2,391	44,374	6,128	5,189	14,303	(D)	25,005	10,692	181.4
Real estate	67,223	22,055	(D)	15,844	(D)	5,156	4,754	0	10,676	4,742	39.9
Rental and leasing (except real estate)	56,501	30,838	(D)	28,530	(D)	33	9,549	(D)	14,329	5,950	141.5
Management of nonbank companies and enterprises ..	166,630	(D)	0	(D)	0	(D)	837	0	18,269	735	15.8
Administration, support, and waste management	144,833	112,674	8,762	103,284	628	5,594	5,441	(D)	61,775	44,951	1,245.6
Health care and social assistance	44,277	44,653	(D)	43,758	(D)	2,115	2,060	(D)	25,674	17,632	319.5
Accommodation and food services	104,436	72,893	2,878	69,530	486	5,901	7,220	(D)	41,849	27,050	1,279.7
Accommodation	47,413	19,220	(D)	19,181	(D)	1,267	3,784	0	12,071	6,724	279.0
Food services and drinking places	57,023	53,673	(D)	50,348	(D)	4,634	3,436	(D)	29,778	20,327	1,000.7
Miscellaneous services	116,852	(D)	(D)	(D)	(D)	(D)	7,317	269	33,145	19,213	541.3

* Less than $500,000 (+/–).

D Suppressed to avoid disclosure of data of individual companies.

1. Some parents and foreign affiliates primarily in finance and insurance include investment income in sales or gross operating revenues. Most other parents and affiliates consider investment income an incidental revenue source and include it in their income statements in an “other income” category rather than in sales. BEA collects data on investment income to ensure that—whe re it is included in total sales—it is not misclassified as sales of services.

Table 16. Selected Statistics for Nonbank Foreign Affiliates by Country of Affiliate, 2006 and 2007

	2006							2007						
	Millions of dollars							Millions of dollars						
	Total assets	Sales	Net income	U.S. exports of Goods shipped to affiliates	U.S. imports of Goods shipped by affiliates	Compensation of employees	Thousands of employees	Total assets	Sales	Net income	U.S. exports of Goods shipped to affiliates	U.S. imports of Goods shipped by affiliates	Compensation of employees	Thousands of employees
All countries	**12,118,593**	**4,793,319**	**727,625**	**237,553**	**307,165**	**436,050**	**11,149.9**	**14,201,291**	**5,517,143**	**846,753**	**257,660**	**331,934**	**475,595**	**11,737.5**
Canada	**861,894**	**511,932**	**51,776**	**74,541**	**(D)**	**50,584**	**1,104.0**	**1,008,970**	**557,756**	**49,556**	**77,484**	**(D)**	**54,519**	**1,115.2**
Europe	**7,563,029**	**2,434,327**	**398,904**	**58,154**	**69,121**	**254,930**	**4,637.3**	**8,969,832**	**2,837,736**	**480,600**	**67,991**	**81,442**	**276,261**	**4,800.9**
Austria	(D)	(D)	(D)	289	258	2,758	40.6	(D)	(D)	(D)	304	372	3,074	40.1
Belgium	266,319	105,987	14,358	3,426	(D)	10,197	133.9	303,890	123,823	18,899	3,770	4,438	11,341	140.6
Czech Republic	(D)	14,475	1,034	95	230	(D)	L	(D)	(D)	(D)	113	(D)	(D)	L
Denmark	51,045	29,008	4,973	204	(D)	4,600	66.4	(D)	(D)	(D)	204	318	(D)	L
Finland	(D)	(D)	(D)	435	420	1,399	22.9	(D)	13,396	1,050	406	297	1,515	23.8
France	286,132	200,668	9,200	(D)	5,270	33,002	665.4	346,286	228,351	13,257	(D)	6,974	35,380	654.3
Germany	522,267	325,004	17,596	7,804	6,758	46,114	665.2	612,612	357,227	18,891	8,670	(D)	49,194	672.7
Greece	(D)	(D)	(D)	55	3	(D)	L	(D)	(D)	(D)	114	4	(D)	L
Hungary	29,417	15,626	1,225	153	503	1,225	61.3	40,379	22,496	2,198	228	585	1,585	67.3
Ireland	427,640	185,666	46,902	3,493	18,887	5,292	92.3	563,466	224,470	68,701	4,897	21,732	6,438	94.9
Italy	168,123	137,109	9,620	(D)	(D)	14,140	274.6	205,239	155,362	10,812	(D)	2,985	14,817	280.6
Luxembourg	756,680	14,596	56,918	(D)	(D)	958	14.2	873,444	15,283	65,463	305	73	1,009	13.7
Netherlands	1,044,305	232,142	93,098	(D)	(D)	14,764	235.4	1,254,382	258,064	104,569	(D)	(D)	15,460	239.8
Norway	62,338	38,006	4,428	368	577	2,279	32.8	69,088	42,210	5,616	414	817	2,610	34.9
Poland	23,341	24,345	1,569	264	232	2,003	118.8	32,807	32,631	2,472	318	247	2,621	130.2
Portugal	(D)	(D)	(D)	157	124	(D)	K	42,844	14,009	3,483	169	180	(D)	K
Russia	(D)	(D)	(D)	251	2	1,270	77.3	(D)	(D)	(D)	(D)	3	(D)	M
Spain	173,618	95,424	8,161	989	764	10,528	215.6	203,007	109,528	10,345	1,190	1,127	11,579	215.5
Sweden	(D)	51,923	2,341	681	4,744	7,051	106.1	(D)	(D)	(D)	(D)	(D)	(D)	L
Switzerland	401,703	192,645	44,712	7,904	(D)	8,142	109.5	443,721	242,920	49,834	9,677	(D)	8,323	93.3

Table 16. (Continued)

	2006							2007						
	Millions of dollars							Millions of dollars						
	Total assets	**Sales**	**Net income**	**U.S. exports of Goods shipped to affiliates**	**U.S. imports of Goods shipped by affiliates**	**Compensation of employees**	**Thousands of employees**	**Total assets**	**Sales**	**Net income**	**U.S. exports of Goods shipped to affiliates**	**U.S. imports of Goods shipped by affiliates**	**Compensation of employees**	**Thousands of employees**
Turkey	10,721	21,298	1,153	(D)	(D)	1,175	44.3	16,045	26,727	–2,987	(D)	(D)	1,547	48.9
United Kingdom	2,960,005	621,258	59,436	14,366	(D)	81,657	1,367.4	3,497,971	672,000	60,572	14,740	15,858	86,241	1,344.4
Other	81,220	34,177	12,205	202	(D)	2,012	128.2	99,710	44,834	15,776	302	87	2,549	136.9
Latin America and Other Western Hemisphere	**1,670,620**	**558,111**	**132,717**	**49,791**	**65,036**	**38,738**	**2,225.9**	**1,881,001**	**627,995**	**161,979**	**54,828**	**68,163**	**42,668**	**2,360.6**
South America	281,846	220,772	21,427	8,233	(D)	18,596	839.4	367,320	253,638	24,106	9,581	6,347	21,010	884.1
Argentina	40,416	29,075	3,348	1,039	836	2,067	107.8	44,527	34,151	3,179	1,148	783	2,396	124.2
Brazil	124,258	113,035	5,955	4,170	(D)	10,814	465.9	178,215	134,087	11,018	4,548	(D)	12,782	490.5
Chile	31,150	18,415	1,905	480	(D)	1,532	79.8	35,367	20,241	2,012	715	(D)	1,633	76.1
Colombia	14,025	14,381	1,018	(D)	(D)	(D)	L	(D)	(D)	(D)	1,008	1,064	(D)	L
Ecuador	(D)	(D)	(D)	80	(D)	176	8.6	4,638	4,039	4	70	(D)	210	11.6
Peru	18,536	12,147	2,541	183	(D)	688	33.6	24,588	13,896	2,302	255	(D)	935	41.9
Venezuela	44,257	25,961	6,576	1,125	(D)	2,045	77.4	48,159	23,281	3,605	1,571	187	1,451	57.3
Other	(D)	(D)	(D)	(D)	(D)	(D)	J	(D)	(D)	(D)	266	(D)	(D)	J
Central America	233,339	206,223	16,383	39,997	50,269	17,759	1,284.3	264,396	228,929	17,706	43,373	55,340	19,101	1,372.5
Costa Rica	(D)	(D)	(D)	522	1,427	(D)	K	(D)	(D)	(D)	661	1,753	(D)	L
Honduras	(D)	(D)	(D)	(D)	663	(D)	K	2,180	3,791	135	(D)	722	(D)	L
Mexico	178,326	181,923	11,762	37,242	47,660	15,612	1,108.7	207,500	199,571	13,365	39,523	52,245	16,510	1,152.1
Panama	(D)	8,424	3,609	790	(D)	(D)	K	(D)	9,066	3,135	1,066	(D)	(D)	L
Other	5,529	7,532	341	(D)	(D)	415	49.4	7,456	(D)	(D)	(D)	(D)	579	64.8

Table 16. (Continued)

	2006							2007						
	Millions of dollars							Millions of dollars						
	Total assets	Sales	Net income	U.S. exports of Goods shipped to affiliates	U.S. imports of Goods shipped by affiliates	Compensation of employees	Thousands of employees	Total assets	Sales	Net income	U.S. exports of Goods shipped to affiliates	U.S. imports of Goods shipped by affiliates	Compensation of employees	Thousands of employees
Other Western Hemisphere	1,155,435	131,116	94,907	1,561	(D)	2,383	102.2	1,249,285	145,428	120,166	1,874	6,476	2,557	104.0
Barbados	(D)	(D)	(D)	109	(D)	74	1.7	(D)	(D)	(D)	117	(D)	75	1.8
Bermuda	623,897	67,954	54,094	178	13	(D)	J	710,043	75,755	66,458	225	(D)	(D)	K
Dominican Republic	4,687	(D)	(D)	(D)	(D)	(D)	K	6,144	(D)	(D)	(D)	(D)	(D)	K
United Kingdom Islands, Caribbean	363,382	26,741	22,982	164	(D)	302	8.2	349,924	28,954	29,725	197	(*)	312	7.0
Other	(D)	23,678	13,692	(D)	5,239	732	29.3	(D)	26,628	19,923	(D)	(D)	(D)	K
Africa	**139,376**	**84,351**	**19,162**	**1,558**	**(D)**	**4,298**	**188.6**	**164,115**	**97,627**	**22,380**	**1,379**	**(D)**	**5,058**	**206.3**
Egypt	13,398	8,544	1,507	(D)	(D)	368	35.0	16,377	10,395	1,827	22	(D)	404	35.5
Nigeria	(D)	16,513	4,258	8	(D)	(D)	I	(D)	17,917	4,213	5	(D)	(D)	I
South Africa	15,375	22,951	1,576	(D)	(D)	1,971	70.6	22,016	27,940	3,044	(D)	(D)	2,578	83.9
Other	(D)	36,343	11,822	756	2,304	(D)	L	(D)	41,376	13,296	(D)	2,367	(D)	L
Middle East	**126,092**	**79,606**	**17,233**	**969**	**2,581**	**4,654**	**99.8**	**144,942**	**93,966**	**22,005**	**1,166**	**3,102**	**5,532**	**109.6**
Israel	29,860	(D)	(D)	(D)	1,323	2,837	63.0	(D)	(D)	(D)	269	(D)	3,378	66.9
Saudi Arabia	19,558	20,578	5,444	97	(D)	727	15.0	23,237	26,368	7,193	177	(D)	898	16.8
United Arab Emirates	(D)	19,541	546	449	(D)	426	8.9	11,920	17,470	725	(D)	(D)	503	10.5
Other	(D)	(D)	(D)	(D)	(D)	664	12.9	(D)	(D)	(D)	(D)	(D)	752	15.5
Asia and Pacific	**1,757,581**	**1,124,993**	**107,832**	**52,540**	**62,473**	**82,845**	**2,894.2**	**2,032,431**	**1,302,063**	**110,233**	**54,812**	**67,676**	**91,557**	**3,144.8**
Australia	225,696	120,204	15,060	4,731	2,492	16,871	315.0	296,549	159,117	14,855	5,008	2,031	19,141	328.6
China	97,764	115,478	9,798	4,415	6,081	6,148	704.1	128,808	146,172	11,619	4,546	(D)	7,917	792.9

Table 16. (Continued)

	2006							2007						
	Millions of dollars							Millions of dollars						
	Total assets	Sales	Net income	U.S. exports of Goods shipped to affiliates	U.S. imports of Goods shipped by affiliates	Compensation of employees	Thousands of employees	Total assets	Sales	Net income	U.S. exports of Goods shipped to affiliates	U.S. imports of Goods shipped by affiliates	Compensation of employees	Thousands of employees
Hong Kong	197,749	84,446	10,355	5,179	(D)	4,703	124.2	219,394	94,392	10,225	4,905	(D)	5,220	125.0
India	31,834	24,330	1,805	618	(D)	2,982	242.5	50,635	34,839	2,647	626	(D)	4,333	334.8
Indonesia	44,400	23,747	6,122	385	(D)	1,320	105.1	58,764	27,352	7,195	351	(D)	1,649	107.1
Japan	621,842	296,176	15,386	12,328	7,556	31,694	594.1	653,755	299,492	12,645	12,438	6,680	31,739	612.9
Korea, Republic of	86,901	80,343	5,696	3,010	2,849	5,973	125.1	99,704	99,451	6,274	(D)	3,064	6,421	121.8
Malaysia	38,802	49,090	4,612	(D)	14,913	1,703	130.9	47,230	53,538	5,007	2,694	(D)	1,755	114.5
New Zealand	12,829	12,637	780	225	68	1,293	33.4	15,005	13,509	801	332	122	1,397	32.7
Philippines	23,207	15,635	1,573	1,400	954	915	106.7	23,863	16,501	1,532	1,444	1,044	1,084	127.3
Singapore	219,507	208,593	28,902	(D)	(D)	4,735	128.6	254,732	254,348	29,037	(D)	(D)	5,563	139.1
Taiwan	92,762	41,094	2,349	3,658	(D)	2,393	94.6	106,645	44,037	3,109	3,390	(D)	2,630	104.3
Thailand	45,221	42,887	3,559	1,139	3,718	1,416	146.8	51,193	46,268	3,424	1,550	5,288	1,675	147.2
Other	19,066	10,333	1,835	262	3	699	43.1	26,153	13,047	1,863	263	3	1,034	56.7
Addenda:														
European Union(25)[1]	6,960,874	2,124,256	334,875	49,289	63,593	241,040	4,294.7							
European Union(27)[2]								8,280,859	2,387,096	401,760	57,102	73,726	258,697	4,350.3
OPEC[3]	222,997	132,739	32,588	2,169	3,862	5,639	227.2	285,188	157,509	41,010	3,160	3,735	6,076	219.5

* Less than $500,000 (+/–). , D Suppressed to avoid disclosure of data of individual companies.

1. The European Union (25) comprises Austria, Belgium, Cyprus, the Czech Republic, Denmark, Estonia, Finland, France, Germany, Greece, Hungary, Ireland, Italy, Latvia, Lithuania, Luxembourg, Malta, the Netherlands, Poland, Portugal, Slovakia, Slovenia, Spain, Sweden, and the United Kingdom.
2. The European Union (27) is comprised of the European Union (25) and the 2 countries—Bulgaria and Romania— that joined the Union in January 2007.
3. OPEC is the Organization of Petroleum Exporting Countries. In 2006, its members were Algeria, Indonesia, Iran, Iraq, Kuwait, Libya, Nigeria, Qatar, Saudi Arabia, the United Arab Emirates, and Venezuela. In 2007, Angola became a member.

Note. The following ranges are given in employment cells that are suppressed: A—1 to 499; F—500 to 999; G—1,000 to 2,499; H—2,500 to 4,999; I—5,000 to 9,999; J—10,000 to 24,999; K—25,000 to 49,999; L—50,000 to 99,999; M— 100,000 or more.

Table 17.1. Selected Statistics for Majority-Owned Nonbank Foreign Affiliates by Country of Affiliate, 2006

	Millions of dollars												
	Total assets	Sales				Net income	Capital expenditures	Research and development expenditures	U.S.exports of goods shipped to MOFAs	U.S. imports of goods shipped by MOFAs	Value added	Compensation of employees	Thousands of employees
		Total	Goods	Services	Investment income[1]								
All countries	**11,301,182**	**4,169,002**	**3,339,030**	**683,599**	**146,373**	**667,349**	**155,078**	**29,583**	**229,246**	**285,631**	**1,001,206**	**390,969**	**9,617.4**
Canada	**842,480**	**492,917**	**407,916**	**70,099**	**14,902**	**50,135**	**27,508**	**2,439**	**73,035**	**97,387**	**108,051**	**49,252**	**1,086.2**
Europe	**7,175,067**	**2,177,263**	**1,724,605**	**372,177**	**80,481**	**376,482**	**63,663**	**19,326**	**56,583**	**68,152**	**546,313**	**234,466**	**4,143.4**
Austria	31,907	19,503	16,845	2,505	153	3,534	539	313	289	258	5,342	2,745	40.4
Belgium	249,021	99,566	86,618	8,403	4,545	13,165	1,855	961	3,423	2,785	21,584	9,403	125.8
Czech Republic	12,929	13,545	12,199	1,100	246	948	494	71	93	230	3,612	1,152	66.4
Denmark	33,549	15,051	11,327	3,532	192	4,386	513	148	204	316	6,168	2,913	39.4
Finland	18,495	13,729	11,762	1,830	137	595	246	113	435	420	3,239	1,384	22.7
France	265,056	186,865	152,747	31,577	2,541	7,662	4,335	1,518	4,443	5,106	50,136	31,031	601.8
Germany	470,235	283,043	244,318	35,458	3,267	14,648	7,776	4,947	7,759	6,611	82,932	42,625	606.1
Greece	9,294	6,941	5,962	843	136	363	127	41	55	3	2,977	734	16.6
Hungary	28,899	15,278	12,539	2,157	582	1,205	654	36	153	503	3,416	1,212	60.6
Ireland	426,558	185,243	142,556	37,976	4,711	46,887	3,637	1,074	3,489	18,887	46,821	5,243	91.5
Italy	131,310	112,939	95,082	16,951	906	5,262	2,758	702	2,354	2,392	30,187	12,758	241.3
Luxembourg	745,567	14,170	7,403	4,104	2,663	56,840	137	268	322	(D)	1,350	902	13.4
Netherlands	996,161	169,942	139,245	24,136	6,561	89,680	3,529	536	8,278	5,020	28,973	13,596	220.0
Norway	60,789	36,954	33,478	3,341	135	4,240	3,175	41	368	577	16,889	2,173	29.6
Poland	21,880	23,506	21,385	1,876	245	1,491	891	74	264	232	6,577	1,853	110.8
Portugal	35,519	10,602	8,883	1,596	123	2,297	388	23	157	124	4,194	1,133	29.1
Russia	14,887	18,529	16,821	1,687	21	1,258	1,224	82	251	2	4,101	1,174	72.5
Spain	143,971	81,257	69,917	10,603	737	6,674	2,857	278	989	760	17,275	9,675	194.2

Table 17.1 (Continued)

	Millions of dollars												
	Total assets	Sales				Net income	Capital expenditures	Research and development expenditures	U.S.exports of goods shipped to MOFAs	U.S. imports of goods shipped by MOFAs	Value added	Compensation of employees	Thousands of employees
		Total	Goods	Services	Investment income[1]								
Sweden	110,608	51,834	45,228	5,442	1,164	2,331	1,363	1,524	681	4,744	10,886	7,033	105.8
Switzerland	396,241	186,611	164,107	19,539	2,965	44,460	2,220	947	7,894	4,685	23,402	6,917	77.9
Turkey	8,315	18,803	18,030	747	26	962	229	36	180	89	5,779	1,063	40.0
United Kingdom	2,885,972	581,073	378,682	154,274	48,117	55,807	20,496	5,551	14,297	14,240	154,997	75,861	1,216.8
Other	77,906	32,278	29,470	2,499	309	11,787	4,219	41	202	(D)	15,476	1,883	120.8
Latin America and Other Western Hemisphere	**1,505,060**	**477,908**	**376,900**	**78,133**	**22,875**	**119,991**	**19,474**	**1,046**	**47,514**	**60,509**	**107,121**	**32,714**	**1,851.7**
South America	240,019	197,213	163,054	30,974	3,185	17,716	9,632	636	7,939	7,392	53,941	16,892	763.1
Argentina	37,143	27,278	23,131	3,918	229	2,944	1,973	31	1,038	836	9,823	1,980	103.8
Brazil	112,949	106,501	89,162	15,234	2,105	5,312	4,148	574	3,936	2,529	24,346	10,339	433.2
Chile	24,879	14,792	9,905	4,594	293	1,573	620	7	479	439	4,787	1,256	68.4
Colombia	13,488	14,147	12,761	1,294	92	991	680	7	919	(D)	3,848	1,051	49.7
Ecuador	3,137	3,023	2,654	322	47	177	189	(*)	80	(D)	686	150	7.2
Peru	14,731	10,446	9,080	1,322	44	2,331	1,249	3	183	1,346	4,280	594	30.5
Venezuela	29,282	16,973	12,870	3,841	262	4,218	613	12	1,087	888	5,478	1,330	58.9
Other	4,411	4,053	3,491	448	114	169	160	0	217	(D)	692	192	11.4
Central America	164,090	164,930	146,064	16,345	2,521	10,071	6,481	(D)	38,107	47,449	32,304	14,369	1,025.2
Costa Rica	6,557	4,421	4,221	200	0	554	158	8	522	1,427	1,272	569	36.8
Honduras	1,526	2,561	2,528	27	6	65	43	0	690	663	596	245	32.9

Table 17.1 (Continued)

	Millions of dollars												
	Total assets	Sales				Net income	Capital expenditures	Research and development expenditures	U.S.exports of goods shipped to MOFAs	U.S. imports of goods shipped by MOFAs	Value added	Compensation of employees	Thousands of employees
		Total	Goods	Services	Investment income[1]								
Mexico	144,714	147,867	131,272	14,130	2,465	8,904	5,980	(D)	35,392	44,924	28,273	12,925	900.4
Panama	6,550	3,478	2,614	826	38	267	123	(*)	790	(D)	599	283	17.6
Other	4,743	6,603	5,427	1,162	14	281	177	(*)	713	(D)	1,564	345	37.6
Other Western Hemisphere	1,100,950	115,765	67,782	30,814	17,169	92,204	3,362	(D)	1,468	5,668	20,876	1,454	63.4
Barbados	27,555	7,287	5,886	980	421	3,419	(D)	0	109	(D)	3,180	51	1.2
Bermuda	594,802	58,531	32,608	18,313	7,610	52,232	748	2	178	13	6,735	223	2.9
Dominican Republic.	3,669	4,133	3,481	651	1	568	48	(*)	262	265	1,254	399	35.4
United Kingdom Islands, Caribbean	346,572	25,702	12,741	5,330	7,631	22,833	384	(D)	163	(D)	3,436	298	7.8
Other	128,352	20,112	13,065	5,540	1,507	13,153	(D)	(D)	756	5,239	6,272	483	16.1
Africa	**131,550**	**79,115**	**69,862**	**9,064**	**189**	**18,154**	**11,172**	**67**	**1,444**	**3,088**	**42,332**	**3,994**	**160.6**
Egypt	11,099	6,846	6,231	606	9	1,114	736	4	22	(D)	2,857	281	21.2
Nigeria	27,974	16,377	(D)	(D)	(D)	3,840	(D)	2	5	(D)	13,513	425	7.3
South Africa	13,312	20,827	18,496	2,230	101	1,488	381	53	663	395	5,483	1,810	62.3
Other	79,166	35,066	(D)	(D)	(D)	11,711	(D)	7	755	2,304	20,479	1,478	69.7
Middle East	**71,692**	**32,493**	**26,268**	**5,904**	**321**	**6,775**	**3,838**	**840**	**847**	**2,187**	**13,176**	**3,140**	**69.2**
Israel	22,795	10,538	8,683	1,821	34	1,237	974	839	307	1,323	3,859	2,081	48.1
Saudi Arabia	6,717	2,233	1,384	841	8	1,630	20	(*)	4	(*)	361	206	4.3
United Arab Emirates	6,905	10,033	9,094	907	32	432	(D)	1	449	(D)	3,636	383	7.5

Table 17.1 (Continued)

	Millions of dollars												
		Sales											
	Total assets	Total	Goods	Services	Investment income[1]	Net income	Capital expenditures	Research and development expenditures	U.S.exports of goods shipped to MOFAs	U.S. imports of goods shipped by MOFAs	Value added	Compensation of employees	Thousands of employees
Other	35,275	9,687	7,107	2,335	245	3,476	(D)	0	87	(D)	5,320	469	9.3
Asia and Pacific	**1,575,332**	**909,307**	**733,480**	**148,221**	**27,606**	**95,812**	**29,423**	**5,864**	**49,824**	**54,307**	**184,213**	**67,403**	**2,306.3**
Australia	214,579	100,139	73,752	23,068	3,319	14,381	4,431	718	4,672	2,490	37,821	15,547	280.7
China	83,680	96,078	87,305	8,435	338	8,407	4,532	759	3,566	5,533	18,489	5,525	591.5
Hong Kong	193,899	83,267	63,074	14,685	5,508	10,386	574	108	5,173	7,928	10,232	4,527	116.9
India	25,720	20,702	15,996	4,255	451	1,534	1,051	337	594	564	5,483	2,655	215.8
Indonesia	38,691	19,438	17,827	1,329	282	5,669	1,594	11	382	212	11,836	1,153	90.2
Japan	545,410	187,985	121,510	54,915	11,560	11,460	5,427	1,862	11,604	1,459	38,328	20,672	280.6
Malaysia	34,646	43,269	41,052	2,027	190	4,049	2,208	252	2,846	14,909	7,911	1,641	127.9
Philippines	21,482	14,029	11,727	2,071	231	1,492	645	22	1,399	953	3,938	855	100.5
Singapore	211,170	198,640	188,189	9,332	1,119	27,347	1,408	845	11,747	12,056	17,446	4,461	116.0
Taiwan	84,562	38,510	24,561	11,666	2,283	2,252	1,184	123	3,639	1,748	5,849	2,239	85.9
Thailand	41,242	39,670	35,270	3,309	1,091	3,316	1,746	47	1,139	3,718	8,715	1,278	124.3
Other	17,649	9,015	4,728	4,169	118	1,717	2,171	1	262	3	4,345	672	38.0
Addenda:													
European Union(25)[2]	6,628,029	1,893,732	1,471,292	345,174	77,266	315,075	52,980	18,209	47,771	62,767	483,944	222,205	3,850.8
OPEC[3]	152,583	77,120	66,828	9,494	798	19,371	8,945	26	2,020	2,133	41,828	4,006	177.3

MOFAs Majority-owned foreign affiliates * Less than $500,000 (+/–).

D Suppressed to avoid disclosure of data of individual companies. OPEC Organization of Petroleum Exporting Countries

1. See footnote 1 to table 15.1.
2. See footnote 1 to table 16.
3. See footnote 3 to table 16.

Table 17.2. Selected Statistics for Majority-Owned Nonbank Foreign Affiliates by Country of Affiliate, 2007

	Millions of dollars												
	Total assets	Sales				Net income	Capital expenditures	Research and development expenditures	U.S. exports of goods shipped to MOFAs	U.S. imports of goods shipped by MOFAs	Value added	Compensation of employees	Thousands of employees
		Total	Goods	Services	Investment income[1]								
All countries	**13,180,221**	**4,736,009**	**3,802,171**	**763,484**	**170,354**	**765,240**	**169,074**	**35,019**	**247,642**	**312,405**	**1,117,585**	**425,535**	**10,016.6**
Canada	**964,240**	**537,033**	**443,652**	**76,253**	**17,128**	**48,525**	**25,497**	**2,729**	**75,236**	**101,107**	**116,180**	**53,242**	**1,099.2**
Europe	**8,466,519**	**2,488,777**	**1,977,462**	**416,823**	**94,492**	**441,220**	**73,504**	**23,142**	**66,164**	**80,530**	**610,921**	**252,916**	**4,184.5**
Austria	35,100	22,240	19,354	2,723	163	3,747	685	455	304	372	6,026	3,056	39.6
Belgium	288,904	117,545	100,842	10,962	5,741	14,964	2,472	1,197	3,769	4,438	23,682	10,301	127.4
Czech Republic	15,333	15,860	14,177	1,433	250	840	684	102	113	484	4,312	1,439	73.0
Denmark	36,900	16,604	12,551	3,875	178	3,990	762	151	204	318	6,038	3,020	37.8
Finland	21,389	13,190	11,139	1,911	140	1,041	474	169	406	297	3,137	1,500	23.6
France	323,954	214,413	175,057	36,223	3,133	12,071	4,936	1,698	5,244	6,793	56,196	33,459	616.1
Germany	552,104	313,905	269,432	40,248	4,225	15,905	11,533	5,970	8,658	7,658	86,649	45,530	610.6
Greece	10,679	8,152	7,004	995	153	430	169	35	114	4	3,533	848	16.6
Hungary	38,633	21,164	17,527	2,830	807	2,119	949	40	228	585	5,014	1,514	64.0
Ireland	559,308	222,482	178,071	37,278	7,133	68,270	4,449	1,513	4,890	21,732	53,842	6,273	92.9
Italy	147,913	127,723	106,853	19,622	1,248	5,182	2,907	668	2,557	2,945	32,508	13,096	243.1
Luxembourg	863,595	14,813	8,609	2,864	3,340	65,331	153	304	305	73	1,200	951	12.9
Netherlands	1,180,344	188,706	151,310	29,456	7,940	97,665	3,656	730	11,136	4,716	29,515	14,221	223.8
Norway	67,504	41,548	37,120	4,216	212	5,485	3,365	46	414	817	16,624	2,547	32.9
Poland	29,058	28,527	25,837	2,352	338	1,947	1,771	80	318	245	8,470	2,365	120.7
Portugal	41,044	11,711	9,457	2,122	132	3,217	399	81	169	180	4,463	1,180	29.2
Russia	20,337	28,118	25,658	2,422	38	2,794	1,603	100	472	3	6,965	1,626	85.9
Spain	177,482	95,281	81,932	12,139	1,210	8,855	2,462	475	1,190	1,123	19,611	10,790	197.1
Sweden	119,041	57,534	50,553	5,541	1,440	7,107	1,477	1,555	840	5,109	13,775	7,222	96.2
Switzerland	438,981	238,939	208,066	28,221	2,652	49,585	2,252	1,160	9,677	6,559	28,950	7,983	83.0
Turkey	11,576	22,319	21,228	1,013	78	1,441	449	54	159	177	7,041	1,302	41.2

Table 17.2 (Continued)

	Millions of dollars												
	Total assets	Sales				Net income	Capital expenditures	Research and development expenditures	U.S. exports of goods shipped to MOFAs	U.S. imports of goods shipped by MOFAs	Value added	Compensation of employees	Thousands of employees
		Total	Goods	Services	Investment income[1]								
United Kingdom	3,391,268	625,442	406,770	165,053	53,619	53,812	20,555	6,522	14,695	15,817	172,310	80,371	1,191.9
Other	96,073	42,562	38,914	3,325	323	15,421	5,340	36	302	86	21,058	2,322	125.0
Latin America and Other Western Hemisphere	**1,702,327**	**541,548**	**428,625**	**88,029**	**24,894**	**148,747**	**22,371**	**1,151**	**52,441**	**64,365**	**123,544**	**36,183**	**1,962.9**
South America	316,074	229,282	190,395	34,525	4,362	20,421	11,335	799	9,274	5,968	65,918	19,543	809.8
Argentina	40,038	31,492	27,286	3,864	342	2,695	2,297	64	1,147	783	10,815	2,174	113.5
Brazil	164,224	126,839	106,412	17,724	2,703	10,406	6,191	629	4,347	2,758	33,090	12,274	469.7
Chile	30,167	16,825	10,301	6,084	440	1,688	763	48	713	186	4,839	1,385	66.8
Colombia	15,029	16,166	14,384	1,603	179	1,325	707	16	1,008	1,063	5,127	1,243	56.6
Ecuador	3,096	3,264	2,891	320	53	–87	121	3	70	(D)	802	157	7.4
Peru	16,878	11,026	9,857	1,117	52	2,019	681	(D)	254	(D)	4,894	741	32.9
Venezuela	40,316	19,209	15,514	3,226	469	2,115	426	20	1,472	187	5,532	1,366	51.7
Other	6,325	4,461	3,750	589	122	260	148	(D)	263	(D)	819	203	11.4
Central America	193,326	183,758	162,033	18,795	2,930	11,634	7,766	342	41,380	52,211	35,744	15,266	1,091.9
Costa Rica	6,822	5,437	4,998	440	–1	594	115	(D)	661	1,753	1,332	577	42.5
Honduras	1,567	3,105	3,049	49	7	63	59	0	1,078	722	668	278	45.6
Mexico	170,372	163,511	144,425	16,214	2,872	10,214	7,338	316	37,574	49,163	31,327	13,697	940.2
Panama	8,618	4,032	2,999	995	38	436	109	1	1,066	(D)	712	319	20.2
Other	5,948	7,674	6,562	1,096	16	328	146	(D)	1,001	(D)	1,705	395	43.5
Other Western Hemisphere	1,192,927	128,508	76,197	34,710	17,601	116,693	3,270	10	1,788	6,186	21,882	1,374	61.1

Table 17.2 (Continued)

	Millions of dollars												
		Sales											
	Total assets	Total	Goods	Services	Investment income[1]	Net income	Capital expenditures	Research and development expenditures	U.S. exports of goods shipped to MOFAs	U.S. imports of goods shipped by MOFAs	Value added	Compensation of employees	Thousands of employees
Barbados	29,323	8,006	6,423	1,183	400	3,507	(D)	(*)	117	(D)	3,223	51	1.2
Bermuda	677,581	65,674	38,108	19,358	8,208	64,238	632	2	225	(D)	7,737	226	3.0
Dominican Republic	4,945	4,574	3,635	939	0	369	116	(*)	466	496	1,084	328	35.5
United Kingdom Islands, Caribbean	334,073	27,871	13,177	7,507	7,187	29,314	363	0	196	(*)	3,394	307	6.6
Other	147,005	22,382	14,854	5,722	1,806	19,266	(D)	8	784	5,522	6,444	462	14.7
Africa	**150,872**	**86,769**	**77,288**	**9,232**	**249**	**19,688**	**10,854**	**65**	**1,325**	**3,445**	**43,269**	**4,304**	**164.7**
Egypt	13,438	8,084	7,317	756	11	1,418	645	3	15	(D)	3,636	306	21.1
Nigeria	32,111	17,643	(D)	(D)	(D)	3,752	(D)	3	3	(D)	13,959	448	7.3
South Africa	16,241	21,436	18,821	2,501	114	1,379	520	53	625	(D)	5,581	2,001	64.6
Other	89,083	39,606	(D)	(D)	(D)	13,139	(D)	5	682	2,367	20,094	1,549	71.6
Middle East	**81,288**	**38,941**	**30,556**	**7,717**	**668**	**8,663**	**4,376**	**948**	**893**	**2,497**	**16,036**	**3,950**	**78.9**
Israel	26,438	13,138	10,724	2,384	30	1,337	1,155	946	265	(D)	4,697	2,645	53.9
Saudi Arabia	8,591	3,089	1,827	1,251	11	2,243	69	(*)	3	2	536	294	5.3
United Arab Emirates	7,301	10,692	9,521	1,133	38	502	156	2	566	(*)	4,437	458	8.9
Other	38,958	12,022	8,484	2,948	590	4,581	2,996	0	58	(D)	6,365	554	10.9
Asia and Pacific	**1,814,975**	**1,042,941**	**844,588**	**165,429**	**32,924**	**98,397**	**32,472**	**6,984**	**51,583**	**60,461**	**207,635**	**74,940**	**2,526.4**
Australia	282,479	130,264	97,079	28,446	4,739	14,142	5,606	1,083	4,929	2,028	44,088	17,689	295.9
China	106,798	117,748	105,872	11,445	431	10,122	4,805	1,141	3,463	7,041	22,429	6,882	679.2
Hong Kong	215,655	93,339	69,211	17,507	6,621	10,385	701	96	4,901	7,571	10,943	5,034	118.3

Table 17.2 (Continued)

	Millions of dollars												Thousands of employees
		Sales											
	Total assets	Total	Goods	Services	Investment income[1]	Net income	Capital expenditures	Research and development expenditures	U.S. exports of goods shipped to MOFAs	U.S. imports of goods shipped by MOFAs	Value added	Compensation of employees	
India	39,597	28,053	21,370	5,896	787	2,287	1,382	449	540	816	7,307	3,691	276.5
Indonesia	52,760	21,248	19,205	1,649	394	6,386	2,264	13	346	315	13,095	1,490	96.2
Japan	571,076	185,303	121,542	51,820	11,941	9,806	4,747	1,980	11,648	1,447	38,954	20,687	302.9
Korea, Republic of	59,315	54,806	45,675	8,020	1,111	3,924	2,013	995	2,386	2,935	12,442	5,384	104.1
Malaysia	42,901	47,167	44,427	2,472	268	4,144	2,163	396	2,687	17,104	8,149	1,686	111.4
New Zealand	12,061	11,443	8,869	2,269	305	529	198	53	331	122	2,813	1,204	28.5
Philippines	21,922	14,833	12,755	1,791	287	1,529	525	45	1,443	1,042	4,158	1,023	121.4
Singapore	244,296	243,168	229,423	11,865	1,880	27,282	2,552	578	13,728	12,629	20,917	5,270	126.7
Taiwan	95,996	40,688	25,729	12,164	2,795	2,803	955	98	3,370	2,119	6,958	2,385	88.8
Thailand	46,273	42,706	37,735	3,788	1,183	3,170	1,415	55	1,550	5,287	9,819	1,523	124.7
Other	23,845	12,175	5,697	6,298	180	1,889	3,146	3	263	3	5,565	993	52.0
Addenda:													
European Union(27)[2]	7,852,303	2,131,648	1,660,859	379,350	91,439	368,224	61,321	21,779	55,337	72,966	535,379	238,682	3,904.1
OPEC[3]	211,644	97,236	84,753	11,019	1,464	25,562	11,856	38	2,782	3,118	51,514	4,989	184.5

MOFAs Majority-owned foreign affiliates * Less than $500,000 (+/–).

D Suppressed to avoid disclosure of data of individual companies. OPEC Organization of Petroleum Exporting Countries

1 See footnote 1 to table 15.1.

2 See footnote 2 to table 16.

3See footnote 3 to table 16.

Table 18.1. Employment of Majority-Owned Nonbank Foreign Affiliates, Country by Industry of Affiliate, 2006
[Thousands of employees]

	All Industries	Mining	Utilities	Manufacturing								Wholesale trade	Information	Finance (except depository institutions) and insurance	Professional, scientific, and technical services	Other industries
				Total	Of Which:											
					Food	Chemicals	Primary and fabricated metals	Machinery	Computers and electronic products	Electrical equipment, appliances, and components	Transportation equipment					
All countries	**9,617.4**	**175.3**	**54.9**	**4,599.3**	**404.4**	**584.4**	**238.2**	**370.5**	**689.4**	**253.1**	**960.3**	**753.6**	**340.9**	**296.8**	**587.3**	**2,809.3**
Canada	**1,086.2**	**21.1**	**5.8**	**369.4**	**38.4**	**42.5**	**21.6**	**20.2**	**19.7**	**8.6**	**98.4**	**74.5**	**20.6**	**26.2**	**55.5**	**513.1**
Europe	**4,143.4**	**31.2**	**22.2**	**1,914.1**	**137.0**	**276.2**	**144.1**	**202.6**	**171.1**	**108.8**	**449.0**	**397.3**	**177.5**	**124.0**	**283.8**	**1,193.4**
Austria	40.4	(*)	0.1	22.6	1.7	1.9	0.5	3.0	2.4	0.5	7.2	7.7	1.7	0.4	3.0	4.8
Belgium	125.8	0.6	(*)	70.7	7.1	16.8	3.8	8.0	1.3	3.0	14.7	14.2	5.0	3.4	9.7	22.3
Czech Republic	66.4	0.4	(*)	53.6	0.6	2.2	2.5	4.0	8.4	5.0	24.2	3.8	1.0	1.2	2.1	4.3
Denmark	39.4	0.2	0.3	15.8	0.9	1.2	0.7	5.0	1.2	0.4	0.1	5.0	0.9	0.4	10.7	6.1
Finland	22.7	0.0	0.0	12.3	0.0	1.2	0.5	2.9	3.2	0.3	0.3	4.1	0.8	0.4	3.5	1.6
France	601.8	0.3	(*)	241.4	15.9	36.5	15.0	30.9	21.1	9.8	39.5	53.6	14.0	7.6	22.0	263.0
Germany	606.1	2.6	I	373.3	12.3	39.3	22.0	41.9	33.7	23.9	124.3	70.8	13.7	9.9	37.6	L
Greece	16.6	(*)	0.0	6.4	1.6	1.8	0.3	0.2	(*)	0.0	0.0	4.0	0.2	1.7	0.6	3.6
Hungary	60.6	(*)	0.2	44.4	1.8	0.7	4.0	2.1	5.5	J	13.0	2.4	4.1	0.4	4.3	5.0
Ireland	91.5	0.1	0.0	53.3	2.0	11.4	0.9	1.6	18.7	1.5	1.0	6.7	6.1	3.2	3.8	18.2
Italy	241.3	0.2	(*)	119.5	3.8	30.4	8.8	18.2	8.8	9.8	19.4	24.8	10.7	5.3	18.5	62.3
Luxembourg	13.4	(*)	0.0	7.4	0.0	0.8	0.6	0.1	0.0	0.0	(*)	0.1	1.7	1.7	0.7	1.7
Netherlands	220.0	4.6	0.0	108.0	18.1	28.3	8.7	10.3	7.4	3.1	8.4	28.2	9.8	5.0	15.9	48.4
Norway	29.6	2.9	(*)	9.0	0.9	0.8	0.7	2.5	0.6	(*)	0.2	3.9	0.5	0.7	1.6	11.0
Poland	110.8	0.0	0.1	82.8	17.1	4.0	5.4	1.8	3.2	4.8	28.7	6.3	1.7	1.1	4.9	13.9
Portugal	29.1	0.0	0.0	17.3	1.9	2.4	0.6	1.9	0.6	0.1	7.6	4.2	1.2	0.7	1.5	4.2
Russia	72.5	I	0.0	33.5	9.3	3.6	I	H	G	0.8	1.1	5.4	0.6	0.4	2.6	J
Spain	194.2	0.1	0.1	102.5	7.6	16.0	7.2	5.8	5.1	8.4	35.0	20.9	6.5	4.9	15.0	44.1

Table 18.1. (Continued)

	All Industries	Mining	Utilities	Manufacturing								Wholesale trade	Information	Finance (except depository institutions) and insurance	Professional, scientific, and technical services	Other industries
					Of Which:											
				Total	Food	Chemicals	Primary and fabricated metals	Machinery	Computers and electronic products	Electrical equipment, appliances, and components	Transportation equipment					
Sweden	105.8	0.0	0.0	55.3	G	4.9	2.5	4.8	H	0.7	28.8	9.3	2.5	1.6	5.8	31.2
Switzerland	77.9	F	0.0	25.7	1.7	7.8	0.8	3.1	3.9	1.7	0.7	28.0	3.7	1.8	6.0	J
Turkey	40.0	(*)	0.1	17.6	G	5.2	0.2	0.1	0.1	(*)	4.1	17.9	0.2	0.5	0.9	2.8
United Kingdom	1,216.8	7.6	5.4	360.7	24.6	54.3	25.1	46.2	36.6	17.5	71.6	70.4	88.3	70.7	109.8	503.8
Other	120.8	H	I	81.1	5.2	4.8	K	H	H	H	19.1	5.7	2.5	0.9	3.3	J
Latin America & Other Western Hemisphere	**1,851.7**	**57.0**	**19.3**	**1,065.3**	**135.5**	**115.0**	**33.0**	**53.9**	**105.1**	**62.3**	**283.9**	**70.2**	**53.5**	**29.2**	**37.3**	**519.9**
South America	763.1	39.4	15.4	398.1	68.1	70.2	14.0	30.1	14.9	17.1	89.0	42.0	30.9	14.8	22.0	200.6
Argentina	103.8	10.1	G	44.7	9.2	11.0	0.5	1.5	0.8	0.2	9.6	3.4	4.5	4.4	3.4	K
Brazil	433.2	2.5	I	281.7	43.8	40.9	11.4	24.9	13.6	16.2	68.1	20.7	17.9	5.5	14.8	L
Chile	68.4	3.2	3.3	11.0	G	4.0	0.3	F	0.2	(*)	0.4	3.8	4.2	1.6	1.4	40.0
Colombia	49.7	6.8	0.0	18.1	3.9	4.0	0.6	0.4	0.2	0.3	G	3.6	0.6	1.4	0.9	18.4
Ecuador	7.2	0.8	(*)	3.8	0.7	0.8	(*)	(*)	(*)	0.0	F	0.9	0.2	0.1	(*)	1.4
Peru	30.5	8.3	0.4	4.6	1.4	1.7	0.2	(*)	(*)	0.0	0.0	5.8	1.4	0.2	0.6	9.3
Venezuela	58.9	6.0	H	30.9	5.6	7.2	0.9	H	(*)	0.4	8.4	2.7	1.0	G	0.8	13.0
Other	11.4	1.8	0.4	3.4	G	0.5	0.1	0.0	0.1	0.0	(*)	1.1	1.1	A	0.1	H
Central America	1,025.2	13.7	1.9	627.1	65.7	41.7	18.5	23.6	90.2	45.2	194.8	26.3	18.5	12.0	14.9	310.8
Costa Rica	36.8	0.0	0.1	19.0	2.3	3.7	0.3	0.0	I	1.5	0.0	0.4	0.2	0.0	2.8	14.2
Honduras	32.9	0.0	0.0	25.2	2.3	0.4	0.1	(*)	0.0	0.0	H	0.2	(*)	0.1	(*)	7.4
Mexico	900.4	13.4	0.3	556.2	57.8	34.4	18.0	23.6	81.9	43.7	M	23.0	17.4	11.0	11.6	267.5
Panama	17.6	0.2	0.0	1.2	0.3	0.6	(*)	0.0	(*)	0.0	0.0	1.3	(*)	0.4	(*)	14.4
Other	37.6	0.1	1.5	25.6	3.0	2.7	0.1	(*)	H	(*)	0.1	1.4	0.8	0.5	0.5	7.3

Table 18.1. (Continued)

	All Industries	Mining	Utilities	Manufacturing								Wholesale trade	Information	Finance (except depository institutions) and insurance	Professional, scientific, and technical services	Other industries
				Total	*Of Which:*											
					Food	Chemicals	Primary and fabricated metals	Machinery	Computers and electronic products	Electrical equipment, appliances, and components	Transportation equipment					
Other Western Hemisphere	63.4	3.9	2.0	40.0	1.6	3.2	0.5	0.2	(*)	0.0	0.1	2.0	4.1	2.4	0.4	8.6
Barbados	1.2	0.1	0.0	0.2	(*)	0.1	(*)	(*)	(*)	0.0	0.1	0.1	(*)	(*)	0.2	0.5
Bermuda	2.9	0.1	(*)	0.3	0.0	0.1	(*)	0.2	(*)	0.0	0.0	0.6	(*)	1.2	0.1	0.6
Dominican Republic	35.4	0.0	0.4	33.3	G	2.0	0.1	0.0	0.0	0.0	0.0	0.5	0.4	0.0	(*)	0.9
United Kingdom Islands, Caribbean	7.8	2.2	A	3.1	0.1	(*)	(*)	0.0	(*)	0.0	0.0	0.1	0.4	0.6	0.1	G
Other	16.1	1.5	G	3.2	A	1.1	0.4	0.0	(*)	0.0	0.0	0.6	3.3	0.6	(*)	I
Africa	**160.6**	**20.0**	**H**	**82.4**	**9.0**	**8.4**	**2.4**	**3.8**	**0.4**	**2.4**	**21.0**	**14.3**	**3.2**	**2.9**	**3.5**	**K**
Egypt	21.2	1.2	0.0	15.2	3.4	1.3	0.4	G	(*)	0.3	0.0	1.3	0.1	0.4	0.1	2.9
Nigeria	7.3	5.6	0.1	0.6	0.0	0.3	(*)	0.1	(*)	0.0	0.0	0.3	(*)	0.0	(*)	0.6
South Africa	62.3	(*)	0.0	35.5	2.6	5.3	1.2	2.5	0.3	2.1	13.6	9.5	2.1	0.7	3.0	11.5
Other	69.7	13.3	H	31.0	3.1	1.4	0.8	A	(*)	0.0	7.4	3.2	0.9	1.8	0.3	J
Middle East	**69.2**	**6.8**	**0.2**	**35.3**	**G**	**2.9**	**0.1**	**5.2**	**18.1**	**0.6**	**(*)**	**3.2**	**3.6**	**1.4**	**8.3**	**10.4**
Israel	48.1	(*)	0.0	30.6	G	2.3	0.0	4.3	17.6	0.6	0.0	1.6	2.8	0.6	6.1	6.5
Saudi Arabia	4.3	1.6	(*)	0.6	0.0	0.2	0.0	0.2	0.2	0.0	(*)	0.4	0.1	0.1	0.4	0.9
United Arab Emirates	7.5	1.7	0.0	2.2	(*)	0.2	0.1	0.8	0.3	(*)	0.0	1.1	0.5	0.5	0.7	1.0
Other	9.3	3.5	0.1	1.9	0.0	0.1	(*)	(*)	0.0	0.0	0.0	0.1	0.2	0.4	1.0	2.1
Asia and Pacific	**2,306.3**	**39.3**	**H**	**1,132.9**	**L**	**139.4**	**37.1**	**84.7**	**374.9**	**70.4**	**108.1**	**194.1**	**82.6**	**113.1**	**198.9**	**M**
Australia	280.7	7.7	0.3	100.0	17.6	13.4	9.9	8.5	3.1	3.6	19.1	26.3	23.1	13.6	27.8	81.9
China	591.5	1.2	0.4	369.0	21.9	43.8	18.8	35.7	134.7	42.5	22.4	28.4	7.5	3.9	11.3	169.8
Hong Kong	116.9	(*)	F	51.0	0.2	1.9	1.2	2.0	6.2	6.7	(*)	18.5	3.9	9.7	8.8	J

Table 18.1. (Continued)

	All Industries	Mining	Utilities	Manufacturing								Wholesale trade	Information	Finance (except depository institutions) and insurance	Professional, scientific, and technical services	Other industries
				Total	Of Which:											
					Food	Chemicals	Primary and fabricated metals	Machinery	Computers and electronic products	Electrical equipment, appliances, and components	Transportation equipment					
India	215.8	1.1	(*)	68.4	2.9	10.3	1.8	16.5	9.0	1.8	12.3	22.6	24.3	7.2	70.8	21.4
Indonesia	90.2	22.0	0.5	57.7	I	7.4	0.0	0.4	0.7	G	1.1	2.1	0.4	2.6	0.6	4.3
Japan	280.6	(*)	0.0	76.4	0.7	27.0	1.1	4.2	21.9	2.4	6.0	38.1	9.9	42.1	36.6	77.4
Korea, Republic of	106.9	(*)	(*)	59.9	1.1	4.1	0.9	5.8	16.8	0.9	25.0	8.9	2.4	5.5	5.6	24.6
Malaysia	127.9	2.0	0.0	93.2	1.0	4.1	0.2	1.1	72.0	H	1.6	7.0	0.8	2.1	2.6	20.4
New Zealand	31.1	0.3	0.1	9.9	H	1.6	0.2	0.7	0.6	0.4	(*)	2.4	2.9	1.4	2.7	11.4
Philippines	100.5	(*)	1.7	59.1	10.7	5.5	0.1	0.4	28.5	4.2	I	3.5	0.6	3.4	16.4	15.6
Singapore	116.0	1.5	(*)	60.4	0.4	5.3	0.3	4.8	36.4	2.3	3.8	14.6	4.8	4.4	9.7	20.5
Taiwan	85.9	0.0	0.0	27.5	0.7	3.9	0.9	1.5	13.0	0.2	2.5	12.0	1.4	11.1	3.6	30.1
Thailand	124.3	2.1	(*)	89.2	14.8	8.2	1.5	3.1	32.0	0.9	7.5	7.1	0.4	5.1	2.3	18.3
Other	38.0	1.3	0.2	11.2	G	2.7	0.3	(*)	(*)	0.0	G	2.6	0.1	1.0	0.1	21.5
Addenda:																
European Union (25)[1]	3,850.8	16.8	15.4	1,784.5	119.3	256.0	125.1	191.0	161.8	106.2	429.8	339.0	170.6	120.2	271.4	1,132.8
OPEC[2]	177.3	40.5	3.9	92.1	11.6	15.3	1.0	4.0	1.2	1.6	9.6	6.8	2.3	4.4	3.4	23.8

* Fewer than 50 employees.

1. See footnote 1 to table 16.

2. See footnote 3 to table 16.

OPEC Organization of Petroleum Exporting Countries

Note. The following ranges are given in employment cells that are suppressed: A—1 to 499; F—500 to 999; G—1,000 to 2,499; H—2,500 to 4,999; I—5,000 to 9,999; J—10,000 to 24,999; K—25,000 to 49,999; L—50,000 to 99,999; M—100,000 or more.

Table 18.2. Employment of Majority-Owned Nonbank Foreign Affiliates, Country by Industry of Affiliate, 2007 [Thousands of employees]

				Manufacturing												
					Of which:											
	All industries	Mining	Utilities	Total	Food	Chemicals	Primary and fabricated metals	Machinery	Computers and electronic products	Electrical equip-ment, appliances, and components	Transpor- tation equipment	Wholesale trade	Information	Finance (except depository institutions) and insurance	Professional, scientific, and technical services	Other industries
All countries	**10,016.6**	**186.9**	**45.3**	**4,682.8**	**428.8**	**615.3**	**229.7**	**396.3**	**695.9**	**243.9**	**973.0**	**775.5**	**354.5**	**318.1**	**621.8**	**3,031.6**
Canada	**1,099.2**	**22.1**	**4.7**	**361.4**	**36.7**	**41.5**	**27.1**	**19.7**	**18.4**	**8.4**	**96.1**	**80.7**	**21.9**	**29.0**	**57.4**	**522.0**
Europe	**4,184.5**	**35.2**	**20.8**	**1,906.5**	**135.8**	**284.5**	**137.2**	**218.2**	**177.3**	**97.2**	**446.6**	**398.9**	**173.2**	**130.9**	**278.6**	**1,240.3**
Austria	39.6	(*)	0.0	22.9	1.6	2.5	0.6	3.2	2.6	0.7	6.4	6.9	1.7	0.4	2.9	4.7
Belgium	127.4	0.6	(*)	69.2	7.1	17.3	3.6	8.4	1.0	2.4	13.9	15.0	5.3	3.4	9.5	24.4
Czech Republic	73.0	0.0	0.1	57.1	0.5	3.1	2.4	4.0	9.3	4.5	25.7	3.6	0.9	G	2.9	I
Denmark	37.8	0.2	0.3	16.5	1.3	1.3	0.7	5.3	1.3	0.4	0.1	5.2	0.8	0.3	10.0	4.5
Finland	23.6	0.0	0.0	12.4	0.0	1.2	0.2	3.0	3.1	0.3	0.3	3.8	0.9	0.4	3.4	2.7
France	616.1	0.3	(*)	225.6	15.3	36.5	15.5	31.5	22.7	9.5	36.5	57.1	10.8	7.8	24.3	290.1
Germany	610.6	3.0	I	372.3	12.5	42.9	19.0	49.0	34.2	21.3	120.5	70.6	13.8	9.8	37.7	L
Greece	16.6	(*)	0.0	6.2	1.5	1.9	0.3	0.2	(*)	0.0	0.0	4.1	0.2	1.9	0.7	3.5
Hungary	64.0	(*)	0.2	45.5	1.2	1.2	4.0	2.3	6.5	J	14.0	2.3	5.5	0.4	5.3	4.8
Ireland	92.9	0.1	0.0	54.9	1.7	14.6	0.9	1.6	19.0	0.9	0.5	7.0	5.6	2.7	5.9	16.6
Italy	243.1	0.2	0.2	117.0	3.6	28.6	6.5	20.2	8.8	8.7	18.8	24.3	11.4	4.3	17.6	67.9
Luxembourg	12.9	(*)	0.0	6.8	0.0	0.8	0.2	0.1	0.0	0.0	(*)	0.1	1.7	1.7	0.8	1.8
Netherlands	223.8	4.9	0.0	108.9	17.8	27.1	8.8	10.0	7.8	2.7	10.4	24.9	10.9	5.6	15.4	53.2
Norway	32.9	3.5	(*)	9.7	(*)	0.8	G	2.4	0.8	(*)	0.2	3.3	0.8	0.9	1.8	12.9
Poland	120.7	0.0	0.1	90.2	17.2	4.2	5.5	2.1	3.5	4.8	32.9	10.0	1.2	1.4	4.1	13.8
Portugal	29.2	0.0	0.0	17.1	1.9	2.4	0.6	1.1	1.3	0.1	7.5	3.4	1.4	0.6	1.4	5.3
Russia	85.9	5.4	0.0	43.2	12.6	4.5	I	I	G	0.3	1.3	5.1	0.6	0.4	2.9	28.3

Table 18.2 (Continued)

	All industries	Mining	Utilities	Manufacturing								Wholesale trade	Information	Finance (except depository institutions) and insurance	Professional, scientific, and technical services	Other industries
				Total	*Of which:*											
					Food	Chemicals	Primary and fabricated metals	Machinery	Computers and electronic products	Electrical equip-ment, appliances, and components	Transpor- tation equipment					
Spain	197.1	0.1	0.1	100.8	8.2	17.5	7.1	6.2	5.1	6.0	32.9	20.3	6.4	5.2	14.4	49.8
Sweden	96.2	0.0	0.0	54.5	1.4	4.5	2.5	5.5	3.8	0.6	27.6	9.1	2.4	1.6	5.7	22.9
Switzerland	83.0	G	0.0	29.1	1.6	8.4	0.8	3.0	5.0	2.0	0.7	28.8	3.9	2.0	6.4	J
Turkey	41.2	(*)	0.1	18.8	2.1	5.4	0.2	0.1	0.2	(*)	4.1	17.3	0.3	0.7	0.5	3.3
United Kingdom	1,191.9	10.4	5.2	346.2	21.8	51.8	24.6	48.7	34.9	16.3	69.5	70.0	82.8	75.8	101.0	500.6
Other	125.0	I	I	81.5	4.8	6.1	22.8	H	I	H	22.8	6.5	4.0	G	4.1	J
Latin America and Other Western Hemisphere	**1,962.9**	**51.1**	**13.0**	**1,108.3**	**151.1**	**121.7**	**25.9**	**55.8**	**111.3**	**61.4**	**290.2**	**74.9**	**59.0**	**31.5**	**45.1**	**580.0**
South America	809.8	33.1	10.8	419.5	83.4	74.5	12.3	31.3	16.6	16.2	90.7	45.2	34.1	16.7	27.5	222.8
Argentina	113.5	5.3	G	48.4	10.3	11.8	0.4	1.6	0.7	0.2	10.9	3.8	5.2	5.8	4.3	K
Brazil	469.7	2.9	I	294.3	54.2	41.7	10.7	25.9	15.4	15.3	69.0	22.8	18.6	5.4	18.8	M
Chile	66.8	3.3	3.1	11.2	G	4.5	0.1	1.0	0.2	(*)	0.6	4.0	4.8	1.5	2.1	36.7
Colombia	56.6	6.0	0.0	19.2	3.9	5.4	0.6	A	0.2	0.3	G	3.7	1.4	1.5	0.9	23.8
Ecuador	7.4	0.7	(*)	3.9	0.7	0.8	(*)	(*)	(*)	0.0	G	0.9	0.2	0.1	(*)	1.4
Peru	32.9	8.6	0.2	5.3	1.4	1.9	0.2	(*)	(*)	0.0	0.0	6.0	1.7	0.3	0.5	10.3
Venezuela	51.7	4.6	0.0	33.5	9.3	7.9	0.2	G	(*)	0.5	7.2	2.9	1.2	1.5	0.7	7.2
Other	11.4	1.7	(*)	3.6	G	0.5	0.1	0.0	0.1	0.0	(*)	1.1	1.1	0.5	0.2	3.3
Central America	1,091.9	14.3	1.7	649.3	66.1	43.5	12.9	24.3	94.6	45.2	199.4	27.5	20.3	12.0	17.0	349.7
Costa Rica	42.5	0.0	0.1	22.2	2.3	3.7	0.1	0.0	I	1.3	0.0	0.4	0.2	0.0	H	J

Table 18.2 (Continued)

				Manufacturing											
					Of which:										
	All industries	Mining	Utilities	Total	Food	Chemicals	Primary and fabricated metals	Machinery	Computers and electronic products	Electrical equip-ment, appliances, and components	Transpor- tation equipment	Wholesale trade	Information	Finance (except depository institutions) and insurance	Professional, scientific, and technical services	Other industries
Honduras	45.6	0.0	0.0	36.4	2.4	0.4	0.0	(*)	0.0	0.0	I	0.6	(*)	0.1	(*)	8.4
Mexico	940.2	14.1	0.2	558.5	57.1	36.1	12.8	24.2	86.3	43.8	194.2	23.5	19.2	11.1	12.8	300.8
Panama	20.2	0.2	0.0	1.2	0.3	0.6	(*)	0.0	(*)	0.0	0.0	1.5	(*)	0.4	(*)	16.9
Other	43.5	0.1	1.4	31.0	3.9	2.8	0.1	(*)	H	(*)	A	1.4	0.8	0.5	A	I
Other Western Hemisphere	61.1	3.6	0.4	39.5	1.6	3.6	0.7	0.2	(*)	0.0	0.1	2.2	4.7	2.8	0.5	7.5
Barbados	1.2	0.1	0.0	0.2	(*)	0.1	(*)	(*)	(*)	0.0	0.1	0.2	(*)	(*)	0.2	0.5
Bermuda	3.0	0.1	(*)	0.3	0.0	0.1	(*)	0.2	(*)	0.0	0.0	0.6	(*)	1.5	0.1	0.4
Dominican Republic	35.5	0.0	0.3	32.9	G	1.9	0.1	0.0	0.0	0.0	0.0	0.5	0.9	0.0	(*)	1.0
United Kingdom Islands, Caribbean	6.6	1.9	0.1	2.4	0.1	(*)	(*)	0.0	(*)	0.0	0.0	0.1	0.4	0.6	0.2	1.0
Other	14.7	1.5	0.0	3.8	A	1.5	0.6	0.0	(*)	0.0	0.0	0.8	3.4	0.6	0.1	4.6
Africa	**164.7**	**21.5**	**H**	**80.7**	**8.9**	**7.9**	**2.0**	**3.9**	**0.5**	**2.3**	**21.2**	**13.0**	**2.8**	**2.9**	**4.7**	**K**
Egypt	21.1	1.4	0.0	14.0	3.6	1.1	0.4	G	(*)	0.3	0.0	1.4	0.1	0.3	0.5	3.3
Nigeria	7.3	5.3	(*)	0.9	0.0	0.7	(*)	0.1	(*)	0.0	0.0	0.3	(*)	0.0	(*)	0.7
South Africa	64.6	(*)	0.0	35.8	2.9	4.5	1.2	2.6	0.4	2.0	13.3	8.1	1.8	0.8	3.9	14.2
Other	71.6	14.7	H	30.0	2.5	1.6	0.5	A	(*)	0.0	7.9	3.2	0.9	1.8	0.3	J
Middle East	**78.9**	**7.1**	**0.2**	**37.0**	**G**	**3.1**	**0.4**	**5.6**	**17.7**	**0.6**	**G**	**4.2**	**4.3**	**1.6**	**10.2**	**14.3**
Israel	53.9	(*)	0.0	32.1	G	2.5	0.3	4.6	17.4	0.6	G	2.1	3.1	0.6	7.0	8.9
Saudi Arabia	5.3	1.8	(*)	0.7	0.0	0.2	0.0	0.2	0.2	0.0	(*)	0.4	0.1	0.1	G	F
United Arab Emirates	8.9	G	0.0	2.3	0.2	0.3	0.1	0.8	(*)	(*)	0.0	1.6	0.8	0.5	1.1	G

Table 18.2 (Continued)

				Manufacturing											
				Of which:											
	All industries	**Mining**	**Utilities**	**Total**	**Food**	**Chemicals**	**Primary and fabricated metals**	**Machinery**	**Computers and electronic products**	**Electrical equip-ment, appliances, and components**	**Transpor- tation equipment**	**Wholesale trade**	**Information**	**Finance (except depository institutions) and insurance**	**Professional, scientific, and technical services**	**Other industries**
Other	10.9	H	0.1	2.0	0.0	0.1	(*)	(*)	0.0	0.0	0.0	0.1	0.2	0.4	G	H
Asia and Pacific	**2,526.4**	**49.9**	**H**	**1,188.9**	**L**	**156.6**	**37.2**	**93.2**	**370.6**	**73.9**	**M**	**203.7**	**93.2**	**122.2**	**225.8**	**M**
Australia	295.9	12.0	0.3	101.3	19.7	13.1	9.9	8.4	3.2	3.5	16.7	25.9	23.5	14.9	29.3	88.8
China	679.2	1.4	0.5	402.8	24.5	47.5	19.9	40.5	140.3	42.1	27.5	38.0	9.4	H	11.8	M
Hong Kong	118.3	(*)	F	48.3	0.2	2.0	0.7	2.0	4.4	6.1	(*)	16.6	4.0	10.0	9.1	K
India	276.5	1.2	(*)	92.9	5.1	20.8	G	18.4	11.4	3.3	J	27.5	29.0	8.1	91.8	25.9
Indonesia	96.2	27.4	0.6	54.9	H	7.4	0.0	0.4	0.7	G	1.1	2.0	0.4	H	0.6	I
Japan	302.9	(*)	0.0	79.2	0.6	26.8	1.5	5.1	24.2	2.5	6.3	34.1	13.7	44.8	36.7	94.4
Korea, Republic of	104.1	(*)	(*)	59.8	1.1	4.7	1.4	5.9	16.5	0.9	24.6	8.7	2.3	5.6	5.6	22.1
Malaysia	111.4	2.0	0.0	81.4	0.9	5.1	0.1	1.5	59.2	H	1.3	7.2	0.8	2.4	3.2	14.4
New Zealand	28.5	0.3	0.1	8.8	G	1.4	0.2	0.7	0.7	0.5	0.4	2.1	G	1.4	2.9	J
Philippines	121.4	(*)	F	70.2	J	5.5	0.1	0.4	26.2	I	I	3.3	0.6	G	18.9	24.9
Singapore	126.7	1.6	(*)	63.3	0.4	6.6	0.3	5.3	36.7	2.3	4.6	15.8	5.0	6.0	9.6	25.5
Taiwan	88.8	0.0	0.0	27.2	0.6	4.0	1.0	1.6	12.8	0.2	2.6	12.3	1.9	12.7	3.6	31.1
Thailand	124.7	2.3	(*)	84.8	12.7	8.8	0.9	3.1	33.9	0.9	7.9	7.5	0.4	5.3	1.7	22.7
Other	52.0	1.6	0.2	14.0	G	2.9	A	(*)	0.3	0.0	0.6	2.6	A	1.0	1.1	K
Addenda:																
European Union (27)[1]	3,904.1	19.9	15.4	1,790.5	118.0	263.8	119.6	205.6	169.9	94.8	439.9	341.5	167.6	126.6	266.7	1,175.9
OPEC[2]	184.5	50.3	0.7	92.5	14.3	16.5	0.3	4.0	1.0	1.6	8.3	7.5	2.8	4.9	4.4	21.4

* Fewer than 50 employees. 1. See footnote 2 to table 16. 2. See footnote 3 to table 16.

OPEC Organization of Petroleum Exporting Countries

Note. The following ranges are given in employment cells that are suppressed: A—1 to 499; F—500 to 999; G—1,000 to 2,499; H—2,500 to 4,999; I—5,000 to 9,999; J—10,000 to 24,999; K—25,000 to 49,999; L—50,000 to 99,999; M—100,000 or more.

Table 19.1. Value Added of Majority-Owned Nonbank Foreign Affiliates, Country by Industry of Affiliate, 2006 [Millions of dollars]

			Manufacturing												
				Of which:											
	All industries	Mining	Utilities	Total	Food	Chemicals	Primary and fabricated metals	Machinery	Computers and electronic products	Electrical equipment, appliances, and components	Transportation equipment	Wholesale trade	Information	Finance(except depository institutions) and insurance	Professional, scientific, and technical services	Other industries
All countries	**1,001,206**	**140,985**	**11,788**	**455,675**	**28,519**	**86,816**	**18,581**	**28,180**	**48,008**	**12,505**	**62,539**	**139,494**	**40,565**	**34,671**	**57,154**	**120,874**
Canada	**108,051**	**17,033**	**653**	**50,923**	**3,773**	**5,933**	**2,243**	**1,893**	**1,333**	**715**	**12,476**	**9,383**	**2,157**	**1,293**	**4,748**	**21,859**
Europe	**546,313**	**40,391**	**4,121**	**273,959**	**15,244**	**53,567**	**11,354**	**19,329**	**21,754**	**8,026**	**33,557**	**87,026**	**27,255**	**11,429**	**34,137**	**67,996**
Austria	5,342	2	27	2,692	341	242	44	348	312	44	788	1,522	286	72	391	350
Belgium	21,584	16	(*)	12,535	834	4,339	285	711	109	331	1,455	3,971	525	200	1,161	3,177
Czech Republic	3,612	6	2	2,527	16	188	73	133	133	96	809	354	90	–21	117	536
Denmark	6,168	1,633	41	1,605	92	131	80	420	155	42	11	866	141	52	1,376	454
Finland	3,239	0	0	1,338	0	267	95	336	165	42	18	1,145	115	(*)	427	213
France	50,136	44	(*)	27,130	1,419	4,976	1,451	3,296	2,111	886	2,934	7,242	1,667	1,369	2,644	10,041
Germany	82,932	1,561	(D)	54,888	1,985	6,135	2,221	4,459	4,348	2,605	11,055	10,573	2,194	666	4,158	(D)
Greece	2,977	2	0	2,161	107	362	–35	15	6	0	0	541	21	117	46	88
Hungary	3,416	2	76	1,970	115	75	205	93	272	(D)	325	345	282	28	297	417
Ireland	46,821	157	0	27,046	359	11,622	45	141	8,090	255	52	4,612	4,334	490	1,097	9,085
Italy	30,187	26	31	19,291	620	3,634	844	1,815	842	673	1,002	4,655	1,102	431	2,054	2,596
Luxembourg	1,350	1	(*)	773	0	163	43	6	0	0	(*)	328	202	–145	61	130
Netherlands	28,973	935	3	16,792	2,460	4,921	575	968	984	288	1,569	4,361	1,516	–115	2,233	3,248
Norway	16,889	12,410	1	2,456	129	123	110	255	86	3	23	652	100	80	205	985
Poland	6,577	0	1	4,984	531	354	196	93	123	98	920	599	148	317	257	271
Portugal	4,194	(*)	0	2,768	109	232	17	135	26	4	253	694	132	21	232	348
Russia	4,101	(D)	(*)	2,402	603	495	(D)	(D)	(D)	9	47	648	26	23	168	(D)
Spain	17,275	24	–43	10,364	665	2,789	1,179	664	255	545	2,716	2,856	509	219	1,406	1,939

Table 19.1 (Continued)

				Manufacturing												
					Of which:											
	All industries	**Mining**	**Utilities**	**Total**	**Food**	**Chemicals**	**Primary and fabricated metals**	**Machinery**	**Computers and electronic products**	**Electrical equipment, appliances, and components**	**Transportation equipment**	**Wholesale trade**	**Information**	**Finance(except depository institutions) and insurance**	**Professional, scientific, and technical services**	**Other industries**
Sweden	10,886	0	0	6,053	(D)	589	271	440	(D)	56	3,176	2,233	238	94	918	1,350
Switzerland	23,402	(D)	0	6,523	224	2,725	72	768	640	394	120	12,739	842	319	1,101	(D)
Turkey	5,779	(*)	38	4,352	(D)	482	19	3	3	1	186	1,206	39	28	37	79
United Kingdom	154,997	13,732	2,250	59,213	4,032	8,349	2,119	3,967	2,754	1,335	5,787	23,634	12,663	6,880	13,643	22,982
Other	15,476	(D)	(D)	4,095	203	372	(D)	(D)	(D)	(D)	311	1,250	82	305	107	(D)
Latin America and Other Western Hemisphere	**107,121**	**18,862**	**4,493**	**47,730**	**5,754**	**10,519**	**1,592**	**2,213**	**2,484**	**1,494**	**9,771**	**13,837**	**3,332**	**4,245**	**2,554**	**12,068**
South America	53,941	12,378	3,741	26,130	3,076	6,315	985	1,325	665	738	4,650	4,963	1,785	408	1,647	2,890
Argentina	9,823	3,973	(D)	4,238	815	981	57	80	28	9	393	336	255	152	118	(D)
Brazil	24,346	191	(D)	16,466	1,665	3,844	836	1,125	629	695	3,507	2,283	973	259	1,120	(D)
Chile	4,787	1,694	832	749	(D)	274	18	(D)	3	(*)	23	754	316	–38	84	397
Colombia	3,848	1,182	0	1,347	169	359	6	14	3	4	(D)	653	13	57	37	558
Ecuador	686	267	11	262	23	50	–3	1	1	0	(D)	116	3	–11	4	35
Peru	4,280	3,343	86	288	35	118	22	3	1	0	0	375	76	22	34	57
Venezuela	5,478	1,489	(D)	2,585	229	662	50	(D)	1	30	473	260	63	(D)	248	311
Other	692	239	24	194	(D)	28	–1	(*)	2	0	3	186	86	(D)	3	(D)
Central America	32,304	2,010	354	19,124	2,594	3,782	491	785	1,502	756	5,118	2,283	1,281	629	686	5,938
Costa Rica	1,272	(*)	–8	1,052	42	195	30	0	(D)	77	0	7	10	0	58	154
Honduras	596	0	0	265	34	12	4	(*)	0	0	(D)	67	(*)	3	(*)	262
Mexico	28,273	1,989	122	17,213	2,412	3,469	457	784	1,240	678	(D)	1,761	1,250	603	613	4,722

Table 19.1 (Contrinued)

				Manufacturing												
					Of which:											
	All industries	**Mining**	**Utilities**	**Total**	**Food**	**Chemicals**	**Primary and fabricated metals**	**Machinery**	**Computers and electronic products**	**Electrical equipment, appliances, and components**	**Transportation equipment**	**Wholesale trade**	**Information**	**Finance(except depository institutions) and insurance**	**Professional, scientific, and technical services**	**Other industries**
Panama	599	13	2	43	3	36	(*)	0	(*)	0	0	80	4	7	7	443
Other	1,564	7	238	551	103	70	1	1	(D)	1	(*)	370	17	17	8	357
Other Western Hemisphere	20,876	4,475	398	2,476	83	422	116	103	317	0	3	6,590	267	3,208	221	3,240
Barbados	3,180	(*)	0	140	14	3	(*)	(*)	120	0	3	2,295	8	259	3	475
Bermuda	6,735	344	(*)	306	0	21	(*)	102	185	0	0	2,402	62	1,388	199	2,035
Dominican Republic	1,254	0	119	1,040	(D)	153	4	0	0	0	0	72	5	0	(*)	17
United Kingdom Islands, Caribbean	3,436	474	(D)	190	14	4	39	1	12	0	0	1,372	151	1,274	13	(D)
Other	6,272	3,657	(D)	800	(D)	240	73	0	(*)	0	0	449	41	287	7	(D)
Africa	**42,332**	**33,148**	**(D)**	**3,217**	**259**	**692**	**94**	**215**	**68**	**92**	**851**	**1,350**	**193**	**233**	**241**	**(D)**
Egypt	2,857	2,330	0	258	44	66	8	(D)	11	5	0	157	7	21	9	75
Nigeria	13,513	13,284	52	79	0	16	–1	4	9	0	0	68	3	(*)	–6	33
South Africa	5,483	65	0	2,077	78	497	44	172	46	87	768	766	161	103	232	2,079
Other	20,479	17,470	(D)	803	137	112	43	(D)	3	0	82	360	22	109	6	(D)
Middle East	**13,176**	**7,531**	**159**	**2,867**	**(D)**	**313**	**9**	**441**	**1,210**	**45**	**–6**	**494**	**561**	**233**	**934**	**396**
Israel	3,859	88	0	2,071	(D)	131	0	363	1,145	41	0	193	476	43	738	250
Saudi Arabia	361	175	1	71	0	28	0	8	41	0	–6	48	10	20	41	–6
United Arab Emirates	3,636	2,857	0	310	6	151	8	69	23	4	0	236	68	74	79	11

Table 19.1 (Continued)

				Manufacturing												
					Of which:											
	All industries	Mining	Utilities	Total	Food	Chemicals	Primary and fabricated metals	Machinery	Computers and electronic products	Electrical equipment, appliances, and components	Transportation equipment	Wholesale trade	Information	Finance(except depository institutions) and insurance	Professional, scientific, and technical services	Other industries
Other	5,320	4,411	158	415	0	2	1	1	0	0	0	17	6	96	77	140
Asia and Pacific	**184,213**	**24,020**	**(D)**	**76,979**	**(D)**	**15,792**	**3,289**	**4,090**	**21,158**	**2,134**	**5,891**	**27,403**	**7,066**	**17,237**	**14,540**	**(D)**
Australia	37,821	6,698	39	14,510	1,652	1,768	2,455	732	250	273	1,378	5,572	2,734	1,941	2,813	3,513
China	18,489	1,701	75	12,346	546	3,166	362	1,128	4,178	814	665	1,740	297	99	830	1,401
Hong Kong	10,232	1	(D)	1,825	24	221	32	157	446	81	7	3,537	411	2,723	1,126	(D)
India	5,483	111	(*)	1,940	64	530	86	302	241	43	297	802	663	49	1,702	215
Indonesia	11,836	8,622	257	2,736	(D)	219	–7	16	5	(D)	10	106	11	104	33	–34
Japan	38,328	4	0	11,807	74	4,768	97	438	2,349	419	572	7,922	1,722	7,611	5,441	3,821
Korea, Republic of	10,923	1	–3	6,644	154	570	95	479	1,828	117	2,128	1,237	217	1,411	709	707
Malaysia	7,911	2,674	(*)	4,301	51	225	12	43	3,560	(D)	13	471	62	95	122	186
New Zealand	2,899	69	2	816	(D)	178	23	40	97	24	2	1,108	186	95	210	412
Philippines	3,938	393	580	1,931	171	381	1	22	837	55	(D)	115	28	110	158	623
Singapore	17,446	282	2	10,636	39	2,632	15	509	5,346	185	428	2,656	549	1,512	868	939
Taiwan	5,849	(*)	0	2,678	40	532	33	92	971	33	118	1,146	159	1,106	381	378
Thailand	8,715	2,725	12	4,405	197	498	63	132	1,004	24	193	673	20	247	139	493
Other	4,345	736	64	403	(D)	103	22	1	45	0	(D)	319	8	134	6	2,675
Addenda:																
European Union (25)[1]	483,944	18,153	3,902	256,108	13,958	49,496	10,864	18,096	20,995	7,619	33,083	71,173	26,203	10,981	32,595	64,829
OPEC[2]	41,828	32,743	830	6,173	302	1,083	51	167	80	41	477	714	167	320	466	415

* Less than $500,000 (+/–).

D Suppressed to avoid disclosure of data of individual companies. OPEC Organization of Petroleum Exporting Countries

1.See footnote 1 to table 16. , 2. See footnote to table 16.

Table 19.2. Value Added of Majority-Owned Nonbank Foreign Affiliates, Country by Industry of Affiliate, 2007 [Millions of dollars]

				Manufacturing												
					Of which:											
	All industries	Mining	Utilities	Total	Food	Chemicals	Primary and fabricated metals	Machinery	Computers and electronic products	Electrical equipment, appliances,and components	Transportation equipment	Wholesale trade	Information	Finance (except depository institutions) and insurance	Professional, scientific, and technical services	Other industries
All countries	**1,117,585**	**152,285**	**11,145**	**509,962**	**30,403**	**107,519**	**21,192**	**32,404**	**50,473**	**13,085**	**71,208**	**151,964**	**45,079**	**51,656**	**61,383**	**134,111**
Canada	**116,180**	**19,241**	**809**	**50,880**	**3,851**	**5,835**	**2,919**	**2,051**	**1,613**	**720**	**11,014**	**10,602**	**2,199**	**1,988**	**5,695**	**24,765**
Europe	**610,921**	**44,634**	**4,089**	**308,403**	**16,099**	**68,968**	**12,641**	**21,577**	**22,702**	**8,115**	**40,019**	**92,152**	**29,229**	**23,510**	**35,669**	**73,237**
Austria	6,026	2	0	3,250	403	390	75	514	364	59	778	1,599	320	115	348	392
Belgium	23,682	17	(*)	13,996	866	4,764	286	835	60	362	1,527	4,795	740	1,425	806	1,903
Czech Republic	4,312	0	20	3,349	18	366	82	180	231	105	874	369	193	(D)	170	(D)
Denmark	6,038	1,551	43	1,818	164	166	77	405	145	48	12	944	100	93	1,247	243
Finland	3,137	0	0	1,630	0	299	43	395	272	51	15	710	124	1	425	248
France	56,196	53	8	28,960	1,563	5,871	1,561	2,987	2,788	902	3,004	8,160	1,553	2,445	2,900	12,118
Germany	86,649	1,209	(D)	58,240	2,138	6,528	2,438	5,226	5,025	2,497	11,881	9,602	2,273	867	4,335	(D)
Greece	3,533	2	0	2,577	113	429	33	16	7	0	0	620	21	158	65	89
Hungary	5,014	20	32	3,457	85	281	251	115	247	(D)	1,312	252	592	28	451	183
Ireland	53,842	181	0	29,443	354	16,416	48	129	5,195	96	91	5,485	4,816	367	1,967	11,583
Italy	32,508	13	24	20,878	661	4,129	768	2,104	989	701	1,160	4,469	1,672	402	1,793	3,257
Luxembourg	1,200	1	(*)	1,557	0	924	21	9	0	0	(*)	283	–641	1,003	78	–1,082
Netherlands	29,515	881	1	17,698	2,032	4,423	677	938	1,928	294	1,790	3,877	1,967	79	2,080	2,932
Norway	16,624	11,490	1	2,887	78	147	(D)	284	141	3	15	578	146	52	228	1,242
Poland	8,470	(*)	4	6,191	620	456	340	112	111	117	1,107	1,199	166	378	222	311
Portugal	4,463	(*)	0	3,031	125	368	19	61	70	4	260	758	113	37	151	373
Russia	6,965	2,028	–1	3,471	893	631	(D)	(D)	(D)	6	224	704	28	28	236	470
Spain	19,611	26	110	12,059	739	3,522	1,397	700	281	544	2,869	2,761	558	489	1,253	2,355

Table 19.2 (Continued)

	All industries	Mining	Utilities	Manufacturing								Wholesale trade	Information	Finance (except depository institutions) and insurance	Professional, scientific, and technical services	Other industries
				Total	*Of which:*											
					Food	Chemicals	Primary and fabricated metals	Machinery	Computers and electronic products	Electrical equipment, appliances,and components	Transportation equipment					
Sweden	13,775	0	0	10,184	187	4,303	283	536	341	77	3,212	883	258	–225	1,309	1,364
Switzerland	28,950	(D)	0	9,732	246	4,928	123	1,207	798	621	131	15,205	1,153	364	1,410	(D)
Turkey	7,041	(*)	33	5,374	226	768	22	3	12	20	195	1,443	46	5	42	98
United Kingdom	172,310	13,501	2,209	63,615	4,430	8,369	2,292	4,477	3,433	1,292	9,142	25,979	12,820	15,207	14,014	24,966
Other	21,058	(D)	(D)	5,009	159	489	1,583	(D)	(D)	(D)	420	1,477	208	(D)	140	(D)
Latin America and Other Western Hemisphere	**123,544**	**18,499**	**4,265**	**57,355**	**6,586**	**13,666**	**1,829**	**2,602**	**2,775**	**1,702**	**12,206**	**17,648**	**4,554**	**5,155**	**3,049**	**13,019**
South America	65,918	11,323	3,759	34,473	3,705	8,806	1,205	1,592	910	816	6,798	7,236	2,536	638	1,977	3,976
Argentina	10,815	3,410	(D)	5,442	1,156	1,201	8	91	25	9	574	424	331	243	125	(D)
Brazil	33,090	296	(D)	21,890	1,682	5,628	1,154	1,368	875	756	4,915	3,788	1,453	323	1,345	(D)
Chile	4,839	1,277	999	941	(D)	373	4	46	3	(*)	66	816	427	–176	115	439
Colombia	5,127	1,588	0	1,562	177	474	6	(D)	3	5	(D)	1,188	10	45	41	694
Ecuador	802	331	–1	322	18	56	(*)	1	1	0	(D)	123	3	–20	4	40
Peru	4,894	3,618	161	406	62	140	26	3	1	0	0	402	97	37	45	128
Venezuela	5,532	568	0	3,650	445	904	7	(D)	1	46	844	279	117	241	300	377
Other	819	234	2	260	(D)	30	–1	(*)	2	0	4	216	97	–55	3	62
Central America	35,744	2,411	367	20,332	2,790	4,375	479	893	1,475	886	5,404	2,571	1,547	350	978	7,187
Costa Rica	1,332	(*)	–10	1,093	46	225	13	0	(D)	30	0	177	10	0	(D)	(D)

Table 19.2 (Continued)

Honduras	668	0	0	284	42	13	0	(*)	0	0	(D)	60	(*)	3	(*)	321
Mexico	31,327	2,388	147	18,254	2,579	4,029	465	892	1,242	855	5,390	1,881	1,523	303	865	5,967
Panama	712	16	3	24	2	16	(*)	0	(*)	0	0	49	4	27	8	581
Other	1,705	7	228	677	121	91	1	1	(D)	1	(D)	404	10	17	(D)	(D)
Other Western Hemisphere	21,882	4,765	139	2,550	92	486	145	117	390	0	3	7,841	471	4,167	93	1,855
Barbados	3,223	(*)	0	135	16	3	(*)	(*)	113	0	3	2,213	9	260	2	603
Bermuda	7,737	342	(*)	474	0	83	(*)	116	278	0	0	3,894	22	1,596	49	1,360
Dominican Republic	1,084	0	119	840	(D)	167	3	0	0	0	0	91	13	0	(*)	21
United Kingdom Islands, Caribbean	3,394	374	18	159	14	4	45	1	–1	0	0	1,131	206	2,061	27	–582
Other	6,444	4,050	2	942	(D)	229	97	0	(*)	0	0	512	221	250	14	453
Africa	**43,269**	**34,081**	**(D)**	**3,252**	**283**	**718**	**95**	**231**	**82**	**109**	**670**	**1,471**	**188**	**264**	**276**	**(D)**
Egypt	3,636	2,976	0	338	47	92	8	(D)	12	5	0	195	7	28	17	73
Nigeria	13,959	13,733	44	100	0	33	–1	4	10	0	0	51	3	(*)	–7	34
South Africa	5,581	44	0	1,960	141	463	54	195	58	104	573	804	156	143	257	2,218
Other	20,094	17,327	(D)	854	94	130	33	(D)	3	0	97	421	22	93	8	(D)
Middle East	**16,036**	**8,885**	**156**	**4,170**	**(D)**	**334**	**33**	**809**	**1,519**	**45**	**(D)**	**688**	**472**	**187**	**984**	**494**
Israel	4,697	110	0	2,856	(D)	135	23	718	1,464	41	(D)	291	338	41	742	319
Saudi Arabia	536	291	1	94	0	30	0	12	51	0	–6	33	11	–7	(D)	(D)
United Arab Emirates	4,437	(D)	0	317	4	161	9	77	4	4	0	346	104	67	115	(D)
Other	6,365	(D)	155	903	0	8	1	1	0	0	0	18	19	85	(D)	(D)
Asia and Pacific	**207,635**	**26,945**	**(D)**	**85,902**	**(D)**	**17,997**	**3,675**	**5,133**	**21,782**	**2,394**	**(D)**	**29,403**	**8,438**	**20,552**	**15,711**	**(D)**
Australia	44,088	7,163	17	16,409	1,684	2,204	2,699	790	245	289	1,678	6,441	2,733	3,673	3,412	4,239
China	22,429	1,933	76	14,409	573	3,379	422	1,463	5,107	825	749	2,513	395	(D)	730	(D)
Hong Kong	10,943	1	(D)	1,916	28	274	31	176	446	142	8	3,314	346	3,862	1,122	(D)
India	7,307	270	(*)	2,808	159	805	(D)	567	249	87	(D)	1,073	744	–141	2,117	436
Indonesia	13,095	9,098	328	3,143	(D)	225	–8	23	6	(D)	11	95	11	(D)	60	(D)

Table 19.2 (Continued)

				Manufacturing											
					Of which:										
	All industries	Mining	Utilities	Total	Food	Chemicals	Primary and fabricated metals	Machinery	Computers and electronic products	Electrical equip-ment, appliances,and components	Transportation equipment	Wholesale trade	Information	Finance (except depository institutions) and insurance	Professional, scientific, and technical services	Other industries
Japan	38,954	4	0	11,631	68	4,802	173	481	2,160	407	518	7,429	2,746	6,880	5,442	4,822
Korea, Republic of	12,442	1	–3	7,895	149	538	142	608	2,081	136	2,764	1,354	221	1,482	729	762
Malaysia	8,149	3,480	(*)	3,545	74	308	5	78	2,688	(D)	8	558	67	297	138	64
New Zealand	2,813	–90	2	841	(D)	178	25	42	113	42	36	1,025	(D)	120	162	(D)
Philippines	4,158	416	(D)	2,196	(D)	464	1	10	854	(D)	(D)	148	29	(D)	254	723
Singapore	20,917	407	2	12,501	22	3,611	23	638	5,505	192	698	3,198	696	1,268	1,040	1,805
Taiwan	6,958	(*)	0	2,958	39	542	39	114	1,063	39	93	1,189	231	1,890	329	361
Thailand	9,819	3,043	20	5,127	221	574	30	142	1,196	26	224	770	20	288	117	433
Other	5,565	1,218	93	523	(D)	93	(D)	1	69	0	27	295	(D)	179	61	(D)
Addenda:																
European Union (27)[1]	535,379	17,481	3,877	285,338	14,597	62,391	11,882	19,838	21,713	7,465	39,428	73,642	27,848	23,050	33,762	70,381
OPEC[2]	51,514	39,964	471	8,170	513	1,361	9	185	71	58	848	843	258	608	589	611

* Less than $500,000 (+/–).

D Suppressed to avoid disclosure of data of individual companies. OPEC Organization of Petroleum Exporting Countries

1. See footnote 2 to table 16.

2. See footnote to table 16.

End Notes

[1] A U.S. MNC comprises a U.S. parent company and its foreign affiliates. For both conceptual and practical reasons, the examination of foreign operations of U.S. MNCs in this article generally focuses on data for majority- owned foreign affiliates (MOFAs) rather than data for all foreign affiliates. Conceptually, most data users prefer using the data for majority-owned affiliates because such affiliates are unambiguously under U.S. control; foreign affiliates that are minority-owned by a U.S. resident could be under the control of foreign investors. In addition, some of the data items necessary for the examination of foreign operations of U.S. MNCs are more easily col- lected for majority-owned affiliates, and most foreign affiliates are majority owned; majority-owned affiliates accounted for 85.3 percent of the employ- ment by all nonbank foreign affiliates in 2007.

[2] Estimates of worldwide GDP excluding the United States are at current prices in U.S. dollars and were obtained from the Economic Statistics sec tion of the United Nations Statistics Division Web site at unstats.un.org/unsd/economic_main.htm; click on "National Accounts Main Aggregates Database," and then click on "Basic Data Selection."

[3] Throughout this article, "finance (except banks) and insurance" refers to "finance (except depository institutions) and insurance," which is the industry title that appears in the tables.

[4] The rate of inflation in 12 major euro area countries and in 15 other major host countries averaged 1.9 percent in 2007. Together, these coun- tries accounted for 78 percent of total value added of foreign affiliates in 2007. The average inflation rate (weighted by foreign affiliate value added) in these countries was derived from data on GDP implicit price deflators from the World Bank Web site. The weighted average U.S.-dollar price of the currencies of these countries in foreign exchange markets increased 6.9 percent in 2007.

[5] For a more complete examination of the R&D activities of U.S. MNCs, see Daniel R. Yorgason, "*Research and Development Activities of U.S. Multinational Companies: Preliminary Results From the 2004 Benchmark Survey,"* SURVEY OF CURRENT BUSINESS 87 (March 2007): 22–39.

[6] See Michael E. Porter, *The Competitive Advantage of Nations* (New York, NY: Free Press, 1990).

[7] In 2007, two-thirds of sales by Chinese manufacturing affiliates were to local customers.

[8] This definition is from Daniel Kaufmann, Aart Kraay, and Pablo Zoido, "Governance Matters," World Bank Policy Research Working Paper no. 2196 (Washington, DC: World Bank, 1999).

[9] These measures of regulatory quality of host governments are available on the World Bank Web site at www.worldbank.org under "Governance Indicators." The construction of these indicators are described in Daniel Kaufmann, Aart Kraay, and Massimo Mastruzzi, "Governance Matters VII: Aggregate and Individual Governance Indicators for 1996–2007," World Bank Policy Research Working Paper No. 4654 (Washington, DC: World Bank, 2006).

[10] See Robert E. Lipsey "Defining and Measuring the Location of FDI Output," National Bureau of Economic Research (NBER) Working Paper no. 12996 (Cambridge, MA: NBER, March 2007).

[11] To translate the value-added estimates that are denominated in foreign currencies into U.S. dollars for international comparisons, PPP exchange rates generally are preferable, because they approximate the number of foreign currency units required in a foreign country to buy the goods and services that are equivalent to those that can be bought in the United States with 1 U.S. dollar. A distinguishing feature of PPP exchange rates is that they are based on the prices of all goods and services produced or sold in a country, both those that are traded internationally and those that are not. For details and for a summary of the original methodology used to derive the estimates of real value added, see Raymond J. Mataloni Jr., "Real Gross Product of U.S. Manufacturing," SURVEY 77 (April 1997): 8–17. A major improvement to the original methodology occurred with the release of the preliminary 2004 estimates when the industry detail of the producer price indexes used for deflation was increased from 6 manufacturing industries to 22 manufacturing industries.

[12] Previously, the estimates were denominated in chained 2002 dollars. The preparation of estimates in chained 2005 dollars was made possible by the release of European Communities and Organisation for Economic Co-Operation and Development (OECD), *Purchasing Power Parities and Real Expenditures: 2005 Benchmark Year* (Paris: OECD, 2008).

[13] See Kazuyuki Motohashi "R&D of Multinationals in China: Structure, Motivations and Regional Difference," Research Institute of Economy, Trade & Industry (RIETI) Discussion Paper Series 06-E-005 (Tokyo: RIETI, February 2006).

Chapter 6

DO INTANGIBLE ASSETS EXPLAIN HIGH U.S. FOREIGN DIRECT INVESTMENT RETURNS?*

*Benjamin Bridgman**

ABSTRACT

U.S. investors abroad receive a higher return on their assets than their counterparts that invest in the United States. I examine the degree to which excluding intangible assets from the measurement of foreign direct investment can account for this gap. Using a growth accounting framework, I estimate intangible capital stocks for foreign-owned affiliates and find that including unmeasured capital reduces the gap by up to two thirds. U.S. affiliates abroad hold a relatively large share of their assets as intangible capital since they are taxed at the relatively high U.S. corporate rate and intangible investment is expensed. Accounting for intangibles reduces a similar gap in British FDI returns by nearly half.

1. INTRODUCTION

Measured U.S. net investment position is negative and has been so for over two decades. However, as shown in Figure 1, U.S. net earnings on foreign-owned assets has been positive despite the fact that the net investment position has been growing more negative over this period.

---

* This is an edited, reformatted and augmented version of a U. S. Bureau of Economic Analysis publication dated September 2008.

* I thank Dennis Fixler, Ralph Kozlow, Ellen McGrattan, Obie Whichard, Dan Yorgason and seminar participants at the 2007 APET meetings, 2008 Midwest Macro Meetings, 2nd World Congress on Index Measures and the 2008 North American Summer Meetings of the Econometrics Society for comments and Andrew Miller, Anna Rahkman and Chris Zwicker for research assistance. The views expressed in this paper are solely those of the author and not necessarily those of the U.S. Bureau of Economic Analysis or the U.S. Department of Commerce. Address: Department of Commerce, Bureau of Economic Analysis, Washington, DC 20230. email: Benjamin.Bridgman@bea.gov. Tel. (202) 606-9991. Fax (202) 606-5366.

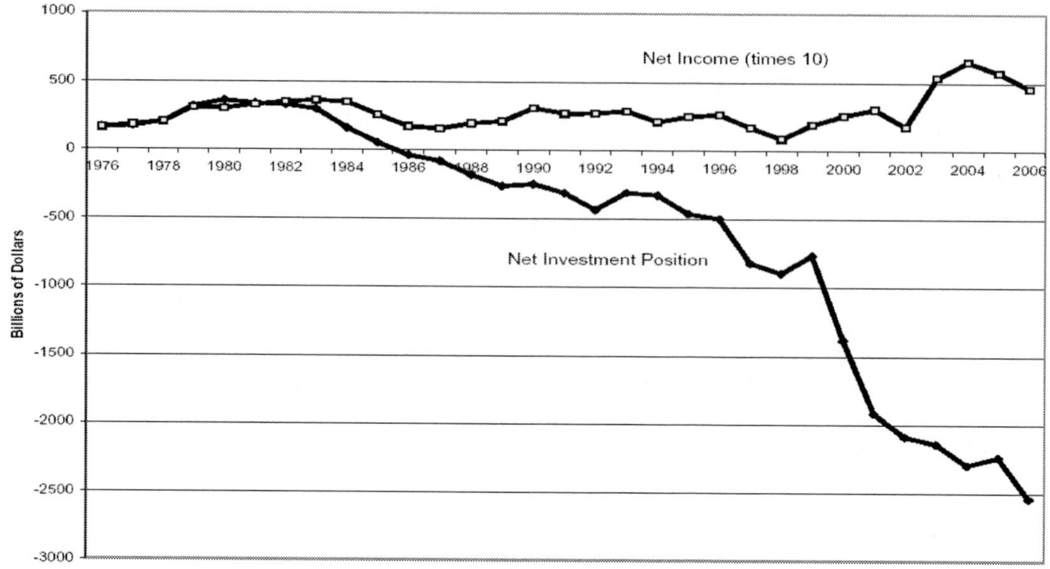

Figure 1. U.S. Net Investment Position and Net Income on Foreign-Owned Assets, 1976- 2006

The reason for the continued positive return is that American investors receive higher returns on their investments abroad than their foreign counterparts do on their U.S. investments. The average inward return on foreign assets between 1982 and 2004 was 4.5 percent compared to 5.7 percent for outward investment[1]. American investors also receive higher returns on U.S. investments than foreigners.

The gap in returns is most severe in direct investment. As can be seen from Figure 2, the gap is due to a large gap in returns for FDI. From 1982 to 2004, outward direct investment earned a 7.6 percent return compared to 2.2 for inward FDI. Non-FDI assets do not show much of a gap, with inward investment earning an average return of 5.2 percent compared to 4.9 for outward investment. The gap in rates of return on foreign investment has been a long standing puzzle. For example, foreign manufacturing firms in the United States have had lower returns than U.S. firms since at least 1951 (Laster & McCauley 1994). In no year do foreign firms have a higher return and the gap has widened with time. Other authors that have analyzed this issue include Landefeld, Lawson & Weinberg (1992), Laster & McCauley (1994), Mataloni (2000), and Hung & Mascaro (2004).

This gap has generated a great deal of interest recently. While returns need not be equal across countries at any given time, the size and persistence of the gap seems quite anomalous. Understanding the nature of the gap is important for analyzing a number of economic issues, such as whether the U.S. current account deficit is sustainable. (See Caballero, Farhi & Gourinchas (2008) and Mendoza, Quadrini & Rios-Rull (2007), among many others.)

Many explanations of this puzzle have been advanced. These include risk compensation, the use of transfer pricing and other methods to avoid taxation (Hines 1999), the use of the dollar as an international standard (Gourinchas & Rey 2006), and provision of liquidity (Caballero et al. 2008), among others. Hausmann & Sturzenegger (2007) suggest that the "dark matter" they use to explain the gap comes from three sources: risk compensation, implicit payment for financial services, and unmeasured intangible capital. This paper explores how much of the gap can be attributed to a novel explanation: differences in intangible asset holdings that result from multinational corporations' (MNC) corporate income taxation.

The National Income and Product Accounts do not include most intangible assets, while they do pick up their returns. Therefore, measured returns are likely to be overstated for countries that invest more in intangible capital relative to those that invest in tangible capital. Portfolio investment captures intangible capital since the price of a share includes the value of its intangible assets (Lev & Sougiannis 1996). Since there is no market price, non-traded firms are valued by a proxy: the purchase price of physical assets adjusted for country specific equity price changes.

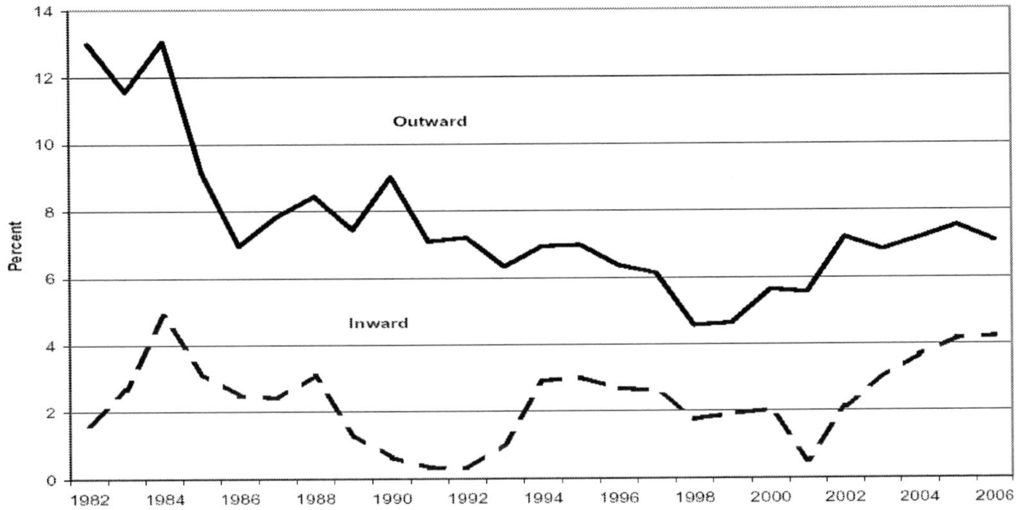

(a) FDI returns

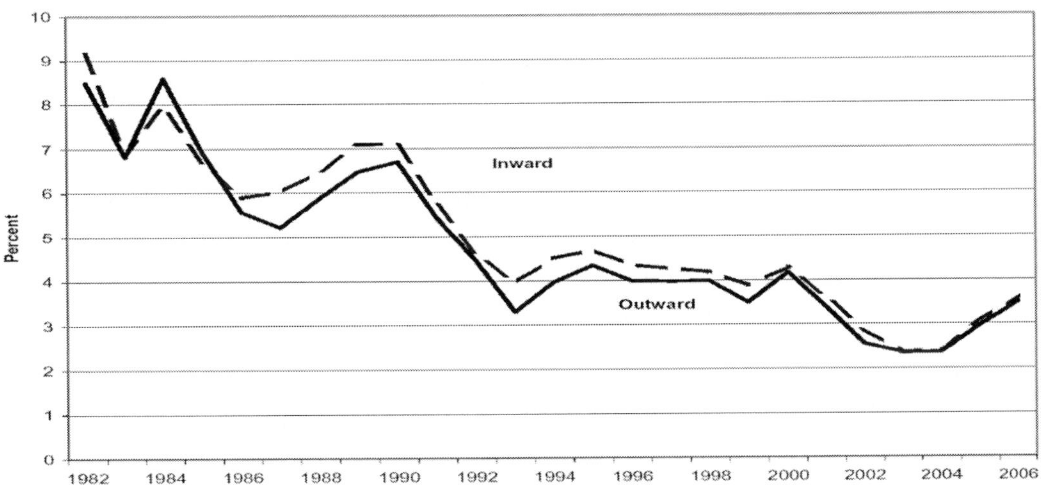

(b) Non-FDI Returns

Figure 2. Returns to Foreign Investment, 1982-2006 (Percent)

The way that MNCs are taxed give an incentive for U.S. based MNCs to hold more of their assets as intangibles. Since intangible investments are expensed while tangible investments are not, corporate income taxes give an incentive to shift asset holdings into intangibles. The United States has had relatively high corporate income taxes. In addition, the United States taxes the worldwide profits of its MNCs at the U.S. rate, with a credit for payments abroad. Therefore they may be subject to a repatriation tax when profits are returned from lower tax jurisdictions. Since this tax payment is a purely domestic transaction, it is not counted in the balance of payments accounts.

I use a growth accounting framework similar to that used by McGrattan & Prescott (2005) to calculate the contribution of the taxation of MNCs on the returns gap through the accumulation of intangible capital. I assume that after-tax rates of return on tangible and intangible capital are equalized and use corporate income tax rates to estimate the stock of intangible capital held by U.S. direct investors abroad and foreign investors in the United States. The estimates are used to adjust the rates of return on FDI assets.

Accounting for intangible asset holdings reduces the U.S. FDI returns gap by up to three quarters. The average returns gap falls from 4.7 to 1.1 percentage points over the period 1990 to 2001. The overall gap in returns is nearly eliminated when the adjusted FDI rates of return are applied to the overall overseas asset portfolio: The total average annual rate of return is 3.7 percent for foreign owned assets in the United States compared to 3.8 percent for U.S. owned assets abroad. I calculate alternative estimates of intangible assets using R&D expenditures as a proxy for intangible investment and find nearly identical results.

I also apply the model to the United Kingdom. Since 1997, the UK has been in a situation similar to that of the United States: It has a negative international investment position with positive net returns due to higher outward FDI returns. Like the United States, the UK uses worldwide taxation. Including intangible assets reduces the UK's average annual gap in FDI returns from 2.6 percent to 1.5 percent over the period 1997 to 2005, nearly half the gap in FDI asset returns. Adjusting the overall foreign asset returns reduces total gap by half, from 0.53 to 0.26 percentage points.

The results suggest that different holdings of intangible assets as a result of corporate income taxes are a first order cause of the gap in international asset returns. They also underline the importance of accounting for intangible assets in the international investment position. Excluding them have a quantitatively important impact on the measurement of international returns.

This paper is part of a growing literature examining the rates return puzzle, which has been discussed above. Other papers have suggested intangible assets as a source of the returns gap. McGrattan & Prescott (2008) use the returns gap in returns to identify differential openness to foreign investment in a growth accounting framework. Kapicka (2008) uses a similar framework to back out the degree of openness to intangible "technology capital." This paper differs in that it uses taxes to identify intangible asset holdings and estimates intangible assets in the United Kingdom. The impact of openness is discussed below.

Hausmann & Sturzenegger (2007) also examine intangible assets, which they colorfully refer to as "Dark Matter." They revalue assets assuming all assets return a reference rate of 5 percent. This paper only assumes that rates of return are equalized across tangible and intangible assets, rather than imposing a rate of return, and uses independent data on tax rates to identify holdings of intangible assets.

The rest of the paper is organized as follows: Section 2 discusses intangible assets. Section 3 presents the model. Section 4 presents the theoretical results while Section 5 presents the empirical results. Section 6 applies the model to the British case and Section 7 the robustness of the results. Section 8 concludes.

2. Why Intangible Capital?

There are a number of reasons to believe intangible assets may help resolve the returns gap puzzle.

The intangible assets explanation is specific to FDI. Returns to portfolio investment do not show the large gap that direct investment does. When valuing portfolio investment, the market takes into account both tangible and intangible assets owned by the firm. This is not true for direct investment. (By using stock market indices to revalue the book value of assets, BEA methodology will capture changes in the relative holding of intangible assets. However, it will not capture persistent differences in the the relative holding of assets types.)

Omitting intangibles can generate very high rates of return on assets. Multinational companies (MNCs) account for most R&D expenditures, suggesting that omitting intangibles may be particularly distorting to the valuation of foreign-owned affiliates.

There is reason to believe that U.S. MNCs hold more of their assets as intangibles. Doms & Jensen (1998) find that U.S. MNC's manufacturing plants are more productive (as measured by total factor productivity) and pay higher wages than foreign-owned U.S. plants. This superior performance is consistent with U.S. MNCs holding relatively higher portfolios of intangible assets. Girma, Thompson & Wright (2002) also find that U.S. owned plants in the United Kingdom are the most productive and pay higher wages.

Finally, the United States is not the only country to show a gap. Meissner & Taylor (2006) finds that gaps occur in many countries. As mentioned above, the United Kingdom has developed a situation similar to the United States. Therefore, general explanations are more likely relative to those that are specific to the United States.

2.1. Alternative Explanations

A number of theories have been put forward to explain the gap. I consider each in turn.

Higher rates of return may be a reflection of the higher risk that U.S. investments face. The United States is a mature market and investors looking for higher returns may look abroad (Hausmann & Sturzenegger 2007). Hung & Mascaro (2004) examine whether the countries U.S. MNCs invest in are risky by looking at their bond ratings. They find that the risk gap is small since most investment is in developed countries with similar risk profiles. However, individual projects that they invest in may be riskier.

The return gap may reflect transfer pricing to reduce profits in high tax countries (Hines 1999). While identifying this effect is difficult, attempts to do so have found only minor revenue losses on the order of one percent of tax liabilities (U.S. Deparment of the Treasury Internal Revenue Service 1999, Bernard, Jensen & Schott 2006).

Gourinchas & Rey (2006) suggest that the higher return reflects the "Exorbitant Privilege," a willingness of foreigners to hold dollar denominated assets since the dollar is an important international currency. This theory does not explain why the gap appears in other countries or why it only affects FDI.

A related theory is that the gap reflects unmeasured exports of U.S. financial services that arise from the United States's superior financial depth (Hausmann & Sturzenegger 2007, Caballero et al. 2008). Curcuru, Dvorak & Warnock (2008) find that there is very little gap in portfolio assets once revisions in the data are properly accounted for and that the gap only exists in FDI assets. Forbes (2008) finds evidence in portfolio investment that low income countries accept low returns since they lack developed financial markets. Most FDI investors in the United States are from high income countries. Further, this theory does not explain why foreign investors accept such a large gap in returns in FDI when the gap in portfolio assets is much smaller.

McGrattan & Prescott (2008) also argue that the returns reflect differential investments in intangible capital, but identify the cause as less financial openness in the United States. This paper is similar in that it also identifies intangibles as the source of the gap, though the mechanism for the difference is taxation rather than financial openness. This explanation is discussed in more detail below.

2.2. What are Intangible Assets?

The intangible assets identified in this paper are those that are created and held by the firm. It does not include intangible public capital such as rule of law and political stability. (Such intangible capital figures prominently in World Bank (2006)). While these may affect returns, intangible capital is identified in the model using the incentives of firms to accumulate such capital. There are a number of different such intangible assets. They include patents, trademarks, trade secrets, and knowledge about organizing a firm (organization capital).

Although investment in intangible capital is accepted as a legitimate investment activity by national accountants, it has been generally excluded due to the difficulty in measuring its production and depreciation. The 1993 System of National Accounts (SNA) manual, which contains the basic methodology for computing national accounts for most countries in the world, says of R&D that "[i]n order to classify such activities as investment type it would be necessary to have clear criteria for delineating them from other activities, to be able to identify and classify the assets produced, to be able to value such assets in an economically meaningful way and to know the rate at which they depreciate over time. In practice, it is difficult to meet all these requirements. By convention, therefore, all the outputs produced by research and development ... are treated as being consumed as intermediate inputs even though some of them may bring future benefits."

National accounting is now moving toward including intangible assets in its es timates. The forthcoming SNA 2008 manual will require that investments in R&D be capitalized. Some intangible assets, such as computer software, have already been added to the U.S. national accounts. The United States also produces periodic R&D satellite accounts (Okubo, Robbins, Moylan, Sliker, Schultz & Mataloni 2006), but does not currently incorporate it into the main accounts (Carson, Grimm & Moylan 1994). However, they will be incorporated into the main accounts in the future.

3. MODEL

3.1. Households

There are I countries, each with a representative household with preferences represented by the utility function:

$$\sum_{t=0}^{\infty} \beta^t u(c^i(t)) \tag{1}$$

where $c^i(t)$ is per capita consumption in country i. Each household is endowed with one unit of labor in each period. The price of consumption in country i is p^i. Lowercase variables refer to per capita quantities while uppercase variables are aggregates. The measure of population in each country N^i grows at the common growth rate γ_N.

3.2. Production

Each country has a representative multinational that has foreign affiliates in all other countries. Output of country i's multinational's affiliate in location j is given by Y_j^i. The parent's output is Y_j^i. (Superscripts refer to ownership and subscripts to location.) output is Output is produced by a Cobb-Douglas production function:

$$Y_j^i \leq (K_j^{m,i})^{\alpha_m} (K_j^{u,i})^{\alpha_u} (A(t) * N_j^i)^{1-\alpha_m-\alpha_u} \tag{2}$$

where K^m and K^u is tangible (measured) and intangible (unmeasured) capital respectively, N_j^i is labor used and A is labor augmenting technological change. Output can be used for investment or consumption:

$$C_j^i(t) + X_j^{m,i} + X_j^{u,i} \leq Y_j^i \tag{3}$$

The inputs into production, capital and labor, are immobile. Consumption can be costlessly traded to any country. The common productivity trend is given by $A(t) = (1+\gamma A)^t$.

The laws of motion for capital are:

$$K_j^{m,i}(t+1) \leq K_j^{m,i}(t)(1-\delta_m) + X_j^{m,i}(t) \tag{4}$$

and

$$K_j^{u,i}(t+1) \leq K_j^{u,i}(t)(1-\delta_u) + X_j^{u,i}(t). \tag{5}$$

Labor N in country j is allocated across the local parent and foreign-owned affiliates:

$$N_j(t) = \sum_{i=1}^{I} N_j^i(t) \tag{6}$$

3.3. Taxation

Corporate income of foreign affiliates may be taxed both in the country it is based in and in the parent's home country. The proceeds of each countries taxes are rebated to the domestic household as lump sum transfer $\Psi^i(t)$. Dividends are given by:

$$d^i(t) = \sum_j p_j(t)\{Y_j^i(t) - X_j^{u,i}(t) - X_j^{m,i}(t) - w_j(t)N_j^i(t) - (\tau_j + \tau_j^{i,f})\pi_j^i\} \tag{7}$$

where τ_j is the government in countryj's corporate income tax on firms in j, $\tau_j^{i,f}$ is the corporate income tax on foreign profits of affiliate in country j of country I's MNC and

$$\pi_j^i = Y_j^i(t) - \delta_m K_j^{m,i}(t) - X_j^{u,i}(t) - w_j(t)N_j^i(t) \tag{8}$$

The government maintains budget balance in each period, so its budget constraint is given by:

$$\Psi^i(t) \leq \sum_{j=1}^{I}\{p_i(t)(\tau_i\pi_i^j) + p_j(t)(\tau_j^{i,f}\pi_j^i)\} \tag{9}$$

Each household i faces the budget constraint:

$$\sum_{t=0}^{\infty} p_i(t)c^i(t) \leq \sum_{t=0}^{\infty} p_i(t)\{d^i(t) + w_i(t) + \Psi^i(t)\} \tag{10}$$

3.4. Equilibrium

The representative household in country i's problem is to maximize utility (equation 1) subject to the budget constraint (equation 10). The representative multinational's problem is to maximize $\sum_{t=0}^{\infty} d^i(t)$, where $d^i(t)$ is given by equation 7, subject to the laws of motion on capital (equations 5 and 4).

The definition of equilibrium is standard.

Definition 3.1. *An equilibrium is sequences of prices $\{p_j(t), w_j(t)\}$ and quantities* $\{Y_j^i(t), C_j^i(t), K_j^{m,i}(t), K_j^{u,i}(t), X_j^{m,i}(t), x_j^{u,i}(t), d_j(t), N_j^i(t)$ *Such that*

1. *Households choose* $\{\frac{C_t^i}{N_t}\}$ *to solve their problem,*
2. *Firms choose* $\{X_j^{m,i}(t), X_j^{u,i}(t), d_j(t), N_j^i(t)\}$ *to solve their problem,*
3. *Allocations are feasible.*

4. Model Results

This section presents the theoretical results of the model.

The first implication of the model is that high rates of corporate income taxes increase the incentive to hold intangible assets. Since investment in intangible capital can be expensed, investment in intangible assets reduce the tax burden. Higher taxes reduce the marginal cost of this investment. From the solution to the firm's problem, we have:

$$1 - \tau_j - \tau_j^{i,f} = \frac{\frac{\alpha_u Y_j^i}{K_j^{u,i}} - \delta_u}{\frac{\alpha_m Y_j^i}{K_j^{m,i}} - \delta_m} \tag{11}$$

With higher taxes, the firm sets the marginal product of intangible capital lower relative to that of tangible capital implying that K^u is higher relative to K^m. Worldwide taxes electively make the tax rates faced by an MNC the maximum of the foreign and domestic rates. Countries with high corporate tax rates and worldwide taxation are likely to hold more of their assets as intangibles. (In effect, high corporate income taxes act as a spur to R&D!) The United States has been on the high end of corporate tax rates, so it is more likely to hold intangible assets.

4.1. Taxes and Returns

There are two basic systems for taxing corporate income of multinationals: territorial and worldwide. Under territorial taxation, foreign subsidiaries pay the taxes of country they are located in and do not have any additional tax burden in the parent country.

Worldwide taxation treats the entire MNC as a unified company that faces taxation in the parent country. All profits in all countries that the MNC has affiliates in are subject to tax in their parent's country. Affiliates must pay taxes in their country of residence on the profits earned locally. Local tax payments are deducted from the total tax bill of the MNC. (Otherwise, an affiliate could face over 100 percent taxation). If the tax rate in the parent's country is lower than in that of the affiliate, the affiliate is not subject to additional tax and the "overpayment" may be used to offset tax burden of other affiliates. If the tax rate is higher, the difference must be paid to the parent's home government. However, the difference is only due when the profits are repatriated in the home country. Table 1 shows the tax basis and average rates for the largest investors in the United States. Generally the statutory rates and average rates are similar. The Netherlands have consistently lower tax rates than the statutory rate. There are a number of tax provisions, such as the deductability of royalty income, that allow multinationals to pay much less than the statutory rate on their Dutch investments. (See van Dijk, Weyzig & Murphy (2006) for details on Dutch tax shelters available to multinationals.)

The return data are net of taxes, so ROA should be equalized. However, worldwide taxation can introduce gaps in rates of return that cause the rates of return in the data to deviate from that of the theory. The model predicts that after-tax rates of return are equalized across affiliates:

$$(r_j^{m,i} - \delta_m)(1 - \tau_j - \tau_j^{i,f}) = (r_{j'}^{m,i} - \delta_m)(1 - \tau_{j'} - \tau_{j'}^{i,f}) \tag{12}$$

They are also equalized between affliates and with the parent:

$$(r_j^{m,i} - \delta_m)(1 - \tau_i) = (r_j^{m,i} - \delta_m)(1 - \tau_j - \tau_j^{i,f}) \tag{13}$$

With worldwide taxation, the repatriation taxes are not recorded in the affiliates accounts: $\tau_j^{i,f}$ is not deducted from their profits since the balance of payments is concerned with cross border transactions. Repatriation taxes are payments of domestically owned firms to the home government. Therefore, some of the tax paid on affiliate profits is recorded in the parent's accounts. This shift increases the affiliates' measured return on assets and reduces the parent's returns, since returns are calculated net of taxes. Therefore, we have:

$$(r_i^{m,i} - \delta_m)(1 - \tau_i) - \sum_j [\frac{K_j^{m,i}}{K_i^{m,i}} \tau_j^{i,f} (r_j^{m,i} - \delta_m)] \leq (r_j^{m,i} - \delta_m)(1 - \tau_j) \tag{14}$$

Table 1. Taxation of Multinationals: Average 1990-2001

Country	Tax Basis	Avg. CIT	Data Avg. CIT
Canada	Territorial	35.9	34.4
France	Territorial	36.9	33.7
Germany	Territorial	54.6	34.2
Japan	Worldwide	47.6	50.3
Netherlands	Territorial	35.0	13.4
United Kingdom	Worldwide	32.0	24.8
United States	Worldwide	39.1	39.1

As shown in Figure 3, the gap between rates paid by U.S. affiliates abroad and the U.S. tax rate has been growing. Corporate tax rates around the world have been falling during this period and investment has shifted to lower tax countries.

4.2. Balanced Growth Path

To examine the effects of multinational taxation on returns, I calculate the balanced growth path equilibrium.

With population growth γN, the economy grows at $1+\gamma_Y=(1+\gamma_A)*(1+\gamma_N)$. Per capita income grows at the common productivity trend γ_A. The composition of an affiliate's asset portfolio is given by:

$$\frac{K_j^{u,i}}{K_j^{m,i}}=\frac{\alpha_u}{\alpha_m}\left(\frac{(\frac{1+\gamma_A}{\beta}-1)(\frac{1}{1-\tau_j-\tau_j^{i,j}})+\delta_m}{\frac{1+\gamma_A}{\beta}-1+\delta_u}\right) \tag{15}$$

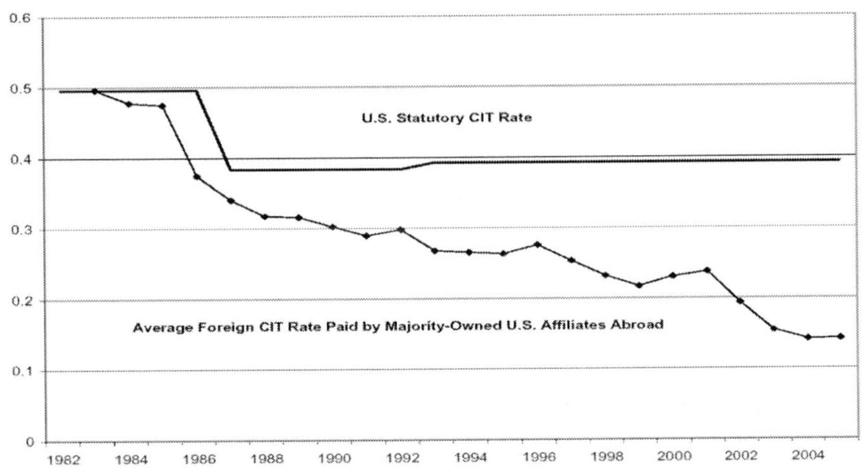

Figure 3. Foreign Corporate Income Tax Rates, 1982-2005

Table 2. Parameter

α_m	α_u	δ_m	δ_u	τ	β	γ_A	γ_N
0.23	0.1	0.05	0.07	0.39	0.98	0.012	0.01

Higher taxes shift the affiliate'stangibles. In the steady state, higher corporate taxes lead to higher pre-tax returns as measured by profits over measured capital $\frac{\pi}{K^m}$. When repatriation taxes are not included, this effect induces a measured rate of return gap.

Proposition 4.1. *On the BGP, if country i has worldwide taxation with* $\tau_j^{i,f} > 0$ *and* $\tau_j^j + \tau_j^{i,f} = \tau_i^i$, *then* $\frac{(1-\tau_j^{i,f}-\tau_j)\pi_j^i}{K_j^{i,m}} > \frac{(1-\tau_i)\pi_i^j}{K_i^{j,m}}$, *measured after-tax rate of return of country I's affliate in territorial taxation country j is higher than j's affliates in country i.*

Proof. The return on measured assets is given by:

$$\frac{(1-\tau_j-\tau_j^f)\pi_j}{K_j^m} = (1-\tau_j-\tau_j^f)[\frac{1}{\alpha_m}(\frac{\frac{1+\gamma_A}{\beta}-1}{1-\tau-\tau^f}+\delta_m)(\alpha_m+\alpha_u-\alpha_u(\frac{\delta_u+\gamma_Y}{\frac{1+\gamma_A}{\beta}-1+\delta_u}))-\delta_m]$$

(16)

The tax rate faced by both affliates is $\tau_j^j + \tau_j^{i,f} = \tau_i^i$ but the $\tau_j^{i,f}$ portion is not measured for country *j*. Therefore, measured ROA for the worldwide taxing country *i* is higher:

$$(1-\tau_i)[\frac{1}{\alpha_m}(\frac{\frac{1+\gamma_A}{\beta}-1}{1-\tau_i-\tau_i^{j,f}}+\delta_m)(\alpha_m+\alpha_u-\alpha_u(\frac{\delta_u+\gamma_Y}{\frac{1+\gamma_A}{\beta}-1+\delta_u}))-\delta_m]$$

(17)

Higher taxes drive up the measured rate of return on tangible assets since there are more unmeasured intangible assets earning returns. Worldwide taxes cause a measured gap since not all affiliates in a country are paying the same tax rate, with territorial tax countries paying the local rate and worldwide tax countries paying their home rate if it is higher. There is a further effect since the Balance of Payments omits the repatriation tax payment.

Table 3. Data and Model, 1990-2001

	Data	Model
Inward measured ROA	1.65	4.73
Outward measured ROA	6.37	5.83
Gap	**4.72**	**1.33**

5. Quantitative Results

This section examines the quantitative effects of different tax treatment. I adjust for the presence of intangible capital and repatriation taxes.

To get a baseline estimate of the effect of taxes on the returns gap, I calibrate the model to estimate intangible capital stocks on the balanced growth path. Capital shares, growth rates and depreciation rates are drawn from McGrattan & Prescott (2008). The tax rate is the average CIT in the United States, including state taxes, from Devereux, Griffith & Klemm (2002). Since U.S. affiliates face repatriation taxes, they are taxed at the domestic rate.

I consolidate FDI across countries to form inward and outward FDI with respect to the United States. Outward investment is subject to repatriation taxes. Over the sample period, U.S. affiliates paid an average of 24.9 percent in corporate income taxes to foreign governments. This implies that the repatriation tax that they face is 14.2 percent.

I do not make any such adjustment for foreign owned affiliates. Most major investor countries use territorial taxation, so are not subject to repatriation taxes. The major investor country with worldwide taxation, the United Kingdom, has a lower tax rate so is also not subject to repatriation taxes on their U.S. investments.

Table 3 compares the model predictions along the balanced growth path for measured rates of returns to the data. Adding intangible capital induces a gap of 1.3 percentage points, about a quarter of the observed gap 4.7 percent.

When these results are applied to the overall asset position, the gap between foreign and U.S. ROA is strongly diminished. Foreigners hold relatively more of their assets in non-FDI assets: FDI assets average 26 percent of inward investment, versus 35 percent for outward. Under the assumption that 1.1 percentage points of the gap is due to the effects of multinational taxation, I reduce U.S. outward FDI ROA by this amount, giving a total of 4.67 for U.S. assets abroad. This reduces the overall gap in the rates of return by a third, from 1.14 to 0.82 percentage points.

In the balanced growth path equilibrium calculated above, after-tax returns are declining in tax rates. Since there are no transaction costs and all countries are the same, rates of return are equalized in the model across countries as well. If there were technological differences or differences in cost of funds, rates of return across countries need not be equalized.

While the model generates a gap in returns, it does not match the low returns on inward investment. In the above analysis, I assumed that the economy was on a balanced growth path. The balanced growth path does not capture the low rates of return on inward investment. I discuss reasons for low returns below.

I relax the balanced growth path assumption and parameterize Equation 11 to generate an estimate of the intangible capital-output ratio to expand observed tangible asset holdings. This equality holds in all equilibria, even off the balanced growth path. Tangible capital data are drawn from the BEA's surveys on foreign direct investment. I use value added to measure output Y and net property, plant and equipment plus inventories to measure tangible capital K^m. The rate of return on assets are adjusted using the expression:

$$ROA_{Adj} = ROA\frac{K^m}{Y}\frac{Y}{K^m + K^u} \tag{18}$$

Table 4. Adjusting FDI Rates of Return, 1990-2001 (Percent)

	Inward	**Outward**
$\frac{K^u}{Y}$	0.9	0.7
$\frac{K^m}{Y}$	1.9	1.3
Unadjusted ROA	1.6	6.4
Intangible Adj. ROA	**1.1**	**3.2**
Repatriation & Intan. Adj. ROA	**1.1**	**2.9**

To account for repatriation taxes, outward ROA is further reduced by the difference between taxes paid abroad and the domestic tax rate: $ROA^{Ad}j * (1 - 0.149)$. The results are reported in Table 4.

The gap between the ROA on direct investment abroad and in the United States in reduced from 4.7 to 1.1 percentage points, or three quarters of the gap. Adding intangibles reduces all rates of returns since the observed returns are spread over more assets. However, U.S. returns are reduced more since those firms devote relatively more of their investment to (unmeasured) intangibles while foreign firms invest in (measured) tangible assets. While foreign owned affiliates in the United States and U.S. affiliates abroad have similar R&D expenditures, foreign owned affiliates are much more (tangible) capital intensive.

A higher share of U.S. owned assets abroad are held as FDI (35 percent) than foreign owned assets in the United States (26 percent). Therefore, a larger portion of U.S. returns are adjusted (downward) by including intangible assets in the overall returns on foreign owned assets. In addition, foreign investors receive slightly higher returns on their non-FDI assets than their American counterparts (4.6 versus 4.3 percent). Replacing the rates of return for FDI with the adjusted rates in the overall return on international assets nearly eliminates the gap in returns. The adjusted annual average ROA for foreign owned assets is 3.7 versus 3.8 for U.S. assets abroad, giving a gap of only 0.1 percent. The unadjusted gap is 1.1 percent.

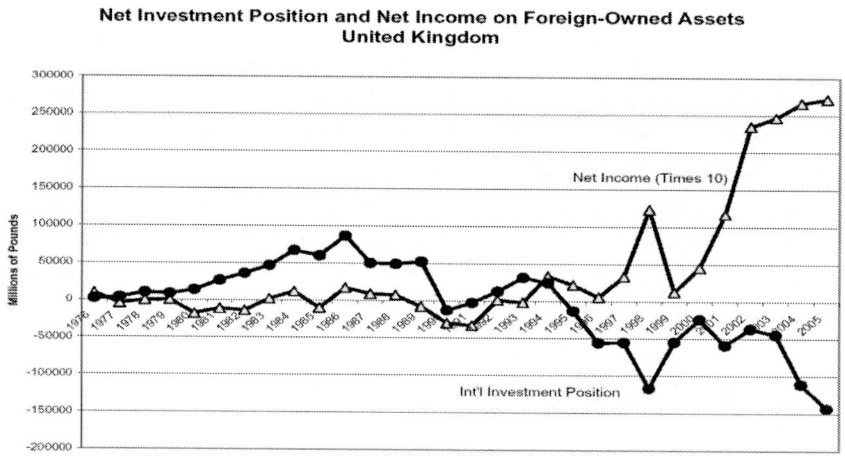

Figure 4. Foreign-Owned Assets in U.K. BOP, 1976-2004

The results provide evidence that intangible assets are a first order source of the FDI returns gap. As shown below, they are robust to a number of checks. However, the estimates are unavoidably imprecise since some of the parameters, such as depreciation of intangible assets, are not directly observable and the methodology does not allow for high frequency estimates. Only estimates of intangible assets based on careful microeconomic data can definitively solve the puzzle.

6. United Kingdom

The United States is not the only country to show a gap in returns. The United Kingdom has a situation very similar to the United States. This section uses the theory to examine this example. The analysis is limited somewhat since the UK does not keep the detailed data on the operations of multinationals that the United States does. However, the available evidence is consistent with multinational taxation being an important part of the explanation of return gap.

As can be seen in Figure 4, since 1997 the United Kingdom developed a situation similar to the U.S. case: positive earnings on a negative international investment position. Like the United States, the positive earnings despite a negative international investment position is due to a gap in ROA, specifically in FDI assets (Figure 5)[2]. The imbalances have been less pronounced in the UK than in the United States, but have been growing recently. The average overall gap in returns from 1997 to 2005 was 0.53 percentage points.

The United Kingdom taxes MNCs using worldwide taxation. Since the UK does not keep data on the balance sheets of its foreign affiliates, we do not know what repatriation taxes, if any, British MNCs face. As an estimate of the taxes they face, I weight the tax rate paid by U.S. affiliates by UK FDI assets for countries that are major destinations for British investment[3]. I use statutory rate from Devereux et al. (2002) for the U.S. rate. As can be seen from Figure 6, UK MNCs faced repatriation taxes over most of the period4. In fact, the data may overstate the tax paid abroad, since it excludes a number of tax havens, such as Bermuda, that have sizable British investment. Further, the British MNCs have a higher share of investment in the Netherlands than U.S. MNCs, increasing the scope for reducing profits in other countries using Dutch tax shelters.

As a baseline, I examine the period from 1997 to 2005, the period in which the UK runs a negative IIP. The returns gap begins in 1987. The late 1980s were of period of significant change in taxes as a result of the Thatcher reforms in the UK and the 1986 tax reform in the United States, the most important destination for British investment. It is not clear what expectations managers at MNCs had about the tax burden they would be facing, especially since investment begins to shift from higher tax countries like France to the low tax destinations like the Netherlands and Ireland. Examining the later period avoids changes in MNC investments that may have accompanied these reforms.

I use the rate of return equalization method rather than calculating the balance growth path since both inward and outward FDI grew rapidly during this period, suggesting that the UK was not on a balanced growth path.

The UK does not collect the data required to do the same adjustments as were done for the United States. As a rough estimate, I adjust the UK rates of return using the average statutory corporate income tax for the UK (0.302) and the estimated tax faced by British affiliates abroad (0.250) for 1997 to 2005. The technology parameters are the same as those used in the U.S. calculation and I use the tangible capital/value added ratio for all British non-financial private corporations from the Blue Book for both inward and outward investment (from the perspective of UK).

The results provide evidence that intangible assets are a first order source of the FDI returns gap. As shown below, they are robust to a number of checks. However, the estimates are unavoidably imprecise since some of the parameters, such as depreciation of intangible assets, are not directly observable and the methodology does not allow for high frequency estimates. Only estimates of intangible assets based on careful microeconomic data can definitively solve the puzzle.

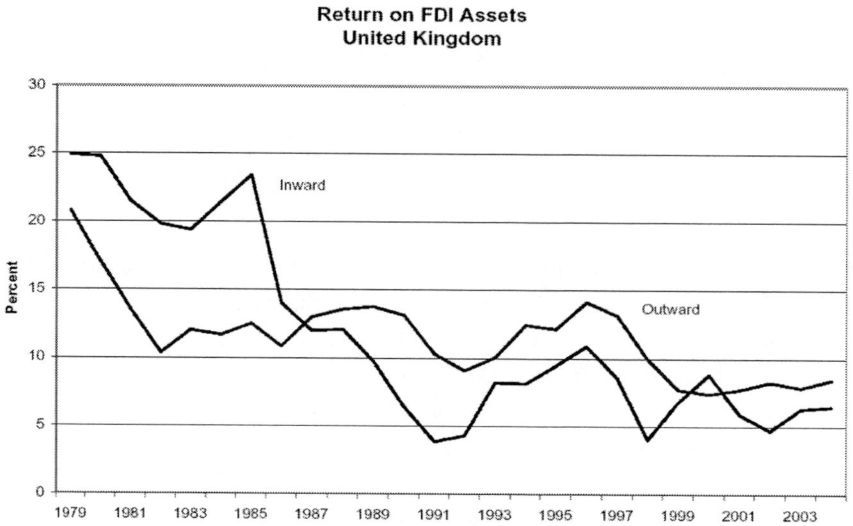

(a) FDI returns

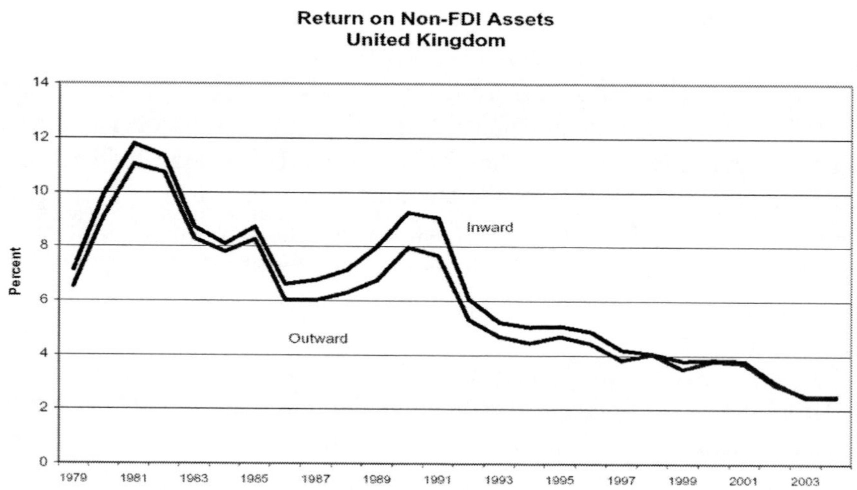

(b) Non-FDI Returns

Figure 5. U.K. Returns to Foreign Investment, 1979-2004 (Percent)

Table 5. Adjusting UK FDI Rates of Return, 1997-2005 (Percent)

	Inward	Outward
$\frac{K^{a}}{Y}$	0.9	0.9
$\frac{K^{m}}{Y}$	2.0	2.0
Unadjusted ROA	6.70	9.26
Intangible Adj. ROA	**4.67**	**6.46**
Repatriation & Intan. Adj. ROA	**4.67**	**6.12**

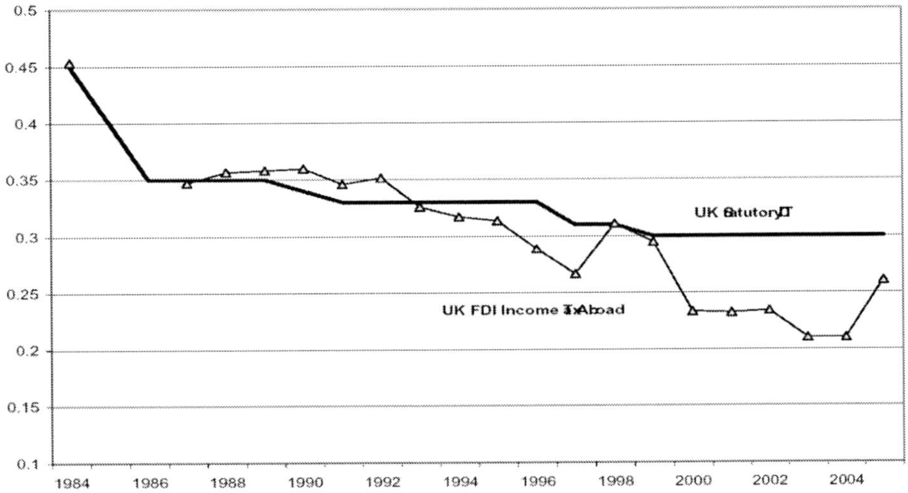

Figure 6. UK Tax Rates, 1984-2005

The results are reported in Table 5. Intangibles close almost half of the gap, dropping it from 2.56 to 1.45 percentage points. This result is robust to different time periods. Expanding the time period to 1987 to 2005 (the entire period that the UK shows a gap) gives similar results. The adjustments reduce the gap from 3.15 to 1.93 percentage points, 40 percent of the gap.

Replacing the adjusted rates of return on FDI in the overall rates of return on foreign owned assets from 1997 to 2005 reducing the gap by half, from 0.53 to 0.26 percentage points. (3.76 percent on outward versus 3.5 percent on inward investment). FDI investment is less important in the UK, both outward (17.4 percent of assets) and inward (10 percent), so the large gap in FDI assets are muted compared to the U.S. case.

While this calculation is necessarily rough, there is additional evidence that intangibles are an important part of the gap. Nickell (2006) has argued that the gap can be explained by the undervaluation of FDI assets, which are valued at book value. Pratten (1996) estimates the estimates the 1991 ratio of market value to book value of British FDI assets abroad and foreign owned assets in the UK to be 1.75 and 1.50 respectively. Kubelec, Orskaug & Tanaka (2007) updates this estimate for 2005 using stock market index changes to obtain 2.05 and 1.65. The higher value of British assets abroad is enough to flip the net international investment position from negative to positive.

As further evidence, it is notable that R&D expenditures as a share of GDP fell during the 1980s, from 1.9 percent in 1981 to 1.5 percent in the mid-1990s, suggesting that expenditures on intangibles fell after corporate taxes were cut.

7. Discussion

This section discusses the validity of the underlying assumptions and the results.

The methodology does not allow for high frequency estimates of intangibles and exclude intangible capital obtained from parents and sister affiliates in other countries. The adjustments use parameter values that are not directly observable to measure assets that are not currently measured. Therefore, they are subject to error. This section presents some checks on the results to see if they are consistent with other data and parameter values. I find that the results hold up under a number of robustness checks.

7.1. Openness

In the model all intangible investment is done locally. For some types of intangibles, this assumption is not very strong. It is unlikely that much of the organization capital identified by Prescott & Visscher (1980), such as job-employee matches and firm specific human capital, is likely the result of investment done outside that affiliate. However, some intangibles (what McGrattan & Prescott (2008) refer to as "technology capital"), such as process innovations, may flow between countries. Unlike physical assets, whose location can easily be determined, intangibles may move within a firm without leaving a trail (Lipsey 2008).

Intangible capital mobility likely strengthens the results. MNCs based in countries with territorial taxation have an incentive to expense their intangible investment in countries with high taxes since it reduces measured profits. Countries with worldwide taxation have less incentive to do so since the tax burden is determined by the MNC's total profits. Shifting profits across does not reduce the tax burden when they are repatriated. Relatively high taxes gives inward investors an incentive to do their intangible investment in their U.S. affiliates, lowering measured U.S. returns. Therefore, high tax locations will appear to have abnormally low returns. The model is a lower bound on the effects of taxes since it does not include this effect.

There is evidence that MNCs perform R&D in the United States for export to other countries. Griffith, Harrison & Reenen (2004) find that U.S. R&D spending flows to British firms if the British firm has a presence in the United States. The United States runs a surplus in royalty payments (Robbins 2006).

McGrattan & Prescott (2008) argue that historically the United States has been relatively closed to foreign investment until the 1970s. Indeed, there have been substantial capital flows into the United States since then. During a transition to a new steady state brought about by opening to foreign capital, foreign-owned assets in the United States may yield low measured returns since investment in intangibles will be higher than in the steady state. Since this investment is expensed, measured returns will be reduced. Part of the lower return is young firms building up organization capital (Mataloni 2000). (For a model of this process, see Atkeson & Kehoe (2005).) This factor very well may be an important part of the solution. Tax differentials do not completely close the gap, nor does the openness. A combination of both may more fully explain the difference.

7.2. Robustness

As a robustness check, I re-estimate U.S. inward and outward foreign intangible capital using a procedure from McGrattan & Prescott (2005). They estimate intangible capital stock for the United States using a growth accounting framework and then estimate another country's intangible capital stocks by assuming that the ratio of the intangible capital-output ratio and R&D expenditure share of output across economies are the same across economies. An advantage of this approach is that we do not need to take a stand on the depreciation rate on intangible capital.

Let RD_j be research and development expenditures. Intangible assets are calculated by comparing affiliate R&D expenditures with those of a reference economy, in this case the U.S. private business sector.

$$\frac{K_j^u}{Y_j} = \frac{K_{US}^u}{Y_{US}} \frac{RD_j}{Y_j} \frac{Y_{US}}{RD_{US}} \tag{19}$$

Table 6 presents the results of this alternative approach. The results are robust to using this method. The results are very similar to the non-balanced growth path estimates of U.S. FDI returns (Table 4). The alternative inward and outward adjusted FDI rates of return are 0.9 and 3.1 percent respectively versus 1.1 and 2.9 percent. The similarity of the gap is remarkable given that the alternative estimates use a different methodology and independent data.

7.3. Taxes

Implementing taxes in the model raises a number of difficulties. While they are represented by a single rate in the model, in reality the corporate tax code is extremely complex. While corporate income taxes are generally not progressive, a major issue is calculating personal income taxes, there are a number of complexities. Different industries may be subject to different tax rates. FDI investments may get tax breaks to encourage the selection of a particular area for investment. The use of tax havens and financial engineering may trim tax burdens. Backus, Henriksen & Storesletten (2008) note that statutory rates do not appear to match very well with actual tax payments or investment behavior.

Table 6. Alternative Adjustment to U.S. Rates of Return, 1990-2001 (Percent)

	U.S. Bus. Sector	**Inward**	**Outward**
$\frac{RD}{Y}$	2.1	5.5	3.2
$\frac{K^m}{Y}$	1	1.9	1.3
$\frac{K^u}{Y}$	0.65	0.88	0.68
Unadjusted ROA	4.1	1.6	6.4
Intangible Adj. ROA	**2.4**	**0.9**	**3.6**
Repatriation + Intang. Adj. ROA	**2.4**	**0.9**	**3.1**

Worldwide taxation introduces additional complexity to the taxes faced by MNCs. Foreign-owned affiliates under territorial taxes largely face the same incentives as domestic firms since they are taxed the same way. Since worldwide taxation can induce repatriation tax liabilities, there may be an incentive to retain earnings strategically (Hines 1999, Desai, Foley & Hines 2001). Kozlow & Abaroa (2006) argue that MNC behavior in response to the

American Jobs Creation Act (AJCA) shows that such strategic behavior is important. Given that such strategic behavior, it is not clear that repatriation taxes should be counted by their full value. The theoretical literature has not developed a consensus. (For example, see Altshuler, Newlon & Randolph (1995) and Altshuler & Grubert (2002).)

It is notable that MNCs appear to be equalizing rates of return according to statutory rates. The average after-tax ROA for U.S. Parents from 1993 to 2001 was 2.9 percent. The pre-tax ROA for Majority-Owned Foreign Affiliates (MOFAs) over that period was 5.1 percent. The implied tax rate on MOFA's profits to set the two rates equal is 43.1 percent, not far from the statutory rate of 39.1 percent. Since affiliates only recorded a tax rate of 24.9 percent, the actual ROA is 3.9 percent. The data are consistent with MNC's equalizing rates of return subject to the home tax rate.

Even if repatriation taxes do not reduce returns by the full amount, the inclusion of intangible assets alone closes the gap a great deal. The fact that affiliates under worldwide taxes hold more retained earnings suggests that repatriation taxes do bind MNC's behavior at least to some degree. The reaction to the AJCA shows that MNC's behavior is not neutral to taxes. Therefore, it is reasonable that different tax systems induce different investment portfolios. Investing in intangible assets provides a partial way around corporate income taxes, which may be used even if financial engineering can be used to reduce the repatriation tax burden.

8. Conclusion

This paper estimates aggregate intangible capital stocks for foreign owned affiliates and suggest a significant role for different holdings of intangible assets due to corporate income taxes. Adjusting rates of return for intangible assets reduces the U.S. FDI returns gap from 4.7 to 1.1 percentage points over the period 1990 to 2001, accounting for about three quarters of the gap. Similar adjustments reduce the British FDI returns gap by 40 percent.

While the results are consistent with intangible assets being an important source of the gap, other factors may account for it. Indeed, the analysis does not account for the full gap indicating that additional factors are at work. A full accounting of the true impact of intangibles will require a careful micro level estimate of these assets.

A. Data Appendix

Table 1

- Average Statutory Corporate Income Tax: Devereux et al. (2002).
- Average Empirical Corporate Income Tax: U.S.: NIPA Table 6.17B. Corporate Profits Before Tax by Industry. Other Countries: USDIA Table III.E.1.

Table 4

- Return on Assets: Payments to direct investment divided by direct investment assets with market value adjustment.
- $\frac{RD}{Y}$: R&D performed by affiliates divided by value added.
- $\frac{K^M}{Y}$ Net gross property, plant and equipment plus inventories divided by value added.

Figure 1

- Assets: International Investment Position, Table 1, Line 1.
- Net Income: Balance of Payments, Table 1, lines 12 and 29.

Figure 2

- FDI Assets: International Investment Position, FDI assets with market pricing adjustment.
- Non-FDI Assets: Total non-financial derivatives assets less FDI.
- Net Income: Balance of Payments, Table 1, lines 12 and 29 less income to FDI.

Figure 3

- Statutory Corporate Income Tax: Devereux et al. (2002).
- Affiliate tax rate: Foreign corporate income tax paid over pre-tax net income, majority owned foreign affiliates.

Figure 4

- IIP: Foreign Direct Investment (Release MA4), U.K. National Statistics Office.
- Net Income: U.K. National Statistics Office, series HJYW-HJYX.

Figure 5

- ROA: U.K. National Statistics Office, series HBOH, HBOI.

REFERENCES

Altshuler, Rosanne & Harry Grubert (2002), 'Repatriation taxes, repatriation strategies and multinational financial policy', *Journal of Public Economics 87*(1), 73–107.

Altshuler, Rosanne, T. Scott Newlon & William C. Randolph (1995), Do repatriation taxes matter?: Evidence from the tax returns of U.S. multinationals, *in* M.Feldstein, J.Hines & G.Hubbard, eds, *'The Effects of International Taxation on Multinational Corporations'*, University of Chicago Press, Chicago, pp. 253–272.

Atkeson, Andrew & Patrick Kehoe (2005), 'Modeling and measuring organization capital', *Journal of Political Economy 113*(5), 1026–1053.

Backus, David, Espen Henriksen & Kjetil Storesletten (2008), 'Taxes and the global allocation of capital', *Journal of Monetary Economics 55*(1), 4861.

Bernard, Andrew, J. Bradford Jensen & Peter Schott (2006), Transfer pricing by U.S. based multinational firms, *Manuscript*, Tuck School of Business, Dartmouth University.

Caballero, Ricardo J., Emmanuel Farhi & Pierre-Olivier Gourinchas (2008), 'An equilibrium model of 'global imbalances' and low interest rates', *American Economic Review 98(1),* 358393.

Carson, Carol S., Bruce T. Grimm & Carol E. Moylan (1994), 'A satellite account for research and development', *Survey of Current Business* pp. 37–71.

Curcuru, Stephanie, Tomas Dvorak & Francis Warnock (2008), 'Cross-border returns differentials', *Quarterly Journal of Economics*.

Desai, Mihir A., C. Fritz Foley & James R. Hines (2001), 'Repatriation taxes and dividend distortions', *National Tax Journal 54(4),* 829–851.

Devereux, Michael P., Rachel Griffith & Alexander Klemm (2002), 'Corporate income tax reforms and international tax competition', *Economic Policy 17(35)*, 451–495.

Doms, Mark & J. Bradford Jensen (1998), Comparing wages, skills, and productivity between domestically owned and foreign-owned manufacturing establishments in the united states, *in* R. E.Baldwin, R. E.Lipsey & J. D.Richardson, eds, *'Geography and Ownership as Bases of Economic Accounting',* University of Chicago Press, Chicago, pp. 235–255.

Forbes, Kristen (2008), Why do foreigners invest in the United States?, *Discussion Paper* 13908, NBER.

Girma, Sourafel, Steve Thompson & Peter W. Wright (2002), 'Why are productivity and wages higher in foreign firms', *Economic and Social Review 33(1)*, 93–100.

Gourinchas, Pierre-Olivier & Helene Rey (2006), From world banker to world venture capitalist: The US external adjustment and the exorbitant privilege, *in* R.Clarida, ed., *'G7 Current Account Imbalances: Sustainability and Adjustment',* University of Chicago Press, Chicago, pp. 11–55.

Griffith, Rachel, Rupert Harrison & John Van Reenen (2004), How special is the special relationship?: Using the impact of U.S. R&D spillovers as a test of technology sourcing, *Discussion Paper* 4698, CEPR.

Hausmann, Ricardo & Frederico Sturzenegger (2007), 'The missing dark matter in the wealth of nations and its implications for global imbalances', *Economic Policy* 22(51), 469518.

Hines, James R. (1999), 'Lessons from behavioral responses to international taxation', *National Tax Journal 52(2)*, 305322.

Hung, Juann H. & Angelo Mascaro (2004), Return on cross-border investment: Why does U.S. investment abroad do better?, *Technical Paper* 2004-17, Congressional Budget Office.

Kapicka, Marek (2008), How important is technology capital?: *Measurement and theory,* mimeo, UCSB.

Kozlow, Ralph & Patricia Abaroa (2006), U.S. multinational companies, dividends, and taxes, mimeo, Bureau of Economic Analysis.

Kubelec, Chris, Bjorn-Erik Orskaug & Misa Tanaka (2007), 'Financial globalization, external balance sheets and economic adjustment', *Bank of England Quarterly Bulletin 47(2),* 244–257.

Landefeld, J. Steven, Ann M. Lawson & Douglas B. Weinberg (1992), 'Rates of return on direct investment', *Survey of Current Business* pp. 79–86.

Laster, David S. & Robert N. McCauley (1994), 'Making sense of the profits of foreign firms in the United States', *FRBNY Quarterly Review* pp. 44–75.

Lev, Baruch & Theodore Sougiannis (1996), 'The capitalization, amortization, and value-relevance of R&D', *Journal of Accounting and Economics 21(1)*, 107–138.

Lipsey, Robert E. (2008), Measuring the location of production in a world of intangible productive assets, FDI, and intrafirm trade, *Working Paper* 14121, NBER.

Mataloni, Raymond (2000), 'An examination of the low rates of return of foreign-owned U.S. companies', *Survey of Current Business* pp. 55–73.

McGrattan, Ellen & Edward C. Prescott (2005), 'Taxes, regulations, and the value of U.S. and U.K. corporations', *Review of Economic Studies 72(3)*, 767–796.

McGrattan, Ellen & Edward C. Prescott (2008), Technology capital and the U.S. current account, *Staff Report* 406, Federal Reserve Bank of Minneapolis.

Meissner, Christopher M. & Alan M. Taylor (2006), Losing our marbles in the new century?: The great rebalancing in historical perspective, *Working Paper* 12580, NBER.

Mendoza, Enrique, Vincenzo Quadrini & Victor Rios-Rull (2007), *Financial integration, financial deepness and global imbalances*, mimeo, University of Minnesota.

Nickell, Stephen (2006), 'The UK current account deficit and all that', *Bank of England Quarterly Bulletin 46(2)*, 231–239.

Okubo, Sumiye, Carol A. Robbins, Carol E. Moylan, Brian K. Sliker, Laura I. Schultz & Lisa S. Mataloni (2006), R&D satellite account: Preliminary estimates, mimeo, Bureau of Economic Analysis and National Science Foundation.

Pratten, Cliff (1996), *The Valuation of Outward and Inward Direct Investment*, Cambridge University.

Prescott, Edward C. & M. Visscher (1980), 'Organization capital', *Journal of Political Economy* 88(3), 446461.

Robbins, Carol (2006), *Measuring payments for the supply and use of intellectual property, mimeo,* Bureau of Economic Analysis.

U.S. Deparment of the Treasury Internal Revenue Service (1999), *Measuring payments for the supply and use of intellectual property,* Publication 3218 (4-1999).

van Dijk, Michiel, Francis Weyzig & Richard Murphy (2006), The Netherlands: A tax haven?, Technical report, SOMO (Centre for Research on Multinational Corporations).

World Bank (2006), *Where is the Wealth of Nations?: Measuring Capital for the 21st Century*, World Bank, Washington.

End Notes

[1] In the paper, "inward" and "outward" are defined from the perspective of the United States.

[2] Unlike the United States, which reports current cost estimates, the UK data only values FDI assets at book value.

[3] The countries are Canada, France, Germany, Ireland, Japan, the Netherlands and the United States. These countries account for about 70 percent of British foreign direct investment assets abroad. Unlike the U.S. case, FDI assets are valued at book value.4Annual international investment position data by country is only available for the UK starting in 1987.

In: Direct Investment Abroad
Editor: Caleb J. Blackwell

ISBN: 978-1-61668-857-8
© 2010 Nova Science Publishers, Inc.

Chapter 7

DIRECT INVESTMENT POSITIONS FOR 2008: COUNTRY AND INDUSTRY DETAIL*

Marilyn Ibarra and Jennifer Koncz

IN 2008, both the U.S. direct investment abroad and foreign direct investment in the United States positions, valued at historical-cost, grew 8 percent. This marked a slowdown in growth for both positions compared with 2007, when the U.S. direct investment abroad—or "outward"—position rose 18 percent and the foreign direct investment in the United States—or "inward"—position rose 15 percent.[1]

The much slower growth in the outward direct investment position reflected a drop in new investment activity abroad by U.S. parent companies.[2] The slowdown in growth in the inward direct investment position reflected the write-downs of financial assets, especially in banking and nonbank finance and insurance, as a result of unsettled conditions in financial markets.

Highlights of U.S. direct investment abroad include the following:

- The increase in the outward direct investment position in 2008 (8 percent) significantly lagged the increase in 2007 (18 percent) and was the smallest since 2005 (4 percent). In 1996–2006, annual growth averaged 12 percent. The slowdown in growth in 2008 reflected lower equity capital flows and a shift in valuation adjustments from positive to negative.
- Reinvested earnings were the largest contributor to the increase in the outward position, as they have been in most years. Reinvested earnings rose 6 percent in 2008 as a result of slightly higher earnings and an increase in the share of earnings reinvested in several industries. Earnings grew 2 percent in 2008; earnings gains in the first half of the year were not fully offset by sharp declines later in the year.
- Net equity investments also contributed to the increase in the outward position although these investments were substantially lower in 2008 than in 2007. The

* This is an edited, reformatted and augmented version of a U. S. Bureau of Economic Analysis publication dated July 2009.

decline in equity investment, much of which was for acquisitions of foreign businesses by U.S. companies, coincided with a decline in global merger and acquisition activity; a lack of available credit, plunging stock markets, and a worldwide financial crisis late in the year undermined companies' ability and incentives to make acquisitions. Intercompany debt inflows and negative valuation adjustments decreased the position.

Highlights of foreign direct investment in the United States include the following:

- The inward direct investment position growth (8 percent) in 2008 significantly lagged the increase (15 percent) in 2007. In 1996–2006, annual growth averaged 12 percent. The slowdown in growth in 2008 reflected the turbulent financial market conditions, which are reflected in large valuation adjustments, that began in the second half of 2007 and persisted throughout 2008.
- Net equity capital investment was the largest component of the increase in the inward position in 2008, as it has been in most years. Boosted by a few large transactions, net equity capital investment grew 61 percent in 2008, the third consecutive year of growth, despite the financial market conditions and a slowdown in economic growth in the United States and in several countries that are important sources of foreign direct investment.
- Reinvested earnings were a substantial component of the increase in the inward position in 2008, as they have been since 2004. Reinvested earnings grew in 2008 despite a decline in earnings because the portion of earnings reinvested increased sharply. Intercompany debt transactions also increased the position, though to a lesser extent. In contrast, valuation adjustments decreased the positio

DATA AVAILABILITY

This article summarizes the preliminary statistics on direct investment positions for 2008. It also presents revised statistics on both outward and inward direct investment for 2006 2007. More detailed statistics on the positions and capital transactions and related income flows for both outward and inward investment will be published in the September 2009 SURVEY OF CURRENT BUSINESS.

Detailed statistics on the outward direct investment position and related capital and income flows for 1982–2008 and statistics on the inward direct investment position and related capital and income flows for 1980–2008 are available on BEA's Web site. To access these files, which can be downloaded at no charge, go to BEA's Web site at www.bea.gov.

For more information on these products and how to access them, see the guide to BEA information on direct investment at www.bea.gov/scb/ account_articles/ international/ iidguide. htm.

This article presents details on the direct investment positions valued at historical-cost by type of capital flow. It also presents details for outward investment by country of foreign affiliate and for inward investment by country of foreign parent.[3] Revisions to previously released statistics are also discussed.

Table A. Direct Investment Positions on a Historical-Cost Basis, 1982–2008

	Billions of dollars		Percent change from preceding year	
Yearend	Outward position [1]	Inward position [2]	Outward position [1]	Inward position [2]
1982	207.8	124.7		
1983	212.2	137.1	2.1	9.9
1984	218.1	164.6	2.8	20.1
1985	238.4	184.6	9.3	12.2
1986	270.5	220.4	13.5	19.4
1987	326.3	263.4	20.6	19.5
1988	347.2	314.8	6.4	19.5
1989	381.8	368.9	10.0	17.2
1990	430.5	394.9	12.8	7.0
1991	467.8	419.1	8.7	6.1
1992	502.1	423.1	7.3	1.0
1993	564.3	467.4	12.4	10.5
1994	612.9	480.7	([3])	([3])
1995	699.0	535.6	14.1	11.4
1996	795.2	598.0	13.8	11.7
1997	871.3	681.8	9.6	14.0
1998	1,000.7	778.4	14.8	14.2
1999	1,216.0	955.7	21.5	22.8
2000	1,316.2	1,256.9	8.2	31.5
2001	1,460.4	1,344.0	10.9	6.9
2002	1,616.5	1,327.2	10.7	–1.3
2003	1,769.6	1,395.2	9.5	5.1
2004	2,160.8	1,520.3	22.1	9.0
2005	2,241.7	1,634.1	3.7	7.5
2006	2,477.3[r]	1,840.5[r]	10.5	12.6
2007	2,916.9[r]	2,109.9[r]	17.7	14.6
2008	3,162.0[p]	2,278.9[p]	8.4	8.0

p Preliminary
r Revised
1. U.S. direct investment position abroad.
2. Foreign direct investment position in the United States.
3. The direct investment positions reflect a discontinuity between 1993 and 1994 because of the reclassification of intercompany debt between parent companies and affiliates that are nondepository financial intermediaries from direct investment to other investment accounts.

U.S. DIRECT INVESTMENT ABROAD

The U.S. direct investment position abroad valued at historical cost—the book value of U.S. direct investors' equity in, and net outstanding loans to, their foreign affiliates—was $3,162.0 billion at the end of 2008 (table A and chart 1). As in previous years, three host countries—the Netherlands, the United Kingdom, and Canada—accounted for over a third of the total position (table 1.2 and chart 2). Positions in the Netherlands and the United Kingdom were more than twice as large as the positions of all other countries except Canada. In 2008, the Netherlands surpassed the United Kingdom as the largest host country, with a U.S. position of $442.9 billion, or 14 percent of the total. In the Netherlands, most of the position increase and nearly 70 percent of the position was accounted for by holding companies, which may have invested the funds in other countries or industries. (See the box "Holding Companies in the Data on U.S. Direct Investment Abroad.") The position in the United Kingdom was $420.9 billion (13 percent), and the position in Canada was $227.3 billion (7 percent).

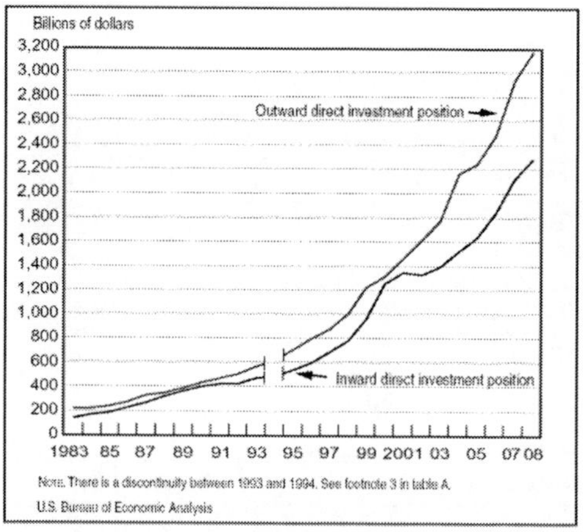

Chart 1. Direct Investment Positions on a Historical-Cost Basis, 1983–2008

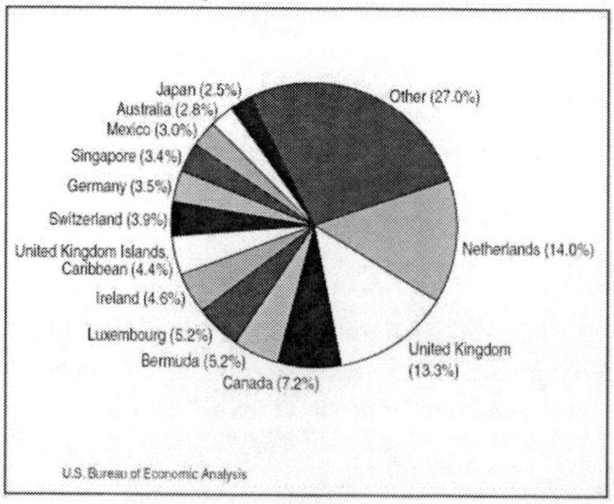

Chart 2. Outward Direct Investment Position by Country of Foreign Affiliate at Yearend 2008

In 2008, the outward direct investment position grew 8 percent, or $245.1 billion, down significantly from the 18 percent growth in 2007. The slowdown in growth reflected lower equity capital flows and a shift in valuation adjustments from positive to negative.

Changes by Component

The $245.1 billion increase in the outward direct investment position was the net result of capital outflows of $311.8 billion and valuation adjustments of –$66.7 billion (table B and chart 3).

Table B. Change in the Outward Direct Investment Position on a Historical-Cost Basis by Component [Billions of dollars]

	2007	2008
Total	439.7	245.1
Capital flows without current-cost adjustment	378.4	311.8
Equity capital	174.9	90.2
Increases	248.9	132.7
Decreases	74.0	42.4
Intercompany debt	–15.3	–9.7
Reinvested earnings without current-cost adjustment	218.8	231.3
Valuation adjustments	61.3	–66.7
Currency translation	54.8	–70.1
Other	6.5	3.4

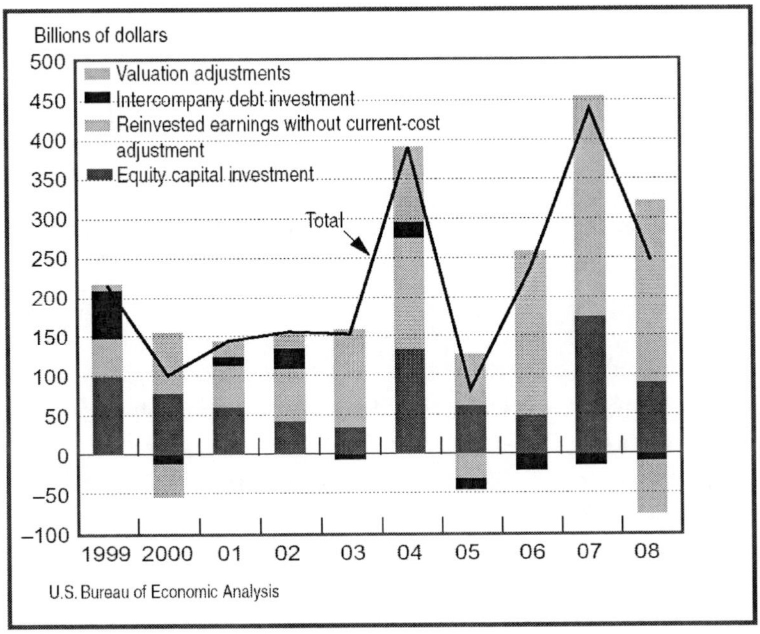

Chart 3. Change in the Outward Direct Investment Position by Component, 1999–2008

Capital flows

Capital outflows for U.S. direct investment abroad were $311.8 billion in 2008, down from $378.4 billion in 2007. Capital flows in 2008 resulted from reinvested earnings of $231.3 billion and net equity capital investment of $90.2 billion, which were partly offset by a $9.7 billion reduction in U.S. parents' net intercompany debt claims on their foreign affiliates.

Equity capital investment. U.S. parents' net equity investment in their foreign affiliates was $90.2 billion in 2008, down sharply from $174.9 billion in 2007. However, the 2008 net equity capital flows were still the fourth highest in the past 10 years. Net equity investment resulted from equity capital increases of $132.7 billion, which were partly offset by equity capital decreases of $42.4 billion. Equity capital increases were down 47 percent from 2007, largely reflecting a slowdown in acquisitions and establishments of new foreign affiliates.[4] Equity capital increases for the acquisition or establishment of new foreign affiliates were $49.2 billion, down from $125.3 billion. Equity capital increases also reflected capital contributions to existing foreign affiliates, which were $83.5 billion, down from $123.6 billion. Equity capital decreases, which reduce the outward position, were down 43 percent from 2007, reflecting a drop in liquidations or selloffs of foreign affiliates and in returns of capital from continuing affiliates.

Equity capital increases for the acquisition or establishment of new affiliates were largest in Europe, particularly in the Netherlands and the United Kingdom. In the Netherlands, the largest increase was in holding companies, whose holdings include retail trade affiliates in Europe and wholesale trade and professional, scientific, and technical services affiliates in Europe and "Latin America and Other Western Hemisphere." In the United Kingdom, the increases were mainly in manufacturing (primarily machinery), "other industries" (particularly electronics retail trade), and "finance (except banks) and insurance."[5]

Among industries, acquisitions of foreign businesses or establishment of new affiliates by U.S. direct investors were largest in "finance (except banks) and insurance," banking, and manufacturing (particularly in machinery and in electrical equipment, appliances, and components manufacturing).

The largest capital contributions were to affiliates in Europe, primarily in the United Kingdom and the Netherlands, and in "Latin America and Other Western Hemisphere," primarily in the "United Kingdom Islands, Caribbean" and Bermuda. By industry, the largest capital contributions were to affiliates in "finance (except banks) and insurance," followed by holding companies, and mining.

In 2008, equity capital decreases due to returns of capital from continuing affiliates were slightly higher than equity capital decreases due to liquidations or selloffs of affiliates. By industry, equity capital decreases were largest in "finance (except banks) and insurance." By region, equity capital decreases were largest in Europe and in Asia and Pacific.

Reinvested earnings. The difference between U.S. parent companies' shares in their foreign affiliates' total earnings and the distributions to the parents from the affiliates' current and cumulative retained earnings—that is, reinvested earnings—increased 6 percent in 2008, to $231.3 billion. Reinvested earnings accounted for more than 90 percent of the increase in the outward position and nearly three-fourths of the capital outflows.

In 2008, reinvested earnings were by far largest for affiliates in holding companies and then in manufacturing (particularly other manufacturing and chemicals), which together accounted for 61 percent of the total. By region, reinvested earnings were largest in Europe, accounting for 56 percent of the worldwide total. Reinvested earnings were particularly large in five European countries: the Netherlands, Ireland, Switzerland, the United Kingdom, and Luxembourg.

ALTERNATIVE MEASURES OF THE DIRECT INVESTMENT POSITIONS

The detailed statistics on the positions of U.S. direct investment abroad and of foreign direct investment in the United States by country and industry are only prepared on a historical-cost basis, so they largely reflect the price levels of earlier periods. The statistics are also prepared on current-cost and market-value bases, but only at an aggregate level. The current-cost statistics value the U.S. and foreign parents' shares of their affiliates' invest ment in plant and equipment, using the current cost of capital equipment; in land, using general price indexes; and in inventories, using estimates of their replacement cost. The market-value statistics value the equity portion of direct investment using indexes of stock market prices.

The historical-cost statistics are not usually adjusted to reflect the changes in the current costs or the replacement costs of tangible assets or in the stock market valuations of firms. Over time, the current costs of tangible assets and the stock market valuations of firms tend to increase. As a result, the historical-cost statistics on the positions tend to be less than the current-cost and market-value statistics on the positions. However, due to the large declines in equity prices, the market value is less for the position of U.S. direct investment abroad in 2008. The current-cost statistics on the position are discussed in "The International Investment Position of the United States at Yearend 2008" in this issue.

Alternative Direct Investment Positions, 2007 and 2008 [Millions of dollars]

Valuation method	Position at yearend 2007 r	Changes in 2008			Position at yearend 2008 p
		Total	Capital flows	Valuation adjustments	
U.S. direct investment abroad:					
Historical cost	2,916,930	245,091	311,796	–66,705	3,162,021
Current cost	3,451,482	247,302	332,012	–84,710	3,698,784
Market value	5,227,962 –	2,156,773	332,012	–2,488,785	3,071,189
Foreign direct investment in the United States:					
Historical cost	2,109,876	169,016	316,112	–147,097	2,278,892
Current cost	2,450,132	196,715	319,737	–123,022	2,646,847
Market value	3,593,291	– 1,036,409	319,737	–1,356,146	2,556,882

p Preliminary
r Revised

The growth in reinvested earnings resulted from a reduction in distributions and slightly higher foreign affiliate earnings. The reinvestment ratio—reinvested earnings relative to current-year earnings—rose from 65 percent in 2007 to 68 percent in 2008. Earnings increased 2 percent in 2008 as an increase in the first half of the year was only partly offset by a decline in the second half.

By industry, the largest increase in earnings was in mining. In addition, a large decrease in losses in banks contributed to the overall increase in earnings of foreign affiliates. In contrast, earnings decreased in several industries, including "finance (except banks) and insurance," holding companies, and information. By region, the largest increases in earnings were in "Latin American and Other Western Hemisphere" (primarily the "United Kingdom Islands, Caribbean") and in Canada.

Intercompany debt investment. U.S. parents' indebtedness to their foreign affiliates increased more than the foreign affiliates' indebtedness to their U.S. parents in 2008. Net intercompany debt inflows from foreign affiliates of $9.7 billion were more than accounted for by inflows from Canada and Asia and Pacific. In Canada, the inflows were largest from mining and manufacturing affiliates. In Asia and Pacific, inflows from "finance (except banks) and insurance" affiliates in Hong Kong and Japan mostly accounted for the regional inflows. By industry, manufacturing more than accounted for the global inflows.

Valuation adjustments

Valuation adjustments of –$66.7 billion reduced the outward direct investment position in 2008. In contrast, positive valuation adjustments of $61.3 billion increased the position in 2007.

The negative adjustments in 2008 resulted mostly from negative currency-translation adjustments as the U.S. dollar appreciated against many major currencies, including the British pound, the Canadian dollar, and the euro, from yearend 2007 to yearend 2008. These currency-translation adjustments were partly offset by $3.4 billion in "other" valuation adjustments.

Changes by Area and by Country

In 2008, the outward direct investment position increased in each of the major areas except Canada (table C). U.S. parents with foreign affiliates in Europe had the largest dollar increase, accounting for 61 percent of the overall increase in the position. Outside of Europe, the largest increases were in "Latin America and Other Western Hemisphere" and Asia and Pacific.

Europe. The position for this region increased $150.4 billion, with reinvested earnings accounting for 85 percent of the increase. Reinvested earnings were particularly large in holding companies and manufacturing (especially chemicals). The positions in three countries—the Netherlands, Ireland, and Switzerland—together accounted for nearly three-fourths of the increase in the position in Europe.

Table C. Change in the Outward Direct Investment Position on a Historical-Cost Basis by Country of Foreign Affiliate

	Change (2007–2008)	
	Billions of dollars	Percent
All countries	245.1	8
Canada	–6.7	–3
Europe *of which:*	150.4	9
Netherlands	53.5	14
Ireland	31.3	27
Switzerland	25.4	26
Germany	10.0	10
Luxembourg	9.5	6
Sweden	8.3	24
Spain	3.0	5
France	4.9	7
United Kingdom	–3.7	–1
Russia	–5.2	–36
Latin America and Other Western Hemisphere *of which:*	55.1	11
United Kingdom Islands, Caribbean	30.7	28
Netherlands Antilles	5.0	77
Mexico	4.4	5
Bermuda	3.6	2
Africa	4.1	13
Middle East	4.2	15
Asia and Pacific *of which:*	37.9	8
China	17.1	60
Singapore	11.7	12
Australia	5.2	6
Japan	–2.7	–3

In the Netherlands, holding companies accounted for four-fifths of the increase, most of it due to reinvested earnings. In Ireland, the increase was widespread by industry. The largest increases were in professional, scientific, and technical services, largely attributable to valuation adjustments, and in holding companies, largely attributable to reinvested earnings. In Switzerland, a large share of the increase was in holding companies; both intercompany debt investment and reinvested earnings were large contributors to the increase.

The position decreased in Russia and the United Kingdom. In Russia, the position decreased by more than a third and was more than accounted for by a decrease in mining, mainly due to valuation adjustments. In the United Kingdom, the decrease was spread over several industries, including manufacturing (particularly petroleum refining and extraction and beverages) and "other industries" (particularly rental and leasing services).

Latin America and Other Western Hemisphere. The position increased $55.1 billion, with reinvested earnings accounting for most of the increase. The "United Kingdom Islands,

Caribbean" had by far the largest increase, $30.7 billion; this increase was mainly in holding companies and in "finance (except banks) and insurance."

Asia and Pacific. The position increased $37.9 billion in 2008. The largest increases were in China, Singapore, and Australia; China alone accounted for 45 percent of the total increase. In China, the largest increase was in banking, due mostly to acquisitions and establishments of new affiliates. In Singapore, the largest increase was in holding companies. In Australia, the increase was more than accounted for by mining.

Within this region, the largest decrease in the position was in Japan, which was more than accounted for by a decrease in "finance (except banks) and insurance."

Middle East and Africa. The $4.2 billion increase in the Middle East position was the largest percentage increase (15 percent) of any region. Increases in the position were widespread by industry and by country; the largest increases were in Qatar, Israel, and Kuwait. In Africa, the $4.1 billion increase was the second largest percentage increase (13 percent) of all regions. Within this region, the largest increases were in Nigeria and Egypt.

Canada. In 2008, the position fell $6.7 billion. The decrease was more than accounted for by negative currency-translation adjustments. The largest decreases were in manufacturing (particularly transportation equipment and chemicals) and in mining.

Holding Companies in the Data on U.S. Direct Investment Abroad

For the past two decades, U.S. parent companies have funneled an increasing share of their direct investments abroad through holding company affiliates.[1] Foreign affiliates classified as holding companies accounted for 36 percent of the U.S. direct investment position abroad in 2008.[2] In 1982, foreign affiliates classified as holding companies accounted for 9 percent of the U.S. direct investment position abroad (chart A). The upward trend of the holding company share is part of a broader trend of indirect ownership in which U.S. parents own foreign affiliates that, in turn, own other foreign affiliates.

One consequence of the rising use of indirect ownership arrangements is that U.S. direct investment abroad statistics on the position and related flows show industry and country patterns that are increasingly different from the industries and countries in which the production and sale of goods and services by foreign affiliates occurs.[3]

Data from ent companies and their foreign affiliates suggest the degree to which indirect ownership structures may affect the country and industry distributions of the outward position data.[4] The statistics on the operations of these foreign affiliates are classified in the country where the affiliate's activity is carried out, and they are classified in the industry that reflects the statistics reflect more closely the countries and industries in which the production of goods and services by foreign affiliates actually occurs than do the statistics classified by the country and industry of the affiliate with which the parent company has a direct position or transaction.

The use of holding company affiliates appears to be the most important reason for differences in the patterns of investment by country or by industry between the position statistics and the operations statistics. However, other factors also contribute, including indirect ownerfunneled ship through other types of affiliates, the fact that the operations statistics, unlike the position statistics, are not adjusted for percentage of U.S. ownership, and duplicapercent tion in some measures of affiliate operations—such as assets and earnings—when affiliates hold equity or debt positions in one another. A comparison of the statistics on the outward direct investment position with the staof tistics on the assets and the net property, plant, and equipment (PP&E) of foreign affiliates for 2006 (the lataffiliates est year for which detailed operations statistics are available) illustrates the differences in distribution between the position statistics and the statistics on the operations. In that year, manufacturing's share of the outward posiand, 18 percent, was similar to its 15 percent share of the assets, but much lower than its 40 percent share of the PP&E, of foreign affiliates. By country, the Netherlands' share of the direct investment position was 11 percent, compared with its 9 percent share of assets and 3 percent share of PP&E.[5]

For further discussion of the effect of holding compaposition nies on the direct investment abroad series, see the "Technical Note" in Maria Borga and Raymond J. Matalaffiliate's oni, Jr., "Direct Investment Positions for 2000: Country and Industry Detail," SURVEY OF CURRENT BUSINESS 81 (July 2001): 23–25.

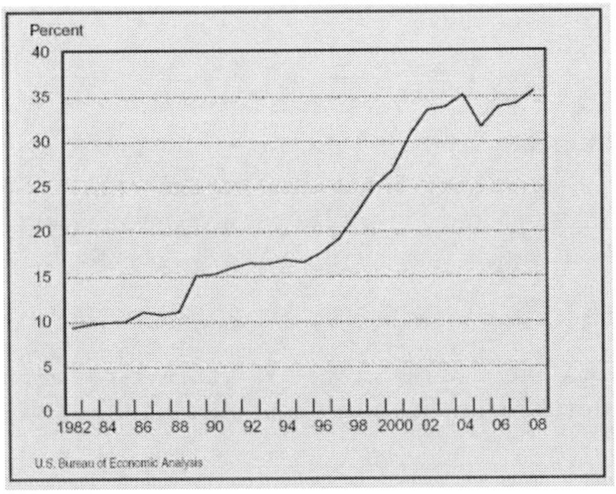

Chart A. Holding Companies' Share of the Outward Direct Investment Position, 1982–2008

[1] A holding company is a company whose primary activity is holding the securities or financial assets of other companies.

[2] In 2008, the share reached a new record high, slightly surpassing the previous record of 35 percent in 2004. The lower shares in 2005–2007 were primarily the result of large earnings distributions (and the resulting negative reinvested earnings) in 2005 associated with the American Jobs Creation Act of 2004. The largest distributions were from holding companies, especially those with parents in chemicals manufacturing.

[3] Statistics on the outward position and related flows are allocated to the industries and countries of the affiliates with which the U.S. parent companies have direct transactions and positions rather than to the industries and countries of the affiliates whose operations the parents

ultimately own or control. This convention follows international guidelines in the International Monetary Fund's *Balance of Payments Manual,* 6th edition.

[4] Besides chain-of-ownership information, data collected on the operations survey include items such as assets, sales, employment, and net property, plant, and equipment.

[5] The statistics used to derive the shares of the assets and the PP&E cover only those foreign affiliates that are majority-owned by U.S. direct investors.

FOREIGN DIRECT INVESTMENT IN THE UNITED STATES

The foreign direct investment position in the United States valued at historical cost—the book value of foreign direct investors' equity in and outstanding loans to, their U.S. affiliates—was $2,278.9 billion at the end of 2008 (table A and chart 1). The United Kingdom accounted for the largest position, $454.1 billion, or 20 percent of the total, followed by Japan and the Netherlands, which each accounted for 11 percent of the total with positions of $259.6 billion and $259.4 billion, respectively (table 2.2 and chart 4). The next largest positions were for Canada (10 percent) and Germany (9 percent).

In 2008, the inward direct investment position increased 8 percent, or $169.0 billion, down markedly from the 15 percent increase in 2007. The slower growth in 2008 was the result of larger negative valuation adjustments and a decrease in net intercompany debt investment. These changes more than offset a sizable increase in equity capital and a much smaller increase in reinvested earnings.

Changes by Component

The $169.0 billion increase in the inward direct investment position resulted from capital inflows of $316.1 billion, which were partly offset by negative valuation adjustments of $147.1 billion (table D and chart 5).

Table D. Change in the Inward Direct Investment Position on a Historical-Cost Basis by Component [Billions of dollars]

	2007	2008
Total	269.4	169.0
Capital flows without current-cost adjustment	271.2	316.1
Equity capital	155.4	250.2
Increases	240.6	288.2
Decreases	85.3	38.0
Intercompany debt	71.0	15.0
Reinvested earnings without current-cost adjustment	44.8	51.0
Valuation adjustments	–1.8	–147.1
Currency translation	4.9	–6.4
Other	–6.6	–140.7

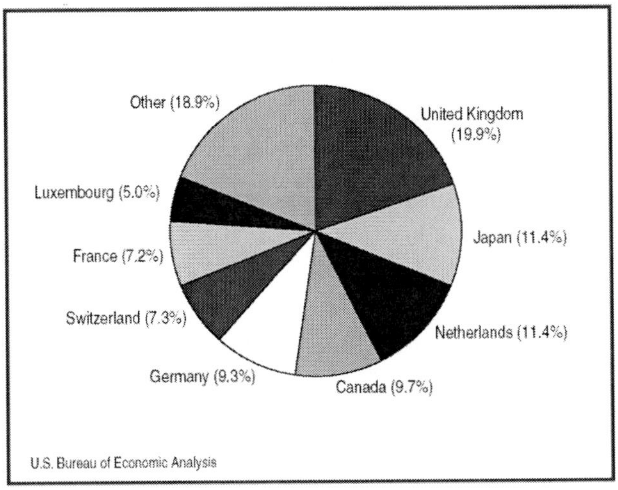

Chart 4. Inward Direct Investment Position by Country of Each Member of the Foreign Parent Group at Yearend 2008

Capital flows

Capital inflows for foreign direct investment in the United States were $316.1 billion in 2008, up from $271.2 billion in 2007. Capital flows in 2008 consisted of $250.2 billion in net equity capital investment, $51.0 billion in reinvested earnings, and $15.0 billion in net intercompany debt investment.

Equity capital investment. Net equity capital investment by foreign parents in their U.S. affiliates was $250.2 billion in 2008, up from $155.4 billion in 2007 and nearly as high as in 2000, when net equity investments peaked at $259.6 billion. In 2008, net equity capital investment resulted from $288.2 billion in equity capital increases and partly offsetting equity capital decreases of $38.0 billion. Boosted by a few large transactions, equity capital increases were up 20 percent in 2008, as foreign investors' expenditures to acquire U.S. businesses increased despite tightening credit conditions, slower growth in the United States and countries that are important sources of direct investment, and a slowdown in worldwide merger activity. Acquisitions in 2008 were broadly based by industry.[6] Equity capital increases in 2008 also reflected capital contributions made by foreign parents to their existing U.S. affiliates, especially those in "finance (except banks) and insurance" and in banking. Many of these affiliates suffered capital losses in 2008. Equity capital decreases, which decrease the inward position, were down 55 percent from 2007, as there were fewer large selloffs of U.S. affiliates and returns of capital in 2008.

Equity capital increases in 2008 were widespread by industry and by country of foreign parent. The largest increases were in manufacturing and in "finance (except banks) and insurance," which together accounted for 58 percent of equity capital increases in 2008. Within manufacturing, equity capital increases were largest in "other" manufacturing, especially beverages and tobacco products, and in chemicals; increases in both were mostly attributable to acquisitions of U.S. businesses. European investors accounted for more than three-quarters of the equity increase in manufacturing. In "finance (except banks) and insurance," equity capital increases were broadly based by country of foreign parent and reflected both acquisitions, especially in insurance, and capital contributions to existing affiliates, especially in nonbank finance. Overall, by country, the largest equity increases were from the Netherlands, the United Kingdom, Japan, and Canada. Equity capital decreases were widely dispersed by industry and by country.

Reinvested earnings. The foreign parent's share of U.S. affiliates' current-period earnings less distributions to the parents from affiliates' current and cumulative retained earnings—that is, reinvested earnings—added $51.0 billion to the inward direct investment position in 2008. Reinvested earnings were up 14 percent from 2007 despite a small decline in reinvested earnings have contributed substantially to growth in the inward investment position.

Reinvested earnings were largest for affiliates in "finance (except banks) and insurance," in wholesale trade, and in "other industries," which together more than accounted for the overall total. Within "other industries," reinvested earnings were largest in mining. By country, reinvested earnings were largest for affiliates with parents in Switzerland, the United Kingdom, and France.

Earnings reinvested in U.S. affiliates increased 14 percent in 2008 despite a $3.7 billion, or 4 percent, decrease in earnings, to $93.2 billion. This marked the second consecutive year of decline in affiliates' earnings, which peaked at $126.3 billion in 2006. The decline in 2008 was in line with a 15 percent contraction in U.S. corporate profits.[7] U.S. affiliates' earnings were down in several industries but banks—which suffered a sharp increase in losses as a result of turmoil in financial markets—more than accounted for the overall decline. The reinvestment ratio—the ratio of reinvested earnings to total earnings—was 55 percent in 2008, up from 46 percent in 2007, as distributions to foreign parents fell more sharply than earnings. The largest increase in reinvested earnings was in "finance (except banks) and insurance," reflecting both improved earnings and reduced distributions to foreign parents.[8]

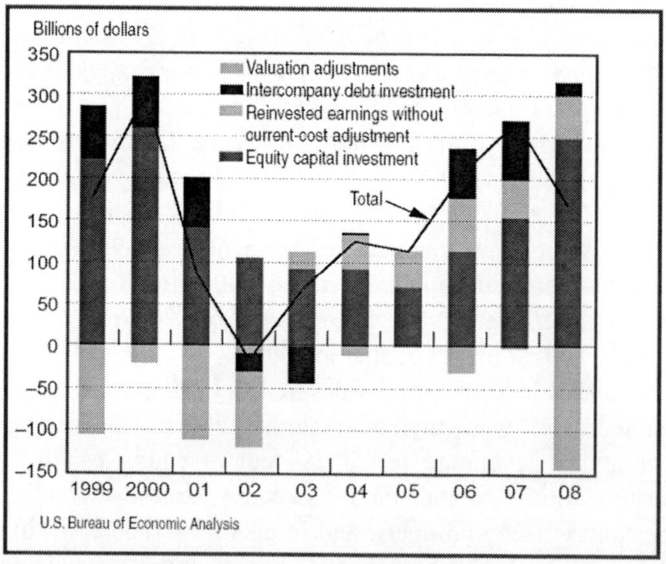

Chart 5. Change in the Inward Direct Investment Position by Component, 1999–2008

Intercompany debt investment. Borrowing and lending transactions between U.S. affiliates and foreign parent groups increased the inward direct investment position $15.0 billion in 2008, compared with $71.0 billion in 2007. Net debt investment in 2008 resulted from a $17.3 billion increase in U.S. affiliates' debt obligations to their foreign parents or other members of the foreign parent group, which was partly offset by a $2.3 billion increase in affiliates' debt claims on foreign parent group members. Net debt investment was held down by several sizable transactions in which U.S. affiliates paid down their debts. The largest increase in position due to net debt investment in 2008 was for affiliates in "finance (except banks) and insurance," followed by those in "other industries," especially utilities. By country, the "United Kingdom Islands, Caribbean" contributed most to the increase in the net intercompany debt position, followed by the United Kingdom and the Netherlands.

KEY TERMS

For a more detailed discussion of the terms in this box, see *Foreign Direct Investment in the United States: Final Results From the 2002 Benchmark Survey* and *U.S. Direct Investment Abroad: Final Results From the 2004 Benchmark Survey.* These methodologies are also available on BEA's Web site at www.bea.gov.

Direct Investment

This is investment in which a resident (in the broad legal sense, including a company) of one country obtains a lasting interest in, and a degree of influence over the management of, a business enterprise in another country. In the United States (and in the international statistical guidelines), the criterion used to define direct investment is ownership of at least 10 percent of the voting securities of an incorporated business enterprise or the equivalent interest in an unincorporated business enterprise.

U.S. direct investment abroad (outward direct investment) represents the ownership or control, directly or indirectly, by one U.S. resident (**U.S. parent**) of at least 10 percent of a foreign business enterprise, which is called a **foreign affiliate**.

Foreign direct investment in the United States (inward direct investment) represents the ownership or control, directly or indirectly, by one foreign resident (**foreign parent**) of at least 10 percent of a U.S. business enterprise, which is called a **U.S. affiliate.** Foreign direct investment includes equity and net debt investments by the foreign parent as well as net debt investments by any other members of the **foreign parent group.** The foreign parent group consists of (1) the foreign parent, (2) any foreign person (including a company), proceeding up the foreign parent's ownership chain, that owns more than 50 percent of the person below it, up to and including the **ultimate beneficial owner (UBO),** and (3) any foreign person, proceeding down the ownership chain(s) of each of these members, that is owned more than 50 percent by the person above it.

The UBO of a U.S. affiliate is the first person that is not more than 50 percent owned by another person in the affiliate's ownership chain beginning with the foreign parent. The UBO ultimately owns or controls the affiliate and derives the benefits and assumes the risks associated with ownership or control. Unlike the foreign parent, the UBO of a U.S. affiliate may be located in the United States.

Direct Investment Position

This is the value of direct investors' equity in, and net outstanding loans to, their affiliates. The direct investment position may be viewed as the direct investor's net financial claims on their affiliates. BEA prepares statistics of the positions for outward direct investment and for inward direct investment at historical cost, current cost, and market value. This article features the **historical-cost** measure. This valuation is principally derived from the books of affiliates and generally reflects the acquisition cost of the investments, cumulative reinvested earnings, and cumulative depreciation of fixed assets. Historical-cost statistics are consistent with U.S. generally accepted accounting principles (GAAP) in most areas. GAAP, however, values the holdings of most financial instruments at current-period prices rather than at historical cost. See the box "Alternative Measures of the Direct Investment Positions."

Direct investment capital flows arise from transactions that change financial claims (assets) and liabilities between U.S. parents and their foreign affiliates or between U.S. affiliates and their foreign parents. Capital **outflows** arise from transactions that increase

U.S. assets or decrease U.S. liabilities. Capital **inflows** arise from transactions that decrease U.S. assets or increase U.S. liabilities. Direct investment capital flows consist of equity capital investment, intercompany debt investment, and reinvested earnings.

Equity capital investment is the difference between equity capital increases and decreases. Equity capital increases arise from (1) parents' establishments of new affiliates, (2) payments by parents to unaffiliated parties for the purchase of capital stock or other equity interests when they acquire an existing business, (3) payments to acquire additional ownership interests in their affiliates, and (4) capital contributions to their affiliates. Equity capital decreases are the funds parents receive when they reduce their equity interest in their affiliates.

Intercompany debt investment results from changes in net outstanding loans between parents (or, for inward investment, other foreign parent group members) and their affiliates, including loans by parents to affiliates and loans by affiliates to parents.

Reinvested earnings (without current-cost adjustment) are the parents' share of the current-period operating earnings of their affiliates less distributions of earnings that affiliates make to their parents. A related measure of reinvested earnings is featured in the international transactions accounts; this measure includes a **current-cost adjustment** that reflects current-period prices. This adjustment converts depreciation charges to a current-cost, or replacement-cost, basis; it adds charges for depletion of natural resources back to income and reinvested earnings, because these charges are not treated as production costs in the national income and product accounts; and it reallocates expenses for mineral exploration and development across periods, so that they are written off over their economic lives rather than all at once.

Various **valuation adjustments** to the historical-cost position are made to account for the differences between changes in the historical-cost positions, which are measured at book value, and direct investment capital flows, which are measured at transaction value. (Unlike the positions on current-cost and market-value bases, the historical-cost position is not usually adjusted to account for changes in the replacement cost of the tangible assets of affiliates or in the market value of parent companies' equity in affiliates.)

Valuation adjustments to the historical-cost position consist of **currency-translation adjustments** and **"other" adjustments.** Currency-translation adjustments account for changes in the exchange rates that are used to translate affiliates' foreign-currency-denominated assets and liabilities into U.S. dollars. "Other" valuation adjustments account for (1) differences between the proceeds from the sale or liquidation of affiliates and their book values, (2) differences between the purchase prices of affiliates and their book values, (3) writeoffs resulting from uncompensated expropriations of affiliates, (4) the reclassification of investment positions between direct investment and other investment, and (5) capital gains and losses (excluding currency-translation adjustments) on transactions, such as the sale of assets (excluding inventories) or capital gains and losses that represent the revaluation of the assets of ongoing affiliates for reasons other than exchange-rate changes, such as the write-down of assets. In addition, for individual industries, offsetting adjustments may be made to effect changes in the industry classification of an affiliate. For individual countries, offsetting adjustments are made when the political boundaries of countries change. In addition, for inward direct investment, offsetting adjustments are made when transactions between foreign residents result in a change in the country of the foreign parent.

Valuation adjustments

Valuation adjustments decreased the inward position $147.1 billion in 2008 after decreasing it $1.8 billion in 2007. Valuation adjustments consisted of –$6.4 billion in currency-translation adjustments and –$140.7 billion in "other" valuation adjustments, which were largely attributable to capital losses. Negative valuation adjustments were largest, by far, in "finance (except banks) and insurance" and in banking. These industries were hit particularly hard by widespread writedowns of financial assets as a result of the unsettled financial market conditions that began in the second half of 2007.

Changes by Area and by Country

In 2008, Europe accounted for 68 percent of the overall increase in the inward direct investment position (table E). The increase in the position for Asia and Pacific was also substantial, accounting for 27 percent of the overall increase.[9]

Europe. The position increased $115.3 billion. Much of the increase was attributable to increases in the position for the Netherlands and the United Kingdom, which together accounted for more than two- thirds of the region's increase. There were also large increases for Hungary, Switzerland, and Spain.

The position for the Netherlands increased $51.2 billion. The largest increase was in manufacturing, followed by wholesale trade and information. Within manufacturing, acquisitions in “other” manufacturing, especially beverages and tobacco products, contributed most to the increase. Acquisitions also boosted the position in wholesale trade.

For the United Kingdom, the $27.6 billion increase was broadly based by industry. The largest increases were in wholesale trade and in manufacturing, especially “other” manufacturing and transportation equipment. In “other” manufacturing, much of the increase was in medical equipment and in petroleum.

The position for Hungary increased $17.5 billion, to $62.5 billion. The increase reflected many cases in which U.S. affiliates were owned by foreign parents in parent groups. The position for Switzerland increased $12.4 billion, mainly in manufacturing; the largest increase within manufacturing was in “other” manufacturing, especially medical equipment. In percentage terms, the position for Finland more than doubled, mainly because of acquisitions.

In contrast to these increases, the position for some countries within Europe decreased. The largest decreases were for Luxembourg and Sweden, which decreased $7.3 billion and $7.1 billion, respectively, and were mainly due to changes in the accounts of existing affiliates; outflows on intercompany debt payables contributed most to the changes.

Asia and Pacific. The position increased $46.1 billion in 2008. The position for Japan increased $29.1 billion, accounting for 63 percent of the region’s increase. For Japan, increases were widespread by industry. The largest increases were in manufacturing, in wholesale trade, and in “finance (except banks) and insurance.” Within manufacturing, chemicals had the largest increase, which was mainly due to acquisitions. Acquisitions were also the main cause of increases in wholesale trade and in “finance (except banks) and insurance.”

The increase in position for Australia was also sizable. Much of the $14.1 billion increase was attributable to “other industries,” including transportation and mining.

Canada. The position increased $13.9 billion and was largely attributable to increases in banking and in information. In both industries, acquisitions were the main contributor to the increase.

Middle East and Africa. The position for Africa increased $0.6 billion, with manufacturing contributing most to the change. In contrast, the position for the Middle East decreased $0.4 billion, reflecting decreases in real estate and rental and leasing and in banking.

Latin America and Other Western Hemisphere. The position decreased $6.6 billion. The “United Kingdom Islands, Caribbean” more than accounted for the change, with a $12.8 billion decrease.

Table E. Change in the Inward Direct Investment Position on a Historical-Cost Basis by Country of Each Member of the Foreign Parent Group

	Change (2007–2008)	
	Billions of dollars	**Percent**
All countries	169.0	8
Canada	13.9	7
Europe	115.3	8
Of which:		
Netherlands	51.2	25
United Kingdom	27.6	6
Hungary	17.5	39
Switzerland	12.4	8
Spain	11.2	41
Finland	7.1	131
Italy	4.3	32
France	3.3	2
Germany	–3.0	–1
	Change (2007–2008)	
	Billions of dollars	**Percent**
Belgium	–5.1	–21
Sweden	–7.1	–17
Luxembourg	–7.3	–6
Latin America and Other Western Hemisphere *of which:*	–6.6	–12
Bermuda	6.1	129
United Kingdom Islands, Caribbean	–12.8	–37
Africa	0.6	43
Middle East	–0.4	–3
Asia and Pacific	46.1	14
Of which:		
Japan	29.1	13
Australia	14.1	28

ACKNOWLEDGMENTS

The statistics on the U.S. direct investment position abroad are largely based on data from BEA's quarterly survey of transactions between U.S. parent companies and their foreign affiliates. The survey was conducted under the supervision of Mark W. New, who was assisted by Iris Branscome, Laura A. Downey, David L. Grayton, Marie K. Laddomada, Sherry Lee, Louis C. Luu, Leila C. Morrison, and Dwayne Torney. Computer programming for data estimation and tabulation was provided by Marie Colosimo.

The statistics on the foreign direct investment position in the United States are based largely on data from BEA's quarterly survey of transactions between U.S. affiliates of foreign companies and their foreign parents. The survey was conducted under the supervision of Gregory G. Fouch, who was assisted by Peter J. Fox, Barbara C. Huang, Susan M. LaPorte, Robert L. Rosholt, and Helen P. Yiu. Computer programming for data estimation and tabulation was provided by Karen E. Poffel and Paula D. Brown.

REVISIONS

The statistics on direct investment positions presented in this article for 2008 are preliminary. The revised statistics for both outward and inward direct investment positions and related capital flows for 2006–2007 incorporate new survey data collected in BEA's quarterly surveys of transactions between parents and their affiliates and in annual surveys of multinational companies' financial and operating data.[10]

The historical-cost outward direct investment position for 2006 was revised up $22.6 billion, to $2,477.3 billion. The upward revision was attributable to a $20.0 billion revision to valuation adjustments from negative to positive and a $2.6 billion upward revision to capital flows. The outward position for 2007 was revised up $125.7 billion, to $2,916.9 billion. The revision was the result of the $22.6 billion upward revision to the 2006 position, a $64.6 billion upward revision to 2007 capital flows, and a $38.5 billion upward revision to 2007 valuation adjustments.

The historical-cost inward direct investment position for 2006 was revised down $3.4 billion, to $1,840.5 billion. The small downward revision resulted from a $3.9 billion downward revision to valuation adjustments and a partly offsetting upward revision of $0.4 billion to capital inflows. The inward position for 2007 was revised up $16.8 billion, to $2,109.9 billion. The revision was the net result of a $38.3 billion upward revision to capital inflows, which was partly offset by an $18.1 billion downward revision to valuation adjustments and the $3.4 billion downward revision to the 2006 position.

Table 1.1. U.S. Direct Investment Position Abroad on a Historical-Cost Basis, 2007 [Millions of Dollars]

			Manufacturing															
	All industries	Mining	Total	Food	Chem- icals	Primary and fabricated metals	Machinery	Computers and electronic products	Electrical equipment, appliances, And Components	Transportation equipment	Other manufacturing	Wholesale trade	Infor mation	Depository instituions	Finance (except depository institutions and insurance	Professional, scientific, and Technical services	Holding companies (nonbank)	Other industries
All countries	**2,916,930**	**143,430**	**493,064**	**39,100**	**102,678**	**22,389**	**32,397**	**69,159**	**18,909**	**58,768**	**149,664**	**154,780**	**114,578**	**127,047**	**617,312**	**68,978**	**998,618**	**199,123**
Canada	**233,971**	**27,794**	**78,059**	**3,729**	**13,432**	**4,633**	**4,476**	**4,352**	**2,333**	**12,618**	**32,487**	**17,346**	**4,118**	**3,649**	**30,011**	**9,114**	**29,867**	**34,013**
Europe [1]	**1,659,499**	**42,832**	**241,498**	**25,924**	**54,300**	**12,410**	**18,328**	**24,459**	**11,660**	**26,656**	**67,762**	**86,986**	**77,387**	**86,348**	**310,123**	**43,385**	**660,673**	**110,268**
Austria	16,527	1	4,009	1	236	(D)	289	(D)	(D)	1,294	96	2,548	–110	1	(D)	341	6,991	(D)
Belgium	62,959	14	18,963	309	8,901	568	237	665	864	930	6,489	6,066	–716	(D)	28,778	2,009	2,810	(D)
Czech Republic	4,180	0	1,850	20	92	67	168	67	120	967	349	51	208	1,466	591	27	(D)	(D)
Denmark	8,273	6	3,576	130	13	47	253	921	53	2	2,156	1,093	614	(D)	322	159	2,051	(D)
Finland	2,196	0	950	0	124	34	(D)	158	(D)	(D)	140	819	147	0	25	87	2	165
France	70,113	96	28,502	6,058	3,529	3,938	1,825	1,960	181	2,307	8,704	4,525	1,633	2,514	7,683	2,022	11,990	11,148
Germany	100,806	732	29,446	726	5,301	2,247	3,164	4,301	1,927	7,791	3,988	10,008	2,759	2,574	13,688	4,439	30,394	6,766
Greece	2,116	–4	540	61	(D)	0	1	14	0	0	(D)	736	44	–119	659	11	240	9
Hungary	4,302	(D)	826	145	122	15	69	53	–4	146	280	257	64	(D)	75	71	(D)	777
Ireland	114,876	(D)	15,693	212	4,851	223	344	4,133	–50	19	5,961	–634	10,651	(D)	23,295	10,489	20,337	22,442
Italy	26,731	30	11,169	813	2,374	525	1,006	1,058	305	1,558	3,529	2,541	2,198	351	3,306	1,068	1,325	4,744
Luxembourg	153,639	163	3,335	0	(D)	(*)	(D)	(D)	(*)	(D)	3,417	2,317	2,208	943	27,025	–24	116,577	1,095
Netherlands	389,430	3,534	26,009	(D)	3,959	985	1,277	1,976	(D)	–187	5,322	13,529	8,879	(D)	49,636	3,374	263,592	(D)
Norway	12,044	8,031	1,564	(D)	173	300	1,241	(D)	–8	0	–48	559	110	(D)	336	172	269	(D)
Poland	15,239	0	4,098	836	841	357	29	146	4	650	1,234	355	507	(D)	1,416	141	(D)	(D)
Portugal	3,123	1	692	10	124	12	(D)	73	15	361	(D)	716	100	0	413	39	126	1,036
Russia	14,404	10,171	2,213	1,151	134	(D)	(*)	51	4	149	(D)	493	29	1,057	63	93	(D)	(D)
Spain	66,621	68	10,968	705	4,094	191	178	169	443	1,289	3,899	3,186	412	1,144	7,455	2,123	38,821	2,444

Table 1.1 (Continued)

			Manufacturing															
	All industries	Mining	Total	Food	Chem- icals	Primary and fabricated metals	Machinery	Computers and electronic products	Electrical equipment, appliances, and Components	Transportation equipment	Other manu-facturing	Wholesale trade	Information	Depository instituions	Finance (except depository institutions and insurance	Professional, scientific, and Technical services	Holding companies (nonbank)	Other industries
Sweden	35,120	0	4,192	(D)	346	40	245	834	148	470	(D)	966	196	(D)	8,631	440	17,813	(D)
Switzerland	97,917	139	8,521	147	2,981	158	1,636	1,397	489	271	1,442	17,399	2,244	7,664	5,318	721	50,216	5,695
Turkey	5,974	–3	1,426	48	559	2	3	19	1	305	490	1,551	69	2,643	142	11	(*)	136
United Kingdom	424,612	8,706	61,076	6,302	15,352	2,364	5,870	4,566	2,048	8,000	16,574	16,902	45,034	22,717	121,229	15,528	93,087	40,333
Other	28,299	(D)	1,880	244	(D)	156	92	(D)	20	197	(D)	1,004	106	2,071	(D)	43	4,067	(D)
Latin America and Other Western Hemisphere	**508,711**	**26,053**	**61,187**	**4,982**	**14,572**	**2,450**	**3,198**	**1,840**	**1,486**	**8,868**	**23,791**	**17,989**	**8,224**	**8,032**	**187,482**	**1,902**	**174,210**	**23,632**
South America	103,697	15,530	31,655	1,934	8,966	800	2,292	2,121	54	4,228	11,262	4,311	3,662	6,796	17,584	1,111	18,555	4,493
Argentina	14,061	2,843	2,933	207	1,546	11	144	81	–121	314	752	324	1,178	351	1,128	58	4,650	597
Brazil	47,750	2,899	20,028	1,121	5,213	709	1,920	2,023	58	2,348	6,635	1,649	1,791	3,932	11,221	665	4,987	579
Chile	11,568	1,177	2,351	34	695	3	66	11	(*)	(D)	(D)	896	129	1,214	2,526	137	918	2,220
Colombia	4,496	1,409	1,340	112	409	6	57	(*)	9	(D)	(D)	503	58	(D)	376	31	147	(D)
Ecuador	977	522	147	28	20	(*)	1	3	0	(D)	(D)	107	2	(D)	40	2	(D)	18
Peru	7,551	4,882	509	(D)	191	(D)	4	1	0	0	212	386	210	(D)	130	70	(D)	500
Venezuela	15,748	1,335	4,143	337	820	18	102	–1	108	1,068	1,692	279	43	(D)	2,046	117	7,281	(D)
Other	1,547	463	204	(D)	73	(D)	–3	2	0	24	60	166	251	179	117	32	1	134
Central America	103,122	4,194	25,463	2,912	4,798	873	(D)	(D)	1,432	4,640	(D)	3,600	3,006	21,811	15,942	638	18,050	10,419
Costa Rica	2,265	(*)	1,373	164	171	53	0	(D)	121	0	(D)	8	16	(D)	(D)	125	900	–216
Honduras	640	0	443	–1	10	4	(*)	0	0	43	388	109	(*)	26	13	(*)	–1	48
Mexico	91,259	4,165	22,807	2,609	4,449	822	(D)	(D)	1,311	4,602	(D)	2,780	2,985	(D)	14,645	532	14,497	(D)
Panama	6,509	50	131	35	70	4	0	(*)	0	0	21	433	–6	(D)	765	–25	2,650	(D)
Other	2,449	–21	709	106	97	–11	1	(D)	(*)	–5	(D)	269	11	(D)	(D)	6	4	264

Table 1.1 (Continued)

	All industries	Mining	Manufacturing									Wholesale trade	Information	Depository instituions	Finance (except depository institutions and insurance	Professional, scientific, and Technical services	Holding companies (nonbank)	Other industries
			Total	Food	Chem-icals	Primary and fabricated metals	Machinery	Computers and electronic products	Electrical equipment, appliances, and Components	Transportation equipment	Other manu facturing							
Other Western Hemisphere	301,891	6,329	4,070	136	809	777	(D)	(D)	0	(*)	(D)	10,078	1,556	–20,575	153,956	152	137,605	8,720
Barbados	674	8	287	31	11	9	(*)	237	0	(*)	0	2,112	–1	0	702	(*)	(D)	(D)
Bermuda	162,286	277	965	0	(D)	(*)	(D)	(D)	0	0	96	–941	585	(D)	91,644	136	64,271	(D)
Dominican Republic	766	0	458	64	30	(D)	0	–13	0	0	(D)	130	20	(D)	1	1	(*)	(D)
United Kingdom Islands,Caribbean	108,559	2,270	612	11	43	–37	1	24	0	0	570	8,127	472	–18,927	50,187	92	64,412	1,315
Other	29,606	3,773	1,747	30	(D)	(D)	0	(*)	0	0	(D)	652	481	–1,835	11,422	–76	(D)	(D)
Africa	**32,496**	**14,591**	**3,419**	**128**	**361**	**220**	**281**	**96**	**140**	**1,062**	**1,132**	**1,045**	**134**	**1,750**	**2,237**	**320**	**7,889**	**1,111**
Egypt	7,147	(D)	340	4	–64	8	(D)	5	5	(D)	248	97	2	(D)	23	1	–2	–57
Nigeria	1,433	67	94	19	25	7	(D)	0	0	0	(D)	35	1	(D)	(D)	–1	811	66
South Africa	5,198	(D)	2,343	10	367	181	154	91	135	1,005	399	804	98	615	127	242	(D)	285
Other	18,718	(D)	642	95	33	24	(D)	(*)	0	(D)	(D)	109	34	575	(D)	77	(D)	818
Middle East	**28,256**	**5,613**	**10,528**	**131**	**1,213**	**67**	**405**	**5,217**	**48**	**23**	**3,425**	**1,880**	**1,045**	**553**	**332**	**563**	**7,083**	**659**
Israel	9,464	0	6,256	122	200	0	(D)	5,133	(D)	0	631	837	960	(D)	86	380	715	(D)
Saudi Arabia	5,013	406	(D)	0	(D)	(D)	(D)	(D)	0	23	73	(D)	13	0	(D)	139	3,735	62
United Arab Emirates	2,969	(D)	506	11	115	(D)	(D)	(D)	(D)	0	(D)	(D)	83	(D)	28	52	(D)	86
Other	10,810	(D)	(D)	–2	(D)	0	2	0	0	0	(D)	8	–11	88	(D)	–8	(D)	(D)
Asia and Pacific	**453,997**	**26,547**	**98,373**	**4,207**	**18,799**	**2,610**	**5,709**	**33,194**	**3,244**	**9,543**	**21,067**	**29,534**	**23,671**	**26,715**	**87,127**	**13,694**	**118,896**	**29,440**
Australia	83,346	14,135	13,777	1,497	3,725	1,125	757	750	209	1,682	4,032	3,627	12,217	2,459	11,007	3,939	15,709	6,475
China	28,579	1,772	18,261	690	4,051	575	1,313	6,931	578	1,872	2,251	2,216	516	857	1,315	651	1,280	1,711
Hong Kong	50,199	(*)	3,668	7	648	47	398	1,406	228	33	901	5,739	945	2,921	15,815	2,318	17,165	1,627

Table 1.1 (Continued)

	All industries	Mining	Manufacturing									Wholesale trade	Infor- mation	Depository instituions	Finance (except depository institutions and insurance	Professional, scientific, and Technical services	Holding companies (nonbank)	Other industries
			Total	Food	Chem- icals	Primary and fabricated metals	Machinery	Computers and electronic products	Electrical equipment, appliances, And Components	Transportation equipment	Other manu- facturing							
India	14,540	236	3,106	54	1,373	(D)	662	(D)	179	(D)	(D)	636	3,117	2,552	1,987	1,926	401	578
Indonesia	17,679	5,971	349	–5	244	–5	15	(D)	(D)	–47	(D)	124	–50	(D)	(D)	22	9,439	(D)
Japan	81,923	5	16,888	209	2,672	193	490	3,232	923	2,820	6,348	8,166	4,444	756	35,655	2,075	5,507	8,427
Korea, Republic of	26,854	–1	9,203	924	1,051	181	273	2,816	333	1,161	2,465	1,430	304	10,007	4,055	339	(D)	(D)
Malaysia	13,037	(D)	4,831	37	902	16	109	3,387	3	45	330	192	116	1,160	425	240	2,946	(D)
New Zealand	5,395	332	1,249	(D)	158	31	34	107	(D)	5	(D)	276	242	(D)	1,366	405	(D)	1,046
Philippines	7,066	21	3,920	196	689	11	46	2,232	2	2	742	332	37	510	(D)	270	(D)	463
Singapore	94,810	(D)	14,295	1	1,589	56	1,198	8,887	621	1,019	924	4,248	1,489	2,404	(D)	1,052	(D)	(D)
Taiwan	15,711	(*)	3,616	50	588	95	203	2,127	73	93	387	1,878	270	799	8,305	229	143	470
Thailand	8,850	187	4,716	73	990	121	209	1,010	50	577	1,687	410	22	1,471	1,128	230	125	562
Other	6,010	(D)	492	(D)	120	(D)	1	98	0	(D)	(D)	259	1	345	(D)	1	118	4,348
Addenda:																		
European Union (27) [2]	1,504,444	15,092	227,205	24,471	50,427	11,889	15,408	23,102	11,173	25,886	64,849	66,236	74,920	72,677	296,516	42,379	606,892	102,528
OPEC [3]	59,776	15,175	8,833	373	2,077	87	403	91	135	1,043	4,625	1,484	108	(D)	2,810	347	27,946	(D)

* A nonzero value between –$500,000 and $500,000. , D Suppressed to avoid disclosure of data of individual companies.

1. In 2007, the “Euro area” includes Austria, Belgium, Finland, France, Germany, Greece, Ireland, Italy, Luxembourg, the Netherlands, Portugal, Slovenia and Spain. For 2007, the U.S. direct investment position in the “Euro area” was $1,009,292 million.
2. The European Union (27) comprises Austria, Belgium, Bulgaria, Cyprus, the Czech Republic, Denmark, Estonia, Finland, France, Germany, Greece, Hungary, Ireland, Italy, Latvia, Lithuania, Luxembourg, Malta, the Netherlands, Poland, Portugal, Romania, Slovakia, Slovenia, Spain, Sweden, and the United Kingdom.
3. OPEC is the Organization of Petroleum Exporting Countries. In 2007, its members were Algeria, Angola, Indonesia, Iran, Iraq, Kuwait, Libya, Nigeria, Qatar, Saudi Arabia, the United Arab Emirates, and Venezuela.

Note. Estimates for 2007 are revised.

Table 1.2. U.S. Direct Investment Position Abroad on a Historical-Cost Basis, 2008 [Millions of dollars]

	All industries	Mining	Manufacturing										Information	Depository institutions	Finance (except depository institutions) and insurance	Professional, scientific, and Technical services	Holding companies (nonbank)	Other industries
			Total	Food	Chemicals	Primary and Fabricated metals	Machinery	Computers and Electroni products	Electrical equipment, appliances, and components	Transportation equipment	Other manufacturing	Wholesale trade						
All countries	**3,162,021**	**151,859**	**512,293**	**41,802**	**108,049**	**24,038**	**36,807**	**76,453**	**24,095**	**51,774**	**149,275**	**178,213**	**121,864**	**141,557**	**634,046**	**81,242**	**1,128,538**	**212,409**
Canada	**227,298**	**23,778**	**72,523**	**4,394**	**10,384**	**5,427**	**4,211**	**4,611**	**2,515**	**7,813**	**33,168**	**18,332**	**4,113**	**3,676**	**32,728**	**8,164**	**30,511**	**33,472**
Europe [1]	**1,809,876**	**38,508**	**259,844**	**27,489**	**62,253**	**12,777**	**21,561**	**28,344**	**16,156**	**23,802**	**67,463**	**99,980**	**80,971**	**80,823**	**328,307**	**53,845**	**750,883**	**116,716**
Austria	17,518	1	4,637	1	232	(D)	301	(D)	(D)	1,477	118	2,554	–121	(D)	2,094	401	7,360	(D)
Belgium	65,054	15	20,058	369	8,816	481	259	796	1,025	1,017	7,295	6,234	–758	(D)	31,434	1,811	2,857	(D)
Czech Republic	4,654	(D)	1,808	39	90	94	(D)	103	(D)	795	313	141	208	(D)	724	31	37	–51
Denmark	10,393	28	3,871	(D)	47	52	173	893	67	2	(D)	1,338	1,040	(D)	299	176	1,973	(D)
Finland	2,298	0	949	–1	109	28	(D)	(D)	(D)	(D)	66	797	156	(D)	26	102	–20	(D)
France	75,040	99	29,207	6,188	3,985	3,641	1,562	2,042	161	1,978	9,650	4,850	2,250	2,059	9,201	2,602	12,398	12,375
Germany	110,784	413	33,993	837	6,538	2,523	3,577	5,039	1,485	7,160	6,834	10,501	2,495	2,321	14,441	5,401	32,769	8,450
Greece	2,125	–5	729	(D)	139	0	1	10	0	0	(D)	717	24	–119	553	12	(D)	(D)
Hungary	5,103	74	815	158	116	19	80	34	–11	190	230	287	40	(D)	63	87	291	(D)
Ireland	146,194	(D)	19,051	261	7,252	199	385	4,379	(D)	31	(D)	1,249	15,723	10,227	24,235	(D)	27,596	26,588
Italy	28,653	60	11,684	740	2,176	587	1,336	1,423	305	1,614	3,500	3,153	1,967	412	3,071	1,160	1,925	5,221
Luxembourg	163,167	163	6,305	0	(D)	(*)	(D)	163	(*)	169	(D)	2,684	1,734	1,033	30,383	80	120,320	467
Netherlands	442,926	4,372	33,026	(D)	(D)	1,094	1,846	2,524	(D)	–138	4,521	17,120	8,099	(D)	49,629	(D)	306,257	(D)
Norway	10,889	6,037	1,862	(D)	167	(D)	1,190	48	–6	5	(D)	715	810	(D)	282	232	19	(D)
Poland	15,597	0	4,420	879	968	465	23	144	–5	557	1,388	454	586	(D)	1,343	164	(D)	(D)
Portugal	3,397	1	728	12	138	12	(D)	149	15	295	(D)	782	115	0	443	88	149	1,091
Russia	9,157	4,165	2,768	1,665	60	(D)	43	52	5	–95	(D)	461	64	1,217	–20	123	(D)	(D)
Spain	69,649	78	11,379	849	4,677	214	216	261	406	742	4,015	3,337	254	986	7,506	2,123	40,850	3,138

Table 1.2. (Continued)

	All industries	Mining	Manufacturing									Wholesale trade	Information	Depository institutions	Finance (except depository institutions) and insurance	Professional, scientific, and Technical services	Holding companies (nonbank)	Other industries
			Total	Food	Chemicals	Primary and Fabricated metals	Machinery	Computers and Electroni products	Electrical equipment, appliances, and components	Transportation equipment	Other manufacturing							
Sweden	43,391	0	3,286	(D)	152	74	321	1,033	184	88	(D)	736	749	(D)	15,618	546	19,862	(D)
Switzerland	123,358	190	8,996	149	2,751	154	1,822	1,476	245	335	2,064	21,423	2,649	7,240	4,844	632	70,100	7,284
Turkey	6,089	–2	1,507	27	655	5	3	19	1	334	464	1,749	–42	2,703	65	20	–4	93
United Kingdom	420,873	9,015	56,685	6,332	15,929	2,371	7,649	5,160	2,032	7,004	10,209	17,689	42,867	19,727	122,854	13,913	101,062	37,060
Other	33,568	(D)	2,078	324	(D)	152	94	(D)	67	(D)	728	1,009	64	2,237	9,218	104	5,138	(D)
Latin America and Other Western Hemisphere	**563,809**	**30,691**	**60,709**	**5,050**	**14,228**	**2,790**	**3,680**	**1,426**	**1,433**	**9,876**	**22,226**	**24,265**	**8,609**	**12,699**	**195,083**	**2,078**	**204,950**	**24,724**
South America	108,231	18,402	32,233	2,098	9,273	902	2,597	2,074	85	4,859	10,345	3,803	4,068	6,272	18,036	1,174	20,051	4,193
Argentina	15,195	3,040	3,363	112	1,887	13	183	87	–134	494	722	426	1,285	450	1,133	77	4,691	731
Brazil	45,500	2,224	20,357	1,277	4,607	772	2,157	1,970	51	2,783	6,740	980	2,210	3,096	9,286	616	6,287	444
Chile	12,613	1,058	2,238	33	748	6	72	11	(D)	(D)	(D)	968	127	1,394	3,978	129	617	2,104
Colombia	6,263	3,234	1,333	99	433	6	69	(*)	(D)	(D)	(D)	466	41	(D)	355	37	149	(D)
Ecuador	1,276	679	166	41	30	(*)	1	3	0	(D)	(D)	124	2	(D)	46	2	(D)	17
Peru	8,458	6,276	580	(D)	256	(D)	4	1	0	0	224	324	63	432	109	76	(D)	(D)
Venezuela	17,332	1,381	3,951	419	1,235	(D)	114	–1	(D)	1,156	821	263	81	(D)	3,057	206	7,610	(D)
Other	1,594	509	246	(D)	76	(D)	–3	2	0	26	(D)	252	258	100	72	31	1	123
Central America	110,424	4,908	23,990	2,811	4,447	(D)	(D)	(D)	1,347	5,017	(D)	3,040	2,784	25,189	19,135	572	20,468	10,338
Costa Rica	2,525	(*)	989	169	80	76	0	(D)	126	0	(D)	37	16	(D)	(D)	126	(D)	–238
Honduras	700	0	(D)	9	12	4	(*)	0	0	–9	(D)	58	(*)	(D)	108	(*)	–2	(D)

Table 1.2. (Continued)

	All industries	Mining	Manufacturing									Wholesale trade	Information	Depository institutions	Finance (except depository institutions) and insurance	Professional, scientific, and Technical services	Holding companies (nonbank)	Other industries
			Total	Food	Chemicals	Primary and Fabricated metals	Machinery	Computers and Electroni products	Electrical equipment, appliances, and components	Transportation equipment	Other manufacturing							
Mexico	95,618	4,865	21,821	2,482	4,306	(D)	(D)	(D)	1,221	5,030	9,209	2,361	2,758	(D)	15,736	460	16,865	(D)
Panama	7,243	63	40	36	–23	4	0	(*)	0	0	22	338	–5	(D)	788	–20	(D)	(D)
Other	4,339	–21	(D)	115	73	–11	1	(D)	(*)	–5	(D)	246	15	(D)	(D)	6	–11	261
Other Western Hemisphere	345,153	7,382	4,486	141	508	(D)	(D)	(D)	0	(*)	(D)	17,421	1,757	–18,762	157,912	333	164,432	10,193
Barbados	873	8	366	33	11	9	(*)	311	0	(*)	2	1,974	17	0	861	12	(D)	(D)
Bermuda	165,857	–201	1,303	0	(D)	(*)	(D)	(D)	0	0	132	3,790	632	(D)	81,179	272	72,566	(D)
Dominican Republic	960	0	599	51	56	50	0	–20	0	0	463	137	(D)	(D)	1	1	(*)	10
United Kingdom Islands,																		
Caribbean	139,290	(D)	695	11	44	–39	2	102	0	0	575	10,699	436	–16,963	(D)	98	(D)	1,716
Other	38,174	(D)	1,523	45	(D)	(D)	0	(*)	0	(*)	(D)	821	(D)	–1,997	(D)	–51	(D)	818
Africa	**36,640**	**18,375**	**2,856**	**62**	**367**	**308**	**313**	**95**	**95**	**807**	**809**	**1,157**	**128**	**1,899**	**1,814**	**372**	**8,664**	**1,375**
Egypt	8,771	(D)	111	17	–76	(D)	(D)	5	5	22	(D)	105	–9	(D)	32	1	–17	28
Nigeria	3,393	1,977	72	19	28	(D)	1	0	0	0	(D)	144	1	(D)	(D)	(*)	817	53
South Africa	4,915	(D)	2,069	–9	384	221	183	90	90	755	356	784	110	(D)	135	289	409	305
Other	19,560	(D)	604	35	32	72	(D)	(*)	0	31	(D)	124	26	632	(D)	82	7,455	988
Middle East	**32,488**	**6,518**	**11,763**	**145**	**1,615**	**85**	**416**	**4,959**	**47**	**33**	**4,464**	**2,145**	**1,447**	**720**	**569**	**933**	**7,594**	**799**
Israel	10,153	0	6,411	139	299	0	114	4,956	38	0	865	930	1,343	(D)	103	354	724	(D)
Saudi Arabia	5,382	770	(D)	2	(D)	(D)	(D)	0	0	33	50	(D)	6	0	(D)	293	3,539	144
United Arab Emirates	3,423	415	556	(D)	85	(D)	(D)	3	9	0	(D)	(D)	112	(D)	(D)	200	(D)	102

Table 1.2. (Continued)

	All industries	Mining	Manufacturing									Wholesale trade	Information	Depository institutions	Finance (except depository institutions) and insurance	Professional, scientific, and Technical services	Holding companies (nonbank)	Other industries
			Total	Food	Chemicals	Primary and Fabricated metals	Machinery	Computers and Electroni products	Electrical equipment, appliances, and components	Transportation equipment	Other manufacturing							
Other	13,531	5,333	(D)	(D)	(D)	0	2	0	0	0	(D)	12	–13	65	354	87	(D)	(D)
Asia and Pacific	**491,910**	**33,989**	**104,598**	**4,662**	**19,202**	**2,652**	**6,626**	**37,018**	**3,850**	**9,443**	**21,146**	**32,334**	**26,596**	**41,740**	**75,544**	**15,850**	**125,935**	**35,324**
Australia	88,549	20,342	12,743	1,936	3,598	955	730	738	273	1,479	3,033	3,856	13,100	2,285	11,275	3,762	13,875	7,310
China	45,695	3,014	21,428	730	4,614	609	1,534	8,142	701	2,146	2,951	3,219	223	(D)	1,895	773	1,556	(D)
Hong Kong	51,505	(*)	3,742	2	137	64	640	1,738	229	36	895	6,858	833	3,694	11,535	2,931	19,552	2,360
India	16,104	385	3,149	8	1,579	(D)	658	169	185	80	(D)	793	3,603	(D)	1,731	2,563	238	(D)
Indonesia	17,909	5,895	299	(D)	211	(*)	19	8	(D)	(D)	(D)	154	–76	(D)	758	14	9,552	(D)
Japan	79,235	1	17,380	294	2,723	160	690	3,342	1,176	2,567	6,429	9,036	5,609	1,144	28,032	2,806	5,911	9,316
Korea, Republic of	27,673	–1	9,165	866	1,022	(D)	246	2,333	301	923	(D)	1,812	448	(D)	3,625	332	(D)	(D)
Malaysia	13,291	2,328	5,825	49	962	19	151	4,186	4	79	376	270	74	(D)	466	207	(D)	403
New Zealand	5,266	322	1,339	449	136	36	39	98	(D)	5	(D)	211	303	(D)	1,307	346	(D)	942
Philippines	5,914	24	3,714	131	683	(D)	36	2,446	7	(D)	(D)	228	28	(D)	125	217	(D)	443
Singapore	106,529	589	16,544	4	1,690	66	1,440	10,430	744	1,369	800	3,322	2,130	(D)	6,782	1,329	71,250	(D)
Taiwan	16,604	(*)	3,816	48	713	78	176	2,396	84	50	271	2,018	310	(D)	7,141	295	102	(D)
Thailand	9,128	215	4,945	97	1,043	176	265	883	51	630	1,801	286	9	1,511	946	276	192	749
Other	8,510	874	510	(D)	91	(D)	1	110	0	(D)	(D)	273	1	372	–73	(*)	122	6,432
Addenda:																		
European Union (27) [2]	1,630,785	16,045	244,149	25,518	58,605	12,168	18,464	26,747	15,912	23,183	63,552	74,933	77,498	67,339	314,098	52,773	676,444	107,506
OPEC [3]	69,299	18,726	9,879	528	2,797	177	443	13	191	1,168	4,561	1,909	146	(D)	4,206	828	29,774	(D)

* A nonzero value between –$500,000 and $500,000.

D Suppressed to avoid disclosure of data of individual companies.

1. In 2008, the "Euro area" includes Austria, Belgium, Cyprus, Finland, France, Germany, Greece, Ireland, Italy, Luxem bourg, Malta, the Netherlands, Portugal, Slovenia and Spain. For 2008, the U.S. direct investment position in the "Euro area" was $1,128,529 million.
2. The European Union (27) comprises Austria, Belgium, Bulgaria, Cyprus, the Czech Republic, Denmark, Estonia, Finland, France, Germany, Greece, Hungary, Ireland, Italy, Latvia, Lithuania, Luxembourg, Malta, the Netherlands, Poland, Portugal, Romania, Slovakia, Slovenia, Spain, Sweden, and the United Kingdom
3. OPEC is the Organization of Petroleum Exporting Countries. In 2008, its members were Algeria, Angola, Ecuador, Indonesia, Iran, Iraq, Kuwait, Libya, Nigeria, Qatar, Saudi Arabia, the United Arab Emirates, and Venezuela.

Note. Estimates for 2008 are preliminary.

Table 2.1. Foreign Direct Investment Position in the United States on a Historical-Cost Basis, 2007 [Millions of dollars]

		Manufacturing																
	All industries	Total	Food	Chemicals	Primary and Fabricated metals	Machinery	Computers and Electronic products	Electrical equipment, appliances, and components	Transportation equipment	Other manufacturing	Wholesale trade	Retail trade	Information	Depository institutions	Finance (except depository institutions) and insurance	Real estate and Rental and leasing	Professional, scientific, And technical services	Other industries
All countries	**2,109,876**	**703,146**	**24,225**	**213,483**	**48,897**	**59,110**	**66,599**	**21,507**	**68,314**	**201,012**	**274,587**	**32,688**	**147,043**	**134,332**	**260,735**	**48,526**	**58,770**	**450,049**
Canada	**207,925**	**43,932**	**1,559**	**5,729**	**5,899**	**346**	**4,443**	**–316**	**6,069**	**20,201**	**4,458**	**4,498**	**7,760**	**18,401**	**64,183**	**3,991**	**2,588**	**58,112**
Europe [1]	**1,507,594**	**541,226**	**18,384**	**192,629**	**35,105**	**50,039**	**41,015**	**17,960**	**30,652**	**155,441**	**136,508**	**22,382**	**134,889**	**97,229**	**178,937**	**19,621**	**46,595**	**330,207**
Austria	2,373	1,683	6	(D)	440	277	4	(D)	74	781	(D)	(D)	–1	(D)	(D)	73	(D)	20
Belgium	23,663	9,390	56	(D)	(D)	278	(*)	19	4	–902	5,856	(D)	8	(D)	1,240	230	229	3,376
Denmark	4,709	3,052	(D)	2,216	(D)	882	(D)	(D)	0	(D)	877	5	1	0	(D)	8	(D)	(D)
Finland	5,413	3,289	(D)	600	(D)	1,454	32	(D)	4	1,152	(D)	(D)	0	(D)	1	(D)	(D)	338
France	160,116	69,891	2,071	14,051	1,284	(D)	17,322	(D)	2,548	17,319	9,680	918	16,157	17,540	28,283	432	4,154	13,062
Germany	214,506	51,288	(D)	21,283	4,735	2,093	739	578	13,267	(D)	9,931	3,881	48,402	15,385	35,436	6,680	781	42,723
Ireland	32,679	16,600	1,852	4,709	(D)	4	–1	0	(D)	8,478	149	(D)	(D)	(D)	3,146	(D)	–33	7,357
Italy	13,291	1,100	–39	340	131	362	138	111	75	–18	1,539	1,917	32	621	(D)	198	(D)	(D)
Luxembourg	120,524	57,988	729	15,318	5,962	21,192	519	1,195	(D)	(D)	1,031	(D)	8,567	0	3,716	79	(D)	46,561
Netherlands	208,177	76,101	808	37,287	(D)	(D)	3,921	(D)	2,643	19,482	18,643	(D)	15,904	(D)	57,709	3,084	8,134	27,495
Norway	5,564	–583	0	676	673	(D)	408	0	5	(D)	2,814	(*)	392	5	22	52	972	1,891
Spain	27,511	3,366	(D)	276	(D)	–4	(D)	3	71	908	125	(D)	(D)	19,250	966	148	(D)	(D)
Sweden	42,129	24,102	(*)	(D)	4,085	(D)	(D)	(D)	4,324	1,124	7,023	(D)	585	–254	264	(D)	100	(D)
Switzerland	153,277	98,382	(D)	31,340	2,245	3,899	485	(D)	(D)	(D)	8,146	(D)	12,235	(D)	27,235	(D)	486	7,506
United Kingdom	426,545	96,680	2,342	45,109	4,989	3,825	14,141	515	5,423	20,335	68,636	2,821	19,216	50,496	18,501	4,976	27,063	138,157
Other	67,116	28,896	185	1,985	1,296	(D)	(D)	(D)	203	19,711	475	(D)	10,878	379	1,162	(D)	(D)	21,759

Table 2.1 (Continued)

			Manufacturing															
	All industries	**Total**	**Food**	**Chemicals**	**Primary and Fabricated metals**	**Machinery**	**Computers and Electronic products**	**Electrical equipment, appliances, and components**	**Transportation equipment**	**Other manufacturing**	**Wholesale trade**	**Retail trade**	**Information**	**Depository institutions**	**Finance (except depository institutions) and insurance**	**Real estate and Rental and leasing**	**Professional, scientific, And technical services**	**Other industries**
Latin America and Other Western Hemisphere	**55,816**	**19,726**	**2,193**	**2,658**	**(D)**	**–1,864**	**1,308**	**(D)**	**–110**	**11,313**	**7,648**	**1,378**	**1,096**	**4,253**	**–4,464**	**8,992**	**1,534**	**15,653**
South and Central America	14,021	4,192	2,084	247	1,135	–76	–286	15	–144	1,217	5,225	26	–16	3,480	(D)	(D)	–50	397
Brazil	1,750	698	(D)	–84	93	–22	(D)	–4	47	–48	(D)	(D)	21	490	(D)	55	–32	59
Mexico	6,287	3,413	(D)	232	1,197	–58	–89	29	(D)	727	1,497	(D)	–18	1,121	55	(D)	–6	175
Panama	980	138	0	(D)	(D)	34	(D)	(*)	(D)	(D)	–5	3	(D)	(D)	(D)	(D)	3	256
Venezuela	4,196	96	(*)	–31	–2	–24	–1	(D)	–3	(D)	(D)	(*)	(D)	(D)	–1	20	–6	–3
Other	808	–154	(D)	(D)	(D)	–7	(D)	(D)	–13	315	331	6	–1	699	9	17	–10	–90
Other Western Hemisphere	41,795	15,534	110	2,411	(D)	–1,787	1,593	(D)	33	10,096	2,423	1,352	1,112	772	(D)	(D)	1,585	15,256
Bahamas	598	(D)	(D)	(D)	(D)	0	(*)	0	0	8	7	0	(D)	(D)	–22	401	5	(D)
Bermuda	4,697	11,660	(D)	(D)	68	(D)	(D)	(D)	0	8,138	296	0	136	0	–11,476	(D)	1,206	(D)
Netherlands Antilles	5,574	–214	2	(D)	(D)	1	–2	0	–4	–245	239	(D)	(D)	(D)	–12	907	(D)	4,593
United Kingdom Islands,																		
Caribbean	34,423	5,163	(D)	(D)	(D)	(D)	(D)	(D)	37	2,095	1,634	(D)	1,230	156	9,676	6,847	(D)	7,981
Other	–3,497	(D)	(D)	8	(*)	–1,306	–1	(D)	0	100	246	–1	(D)	(D)	(D)	253	(D)	272
Africa	**1,396**	**–217**	**–1**	**–7**	**(D)**	**(D)**	**(D)**	**(*)**	**–20**	**195**	**585**	**(D)**	**(D)**	**(D)**	**(D)**	**145**	**–2**	**649**
South Africa	243	(D)	–1	–6	(*)	(D)	0	(*)	–11	(D)	(D)	(*)	(D)	0	(D)	(*)	–2	122

Table 2.1. (Continued)

		Manufacturing																
	All industries	Total	Food	Chemicals	Primary and Fabricated metals	Machinery	Computers and Electronic products	Electrical equipment, appliances, and components	Transportation equipment	Other manufacturing	Wholesale trade	Retail trade	Information	Depository institutions	Finance (except depository institutions) and insurance	Real estate and Rental and leasing	Professional, scientific, And technical services	Other industries
Other	1,153	(D)	0	–1	(D)	–1	(D)	(*)	–10	(D)	(D)	(D)	(D)	(D)	(*)	145	(*)	527
Middle East	**15,058**	**1,916**	**8**	**1,039**	**(D)**	**–9**	**(D)**	**2**	**8**	**454**	**6,258**	**(D)**	**(D)**	**1,299**	**(D)**	**2,136**	**23**	**2,303**
Israel	6,556	1,863	8	1,044	6	(*)	414	0	9	383	472	(D)	(D)	(D)	(D)	(D)	75	665
Kuwait	846	2	0	0	0	0	(*)	2	0	0	(D)	0	2	(D)	(D)	(D)	0	(D)
Lebanon	(D)	(*)	0	0	0	0	0	0	0	(*)	(*)	0	0	0	0	(D)	(*)	(D)
Saudi Arabia	(D)	11	0	–2	(D)	–2	(*)	0	0	(D)	(D)	0	6	(D)	2	(D)	(*)	–37
United Arab Emirates	1,527	–29	0	–4	(D)	–7	(*)	0	–1	(D)	–7	(*)	10	(D)	5	(D)	–52	(D)
Other	544	69	0	0	0	0	(D)	0	0	(D)	(D)	0	(D)	(D)	0	47	(*)	(D)
Asia and Pacific	**322,087**	**96,563**	**2,081**	**11,434**	**6,071**	**(D)**	**19,443**	**(D)**	**31,715**	**13,408**	**119,131**	**4,354**	**(D)**	**(D)**	**21,824**	**13,640**	**8,031**	**43,124**
Australia	50,233	3,358	23	(D)	(D)	(D)	–39	–1	–25	2,036	1,949	(D)	306	1,762	4,138	7,314	(D)	30,929
China	916	–231	(*)	–277	126	(*)	12	162	–133	–122	818	1	(*)	(D)	(D)	(*)	71	117
Hong Kong	3,742	1,377	–1	(D)	–1	–5	653	–3	(D)	–16	1,742	(D)	(D)	413	(D)	147	(D)	43
India	2,822	145	51	42	(D)	(D)	(D)	–2	55	11	11	(*)	49	266	(*)	–1	2,147	202
Japan	230,453	78,384	1,555	9,818	2,355	3,861	18,363	1,068	31,782	9,582	101,125	4,359	1,859	8,505	14,737	5,700	5,356	10,430
Korea, Republic of	15,146	(D)	7	38	(D)	–2	(D)	–2	(D)	80	10,624	(D)	(D)	355	162	71	–1	17
Malaysia	490	32	–1	–15	(D)	(D)	61	(*)	6	2	64	0	2	(D)	(*)	(D)	10	343
New Zealand	975	(D)	(D)	(D)	8	5	–9	(*)	–3	(D)	495	0	0	0	1	(D)	–1	13
Singapore	11,707	(D)	(D)	–63	5	(D)	131	16	26	–19	197	(D)	13	351	(D)	193	–3	674
Taiwan	4,746	1,549	–1	32	3	–2	64	(D)	–70	(D)	1,716	(D)	(D)	1,108	70	58	–45	203
Other	857	89	5	–10	1	9	35	–13	39	24	388	(*)	–2	193	29	18	–11	153

Table 2.1. (Continued)

		Manufacturing																
	All industries	Total	Food	Chemicals	Primary and Fabricated metals	Machinery	Computers and Electronic products	Electrical equipment, appliances, and components	Transportation equipment	Other manufacturing	Wholesale trade	Retail trade	Information	Depository institutions	Finance (except depository institutions) and insurance	Real estate and Rental and leasing	Professional, scientific, And technical services	Other industries
Addenda:																		
European Union (27) [2]	1,332,999	438,315	8,916	159,005	31,467	44,792	40,114	17,899	28,946	107,176	125,242	18,252	118,175	103,863	151,442	17,159	42,785	317,766
OPEC [3]	12,741	63	(*)	–41	–7	–38	–1	–7	5	151	8,696	(*)	7	1,377	–5	(D)	–59	(D)

* A nonzero value between –$500,000 and $500,000.

D Suppressed to avoid disclosure of data of individual companies.

1. In 2007, the "Euro area" includes Austria, Belgium, Finland, France, Germany, Greece, Ireland, Italy, Luxembourg, the Netherlands, Portugal, Slovenia, and Spain. For 2007, the "Euro area" direct investment position in the United States was $808,666 million.
2. The European Union (27) comprises Austria, Belgium, Bulgaria, Cyprus, the Czech Republic, Denmark, Estonia, Finland, France, Germany, Greece, Hungary, Ireland, Italy, Latvia, Lithuania, Luxembourg, Malta, the Netherlands, Poland, Portugal, Romania, Slovakia, Slovenia, Spain, Sweden, and the United Kingdom.
3. OPEC is the Organization of Petroleum Exporting Countries. In 2007, its members were Algeria, Angola, Indonesia Iran, Iraq, Kuwait, Libya, Nigeria, Qatar, Saudi Arabia, the United Arab Emirates, and Venezuela.

Note. Estimates for 2007 are revised.

Table 2.2. Foreign Direct Investment Position in the United States on a Historical-Cost Basis, 2008

		Manufacturing																
	All industries	Total	Food	Chemicals	Primary and Fabricated metals	Machinery	Computers and Electronic products	Electrical equipment, appliances, and components	Transportation equipment	Other manufacturing	Wholesale trade	Retail trade	Information	Depository institutions	Finance (except depository institutions) and insurance	Real estate and rental leasing	Professional, scientific, And technical services	Other industries
All countries	**2,278,892**	**795,336**	**25,641**	**217,777**	**48,719**	**75,184**	**63,251**	**23,815**	**64,514**	**276,435**	**312,583**	**44,062**	**157,973**	**119,124**	**248,888**	**51,995**	**62,118**	**486,813**
Canada	**221,870**	**42,851**	**1,992**	**7,273**	**5,393**	**1,359**	**–235**	**–26**	**6,631**	**20,463**	**4,758**	**7,415**	**11,808**	**27,780**	**62,132**	**4,128**	**2,248**	**58,750**
Europe [1]	**1,622,911**	**617,579**	**19,833**	**189,776**	**36,744**	**50,549**	**40,945**	**19,310**	**25,846**	**234,576**	**167,610**	**28,276**	**142,042**	**71,284**	**177,827**	**19,956**	**49,379**	**348,958**
Austria	2,406	1,323	5	(D)	544	369	3	(*)	15	(D)	263	(D)	–6	(D)	1	83	(D)	97
Belgium	18,580	2,245	–9	3,920	(D)	201	2	36	(D)	31	6,147	(D)	4	(D)	1,005	(D)	343	4,687
Denmark	4,992	3,346	(D)	2,383	0	1,087	(D)	0	(*)	–1,377	891	4	(*)	0	(*)	5	(D)	(D)
Finland	12,499	3,495	(D)	506	(D)	1,517	(D)	2	(*)	1,388	(D)	(D)	(D)	(D)	(*)	(D)	(D)	317
France	163,430	75,973	2,197	18,542	1,800	(D)	14,448	(D)	3,691	19,009	10,710	353	16,798	7,559	27,114	385	5,562	18,977
Germany	211,521	55,598	44	28,345	2,047	2,214	529	298	12,969	9,153	16,415	4,390	50,652	4,677	36,254	6,302	850	36,384
Ireland	34,094	16,514	1,492	4,349	(D)	(D)	–8	(*)	(*)	9,067	187	(D)	1,630	(D)	6,644	91	(D)	7,136
Italy	17,575	5,923	97	1,111	(D)	464	(D)	224	(D)	93	1,677	1,641	87	(D)	(D)	(D)	(D)	6,351
Luxembourg	113,248	48,364	852	5,897	6,719	(D)	(D)	1,263	318	(D)	1,204	(D)	9,481	0	2,586	(D)	(D)	49,101
Netherlands	259,385	131,423	(D)	39,632	(D)	(D)	2,644	(D)	(D)	78,424	23,486	4,874	20,133	–760	39,865	3,287	6,980	30,097
Norway	6,755	851	(*)	(D)	(D)	(D)	435	(D)	(D)	(D)	3,715	(*)	358	(D)	1	115	1,193	(D)
Spain	38,662	2,914	9	315	(D)	1	60	(*)	79	(D)	152	(D)	87	19,971	(D)	121	239	11,399
Sweden	35,020	24,660	(*)	(D)	4,598	3,851	(D)	(D)	(D)	1,306	8,070	95	612	(D)	248	(D)	(D)	1,228
Switzerland	165,697	107,154	10,176	26,575	2,928	4,428	439	24	(D)	(D)	7,184	4,050	(D)	(D)	31,522	2,351	687	9,324
United Kingdom	454,123	102,800	3,016	44,927	5,562	3,844	13,916	484	7,627	23,425	78,758	2,809	21,033	47,882	26,420	5,153	28,805	140,462
Other	84,922	34,996	(D)	(D)	3,700	(D)	(D)	(D)	169	(D)	(D)	3,055	8,907	321	(D)	470	(D)	32,267

Table 2.2. (Continued)

			Manufacturing																
	All industries	Total	Food	Chemicals	Primary and Fabricated metals	Machinery	Computers and Electronic products	Electrical equipment, appliances, And components	Transportation equipment	Other manufacturing	Wholesale trade	Retail trade	Information	Depository institutions	Finance (except depository institutions) and insurance	Real estate and rental leasing	Professional, scientific, And technical services	Other industries
Latin America and Other Western Hemisphere	**49,233**	**25,421**	**2,236**	**2,278**	**2,143**	**(D)**	**1,547**	**(D)**	**–486**	**5,904**	**8,069**	**2,100**	**664**	**4,115**	**–19,829**	**10,261**	**1,766**	**16,664**
South and Central America	15,609	5,130	2,059	481	1,596	172	–168	(D)	–564	(D)	6,495	10	–119	3,315	298	475	–83	89
Brazil	778	85	(D)	–79	(D)	–22	11	–7	28	–37	(D)	(D)	20	514	14	48	–34	–133
Mexico	7,948	5,126	1,946	546	1,718	263	–88	(D)	(D)	1,272	1,760	(D)	–119	1,115	77	(D)	–31	1
Panama	881	54	0	(D)	(D)	(*)	(D)	(*)	(D)	14	–11	2	–6	(D)	198	(D)	4	261
Venezuela	4,563	–168	–5	–40	–2	–24	–4	(D)	(D)	28	(D)	(*)	–8	(D)	1	11	–5	–6
Other	1,439	32	(D)	(D)	–49	–45	(D)	–2	–7	(D)	733	8	–6	688	7	27	–16	–36
Other Western Hemisphere	33,623	20,291	177	1,797	547	(D)	1,715	(D)	78	(D)	1,575	2,090	783	800	–20,126	9,785	1,849	16,576
Bahamas	81	82	(D)	(D)	(D)	0	(*)	0	0	(*)	(D)	(*)	(D)	(D)	–3	(D)	5	–805
Bermuda	10,750	16,156	(D)	1,354	(D)	(D)	(D)	(D)	0	(D)	248	0	(D)	0	–11,965	(D)	1,411	4,677
Netherlands Antilles	6,266	(D)	2	(D)	(D)	(*)	–2	0	–4	–245	(D)	(D)	(D)	(D)	1	884	(*)	5,139
United Kingdom Islands, Caribbean	21,604	3,858	(D)	(D)	(D)	204	(D)	7	81	1,340	(D)	2,074	931	161	(D)	8,235	429	7,347
Other	–5,077	(D)	–1	(D)	(D)	(D)	(*)	0	0	99	(D)	(D)	(D)	(D)	(D)	246	5	219
Africa	**2,002**	**427**	**–2**	**–8**	**(D)**	**3**	**(D)**	**(*)**	**(D)**	**358**	**493**	**–1**	**8**	**(D)**	**(D)**	**(D)**	**(D)**	**878**

Table 2.2. (Continued)

		Manufacturing																
	All industries	Total	Food	Chemicals	Primary and Fabricated metals	Machinery	Computers and Electronic products	Electrical equipment, appliances, And components	Transportation equipment	Other manufacturing	Wholesale trade	Retail trade	Information	Depository Institutions	Finance (except depository institutions) and insurance	Real estate and rental leasing	Professional, scientific, And technical services	Other industries
South Africa	643	–89	–2	–6	–1	3	0	(*)	4	–86	(D)	(*)	(D)	0	(D)	–2	–3	(D)
Other	1,359	516	(*)	–1	(D)	(*)	(D)	(*)	(D)	444	(D)	–1	(D)	(D)	(*)	(D)	(D)	(D)
Middle East	**14,676**	**2,747**	**(D)**	**(D)**	**(D)**	**–2**	**(D)**	**1**	**(D)**	**441**	**5,868**	**(D)**	**952**	**(D)**	**(D)**	**(D)**	**(D)**	**4,354**
Israel	6,143	2,708	(D)	(D)	(D)	0	(D)	–1	(D)	(D)	(D)	(D)	995	250	(D)	147	76	1,257
Kuwait	359	2	0	0	0	0	(*)	2	0	0	(D)	0	2	(D)	(D)	(D)	0	(D)
Lebanon	(D)	(*)	0	0	0	0	0	0	0	(*)	(*)	0	0	0	0	(D)	–1	(D)
Saudi Arabia	(D)	14	0	–1	(*)	–2	0	0	–1	17	(D)	0	6	(D)	2	30	(*)	(D)
United Arab Emirates	2,744	(D)	0	(D)	(*)	(*)	(*)	0	–6	(D)	(D)	(*)	(D)	(D)	1	170	(D)	2,613
Other	272	(D)	0	0	0	0	0	0	0	(D)	(D)	0	(D)	(D)	0	(D)	(*)	338
Asia and Pacific	**368,200**	**106,312**	**(D)**	**(D)**	**4,275**	**(D)**	**20,457**	**(D)**	**32,513**	**14,694**	**125,785**	**(D)**	**2,499**	**(D)**	**28,501**	**17,084**	**8,660**	**57,208**
Australia	64,316	5,224	34	1,000	1,400	238	–12	5	–31	2,591	1,469	1	(D)	3,055	4,922	(D)	593	41,094
China	1,235	–384	–3	–272	125	–34	–7	118	–174	–136	1,092	–5	(D)	(D)	16	–2	(D)	99
Hong Kong	3,973	1,494	–1	(D)	–7	1	(D)	–4	1	6	1,772	(D)	(D)	456	4	143	(D)	108
India	4,527	151	–1	81	(D)	(D)	(D)	–4	38	74	1	(*)	56	357	–1	–4	2,902	1,066
Japan	259,569	86,952	1,562	15,264	2,628	4,183	19,012	1,369	32,609	10,326	108,278	6,108	1,814	10,344	21,690	6,918	4,957	12,509
Korea, Republic of	15,632	(D)	4	39	95	(D)	(D)	–1	84	79	(D)	(D)	(D)	212	152	78	–4	(D)
Malaysia	395	7	1	–17	(D)	(D)	27	(*)	5	11	68	(D)	3	(D)	(*)	(D)	2	258
New Zealand	1,062	(D)	(D)	(*)	8	3	–9	0	–2	(D)	461	0	(D)	0	1	(D)	–2	18
Singapore	12,718	(D)	–39	1	8	(D)	370	51	16	–56	251	–4	8	382	(D)	(D)	36	1,153
Taiwan	3,900	1,425	–2	13	5	(D)	71	(D)	–75	(D)	(D)	35	59	884	(D)	10	–37	269
Other	874	23	5	–15	–2	(*)	27	–27	43	–7	581	(*)	(*)	201	(D)	(D)	–10	(D)

Table 2.2. (Continued)

			Manufacturing																
	All industries	**Total**	**Food**	**Chemicals**	**Primary and Fabricated metals**	**Machinery**	**Computers and Electronic products**	**Electrical equipment, appliances, And components**	**Transportation equipment**	**Other manufacturing**	**Wholesale trade**	**Retail trade**	**Information**	**Depository institu tions**	**Finance (except depository institutions) and insurance**	**Real estate and rental leasing**	**Professional, scientific, And technical services**	**Other industries**
Addenda:																		
European Union (27) [2]	1,434,060	503,714	9,620	159,803	31,697	45,172	40,061	19,260	24,296	173,805	156,455	23,680	126,081	79,536	146,033	17,409	45,148	336,004
OPEC [3]	13,345	–177	–5	–70	–37	–28	–3	(D)	(D)	79	9,026	(*)	11	1,258	(D)	255	(D)	2,960

* A nonzero value between –$500,000 and $500,000.

D Suppressed to avoid disclosure of data of individual companies.

1. In 2008, the “Euro area” includes Austria, Belgium, Cyprus, Finland, France, Germany, Greece, Ireland, Italy, Luxem- bourg, Malta, the Netherlands, Portugal, Slovenia, and Spain. For 2008, the “Euro area” direct investment position in the United States was $872,104 million.
2. The European Union (27) comprises Austria, Belgium, Bulgaria, Cyprus, the Czech Republic, Denmark, Estonia, Finland, France, Germany, Greece, Hungary, Ireland, Italy, Latvia, Lithuania, Luxembourg, Malta, the Netherlands, Poland, Portugal, Romania, Slovakia, Slovenia, Spain, Sweden, the United Kingdom.
3. OPEC is the Organization of Petroleum Exporting Countries. In 2008, its members were Algeria, Angola, Ecuador, Indonesia, Iran, Iraq, Kuwait, Libya, Nigeria, Qatar, Saudi Arabia, the United Arab Emirates, and Venezuela.

Note. Estimates for 2008 are preliminary.

End Notes

[1] In this article, "outward direct investment" and "outward" are short- hand for "U.S. direct investment abroad." Likewise, "inward direct invest- ment" or "inward" are shorthand for "foreign direct investment in the United States."

[2] The measure of direct investment capital flows used in this article differs from the measure of direct investment capital flows used in the interna- tional transaction accounts because the reinvested earnings component of capital flows included here excludes a current-cost adjustment. See the box "Key Terms" for more information. In this article, "(direct investment) capital flows" is shorthand for "(direct investment) capital flows without current-cost adjustment" and "reinvested earnings" is shorthand for "reinvested earnings without current-cost adjustment."

[3] The outward direct investment position and related capital flow statistics are classified by country of the foreign affiliate with which the U.S. parent has direct transactions and positions. The inward direct investment position and related capital flow statistics are classified by country of the foreign parent or of other members of the foreign parent group that have direct transactions and positions with the U.S. affiliate.

[4] The falloff in equity capital increases coincided with a drop of nearly a third in the volume of global mergers and acquisitions in 2008, according to data from Thompson Reuters.

[5] In this article, "banks" refers to "depository institutions," which is the industry title that appears in the tables.

[6] According to data from total outlays to acquire or establish U.S. businesses, which include those financed by capital inflows from foreign parents, were $260.4 billion in 2008, up slightly from 2007. See Thomas Anderson, "Foreign Direct Investment in the United States: New Investment in 2008," SURVEY OF CURRENT BUSINESS 89 (June 2009): 54–61. The new investment data include only those transactions in which U.S. businesses are newly acquired or established by foreign direct investors, regardless of the source of funding. Changes in the inward direct investment position differ from new investment outlays by excluding investment financed by sources other than the foreign parent group and by including transactions that fund ongoing operations of U.S. affiliates, subtractions from investment as well as additions, and valuation adjustments. Despite these differences, the two types of data are related because any outlays to acquire or establish U.S. businesses that are funded by foreign parent groups are included in the capital transactions that largely determine the changes in the inward direct investment position. It is of note that although foreign parent-funded outlays to acquire or establish U.S. businesses typically appear in the direct investment capital transactions as equity investments, these transactions are sometimes funded in part, or in whole, by debt investment from the foreign parent. According to data from the new investment survey, foreign parent groups financed nearly 90 percent of total outlays to acquire or establish U.S. businesses in 2008.

[7] The measure of U.S. corporate profits referenced here excludes inventory valuation and capital consumption adjustments as does the measure of affiliates' earnings discussed in this article (see table 1.12 of the national income and product accounts).

[8] The measure of affiliate earnings discussed here reflects income earned as a result of current production and excludes capital gains and losses; capitalgains and losses of U.S. affiliates are included in "other" valuation adjustments made to the position.

[9] In this article, the statistics on the inward direct investment position are classified by country of foreign parent or of other members of the foreign parent group that have direct transactions and positions with the U.S. affiliate, which is consistent with international standards. Statistics classified on this basis may be higher or lower than those classified by country of ultimate beneficial owner (UBO) for certain countries, particularly when investments have been channeled through affiliates in financial centers in other countries. For tabulations on both bases through 2007 (preliminary), see table 17 in "Direct Investment, 2004–2007: Detailed Historical-Cost Positions and Related Capital and Income Flows" SURVEY 88 (September 2008): 120. Revised statistics for 2006 and 2007 as well as preliminary statistics for 2008 on both bases will be published in the September 2009 SURVEY.

[10] For the previously published statistics, see Marilyn Ibarra and Jennifer Koncz, "Direct Investment Positions for 2007: Country and Industry Detail," SURVEY 88 (July 2008): 20–35.

INDEX

A

accommodation, 120, 131
accountability, 16, 17, 38
accounting, 15, 49, 90, 133, 186, 188, 202, 213, 214, 215, 222, 223, 224
acquisitions, viii, 21, 23, 26, 28, 30, 40, 44, 54, 55, 56, 57, 59, 60, 62, 67, 68, 75, 76, 78, 80, 82, 94, 97, 208, 212, 216, 219, 224, 244
adjustment, 106, 107, 195, 203, 204, 211, 218, 222, 244
advertising, 26, 127
aerospace, 31, 65, 72, 99, 127, 128
Africa, 4, 13, 18, 130, 131, 134, 143, 155, 159, 163, 167, 171, 175, 179, 215, 216, 224, 225, 229, 233, 237, 241
agriculture, 71, 77, 127
air carriers, 49
airports, 71, 89
Algeria, 156, 230, 235, 239, 243
alloys, 87
amortization, 205
Angola, 156, 230, 235, 239, 243
annual rate, 116, 117, 186
apparel, 144, 149
appetite, 103, 104
Arab world, 90
Argentina, 136, 154, 158, 162, 166, 170, 174, 178, 228, 232
Asia, vii, 4, 9, 11, 13, 121, 130, 131, 134, 140, 143, 155, 160, 163, 167, 172, 176, 179, 212, 214, 215, 216, 223, 224, 225, 229, 234, 238, 242
assessment, 11, 46, 56, 111
assumptions, 199
Attorney General, 45
attractiveness, 103, 133
auditing, 24, 42
Australia, 130, 131, 136, 138, 143, 155, 160, 163, 167, 172, 176, 179, 215, 216, 224, 225, 229, 234, 238, 242
Austria, 136, 138, 153, 156, 157, 161, 165, 169, 173, 177, 227, 230, 231, 235, 236, 239, 240, 243
authority, vii, 9, 10, 13, 14, 16, 17, 26, 27, 36, 44, 47, 53, 54, 70, 72, 77, 80, 81, 85, 90, 94, 99, 133
availability, 98, 133

B

Bahrain, 92
balance of payments, 8, 186, 192
balance sheet, 102, 118, 197, 204
Bank of England, 204, 205
banking, ix, 5, 65, 82, 83, 118, 131, 207, 212, 216, 219, 223, 224
bankruptcy, 76, 104
banks, 12, 72, 80, 114, 118, 126, 131, 181, 212, 214, 216, 219, 220, 221, 223, 224, 244
Barbados, 155, 159, 163, 167, 171, 175, 179, 229, 233
barriers, 42, 75, 91, 92
BEA, viii, ix, 6, 101, 102, 103, 104, 110, 111, 113, 117, 121, 125, 129, 132, 137, 142, 148, 152, 187, 195, 208, 221, 222, 225, 226
behavior, 97, 109, 201, 202
Beijing, 53
Belgium, 3, 42, 136, 153, 156, 157, 161, 165, 169, 173, 177, 225, 227, 230, 231, 235, 236, 239, 240, 243
biological weapons, 98
biotechnology, 127
board members, 22, 25, 35, 39, 63, 78, 79
borrowing, 102, 104, 105, 108
Brazil, 3, 114, 115, 130, 131, 136, 142, 154, 158, 162, 166, 170, 174, 178, 228, 232, 237, 241
Bulgaria, 138, 156, 230, 235, 239, 243
business environment, 76, 92

buyer, 22, 25, 35

C

Canada, viii, 3, 5, 21, 23, 24, 25, 28, 29, 30, 33, 35, 37, 38, 39, 41, 42, 48, 49, 50, 51, 97, 98, 130, 131, 132, 134, 136, 137, 138, 142, 153, 157, 161, 165, 169, 173, 177, 192, 205, 210, 214, 215, 216, 218, 220, 224, 225, 227, 231, 236, 240
capital consumption, 244
capital controls, viii, 101, 108, 110
capital expenditure, ix, 113, 114, 132
capital flows, 132, 200, 207, 211, 212, 223, 226, 244
capital gains, 223, 244
capital inflow, 218, 226, 244
capital intensive, 18, 196
capital markets, 13, 18, 102, 104, 105, 107, 108, 109, 110
capital mobility, 200
capital outflow, 211, 212
capitalism, 41
carbon, 16
Caribbean, 13, 17, 118, 119, 155, 159, 163, 167, 171, 175, 179, 212, 214, 215, 216, 221, 224, 225, 229, 233, 237, 241
central bank, 38
certification, 63
Chile, 3, 136, 154, 158, 162, 166, 170, 174, 178, 228, 232
China, viii, 4, 21, 24, 28, 29, 30, 33, 35, 36, 38, 39, 41, 42, 52, 53, 54, 55, 56, 57, 58, 59, 60, 83, 115, 130, 131, 133, 137, 140, 143, 155, 160, 163, 167, 172, 176, 179, 181, 215, 216, 229, 234, 238, 242
Chinese medicine, 54
citizenship, 22, 25, 35, 39, 95
civil law, 29, 85
classification, 223
clean energy, 17
cleaning, 144, 149
climate change, 16
coal, 55, 65, 71, 97, 120, 123, 144, 149
coding, 87
Colombia, 136, 154, 158, 162, 166, 170, 174, 178, 228, 232
combined effect, 120
command economy, 83
commerce, 42, 97
commercial ties, 103
commodity, 74, 147, 151
common law, 29, 48, 85
Communist Party, 57, 60
compensation, 132, 184
competing interests, 57
competition, 30, 36, 37, 38, 40, 50, 53, 82, 94, 98, 204
competitive advantage, 124
competitor, 56
competitors, 41, 57, 124
complexity, 52, 201
compliance, 46, 72
components, 8, 32, 77, 90, 120, 123, 126, 127, 128, 130, 131, 135, 140, 143, 145, 150, 165, 166, 167, 168, 169, 170, 171, 172, 173, 174, 175, 176, 177, 178, 180, 212, 231, 232, 233, 234, 236, 237, 238, 239, 240, 241, 242, 243
composition, 104, 127, 193
compounds, 144, 149
computer software, 188
concentration, 124, 127
confidentiality, 51, 103
Congress, iv, vii, 1, 9, 10, 13, 16, 17, 18, 19, 24, 29, 30, 41, 47, 53, 60, 98, 183
Congressional Budget Office, 204
consensus, 67, 202
construction, 30, 54, 57, 74, 97, 127, 145, 150, 181
consulting, 12, 147, 151
consumers, 7, 124
consumption, 189
control, 7, 23, 26, 27, 28, 34, 36, 37, 41, 46, 47, 53, 55, 59, 63, 67, 69, 75, 79, 82, 85, 89, 91, 95, 97, 98, 99, 103, 104, 105, 107, 108, 141, 181, 218, 221, 222
conversion, 12, 31, 77
corporate governance, 50, 97
corporations, 11, 70, 106, 197, 205
Costa Rica, 136, 154, 158, 162, 166, 170, 174, 178, 228, 232
costs, 7, 60, 103, 104, 105, 106, 107, 109, 142, 213
Council of Ministers, 90
counterterrorism, 46
country of origin, 124
credit, vii, viii, 9, 10, 11, 13, 14, 15, 16, 18, 74, 104, 105, 110, 118, 126, 186, 208, 219
credit market, 104, 105
critical infrastructure, 45, 46, 82, 98
cross-border investment, 42, 204
crowding out, 17
Cuba, 17
cultural heritage, 38, 50
currency, viii, 2, 10, 12, 60, 71, 101, 108, 109, 110, 181, 188, 214, 216, 223
current account, 132, 184, 205
current account deficit, 184, 205
current prices, 181
customers, viii, 68, 101, 133, 140, 181
Cyprus, 156, 230, 235, 239, 243

Czech Republic, 136, 138, 153, 156, 157, 161, 165, 169, 173, 177, 227, 230, 231, 235, 239, 243

D

dark matter, 184, 204
data processing, 127, 129, 147, 151
debt, 2, 13, 15, 105, 110, 208, 209, 211, 212, 214, 215, 217, 218, 219, 221, 222, 224, 244
debts, 221
decentralization, 103
decisions, 22, 25, 35, 37, 38, 40, 41, 70, 73, 95, 96, 98, 102, 103, 104, 106, 107, 110, 133
defense, 22, 24, 25, 27, 28, 31, 32, 33, 34, 35, 37, 38, 39, 50, 55, 62, 63, 67, 68, 71, 72, 77, 84, 89, 94, 96, 97, 98, 99
definition, 54, 58, 181, 191
denial, 40, 56, 62, 64, 73, 86, 88
Denmark, 136, 138, 153, 156, 157, 161, 165, 169, 173, 177, 227, 230, 231, 235, 236, 239, 240, 243
Department of Commerce, 1, 2, 4, 26, 73, 183
deposits, 32
depreciation, 109, 120, 188, 194, 196, 197, 201, 222
devaluation, 2, 12
developed countries, vii, 1, 5, 7, 10, 18, 187
developing countries, vii, 1, 5, 10, 12, 15, 18
developing nations, vii, 9, 10
diffusion, 124
direct foreign investment, 92
directors, 53, 91, 95
disclosure, 123, 135, 143, 148, 152, 156, 160, 164, 176, 180, 230, 234, 239, 243
discrimination, 61, 66
distortions, viii, 101, 108, 204
distribution, 1, 2, 37, 55, 81, 97, 119, 129, 146, 151, 217
District of Columbia, 141
diversity, 24, 37, 41
domestic investment, 17, 31, 70, 80
dominance, 124
Dominican Republic, 155, 159, 163, 167, 171, 175, 179, 229, 233
downsizing, 6
draft, 22, 25, 32, 38, 84, 86, 87, 89
dual-use items, 63
Duma, 32, 84, 86

E

earnings, 1, 2, 8, 106, 107, 183, 197, 201, 207, 208, 211, 212, 214, 215, 217, 218, 219, 220, 222, 244
Eastern Europe, 13
economic activity, 6, 7, 50
economic cooperation, 53
economic development, 18, 54, 56, 58
economic downturn, 75
economic growth, 2, 5, 6, 28, 57, 58, 60, 91, 107, 131, 208
economic policy, 53
economic reform, 52, 83
economic reforms, 83
economic transformation, 18
economic union, 5
economies of scale, 124
Ecuador, 136, 154, 158, 162, 166, 170, 174, 178, 228, 232, 235, 243
Egypt, 136, 155, 159, 163, 167, 171, 175, 179, 216, 229, 233
electricity, 71, 77, 81
emerging markets, 109
employees, 18, 28, 41, 103, 117, 119, 132, 134, 135, 142, 144, 145, 146, 147, 148, 149, 150, 151, 152, 153, 154, 155, 156, 157, 158, 159, 160, 161, 162, 163, 164, 165, 168, 169, 172
employment, vii, ix, 5, 6, 7, 9, 10, 50, 51, 52, 69, 75, 80, 113, 114, 118, 119, 120, 121, 125, 127, 129, 132, 133, 141, 142, 156, 168, 172, 218
employment growth, 114
energy, 13, 16, 17, 22, 25, 31, 32, 35, 36, 37, 46, 47, 60, 65, 70, 71, 82, 83, 97, 127
Energy Independence and Security Act, 17
energy supply, 97
entrepreneurship, 69
environmental impact, 16
environmental protection, 58
equilibrium, 191, 193, 195, 204
equity, 2, 8, 11, 12, 13, 15, 30, 41, 52, 57, 66, 69, 72, 73, 75, 76, 97, 106, 137, 185, 207, 208, 210, 211, 212, 213, 217, 218, 219, 221, 222, 223, 244
Estonia, 156, 230, 235, 239, 243
EU, 22, 36, 37, 38, 61, 62, 63, 65, 68, 79, 82, 98
Eurasia, 42
Euro, 230, 235, 239, 243
Europe, 3, 5, 38, 114, 130, 131, 134, 142, 153, 157, 161, 165, 169, 173, 177, 212, 213, 214, 215, 223, 224, 225, 227, 231, 236, 240
European Commission, 30, 37, 38, 40, 42, 62, 98
European Community, 22, 30, 37, 61, 65, 98, 99
European Court of Justice, 22, 30, 36, 62, 64, 83, 95
European Union, 22, 36, 37, 38, 40, 42, 61, 65, 81, 82, 94, 96, 98, 156, 160, 164, 168, 172, 176, 180, 230, 234, 235, 239, 243
exchange rate, 120, 137, 181, 223
Executive Order, 45
exercise, 13, 27, 78, 99
expenditures, ix, 52, 109, 113, 114, 115, 116, 127, 129, 132, 140, 141, 144, 145, 146, 147, 148, 149,

150, 151, 152, 157, 158, 159, 160, 161, 162, 163, 164, 186, 187, 196, 199, 201, 219
explosives, 31, 62, 63, 65, 67, 72, 87
exports, 5, 7, 50, 109, 115, 121, 122, 132, 153, 154, 155, 156, 157, 158, 159, 160, 161, 162, 163, 164, 188
exposure, 15, 107, 109
external financing, 104
extraction, 87, 89, 108, 131, 133, 144, 149, 215

F

failure, 39, 40, 59, 68
FAS, 23, 84, 85, 86, 87, 89
FDI, ix, 23, 25, 33, 34, 48, 52, 60, 61, 65, 69, 73, 74, 75, 79, 83, 89, 90, 93, 181, 183, 184, 185, 186, 187, 188, 194, 195, 196, 197, 198, 199, 201, 202, 203, 205
FDI inflow, 52, 60, 65, 69, 74, 79, 83, 89, 93
fear, 40, 41, 59, 76
federal law, 91
Federal Security Service, 86
feedback, 40, 124
FEMA, 23, 70, 72
fibers, 144, 149
finance, viii, ix, 5, 7, 10, 11, 15, 18, 49, 101, 105, 107, 114, 126, 131, 147, 148, 151, 152, 181, 207, 212, 214, 216, 219, 220, 221, 223, 224
financial crisis, 5, 15, 19, 78, 126, 208
financial distress, 76
financial institutions, 11
financial intermediaries, 12, 209
financial markets, ix, 188, 207, 220
financial records, 102
financial resources, 10, 109
financial sector, 15, 28, 38, 49, 70, 72, 80, 81
financing, vii, 9, 10, 11, 12, 13, 15, 16, 102, 104, 105, 106, 107, 108, 109
Finland, 136, 138, 153, 156, 157, 161, 165, 169, 173, 177, 224, 225, 227, 230, 231, 235, 236, 239, 240, 243
firms, vii, viii, 1, 2, 5, 6, 7, 10, 11, 12, 13, 18, 24, 26, 40, 42, 50, 51, 56, 60, 63, 75, 80, 101, 102, 104, 105, 106, 107, 108, 109, 110, 124, 133, 137, 184, 185, 188, 192, 196, 200, 201, 213
fiscal surpluses, 38
fishing, 87, 148, 152
fluctuations, viii, 101
food, 120, 123, 127, 131, 148, 152
foreign assistance, 10
foreign direct investment, vii, ix, 1, 23, 24, 25, 27, 30, 32, 40, 42, 48, 61, 91, 92, 94, 97, 108, 110, 121, 133, 183, 195, 205, 207, 208, 213, 218, 219, 225, 244
foreign exchange, 38, 60, 62, 70, 99, 181
foreign exchange market, 70, 181
foreign firms, 2, 7, 41, 57, 76, 184, 196, 204, 205
foreign nationals, 72
foreign person, 122, 221
foreign policy, vii, 9, 11, 18
France, viii, 3, 21, 24, 28, 29, 30, 33, 35, 36, 37, 38, 39, 41, 42, 48, 49, 60, 61, 62, 63, 64, 65, 75, 98, 130, 136, 138, 142, 153, 156, 157, 161, 165, 169, 173, 177, 192, 197, 205, 215, 220, 225, 227, 230, 231, 235, 236, 239, 240, 243
free trade, 23, 91
funding, viii, 9, 13, 14, 16, 244
funds, 5, 11, 13, 14, 15, 16, 17, 18, 22, 25, 31, 35, 37, 38, 50, 62, 65, 72, 83, 97, 99, 106, 132, 195, 210, 222

G

gambling, 62, 63, 71, 98
GDP, ix, 6, 7, 23, 48, 52, 61, 65, 69, 75, 79, 83, 90, 92, 93, 113, 114, 120, 129, 133, 136, 137, 181, 199
generation, 55, 71, 92, 97, 124, 127
Germany, viii, 3, 21, 24, 25, 28, 29, 31, 33, 35, 37, 38, 39, 41, 42, 61, 65, 66, 67, 68, 69, 75, 99, 124, 130, 132, 136, 137, 138, 140, 142, 153, 156, 157, 161, 165, 169, 173, 177, 192, 205, 215, 218, 225, 227, 230, 231, 235, 236, 239, 240, 243
global markets, 127
globalization, 102, 104, 204
goals, 10, 11, 18
goods and services, 142, 181, 216
governance, 50, 133
ggovernment budget, 83
government policy, 103
government procurement, 91
Greece, 136, 138, 153, 156, 157, 161, 165, 169, 173, 177, 227, 230, 231, 235, 239, 243
grids, 81, 82
gross domestic product, ix, 6, 23, 48, 113, 118
groups, 15, 75, 121, 122, 126, 221, 224, 244
growth, ix, 2, 6, 58, 60, 69, 108, 109, 113, 114, 115, 120, 126, 127, 129, 137, 140, 141, 183, 186, 189, 193, 194, 195, 197, 200, 201, 207, 208, 211, 214, 218, 219, 220
growth accounting, ix, 183, 186, 200
growth rate, 69, 108, 109, 114, 189, 194
guidance, 10, 76, 97
guidelines, 38, 50, 72, 103, 218, 221

H

harm, viii, 21, 75, 77, 81, 94

health, 11, 81, 82
holding company, 216, 217
Honduras, 136, 154, 158, 162, 166, 171, 174, 179, 228, 232
Hong Kong, 118, 119, 136, 156, 160, 163, 167, 172, 176, 179, 214, 229, 234, 238, 242
host, 25, 40, 120, 129, 133, 137, 140, 181, 210
housing, 71, 99
human capital, 200
human resources, 98
humanitarian aid, 10
Hungary, 136, 138, 153, 156, 157, 161, 165, 169, 173, 177, 223, 224, 225, 227, 230, 231, 235, 239, 243
hunting, 148, 152

I

imbalances, 197, 204, 205
IMF, 23, 38, 42, 97
implementation, viii, 21, 24, 51, 85, 86
imports, 5, 7, 115, 121, 122, 123, 132, 153, 154, 155, 156, 157, 158, 159, 160, 161, 162, 163, 164
in transition, 10, 56
incentives, 5, 57, 103, 107, 108, 188, 201, 208
inclusion, 118, 202
income tax, 108, 185, 186, 190, 191, 194, 197, 201, 202, 203, 204
independence, 69
India, viii, 21, 24, 28, 29, 31, 33, 35, 36, 37, 38, 39, 41, 42, 69, 70, 71, 72, 73, 74, 137, 156, 160, 164, 168, 172, 176, 179, 230, 234, 238, 242
indicators, 132, 133, 181
indices, 187
Indonesia, 136, 156, 160, 164, 168, 172, 176, 179, 230, 234, 235, 239, 243
industrial policy, 52, 54, 60
inflation, 2, 105, 120, 181
informal practices, 92
information technology, 63
infrastructure, 5, 10, 11, 31, 37, 38, 45, 65, 71, 83, 124, 133
insight, viii, 101
institutions, 11, 72, 79, 104, 120, 123, 126, 127, 128, 130, 133, 135, 143, 147, 151, 165, 166, 167, 168, 169, 170, 171, 172, 173, 174, 175, 176, 177, 178, 180, 181, 227, 228, 229, 230, 231, 232, 233, 234, 236, 237, 238, 239, 240, 241, 242, 243, 244
instruments, 38, 127, 145, 150, 222
intellectual property, 103, 124, 133, 205
intelligence, 50, 67
interest groups, 93
interest margins, 126
interest rates, 2, 104, 204
interference, 57
internal financing, 104
Internal Revenue Service, 187, 205
international investment, 78, 132, 186, 197, 199, 205
International Monetary Fund, 23, 38, 42, 218
international standards, 244
international trade, 52
internet, 127, 129
intervention, 36, 57, 94, 96, 99
investment bank, 11, 131
investment capital, 222, 244
investment incentive, 10
investors, viii, ix, 2, 11, 12, 13, 17, 21, 24, 25, 30, 32, 36, 37, 38, 39, 49, 51, 54, 55, 56, 61, 62, 65, 66, 69, 71, 72, 73, 75, 76, 78, 82, 83, 84, 85, 86, 89, 92, 99, 108, 181, 183, 184, 186, 187, 188, 192, 196, 200, 210, 212, 218, 219, 222, 244
IPO, 23, 76
Iran, 81, 156, 230, 235, 239, 243
Iraq, 14, 17, 156, 230, 235, 239, 243
Ireland, 3, 133, 136, 138, 153, 156, 157, 161, 165, 169, 173, 177, 197, 205, 213, 214, 215, 227, 230, 231, 235, 236, 239, 240, 243
Israel, 136, 155, 159, 163, 167, 171, 175, 179, 216, 229, 233, 238, 242
Italy, 3, 136, 138, 153, 156, 157, 161, 165, 169, 173, 177, 225, 227, 230, 231, 235, 236, 239, 240, 243

J

Japan, viii, 4, 21, 24, 25, 28, 29, 31, 33, 35, 36, 37, 38, 39, 41, 42, 74, 75, 76, 77, 78, 99, 130, 136, 138, 143, 156, 160, 164, 168, 172, 176, 180, 192, 205, 214, 215, 216, 218, 220, 224, 225, 230, 234, 238, 242
jobs, vii, 1, 5, 6, 7, 57, 58
joint ventures, 11, 52, 89, 90, 102, 103, 110
jurisdiction, 36, 48, 56, 64, 73, 78, 79, 97

K

keiretsu, 75
Korea, 4, 136, 156, 164, 168, 172, 176, 180, 230, 234, 238, 242
Kuwait, 92, 156, 216, 230, 235, 238, 239, 242, 243

L

labor, vii, 1, 6, 7, 18, 60, 91, 92, 124, 142, 189
land, 32, 91, 213
language, 14, 24, 41, 65
Latin America, 5, 13, 18, 114, 121, 130, 131, 134, 137, 142, 154, 158, 162, 166, 170, 174, 178, 212, 214, 215, 224, 225, 228, 232, 237, 241
Latvia, 156, 230, 235, 239, 243

laws, viii, 21, 22, 24, 27, 28, 29, 30, 32, 33, 34, 37, 40, 41, 42, 47, 49, 53, 54, 55, 57, 65, 67, 70, 75, 82, 85, 89, 91, 92, 93, 94, 124, 141, 189, 191
lawyers, 64, 67, 79, 83, 86, 87
Lebanon, 238, 242
legal protection, 104
legislation, 11, 16, 17, 32, 65, 81, 84, 88
liberalization, 31, 69, 70, 74, 93, 103, 108
licenses, 72, 78, 87, 89
likelihood, 40, 41, 57, 64
line, 13, 16, 125, 129, 130, 139, 220
liquidity, 15, 184
Lithuania, 138, 156, 230, 235, 239, 243
loans, 8, 10, 11, 12, 14, 15, 75, 104, 210, 218, 222
local government, 35, 57, 81

M

machinery, 57, 59, 60, 83, 87, 127, 145, 150, 212
macroeconomic management, 53
maintenance, 39, 77, 99
Malaysia, 136, 156, 160, 164, 168, 172, 176, 180, 230, 234, 238, 242
malfeasance, 107
management, 10, 16, 26, 35, 49, 52, 53, 75, 77, 80, 99, 221
manufacturer, 31, 66, 75
manufacturing, vii, 1, 5, 6, 7, 32, 49, 52, 54, 55, 58, 72, 77, 94, 97, 99, 114, 120, 121, 123, 124, 127, 131, 133, 137, 140, 141, 146, 150, 181, 184, 187, 204, 212, 214, 215, 216, 217, 219, 223, 224, 227, 231, 232, 233, 234, 236, 237, 238, 239, 240, 241, 242, 243
marginal product, 191
market, viii, 2, 5, 6, 8, 10, 11, 13, 18, 27, 28, 29, 33, 38, 49, 50, 52, 53, 55, 58, 59, 68, 72, 75, 81, 82, 83, 85, 92, 94, 99, 101, 104, 107, 109, 126, 131, 137, 140, 185, 187, 199, 203, 208, 213, 222, 223
market economy, 49
market failure, 18
market position, 6
market share, 55, 58, 68, 94
market-based economy, 83
marketing, 62, 140
markets, viii, 6, 7, 13, 15, 18, 50, 52, 53, 68, 101, 102, 104, 105, 110, 127, 133
martial law, 88
measurement, ix, 104, 125, 129, 183, 186
measures, ix, 15, 16, 38, 58, 72, 75, 76, 88, 98, 109, 113, 132, 181, 217
media, 13, 31, 38, 54, 59, 65, 71, 89, 94, 95, 98, 145, 150
mergers, 30, 40, 55, 56, 57, 59, 60, 62, 76, 78, 80, 81, 82, 94, 97, 244
metals, 54, 87, 120, 123, 126, 128, 130, 135, 143, 145, 149, 165, 166, 167, 168, 169, 170, 171, 172, 173, 174, 175, 176, 177, 178, 180, 227, 228, 229, 230, 231, 232, 233, 234, 236, 237, 238, 239, 240, 241, 242, 243
Mexico, 3, 115, 130, 136, 138, 142, 154, 159, 162, 166, 171, 174, 179, 215, 228, 233, 237, 241
Middle East, vii, 9, 11, 13, 18, 90, 114, 130, 131, 134, 143, 155, 159, 163, 167, 171, 175, 179, 215, 216, 224, 225, 229, 233, 238, 242
military, 31, 32, 37, 39, 47, 63, 66, 67, 87, 88, 89, 92, 94, 98, 99
mining, 51, 52, 54, 71, 74, 127, 131, 145, 150, 212, 214, 215, 216, 220, 224
minority, 13, 83, 95, 102, 103, 122, 181
model, 186, 187, 188, 191, 192, 194, 195, 200, 201, 204
money, 7, 60, 78, 98
money supply, 60
monopoly, 28, 34, 36, 81, 82, 84, 85, 86, 87, 88, 89, 94
motion, 189, 191
motivation, 35, 106
movement, 36, 61, 62, 65, 66, 83, 99
multinational companies, viii, ix, 101, 113, 121, 132, 141, 204, 226
multinational corporations, 6, 7, 107, 185
multinational firms, viii, 5, 101, 102, 103, 104, 105, 106, 107, 108, 109, 110, 111, 204
music, 50

N

NAFTA, 23, 49
nation, 48, 49, 75, 82, 92
national emergency, 97
national income, 132, 222, 244
national interests, 37, 40, 50, 52, 85, 88, 94
national security, viii, 21, 22, 23, 24, 25, 26, 27, 28, 29, 30, 31, 32, 34, 35, 36, 37, 39, 40, 44, 45, 46, 47, 49, 50, 51, 54, 55, 56, 58, 60, 61, 62, 63, 67, 68, 71, 74, 77, 79, 80, 81, 84, 85, 86, 87, 88, 92, 93, 94, 95, 97, 98
National Security Council, 31, 45, 74
nationalism, 38, 59
nationality, 78, 82, 99
natural gas, 32, 89, 90, 91, 92, 131
natural resources, 133, 222
negative consequences, 110
net investment, 183
New Zealand, 136, 156, 164, 168, 172, 176, 180, 230, 234, 238, 242
Nigeria, 136, 155, 156, 159, 163, 167, 171, 175, 179, 216, 229, 230, 233, 235, 239, 243

North Africa, vii, 9, 11
North America, 23, 49, 183
North American Free Trade Agreement, 23, 49
Norway, 136, 138, 153, 157, 161, 165, 169, 173, 177, 227, 231, 236, 240

O

objectives, vii, 9, 10, 11, 24, 30, 38, 42, 49, 50, 78
obligate, 13
observations, 42
OECD, 23, 40, 42, 75, 77, 78, 181
oil, 17, 32, 49, 55, 59, 71, 77, 83, 87, 88, 89, 90, 91, 92, 96, 97, 131, 133
openness, 91, 97, 133, 186, 188, 200
order, 1, 2, 6, 13, 28, 31, 33, 34, 35, 37, 44, 45, 49, 61, 62, 75, 77, 79, 94, 107, 108, 109, 137, 186, 187, 188, 196, 197
Organization for Economic Cooperation and Development, 40, 58
overseas investment, 5, 10
Overseas Private Investment Corporation, v, vii, 9, 10, 18, 19
oversight, vii, 9, 13, 16, 17, 28, 33
ownership, 7, 11, 22, 25, 26, 28, 30, 31, 32, 35, 37, 38, 49, 53, 57, 59, 69, 70, 71, 74, 78, 80, 87, 89, 91, 93, 95, 96, 99, 102, 103, 104, 122, 132, 133, 141, 189, 216, 217, 218, 221, 222
ownership structure, 216

P

Pacific, 121, 130, 131, 134, 140, 143, 155, 160, 163, 167, 172, 176, 179, 212, 214, 215, 216, 223, 224, 225, 229, 234, 238, 242
Panama, 154, 159, 162, 166, 171, 175, 179, 228, 233, 237, 241
parameter, 200
parameters, 58, 196, 197
parents, ix, 103, 105, 106, 107, 110, 113, 114, 115, 117, 118, 119, 120, 121, 122, 123, 125, 126, 127, 128, 129, 130, 132, 133, 137, 140, 141, 148, 152, 199, 212, 213, 214, 216, 217, 219, 220, 221, 222, 224, 225, 226, 244
Parliament, 30, 32, 50, 65, 82, 83
partnership, 7, 26, 141
patents, 188
pathogens, 63, 87
penalties, 40, 62, 72, 77, 103
personal relations, 92
personal relationship, 92
Peru, 136, 154, 158, 162, 166, 170, 174, 178, 228, 232
pharmaceuticals, 127, 131
Philippines, 136, 156, 160, 164, 168, 172, 176, 180, 230, 234
planning, 17, 50, 53, 56, 103, 104, 105
Poland, 115, 136, 138, 153, 156, 157, 161, 165, 169, 173, 177, 227, 230, 231, 235, 239, 243
population, 72, 79, 91, 140, 189, 193
population growth, 193
portfolio, 16, 18, 186, 187, 188, 193
portfolio investment, 187, 188
portfolios, 187, 202
ports, 70, 89, 97
Portugal, 136, 138, 153, 156, 157, 161, 165, 169, 173, 177, 227, 230, 231, 235, 239, 243
power, 35, 54, 55, 77, 92, 97, 99, 104, 127
predictability, 38
price changes, 185
price deflator, 120, 181
price index, 181, 213
prices, 107, 120, 131, 132, 137, 181, 191, 213, 222, 223
private investment, 10, 11, 36, 70
private sector, 18, 28, 38, 72, 75, 90, 91, 92
privatization, 29, 31, 70, 81
probability, 31, 77
process innovation, 200
production, viii, 5, 10, 18, 31, 37, 49, 54, 62, 63, 70, 80, 81, 90, 92, 98, 101, 103, 125, 127, 131, 133, 137, 140, 142, 188, 189, 205, 216, 222, 244
production costs, 222
production function, 189
productivity, 50, 51, 52, 189, 193, 204
profit, 38, 76, 108
profitability, 108
profits, 6, 41, 60, 75, 103, 106, 108, 142, 186, 187, 190, 191, 192, 193, 197, 200, 202, 205, 220, 244
program, viii, 10, 11, 13, 14, 15, 101, 102, 103, 146, 151
programming, 126, 225, 226
public capital, 188
public interest, 36, 37, 82, 94, 95, 99
public policy, 99
public safety, 28, 31, 33, 35, 37, 61, 62, 77, 79
Puerto Rico, 141
purchasing power, 137
purchasing power parity, 137

Q

quotas, 53

R

radiation, 87
range, 11, 13, 22, 24, 27, 30, 42, 62, 67, 86, 88, 89

rate of return, 186, 193, 194, 195, 197
raw materials, 5
real assets, 25
real estate, 1, 38, 83, 99, 148, 152, 224
real terms, 120, 137
reality, 93, 201
reason, 58, 75, 79, 82, 83, 109, 184, 187, 217
recession, 5, 76
refining, 31, 215
reflection, 54, 187
reforms, 104, 197, 204
region, 41, 212, 213, 214, 216, 223, 224
regression, 106
regression analysis, 106
regulation, 38, 41, 58, 61, 62, 84, 94, 104, 127
regulations, viii, 21, 24, 27, 28, 30, 31, 32, 40, 41, 42, 44, 47, 49, 52, 53, 54, 55, 56, 57, 58, 59, 60, 62, 67, 68, 70, 72, 78, 80, 92, 98, 103, 124, 205
regulators, 65, 69
regulatory framework, 58
relationship, 24, 25, 41, 46, 58, 90, 133, 204
remittances, 12, 73
renewable energy, vii, 9, 11, 13, 16, 19
reputation, 79, 92
reserves, 10, 15, 38, 65, 89, 90, 99
resistance, 31, 74
resources, 13, 14, 17, 18, 47, 89, 97, 105, 109
restructuring, vii, 1, 41
retail, 31, 38, 70, 71, 74, 83, 114, 120, 121, 123, 127, 131, 212
retained earnings, 202, 212, 220
returns, ix, 13, 15, 75, 183, 184, 185, 186, 187, 188, 192, 193, 194, 195, 196, 197, 198, 200, 201, 202, 203, 204, 212, 219
revaluation, 223
revenue, 12, 148, 152, 187
risk, 10, 12, 13, 15, 18, 57, 94, 105, 124, 133, 184, 187
robustness, 187, 200
Romania, 156, 230, 235, 239, 243
royalty, 192, 200
rubber, 144, 145, 149
rubber products, 144, 145, 149
rule of law, 79, 188
Russia, viii, 21, 24, 28, 29, 32, 34, 36, 37, 38, 39, 41, 42, 83, 84, 85, 86, 87, 88, 89, 137, 153, 157, 161, 165, 169, 173, 177, 215, 227, 231

S

safety, 11, 127
sales, ix, 6, 7, 41, 47, 72, 94, 98, 109, 113, 114, 118, 127, 131, 132, 133, 137, 140, 142, 148, 152, 181, 218
satellite, 188, 204, 205
Saudi Arabia, 92, 133, 137, 155, 156, 159, 163, 167, 171, 175, 179, 229, 230, 233, 235, 238, 239, 242, 243
scientific knowledge, 103
Secretary of Commerce, 45
Secretary of Defense, 45, 47
Secretary of Homeland Security, 45
Secretary of the Treasury, 23, 45, 46, 98
securities, 7, 10, 14, 15, 141, 217, 221
security, viii, 21, 22, 23, 24, 25, 27, 28, 30, 31, 32, 33, 34, 35, 36, 37, 38, 46, 47, 49, 50, 54, 58, 61, 62, 63, 64, 65, 66, 67, 74, 78, 82, 84, 85, 86, 87, 88, 92, 94, 95, 97, 98, 99
security services, 84, 86
semiconductors, 127, 131
Senate, 16, 17, 23, 97
shareholders, 63, 76, 79, 98, 106, 107, 110
shares, 7, 36, 65, 68, 70, 73, 75, 78, 79, 82, 83, 85, 95, 96, 102, 103, 106, 114, 127, 129, 194, 212, 213, 217, 218
Singapore, 83, 118, 119, 131, 133, 136, 156, 160, 164, 168, 172, 176, 180, 215, 216, 230, 234, 238, 242
skills, 10, 69, 204
Slovakia, 156, 230, 235, 239, 243
software, 78, 124, 127
South Africa, 136, 155, 159, 163, 167, 171, 175, 179, 229, 233, 237, 242
South Asia, 13
South Korea, 138
Spain, 3, 136, 139, 153, 156, 157, 161, 165, 170, 173, 177, 215, 223, 225, 227, 230, 231, 235, 236, 239, 240, 243
spillover effects, 110
spillovers, 204
stability, 58, 60, 188
stakeholders, 68
standards, 15, 17, 24, 42, 50, 56, 57, 102, 127
state-owned enterprises, 22, 25, 29, 35, 37, 38, 50, 56, 57, 59, 65, 83, 88, 89, 97
statistics, 111, 121, 132, 135, 208, 209, 213, 216, 217, 218, 222, 225, 226, 244
steel, 97
stock, 2, 8, 36, 48, 49, 52, 60, 61, 65, 69, 72, 74, 75, 78, 79, 83, 90, 93, 97, 132, 186, 187, 199, 200, 208, 213, 222
stock exchange, 36, 72, 78
stock markets, 208
strategic assets, 36, 95
strategies, 133, 140, 203
structuring, 11, 105
sub-Saharan Africa, vii, 9, 11

subsidy, viii, 9, 13, 14
supervision, 38, 81, 225, 226
suppliers, 68, 91
supply, 7, 63, 77, 82, 205
support services, 127
surplus, 15, 75, 200
Sweden, 3, 136, 139, 153, 156, 158, 161, 166, 170, 174, 178, 215, 224, 225, 228, 230, 232, 235, 236, 239, 240, 243
Switzerland, 118, 119, 131, 136, 139, 153, 158, 161, 166, 170, 174, 178, 213, 214, 215, 220, 223, 224, 225, 228, 232, 236, 240

T

Taiwan, 4, 136, 156, 160, 164, 168, 172, 176, 180, 230, 234, 238, 242
takeover, 40, 76, 94, 96
tanks, 31, 42, 99
tax rates, 60, 105, 108, 133, 186, 191, 192, 193, 195, 201
tax reform, 197
tax system, 202
taxation, 106, 107, 184, 186, 188, 191, 192, 193, 194, 195, 197, 200, 201, 204
technical assistance, 10, 12
technological change, 189
technology transfer, 51, 103, 104
telecommunications, 13, 31, 38, 49, 55, 73, 74, 78, 87, 91, 97, 129, 146, 151
telecommunications services, 78
television, 54, 69, 87, 95
tension, 36, 62, 91
terrorism, 10, 12, 17, 98
Thailand, 136, 156, 160, 164, 168, 172, 176, 180, 230, 234
threat, 26, 46, 47, 62, 74, 79, 81, 82, 88, 94, 96, 98
threats, 31, 74, 79, 97
threshold, 35, 89, 98
thresholds, 22, 25, 30, 35, 37, 39, 49, 71, 85, 89, 98
time frame, 22, 25, 33, 34, 35, 39, 47, 62, 64, 85, 88, 97
tobacco, 72, 144, 149, 219, 224
total factor productivity, 187
trade benefits, 10
trade deficit, 7
trade policy, 53
trademarks, 28, 33, 54, 58, 188
traditions, 48, 133
transaction costs, 195
transaction value, 223
transactions, 12, 17, 22, 23, 25, 26, 27, 29, 30, 32, 35, 36, 37, 39, 42, 45, 46, 49, 52, 53, 56, 57, 59, 62, 66, 67, 68, 70, 71, 72, 73, 76, 77, 81, 82, 84, 85, 94, 97, 98, 99, 102, 103, 104, 132, 192, 208, 217, 219, 221, 222, 223, 225, 226, 244
transfer pricing, 103, 184, 187
transformation, 18
transition, 29, 83, 200
translation, 99, 211, 214, 216, 218, 223
transmission, 37, 66
transparency, 16, 17, 24, 38, 50, 54, 56, 58, 59, 85
transport, 65, 77, 81, 82, 99
transportation, 36, 49, 82, 83, 98, 124, 127, 131, 137, 141, 216, 224
transshipment, 47
trial, 58
trust, 41, 57, 80, 94, 141
Turkey, 3, 136, 154, 158, 161, 166, 170, 174, 178, 228, 232

U

U.S. Department of the Treasury, 97
U.S. economy, 2, 5, 6, 7, 23, 106
U.S. Treasury, 10, 14, 15
UK, 3, 4, 23, 93, 94, 95, 96, 99, 186, 196, 197, 198, 199, 205
uncertainty, 40, 59, 66
unions, vii, 1
United Nations, 2, 23, 26, 42, 48, 52, 61, 66, 69, 76, 80, 84, 90, 95, 181
United States, v, vii, viii, ix, 1, 2, 5, 7, 10, 14, 16, 18, 21, 22, 23, 24, 25, 26, 27, 28, 34, 35, 36, 40, 41, 42, 44, 45, 46, 47, 49, 52, 61, 65, 97, 98, 99, 104, 113, 114, 121, 124, 141, 181, 183, 184, 186, 187, 188, 191, 192, 194, 196, 197, 200, 204, 205, 207, 208, 209, 213, 218, 219, 221, 222, 225, 236, 239, 240, 243, 244
universe, 125, 129, 130
universities, 140
updating, 94
uranium, 49, 98

V

vehicles, 31, 67, 99, 131, 146, 150
Venezuela, 81, 136, 154, 156, 158, 162, 166, 170, 174, 178, 228, 230, 232, 235, 237, 239, 241, 243
venture capital, 13, 204
vested interests, 57
violence, 10, 12
volatility, 108
voting, 7, 31, 63, 67, 78, 82, 96, 98, 99, 141, 221

W

wages, vii, 1, 7, 140, 187, 204
war, 63, 66, 67, 68, 75, 78, 98

waste management, 148, 152
wealth, 22, 25, 31, 35, 37, 38, 50, 65, 72, 83, 97, 204
weapons, 31, 37, 54, 63, 66, 67, 68, 77, 87
weapons of mass destruction, 31, 77
Western Europe, 5
wholesale, 7, 49, 123, 131, 212, 220, 223, 224
workers, vii, 1, 7, 11, 17, 92, 118, 119, 120, 125, 129, 132
World Bank, 133, 135, 137, 181, 188, 205
World Trade Organization, 23, 49
World War I, 5, 75
WTO, 23, 49, 98